Holy Ghosts

IRENE TAYLER

HOLY GHOSTS

The Male Muses
of Emily and Charlotte Brontë

COLUMBIA UNIVERSITY PRESS   NEW YORK

COLUMBIA UNIVERSITY PRESS
New York   Chichester, West Susex

Copyright © 1990 Columbia University Press

Library of Congress Cataloging-in-Publication Data

Tayler, Irene.
Holy ghosts : the male muses of Emily and Charlotte Brontë / Irene Tayler.
p. cm.
Includes bibliographical references.
ISBN 0-231-07154-X
ISBN 0-231-07155-8 (pbk.)
1. Brontë, Charlotte, 1816–1855—Criticism and interpretation.
2. Brontë, Emily, 1818–1848—Criticism and interpretation.
3. Feminism and literature—Great Britain—History—19th century.
4. Masculinity (Psychology) in literature.
5. Creation (Literary, artistic, etc.)
6. Romanticism—England.
7. Sex role in literature.
8. Men in literature.
I. Title.
PR4169.T39 1989
823'.809—dc20
89-23929
CIP

Casebound editions of Columbia University Press books are printed on permanent and durable acid-free paper.

Printed in the United States of America
c 10 9 8 7 6 5 4 3 2 1
p 10 9 8 7 6 5 4 3 2 1

CONTENTS

In a way, what follows is not one book but two. There is a complex and fascinating story to tell about the creative development of each of these two major writers, Emily and Charlotte Brontë, and I try to tell each story independently, for itself. But in telling the two stories another dimension is added to each by the fact that the writers were sisters. Charlotte's influence on Emily was at best ambivalent. I argue that Charlotte's invasion of Emily's privacy may have hastened Emily's death, but that it also spurred Emily to write her masterpiece, *Wuthering Heights*. On the other hand Emily's influence on Charlotte was also mixed, oddly achieving its greatest effect from beyond the grave. Following Emily's death Charlotte, alone and in crisis as a writer, immersed herself anew in Emily's writings—editing them, even altering them, and at last finding in them what she needed to write her own greatest work, *Villette*.

Central to this story is how each of the Brontë sisters created a male muse, a Holy Ghost—one that was partly, but only partly, the gender-reversed female muse of their male Romantic predecessors. In calling their muses Holy Ghosts I suggest how the sisters shared the sensibility and language of religious vision and how they affirmed the value of female speech (countering St. Paul's stricture, "I suffer not a woman to teach . . . but to be in silence"). Both Emily and Charlotte do "teach," emphatically so. And although both writers addressed the world at large, each offers a special message to women. Indeed in Charlotte's last work, *Villette,* she demonstrates her point directly in the narrative. At the end of the book, Lucy is far from home, running a girls' school and so bringing to a community of young women the message that woman may speak—*as* woman—with apostolic voice.

Although my topic is unusual among feminists—inquiring into qualities of "maleness" in the female imagination—my thinking has been deeply influenced by American feminist theory and I hope that through this book I have contributed to it some small measure of perception.

I am grateful for the generous help I have received at every stage. A summer stipend from the National Endowment for the Humanities made it possible for me to travel to Haworth and work in the Brontë Parsonage Museum Library during the summer of 1981. There I met Sally Stone-house, then librarian for the Parsonage Collection, who shared not only her bibliographical expertise, but also her time, car, and company in showing me the Yorkshire countryside.

Immensely supportive in a different way was the Thomas Meloy Chair of Rhetoric at M.I.T., of which I was honored to be the first occupant. Funds provided by the Meloy endowment helped me finish this work.

Susan Casteras, Assistant Curator of Paintings at the Yale Center for British Art, gave generously of her knowledge and interest in helping me find the lovely Millais that appears on the dust jacket.

My footnotes cannot by any means record my full indebtedness to other scholars and readers of the Brontës. Some works, like J. Hillis Miller's *The Disappearance of God* and Elaine Showalter's *A Literature of Their Own* (to name only two of many) have colored my way of thinking about their subjects. Other scholars have provided information and ideas absorbed so completely, and over so long a time, that I regret to say I can no longer trace them to offer my thanks.

I am especially grateful to Carolyn Heilbrun, Felicia Bonaparte, and Carl Woodring, who read the finished manuscript and offered well-timed support and superb advice. Among the many friends and colleagues who have read earlier drafts or chapters of the manuscript and given their insights and encouragement, I wish to mention especially Stevie Davies, Barbara Davis, Margaret Higonnet, A. Walton Litz, Mary Oates O'Reilly, Stephen Tapscott, Aileen Ward, and Cynthia Woolf. Special thanks go to my son Jesse for guiding me with sweet patience through the complexities of my various computers.

Finally, and most important, my husband Saul Touster gave me the heart to continue on in my work through times of personal trouble and grief. To him, and to the memory of my mother (who, like Mrs. Brontë and Charlotte, died in her 39th year), I lovingly dedicate this book.

Holy Ghosts

"Is the Holy Ghost any other than an Intellectual Fountain?"

—William Blake

C harlotte and Emily Brontë are sometimes thought of as naifs or primitives, unschooled artists driven by native talent and emotional need, but largely innocent of the complex cultural and aesthetic movements of their time. Nothing could be less true. Though they did live in a remote moorland village, the Brontë children were remarkably well informed in most areas of current interest, from politics to literature and art. Voracious readers, they knew the chief periodicals of their day, whose mannerisms they mimicked and whose views they disputed mock-seriously in their own toy "publications."

And the Brontës were in the mainstream in another, more important, sense. As young readers and writers of Romantic poetry who grew up to become major Victorian novelists, Charlotte's and Emily's individual careers paralleled the large generic shift of their century, for the movement from Romantic to Victorian has long been thought of as a movement from poetry to novel as characteristic genre. But the course the Brontë sisters traced they also altered. Because their imaginations were schooled in Romantic habits of thought, they carried these habits into their own novels and in doing so demonstrated that the novel could do much that had before been considered the province only of poetry.

Finally, and most important, they altered the course of literary history, expanding the genre they employed, because they were women—because as women they had to share yet also challenge their period's assumptions about gender and about the artist's sources of inspiration. Charlotte and Emily each had to develop for herself a working mythology to account for the relationship of her femaleness to her creativity, of her being a woman yet doing "man's work." What these mythologies were and how each sister developed hers and wrote it into her fictions is the story my book has to tell.[1]

Family Life

To understand the evolution of thought in Charlotte's and Emily's works, one must know a few facts about their lives; but as the family history is familiar to many readers I will sketch it only very briefly.

The Brontë children's experience was grounded in catastrophe. In 1821 their mother, Maria Branwell Brontë, died of a painful illness, leaving six little children under eight.[2] Their father, Patrick Brontë, was rector of the Church of England in Haworth, the village where they lived. When in 1824 he sent his four older girls to a school for clergymen's daughters, the two eldest, Maria and Elizabeth, caught fatal infections and in the spring of 1825 followed their mother to the grave. Of those who remained, nine-year-old Charlotte was now the eldest; then came Branwell, not yet eight; then Emily and Anne, six and five.

In their triple bereavement the children turned to each other and to a world of imaginative play that took an important new turn when in June of 1826 (Charlotte was then ten and Emily seven) Patrick brought home for Branwell a dozen toy soldiers from Leeds. These toy figures—tangled as they were in associations of loss and compensation—formed the basis for the complex fantasy that marked the future course of each child's life. To summarize the consequences: this fantasy provided a constant resource for the children, an "infernal" or "nether" world, or "world below," as they came to call it, to which they could escape singly or together; in sharply varying ways it retained this function for each of them right into adulthood. Branwell was eventually overcome by its attractions. So much did he prefer the life of fantasy that when the time came for him to act in the real world, he took refuge instead in liquor, opium, and self-dramatizing self-pity, and by thirty-one was dead of his excesses. Anne took what was in some ways an opposite course. As a young adult she continued the childhood play mostly to please Emily, it would seem; increasingly her energies were dedicated to orthodox religious faith, from which she eventually received great support. She died peacefully, of consumption, at twenty-nine.

But for both Emily and Charlotte, this childhood play formed a kind of spiritual system out of which each sister evolved her own "religion," the set of beliefs that mythologized her role as woman writer.

When Maria Brontë died, her spinster sister came to help the widowed Patrick with his six small children. As he never remarried, "Aunt Branwell" stoically remained in the household for the rest of her life. A rather austere woman, she did what she could to occupy her young nieces with sewing, cooking, and cleaning—the things she believed a young woman should know. But it was "the Young Men," as the children called their toy soldiers, that absorbed their real energies. Each girl had her own special figure that functioned to some extent as her "acting" persona in the group play. Emily's soldier, for example, was for a time named after the explorer Captain William Edward Parry (1790–1855), so that the name "Parry" would sometimes be used as a pseudonym for Emily herself, and "Parrysland" was in their earliest games the name for her own special realm. Similarly Charlotte named her soldier after the duke of Wellington—though her attention soon shifted to his sons, Arthur and Charles Wellesley, whose names she used for pseudonyms in her juvenile writing. Charles being the masculine form of the name Charlotte, for years she signed her prose works with his name. But perhaps because poetry is a more elevated genre—more obviously "man's work" —she distanced herself somewhat more from her poems by attributing them to Arthur. Charles she endowed with characteristics she apparently recognized in herself: a satiric tongue and a certain neurotic defensiveness. Charles' older brother Arthur, on the other hand, she made into her ideal hero: domineering, glamorous, sensual, the very type of masculine Byronic genius.

As embodiments within the world of story of their own creative identities, of their own authorial selves cast outward into male forms, Emily's Parry and Charlotte's Charles and Arthur were early progenitors of the muse that each sister would in time develop: Heathcliff is a descendant of Parry, brought to life on the Yorkshire moors, and Paul Emanuel of *Villette* inherits important elements from each of the Welleseys.

At first the children's games were played among the four young people as a group, with Charlotte and Branwell, as eldest, taking the lead. Together they created miniscule journals modeled on such popular periodicals as *Blackwoods's,* filled with mock-solemn reports of the political, literary, and social goings-on of the city of "Glasstown," the glittering capital of their imaginary "nether world."

But because Charlotte and Emily slept together, for three years the two of them also played the game privately at night, without Anne or Branwell. An historically minded child, Charlotte recorded the beginning of this subset of the group fantasy: "Emily's and my Bed Plays were established the 1st of December 1827" (Charlotte was eleven in 1827, and Emily nine). "Bed Plays mean secret plays; they are very nice ones," she added contentedly.[3] Such secrecy remained important for Emily all her life, but Charlotte relished an audience and loved "publication." Increasingly she not only helped Branwell produce the issues of "The Young Men's Magazine," she also contributed stories and poems of her own. For Charlotte this was a time of eager artistic growth.

After three years the "Bed Plays" with Emily ended suddenly and forever, when in January 1831 Charlotte was sent away to Roe Head, a boarding school that was run by family acquaintances, the Misses Wooler, in a large, comfortable house some twenty miles distant from the parsonage at Haworth. The severance was bitter at first for Charlotte, who well remembered the losses that had attended her one previous experience of school, as we know from her angry account of the "Lowood" establishment in *Jane Eyre*. But she was eager for learning, and Roe Head itself proved a rather homey environment where she met among others Ellen Nussey and Mary Taylor, who became her lifelong friends. Emily, by contrast, never showed any desire for a formal education, never in her life made close friends outside the family, nor ever left home at all except at the sternest commands of duty. While the end to those secret and intimate Bed Plays brought new opportunity to Charlotte, it probably seemed merely another bereavement to Emily.

But however grievous her loss, Emily still had all the comforting resources of home about her. Not the least of these was her quietly unassuming little sister Anne. Emily herself could now take the mentoring role and was for the first time at liberty to become the author of her own imagined world. Accordingly, with Anne's support she embarked on an independent new saga set in the land of "Gondal."

After eighteen months at the Misses Wooler's school, Charlotte returned home, her studies ended. Since Emily's and Anne's new game was by then well established, Charlotte found herself working more than ever in partnership with Branwell. She and he were by this time expanding their territory to include a new realm called Angria, with Charlotte's hero Arthur (now glamorously titled the duke of Zamorna) as king, and Branwell's hero (formerly a pirate with the Branwellian name of Rogue) now called Percy and given a role as Zamorna's treacherous prime minister. For the next three years the two pairs of young people pursued their two similar but separate worlds of make-believe. If Emily and Anne wrote down any stories or poems during this period, these works do not survive. But a good deal survives of Charlotte's and Branwell's imaginings, and what it reveals is that this was a time of mounting rivalry for them as well as for their heroes.

This still relatively happy period ended in July of 1835, when the young people had to begin actively preparing to support themselves.

Branwell was to be an artist, his sisters presumably governesses. Charlotte accordingly returned to Roe Head in the position of teacher, permitted as part of her payment to bring a younger sister to be educated in her turn. Emily was first chosen to accompany her; but within three months Emily was returned to Haworth and Anne was sent off in her place. In a later account Charlotte explained the reason: "Liberty was the breath of Emily's nostrils; . . . . I felt in my heart she would die, if she did not go home, and with this conviction obtained her recall."[4] The liberty Emily required was liberty of mind and spirit, and only in the seclusion of home was she ever able to find it.

But this time Charlotte's stay at the Woolers' school proved nearly as ravaging as Emily's had threatened to be. Charlotte was now at nineteen no longer a student making friends and acquiring knowledge, but a would-be writer struggling to keep her mind alive while teaching "dolts" and "asses." Though she bowed to duty and remained at her job for three years, the fragmentary record of her stay (the so-called "Roe Head Journal") reveals a growing emotional turmoil that finally erupted in an illness that brought her, too, home again, in the spring of 1838. Two subsequent experiences as governess were mercifully briefer, but hardly less hateful.

As young adults all three sisters had experience teaching outside the home, and all agreed that it would be vastly preferable to open a school of their own at the Haworth parsonage. To this end Charlotte and Emily went to study in Brussels in 1842, where they remained for nine months, until called home by Aunt Branwell's death. Then Charlotte returned to Brussels alone for a second stay in 1843. But the school venture never materialized; when the time came to try it, they found themselves unable to attract pupils to their bleak and distant Yorkshire village.

All four of the young Brontës were now in their midtwenties, and all more or less troubled and unhappy. Branwell, sliding into decline, was finally expelled in dishonor from a job as tutor in July of 1845—having apparently attempted, perhaps successfully, an affair with the mother of his pupil—and from then on he made himself more and more a spectacle and a burden until his death in 1848. Anne, who had worked for the same family from which Branwell was expelled, was dismayed and depressed by all she had seen both of the world and of her brother. Emily, ever more deeply confirmed in a spiritual isolation that led her to disclaim all wordly ambition, was entering into the period of her darkest views and finest poetry. And Charlotte, badly shaken by the experience of falling in love with and feeling rejected by the married man who had been her teacher in Brussels, was struggling to curb her lifelong compulsion to worship unworthy creatures (including those of her own imagination) rather than the Creator.

Sometime in the autumn of 1845, in the loaded emotional setting just described, Charlotte stumbled onto Emily's private cache of poems, and read them. Exulting in her sister's talent and the prospect of publishing a volume of poems by all three sisters together (for modest Anne, too, wrote poems), Charlotte eventually persuaded a sore and reluctant Emily to her scheme, and *Poems by Currer, Ellis, and Acton Bell* came out in 1846.

Though anonymity of some kind would certainly have been a precondition for Emily's participation, the actual choice of these names may well have been Charlotte's. The name Bell may have been borrowed from their father's curate Arthur Bell Nicholls (who was later to become Charlotte's husband): this almost-household name would have had the virtue of feeling comfortably familiar to all three sisters. Moreover, like *Brontë* it began with a *B,* and the young women apparently wished to keep their initials intact. But the chief interest of the chosen names lies in their ambiguity of gender. Charlotte later defended this ambiguity on the ground that it was dictated by the sisters' desire to be judged not as "authoresses," but as writers irrespective of gender. Yet of course Charlotte had chosen male personae for her writing long before she could have been animated by that motive, however understandable it might be in itself; and in her poems Emily had for a long time been evolving the concept of a male "God of Visions." The choice of names was thus made in a context where maleness and femaleness was already an issue, independent of audience response. The role of gender in their imaginative life had in fact been critical to both Charlotte and Emily at least since the time of the toy soldiers; and from the first it had been closely tied to their conception of themselves as writers. They were of course by no means the first artists to feel that the mysteries of creative power are somehow entwined with the mysteries of gender, as the history of the figure of the muse attests. But they were among the first women writers to use their works themselves as tools for exploring and—insofar as they found it possible to do so—for resolving the peculiar problems that arise when the possessor of creative power is a woman.

Being and Doing

In her book *The Life of Charlotte Brontë,* Charlotte's friend and first biographer, Elizabeth Gaskell, offered a word of wry sympathy for the fate of Branwell. "There are always peculiar trials in the life of an only boy in a family of girls," Gaskell noted. "He is expected to act a part in life; to *do,* while they are only to *be.*"[5] Gaskell's sympathy was charged with the irony that hindsight brings, for this young man who had been expected to "do" wonderful things—to act a great part in life—had of course done nothing of interest except to be the brother of sisters who *did* act.

However, with regard to the Brontës, Gaskell's observation that girls are expected to "be" and boys to "do" touches on much more than the irony of Branwell's fate; her remark points our attention to an issue that was central for both Emily and Charlotte in their careers as writers.

Although Emily and Charlotte had very different attitudes toward femaleness and maleness, they shared fully the view that the essential characteristic of femaleness was "being," of maleness, "doing"; and each saw in herself both male and female elements. Female "being" both sisters associated with their dead mother. Maria Branwell Brontë, who died when Charlotte was five and Emily three, remained a vivid presence in her daughters' memories and in their sense of themselves and their fates as women. Emily longed to rejoin her mother in a primal union she came to think of as "Undying Life." The transcendent realm was a mother-world for Emily, and it lay behind her, not before her in the unfolding of time. Charlotte, who saw in her mother the model of woman as lovable and loved by the father, longed urgently to be lovable too; yet she did not wish to cling so closely to the mother-world as to die as her mother had died. For Charlotte transcendency lay ahead, at the end of life's journey through the stormy father-world. By the power of her art she repeatedly resurrected strong mother figures who would impel or encourage her on this dangerous passage, and help her to survive it to the end.

Male "doing" Charlotte and Emily both associated with their father Patrick, a vigorous, tough-spirited Irishman and an exemplary survivor who had worked his way to Cambridge and was now not only rector of their village church but also a published writer of religious stories and poems. For both Charlotte and Emily the father-world was the *ac*tual world where we act and are acted upon (and where Branwell, for one, destroyed himself so thoroughly). This was the world of creative ambition, of "doing" in all its range of thrill and menace; the realm of will and power, of audience and art.

Such metaphors of gender as these, distinguishing doing as male and being as female, have for centuries provided grist for political grinding by those who argue that woman's proper function is to be contented, not ambitious; passive, not active; supportive, not creative. Such argument from metaphor is flawed, of course, in that it depends on transforming theoretical concepts, ways of characterizing aspects of the inner life of both men and women, into tools for monitoring women's social behavior and limiting their range of opportunity. But flawed though the argument may be, the Brontë sisters suffered as did many before and after them from some such association between inner elements and outer constraints; it set conditions on their lives and their thinking. The process by which Emily and Charlotte each arrived at her own understanding of her "male" and "female" elements was slow, painful, and arduous; the understandings they reached were correspondingly complex, and also rich in their implications for anyone who would understand how hardships and losses may be transmuted into the great gain that is art.

The Brontës' personal distinction between what I call the mother-world of being and the father-world of doing, and their radical understanding of what this distinction meant, finds a suggestive modern analogue in the work of the eminent British psychologist D. W. Winnicott, who in studying specifically the issue of creativity and its origins observes that both men and women have in their psychological makeup what he calls, for lack of a better term, male and female elements (he rejects the terms active and passive).[6] Despite the obvious differences in conceptual frameworks, his view of these elements in what he calls their "distilled" form is strikingly akin to the Brontës' view. Winnicott sees the female element as that aspect of the infant that does not "relate to" the mother's breast (desiring it, resenting it) but "is" the breast—desirable in itself. One's female element is in effect one's ontological center. "The study of the pure distilled uncontaminated female element leads us to BEING, and this forms the only basis for self-discovery and sense of existing." The male element Winnicott then associates with the instincts and object-relating, the concerns of doing and relating—pursuit, performance, possession. Thus the female element necessarily precedes the male: one must first be, if one is to desire or do. Winnicott closes his discussion of the subject with an emphatic finale: "Now I want to say: 'After being—doing and being done to. But first, being.' "[7]

It is in relation to some such ordering of male and female elements that we may understand the function of the muse for both Brontë sisters.

Given the significance of the female muse in male Romantic poetry, and the immersion of the Brontë sisters in that poetry, it is crucial to understand how each of them transformed this heritage in her self-perception as artist. Charlotte and Emily each quite naturally associated her inner element of "being" with her own female person. Her essence was female. Each likewise associated her capacity for "doing" with some instrumental, "male" element in herself. In its maleness this element inevitably incorporated aspects of Patrick and (to a lesser extent) Branwell, the men both sisters knew best. But it is only as the woman-writer's *own* capacity that this element may be called a muse. Each sister gave her male muse various human forms within her fictions; we will see him in Heathcliff, and to some extent in the various "masters" of Charlotte's novels. But the muse also had for each sister a spiritual or divine dimension, which each eventually associated with the Holy Ghost or inspiring breath of God.

Emily was more ambivalent than was Charlotte about the male element in herself. Insofar as Emily felt her muse impelling her forward into the father-world of ambition and achievement, she judged him to be an alien and often subversive force, a fragmenter of her primal, female being. Increasingly she rejoiced in her muse only insofar as she felt him to be a messenger recalling her to her original wholeness. This is another way of saying that she eventually saw her male element as a lost and straying part of her wholeness, active because detached from his female source. Increasingly it was Emily's view that the muse's only proper function was to come home like a prodigal son, to be gathered to a glorious rest in the fullness of original being. But of course art is act. It is the "doer" in us that writes books and builds cities, whether that doer be housed in man or woman. It may have been Emily's sense of the maleness of "doing" that led her to speak *Wuthering Heights* through the voice of the citified Lockwood, an embodiment of the decadent qualities of man the doer, artificial rather than artistic. But the driving force of the book is Heathcliff's; he binds the novel's two halves together. His fierce, pitiless wolfishness reflects the violent energy through which Emily wrote her novel. Although she felt at best ambivalent about her male element in its separateness, she nonetheless fully released and empowered it for this, her near-final act of art.

These matters I will treat in more detail later. For now what I want to note is Emily's attitude toward her muse, which is expressed in the fact that within the fiction Heathcliff, who represents this male element, is after Catherine's death mere beingless motion. As if in parody of rampant masculinity he struggles to possess, dominate, tyrannize, punish.

But he knows his inner emptiness; and given the chance to recover his being—his "life," his "soul"—he abandons all motion in order to join Catherine in the grave.

Charlotte too was ambivalent about the male element in herself, but on different grounds. All her life she longed passionately to be loved by a creative and charismatic man and at the same time to be creative and charismatic herself: to be a beloved "being" like her mother, but also to be a "doer" like her father. For most of her life she fought the dread conviction that these two desires must be ever in irresolvable conflict, that her muse might be wicked, even morbid, and that releasing him was sure to render her unwomanly and unlovable. It seemed that her creative impulses must be stifled or her heart starved. Only in her last years (and partly in response to a renewed understanding of her now-dead sister Emily's work) did she begin to solve her problem by imagining a male figure who could both love the woman in her and at the same time arouse, encourage, and redeem her "masculine" powers.

In a sense Emily's position was more radically feminist than Charlotte's: to the end, Emily valued female being as the root and goal of her life. But it was Charlotte who insisted that women have the right to live as fully as men do, and that in order to act on this right, women must "do" as men do, they must reach for what the world offers or represents, must move toward a God who is male in that He is not the origin but rather the destination of life's journey. For Charlotte life was not circular but linear; it did not move from mother to Mother, but from mother to Father. Charlotte's whole creative life was spent in the effort to conceive a muse who might empower her art and at the same time cherish her being.

By the end of their lives both Charlotte and Emily saw some emanation of Godhead, in Christian terms the Holy Ghost, as the source of their creativity; but their God was surely—especially in Emily's case—no orthodox deity. They arrived at their respective mythologies through the same painful process by which they arrived at their views concerning the male and female elements of their own inner makeup. The two processes are in fact inseparable, and will be studied together.

Contrasts Between Emily and Charlotte

Once Emily came to associate all "doing" with her alienated masculine element and with the father-world outside her, it followed that the practice of art brought her not closer to wholeness and immortality, but farther from it. Her mythology moved in the direction of mysticism, with ties to visionary Romanticism.

But Charlotte was far less prepared than Emily to accede to mystical views, nor did she approve the terms of her sister's reformulation of them, or its results, which she rightly saw as profoundly disruptive of the social and domestic values that she herself held very dear. Charlotte's art served a very different function for her life and spirit than Emily's did for hers. The differences have far-reaching implications for the life each sister lived, for the kind of work she did, and for the place each came to hold in literary history.

As with the Romantic poets she had read from childhood, Emily's most absorbing subject was invariably herself: specifically the location, growth, and potential of her own imaginative power, its appearances and disappearances, its relationship to her life and to her art. One critic has remarked that for Blake and Wordsworth "the pleasures of poetry were only forepleasures, in the sense that poems, finally, were scaffoldings for a more imaginative vision, and not ends in themselves."[8] So also for Emily—and in prose as well as poems—though perhaps she would have reversed the sequence as Shelley did in observing that "when composition begins, inspiration is already on the decline, and the most glorious poetry that has ever been communicated to the world is probably a feeble shadow of the original conception of the Poet."[9] But none of those earlier Romantic poets' work, however internal their focus, is as closeted and self-referential as Emily's, nor was their experience of the world as hermetic. Emily sought no audience; she formed few human attachments, and expressed increasing hostility and contempt for the world of human relationships, whether sexual or social; ultimately she eschewed "scaffoldings" and "feeble shadows" altogether, seeking exclusively the direct company of her visionary conception itself. That way, of course, lie solipsism and silence.

In many ways Charlotte could not have been more different: she was intent on publication, hungered for recognition and approval, made close friends and kept them all her life, delighted in companionship, and fell in love at least twice.[10] She too almost always took herself as the subject of her writing, but in doing so she typically drew on literal autobiography —that is, on the external events of her life—while Emily never did. Charlotte's trip to Brussels is recorded twice—first in *The Professor,* then again in *Villette.* Yorkshire acquaintances were able to identify the author of *Shirley* by the book's many revealing anecdotes and details of character and setting. And quarrels raged for years after Charlotte's death over whether her bitter indictment of "Lowood" in *Jane Eyre* was justified by the facts.

Probably the most interesting difference between the kinds of "self" treated in Emily's work and in Charlotte's parallels the difference between their attitudes toward their father, indeed toward fatherly persons and authority altogether. A telling index to this particular difference lies in their contrasting responses to the schoolgirl status they had to assume when in 1842, at the ages of twenty-four (Emily) and twenty-six (Charlotte), they went to Brussels to improve their French and German. Emily worked like a horse, but hated it; she and their teacher, M. Heger, didn't "draw well together at all." Charlotte on the other hand reveled in this opportunity to study under a confident and accomplished educator: "I think I am never unhappy; my present life is so delightful, so congenial to my own nature."[11] Once Emily returned home after nine months she stayed there gratefully for the rest of her life; but Charlotte seized the opportunity to return a second time to Brussels and on this second visit fell hopelessly in love with M. Heger. Fatherly not only in his role as teacher and in his authoritative manner of instruction, he was also literally a father—a quite settled married man with several children. He returned Charlotte's passion not at all.

But the seeds of the sisters' differing responses to M. Heger must have been planted much earlier in life. And although we can't hope to uncover them altogether, various kinds of evidence do remain as bases for speculation. The theme of the abandoned child that runs through the work of both Emily and Charlotte reflects of course the facts of their early life— the successive deaths of their mother and their two mothering elder sisters, and concomitant disappointment in a father whom his daughters appear to have experienced as disturbingly aloof. The effect on Emily of her brief experience of mother-love, followed by such a sharp succession of losses, was that she retained all her life a strikingly direct access to primordial feeling, unsoftened by time and unscreened by convention.[12] Charlotte, perhaps partly because she was two years older than her sister, responded differently to her losses; among other things she seems always to have sorted her feelings carefully, trying to repress the less acceptable ones, or at least to hide them from view. Emily, then, was disposed to speak as if to no audience but herself, whereas Charlotte's speech was tuned always to other ears. Emily's poetry indicates that she found in her natural surroundings some of the joy and comfort that she missed from her departed human mother. This comfort and her resulting self-sufficiency may have helped encourage her to feel that she could do equally well without the father. Certainly that radical "liberty," whose importance to her has been so much emphasized by her chroniclers from Charlotte on down, is in one sense the liberty of the orphan—the lonely freedom of the parentless child. One price of such freedom is expressed in her work by the way her hatred of authority is seconded by her firm commitment to a narrow world that she could master ("the world within," in Emily's own phrase), to the exclusion of any more expansive one in which her mastery might be too sharply challenged.[13]

I have said that Emily's was a Romantic muse. Thus is should not surprise us that one of his functions in her work was to dramatize her wish to die, a wish commonly expressed (though often metaphorically) in Romantic poetry. Some such longing is likely to inhere in any yearning for transcendence, where transcendence is conceived of as residing within rather than above or beyond the self.[14] Hence the long-recognized association of high Romantic argument with the dangers of narcissism and solipsism. Emily was disposed to approve and embrace such "Romantic" attitudes not only on intellectual grounds but even by what might be thought of as the disturbances in her personality: the presence of unvitiated primordial feeling, the defensive narrowing of her world, the suicidal impulse. She came, that is, to her reading of Romantic poetry with an already deep-rooted disposition to rebel against the limitations of life, against the authority not only of parent and teacher, but of all received opinion, a deep suspicion of all forms of power or thought whose source is not the self—perhaps especially in that these tended, in the world of her experience, to be associated with the masculine.

Charlotte's disposition was different. Because as eldest surviving daughter she seems to have hoped that she might in some way replace her mother at her father's side, Charlotte had always to see the "beloved" as forbidden or inaccessible. This pattern is expressed in Charlotte's life by her attachments first to her married teacher and later to her charming but emotionally elusive publisher, neither of whom, she well knew, was romantically available to her. The same pattern orders her art, for even when her heroines are successful in love, they must surmount great obstacles. Even Charlotte's love of Emily fell into the same pattern. Emily's traits of sternness and withdrawal, because they were traits associated by Charlotte with the masculine, the father, were actually a source of great attraction for Charlotte even as she deplored their consequences. In a letter written not long before Emily's death, Charlotte lamented her sister's intransigent refusal of medical aid, or even of sympathy; yet confided, "I think a certain harshness in her powerful and peculiar character only makes me cling to her more."[15]

In editing Emily's work after her death, Charlotte came to understand her sister's thinking more fully than she had while Emily was living. Much of what she saw pained her. But she did learn from Emily's example how to develop a male muse—though not, in Charlotte's case, a Romantic muse. Rather Charlotte's was that ultimate Victorian paterfamilias, Godhead itself: God-with-us, Emanuel. "Who prizes you if I do not? Who is your friend if not Emanuel?" Paul Emanuel inquires of Lucy at the end of *Villette*. She has already assured him in ringing biblical language that she will use her "talent" well—that she "will be your faithful steward. . . . I trust at your coming the account will be ready." Now, when she yields up her last lingering doubts of his love, he rewards her with "one deep spell of peace." "He gathered me near his heart. I was full of faults; he took them and me all home. . . . 'Lucy . . . Be my dearest, first on earth.' " Beloved of the ultimate Father, resting in the bosom of Abraham, she claims at last the full acceptance and security of what Wordsworth called "God who is our home."

Like Emily's Heathcliff, Paul Emanuel was modeled on the "visions" of his author's "meditations." But the two novels that resulted are very different in kind. For Emily, Christian mystery is subsumed to the logic of Romantic doctrine: the truth of earth being death, the body must be shuffled off in pursuit of the Absolute. For Charlotte, Pauline celibacy is subsumed to the logic of personal experience. The sexual love of man is dangerous; for women who wish to survive and also to do creative work, such love must be resigned (or redesigned) in favor of the love of God. In *Villette*, though the implications of action are enlarged by rich and complex systems of imagery and allusion to which we must be constantly alert if we are to grasp the underlying movement of the book, the overall organization is still that of traditional narrative. "Meaning" unfolds sequentially, in essentially the same way that story unfolds. By contrast *Wuthering Heights* must be read as one reads Blake's *Milton*, Byron's *Manfred*, or Shelley's *Prometheus Unbound*—that is, as visionary poetry whose subject is creative genius itself, in this case specifically a *woman's* creative genius. Although, as has been amply and often demonstrated, Emily worked out such details as chronology, topography, and dialect with rigorous care, these details create patterns and rhythms that order the novel internally and direct the reader inward into its visionary center. The details are not important as threads binding the novel's meaning to a particular geographical place or historical moment. Rather Emily's "realism," her almost fanatical attention to accuracy and order, recalls Blake's assertion that "he who wishes to see a Vision, a perfect whole, / Must see it in its Minute Particulars, Organiz'd" (*Jerusalem*, plate 91).

In Charlotte's novels, on the other hand, setting and chronology point us outward to the world of time and space. This is especially true of *Shirley,* where Charlotte's large ambition was to show that the condition of English women reflected or embodied the condition of England itself, a condition she explored, in turn, through the medium of the Luddite disturbances that shook Yorkshire in the years just before she was born. On the opening page of the novel she warns her reader not to expect "poetry": "Calm your expectations. . . . Something real, cool, and solid, lies before you." And in preparing to write it Charlotte did some research on the real and solid, among other things sending away for the files of the *Leeds Mercury* for the years 1812, 1813, and 1814: clearly not the stuff of poetry in the Romantic sense of the word—that is, of language as it reaches toward what is ultimately beyond speech. Rather it is the utterly appropriate subject of the language of everyday life. In this sense Charlotte's work tended toward prose, Emily's toward poetry.

Poetic Vision and the Novel

For the Romantics, "poetry" was the language of eternity rather than of time, of the transcendent rather than of the mundane. As such it could of course never capture or contain its subject completely, but only point us toward what must remain essentially ineffable; but that pointing was at least more than mere "prose" could do. Accordingly any human experience that took on spiritual dimension might be considered "poetic" (contrast "prosaic"). Given such powers, the word *poetry* opened itself to broad figurative possibilities. The Oxford English Dictionary credits Milton with the first figurative use of the word *poem,* citing "An Apology for Smectymnuus," in which Milton made his famous claim that "he who would not be frustrate of his hope to write well hereafter in laudable things, ought himselfe to be a true Poem, that is a composition and patterne of the best and honourablest things." This claim was indeed the germ of Wordsworth's concept of the silent poet, whereby one might be a "poet" and yet never write a line. After Milton, figurative uses of the terms *poet* and *poetry* abound. The Brontës' contemporary Charles Kingsley is really only extending a little the implications of this figurative flexibility when he writes, in a letter of 1843, that "If we can but keep alive a spiritual meaning in every little action, we shall have no need to write poetry—our life will be the real poem."[16]

For the Romantics, then, to be a poet was to grasp "spiritual meaning," to make of words an opening into the realm beyond words—

ultimately to point one's self or one's audience toward the "eternal Silence" in whose being our years of life are but noisy moments (Wordsworth). In "A Defence of Poetry," Shelley wrote that "A poem is the very image of life expressed in its eternal truth"; similarly, for Blake "Vision" is "a Representation of what Eternally Exists, Really & Unchangeably." Blake's "Vision" and Shelley's "poem" stand in contrast to any art that would copy the shifting surface appearances of the phenomenal world. As Shelley explains, a poem is "universal," it is "the creation of actions according to the unchangeable forms of human nature," whereas "a story is a catalogue of detached facts, which have no other bond of connexion than time, place, circumstance, cause and effect."

This distinction between poem and story certainly suggests the difference between Emily's work and Charlotte's, between Romantic poetry and Victorian novel.[17] But it is suggestion only, not a firm distinction, because by the end of the nineteenth century the novel had assimilated the chief goals and methods of Romantic poetry; novelists had discovered that they could accommodate poetic vision to the exigencies of character and plot, of human action unfolding in space and time. In this process of discovery Emily and Charlotte Brontë both were central— Emily in applying the visionary mode to a prose narrative whose subject was her relation as woman artist to her own creative power, and Charlotte in recognizing what Emily had done and carrying her knowledge back into the mainstream of the nineteenth-century novel. *Wuthering Heights* could be misread as crude Yorkshire Gothic. But few novelists, after *Villette,* doubted the capacity of the novel as a genre to deal with the experience of creativity or the spiritual life, to be "poetic" in the Romantic sense of the word. The differences between Emily and Charlotte are in this sense as much a matter of continuity as of contrast; their works mark successive moments in an evolution whose direction they helped alter toward the "poetic," the "lyric," the "experimental," the "modern" novel. From the Brontë root grow flowerings as diverse as Eliot, Hardy, Conrad, Woolf, Lawrence, Faulkner, and Toni Morrison.

In the Brontës, then, a broad set of issues concerning theology, aesthetics, gender, and genre converges—each issue important in itself, yet complicated in its significance by the way it interconnects with the others. The threat to man's immortality that accompanied the growing secularism and skepticism implied in the term "the death of God" focused the attention of the male Romantic poets on their muses, on art and inspiration as means to transcendence. But the concurrent rise to prominence of women as both authors and subjects of art required an unsettling new consideration of the way genders are assigned or assumed in our concepts of creativity and creation, of artist and muse. Finally, when narrative prose began to replace poetry as the dominant literary form in the nineteenth century, traditional assumptions about the limits of genre were challenged. The increasingly popular genre, the novel, proved quite capable of treating the favorite themes of Romantic poetry, capable even of incorporating "the visionary" both as subject and as literary technique.[18]

The heightened fear of death and the anxiety about the prospects for immortality that were common to the Romantics generally were felt with special force and poignance by the Brontës. Their early youth was such a shattering succession of family losses that Emily, at least, was drawn to a version of the Neoplatonic position familiar to her and to us from such strains of Romantic poetry as Wordsworth's Intimations Ode: "Our birth is but a sleep and a forgetting." The "doing" of mortal action was in her view a kind of reenactment of our "undoing." The same concern brought Charlotte to a different conclusion. Being, as she saw it, was charged with doing: not to do meant, for her, not fully to be. Not only did she regard temporal action as necessary to the creating of art, but she saw artistic act as the model of all life's pilgrimage, of that journey which every soul must make—woman's as well as man's—on its way to the presence of God.

We will see—especially in Charlotte's case—how for each Brontë sister the muse was linked with Godhead. Emily's muse pointed her away from both worldly community and the practical practice of art, to a religion of solitude and silence. But Charlotte clung tenaciously to belief in a more traditional Divinity, though she feared that in this world He often hid His face from ambitious women like herself. From Emily she learned that it might be both necessary and possible to evoke divine presence through her own creative power. This perception she passed on to her descendants in the field of nineteenth-century fiction. Charlotte, rather than Emily, could do so because she had no interest in rejoining divinity at its source in the "O" of silence, death, and eternity (the sphere of poetry, as Shelley understood it: of the universal, ineffable, unchanging). Rather, Charlotte was eager to draw the divine Word into the world of words, into the timely and particular realm of creation, incarnation, the personal experience of the individual living woman who was herself. This is the world of traditional narrative, of Shelley's "story"—but crossed with "poetry" to achieve a new and enlarged form.

ONE

Emily Brontë's Poetry

"Whither is fled the visionary gleam?
Where is it now, the glory and the dream?"

—Intimations Ode, William Wordsworth

"Cut off from hope in early day,
From power and glory cut away."

—#14, Emily Brontë[1]

For the male Romantic poets whose work Emily Brontë knew early and well, life is a process of estrangement from transcendent origins, a story of lost glory and dream, in Wordsworth's famous phrasing. So it seemed also to Emily, which may be one reason Romantic poetry appealed to her so strongly and served as her model in so many and such complex ways. As a model, it presented her with great opportunities for self-expression, but also with great difficulties.

The Romantic Poet's Muse

In their effort to recount the loss of glory or to evoke recovery or compensation, the male Romantics all turned to some woman or women —figures whom they did not generally call "muses," partly no doubt because these were in the first instance literal women, real sisters, wives, or lovers. Yet as females who filled the traditional inspiring role of muses for the poets who invoked them, they typically also appeared within the works they inspired, transmuted into fictional representations of aspects of the poetic imagination, much in the way muses have always done. Among these Romantic muses one thinks for example of Blake's Catherine/Enitharmon, tincturing the artist's outlines "with beams of blushing love"; of Wordsworth's Dorothy, the "Sister of my Soul!" who "preserv'd me still a poet"[2] and who lives and dies as "Lucy" in the poems themselves; of Shelley's "veiled maid" or his "heart's sister," who assumed a succession of inspiring human forms from Harriet Grove to Jane Williams.[3] The case for all such muses, both fictional and actual, is suggestively defined by Jerome McGann in a comment on Byron's literary treatment of women. "The female counterparts of Byron's heroes," he writes, "correspond exactly to the state of the hero's soul which they inhabit. They objectify the passionate impulses in the man whose imagination made them what they are. This is as much to say that none of them are truly 'persons.' "[4] In this respect art seems to have mimicked life: most of the Romantic poets drafted their sisters, wives, and lovers into the service of their art. Like the females of their poetic fictions, these women were for the purposes of the male creative imagination less persons than personae of the poet, doubles or projections of himself, and especially of that lost transcendent self who lived amid "the glory and the dream." So Wordsworth turns to Dorothy at the end of "Tintern Abbey" to "behold in thee what I once was."

Contemporary literary theorists argue that language is constructed over an absence, specifically the absence of the mother from whom we all separated as young children in learning to speak and in adapting ourselves to our roles within culture. And feminists have been concerned about the ways in which this makes of language a peculiarly masculine tool, whose function it is to represent the mother/female figuratively (in words) while keeping her distanced, excluding her presence except through language—through the words that replace her by naming her. It is assumed in this view that the position of human women parallels that of the natural world (Mother Earth, Mother Nature) in being the absent Other that is replaced by words and not the (male) voice that can speak them.[5] Perhaps this myth of language helps explain the way Catherine Blake, Dorothy Wordsworth, and others entered their husbands' and brothers' texts.

But it is also true, and in ways that go beyond myth, that in the mother's womb and later at her breast we all learned our first lessons of happiness. In the idiom of "being" and "doing," it was there, at womb and breast, that each of us first learned what it was to "be," and experienced the ineffable (literally, *unspeakable*) joy of being at one with the world which was our mother. If speaking is "doing," and implies separation from that world, then poetry must inevitably be a record of loss; and so the Romantics did perceive it, as I have already observed. In these terms we may understand the Romantic muse not so much as a drafted wife or sister, but more as a figurative presence standing in for the missing mother, or more accurately for each poet's (long since forfeited) experience of primary identification with his own mother. As such the muse is a signifier, replacing the objective world whose very being threatens language, and at the same time a projection of the poet's own inner female element, his "being" from which he has split off as part of the price of growing up male—of becoming not a "mother" but a *man.* Quite appropriately then, this Romantic muse regularly appears as the poet's literal or figurative sister, the mirroring double of himself, and yet the beloved mediator through whom he can remain in touch with all that is beyond himself. She is the human-formed locus of both earth and eternity, both Mother Nature and the Heaven that lay about the poet in his infancy, his own recollected Paradise (cf. Coleridge's speaker who has "drunk the milk of Paradise").

In order to understand the situation Emily encountered as a woman reading and later writing Romantic poetry, to see what work she had to do to find a voice and make a place for herself within that aesthetic tradition, we should look rather closely at this matter of gender roles as the Romantics themselves perceived it. We have seen that it is consonant in certain ways with our modern literary theory, but it differs in its emphases.

Shelley was the poet with whom Emily had the closest affinity, and the imagery he drew on to talk of love is directly pertinent here. "What is Love?" he queries in a fragmentary essay: "ask him who adores, what is God?"[6] The atheist Shelley is invoking no conventionality here, but rather indicating the dimensions of his topic. For him "Nothing exists but as it is perceived," and to perceive in the spirit of love is to concentrate all worthiness into a mirroring figure, the projected likeness of one's own "best" being. Love is the thirsting after this figure. To slake that thirst is to unite with the beloved—a union that the language of sexuality helps convey, but only by metaphor. Ultimately the redemptive union can result (somewhat as it does in Blake) only when one relinquishes all resistant separateness, all selfish jealousy or even individual will. In such a state doing is subsumed into being; one does not act but *becomes,* in a union that recalls the infant slaking its thirst at the breast.

Indeed, "to thirst" was a verb with special resonance for many romantics, for whom it denoted a yearning toward greater fullness of being. Consider the implications of Keats' "parching tongue," or how for Coleridge drought emblemizes the Ancient Mariner's spiritual isolation and emptiness. Similarly Shelley repeatedly used thirst to figure the longing for transcendence—as in one of his notes to "Hellas," where he comments on "our inextinguishable thirst for immortality," and in "On Love," where he says that we conceive a perfect "Paradise" circled in a "soul within our soul" to which we "eagerly refer all sensations, thirsting that they should resemble or correspond with it." If we recall Winnicott's description of the female element as that which "is" the breast, the male element as that which desires it, we may better understand why Shelley saw infant thirst as the initiating model of all human longing. "We are born into the world," writes Shelley, "and there is something within us which from the instant that we live and move thirsts after its likeness. It is probably in correspondence with this law that the infant drains milk from the bosom of its mother." His point is of course that the breast is our first object of desire, the first object in whose desirableness we recognize the image of our own "best" being, our inward "Paradise." Shelley does not suggest here that this paradise is modeled on our memory of the womb, but he hints at it in "Epipsychidion," where the perfect isle to which the poet will take his "heart's sister" conflates to a "soul within a soul" whose deep music seems "Like echoes of an antenatal dream." Thus, in crude declension of this figure, the island paradise is a geographical form of the sister-muse, who is the human form of the mother's breast, which the infant poet had once assumed was himself and now sees as the emblem of his "best" self, his paradisal "being," which he thirsts to reclaim.

Given these views it should not surprise us that Shelley, like Wordsworth, considered that children are graced with a special confidence in their own being, a sense of unbroken union with their world. This sense must fade with time: "in living we lose the apprehension of life," Shelley wrote in his fragmentary essay "On Life."[7] Only some persons "who are in this respect always children" manage to recover in "reverie" the feeling of being "dissolved into the surrounding universe, or as if the surrounding universe were absorbed into their being." Thus is the infant the poet-nascent, for whom the mother-world is still a part of the self. From this state of fullness or plenitude Shelley and Wordsworth both agree that the story of life with all its getting and spending can only record fallings away, vanishings. This explains why the Romantics were all somewhat ambivalent about the value of words, especially in matters of transcendence, of "high Romantic argument." It may be that the process of gender identity and acculturation that made the male poet both a man and a poet required him to distance himself from his female origins and being. But for a Romantic, the aim of poetry is to recover just those experiences from which he is distanced. In Wordsworth's phrase, these are the "first affections," which

> have power to make
> Our noisy years seem moments in the being
> Of the eternal Silence.

We have seen that the male Romantic artist's female muse embodies both temporal and eternal being. The famed Romantic love of nature reminds us that Mother Earth was one aspect of the desirable female being that these ardent doers so eagerly sought ("both what they half create / And what perceive"). Yet to the immortal soul she is a foster mother only, a "homely Nurse," as Wordsworth wrote in the Intimations Ode. Moreover, to embrace Mother Earth directly is to make of her bosom a grave, just as modern theorists argue that to accede to the natural world would be to render language impotent and destroy culture. In his ambitious meditation on the history of poetic myths, Robert Graves wrote that all poetry is religious invocation of the muse, "the Mother of all living . . . whose embrace is death."[8] The muse as literal woman—a Dorothy Wordsworth, or even better a Lucy (as fictional variant of the actual sister)—thus offers a safer object of love; she represents the sum of all being, yet her dimensions are sufficiently human to allow of human embrace, and as poetic topic she is safely encoded in language. In this way the male artist's female muse offers him a way to encounter both Mother Earth and lost Edenic paradise in a form that is not annihilative but restorative. She has the desired maternal attributes yet is more like a sister than like a parent whose power is so great as to subsume or destroy the mortal poet. As goddess, the Romantic muse is present proof that divinity still lives within the poet as well as beyond him. As Shelley says of Emilia Viviani in "Epipsychidion," she is "a mortal shape indeed" and yet her attributes "cannot die." Thus even if God the Father be dead, as Nietzsche was soon to proclaim, still the artist as doer may father forth his own immortality by projecting his inmost self onto the female muse who "bears" it not into the world of earth and death but into Milton's "Heav'n of Heav'ns," that infinitude which Wordsworth calls "our being's heart and home."

Emily's Male Muse

To turn from the male Romantic poets to Emily Brontë is to recognize that this formulation of the muse's meaning cannot account for a woman poet's needs and experience. Robert Graves points to the problem for woman in the Romantic tradition most starkly when he states that "woman is not a poet: she is either a Muse or she is nothing." Having said so much, however, he hurries to clarify his meaning. It is not, he insists, that a woman should not write poems, but rather "that she should write as a woman, not as if she were an honorary man." He means, apparently, that she must not love the muse but be the muse, be in herself "the Mother of all Living . . . whose embrace is death." As woman she must either serve as the silent inspirer of male poets, or else write "as a woman" with what Graves calls "antique authority: . . . impartial, loving, cruel, wise."⁹

Perhaps Emily Brontë as poet and even as poetic novelist fulfilled something of Graves' ambition for the woman who would write "as a woman." Certainly she was prepared, as Graves insists all poets must be, to forgo domesticity (the connubial hearth) as a value for herself. But in facing the problem of what it might mean to "be" as a woman and yet also to "do" as an artist, Emily discovered that she must have what Graves denies she could have—namely a muse of her own: a figure to embody her *male* element. To understand that need, let us take a brief look at the Romantic woman artist's situation as Emily faced it.

Sharing as Emily did the general perspectives of Romantic philosophy, and the correlate aesthetic assumption that art is itself the tacit subject of art, that central to every poem is the poet's encounter with the experience of creativity itself, Emily had to face the issue of gender quite directly—just as we must now, in looking back at her. What could it mean for a female artist to have a Romantic muse? To envision a "heart's brother," or "brother of my soul"? Would he then stand as the safely mediating representative of a beloved but dangerous father—Father Nature? Our Father who art in Heaven? Can the female child "mother" the woman-artist? Or if not, what can be woman's comparable access to transcendence or immortality?

Emily's art reveals that she struggled with precisely these questions. As we might expect, they did not and could not resolve themselves along gender lines consistently parallel to those of the male artist; her relationship to her inner elements of being and doing will differ from his, insofar as these metaphors of gender derive from the human sexes. Emily's work is important to the history of ideas because she appeared near the end of the Romantic period, when (in Shelley's phrase) "The cloud of mind" was "discharging its collected lightening." In that stormy time the upheavals of revolution in every sphere had thrown into fresh relief some of our deepest and most unquestioned assumptions about what it means to be human, and specifically about the nature and power of the human mind or spirit: that is, about our relation to the (presumed male)

Creator on the one hand, and on the other to His (presumed female) Creation. At this moment, then, appeared a woman artist of great intellectual power and creative energy, who was prepared in general to assent to the views of the new age but could not avoid questioning the metaphoric system in which they still resided. In matters such as these, where ontological, aesthetic, psychoanalytic, and religious perspectives all converge, idea can hardly be disentangled from its medium in metaphor. Words shape the thought they clothe, tenor resides in vehicle. To challenge metaphor, then, is to challenge all: no wonder her audience found Emily Brontë's work disturbing.[10]

The first audience to find it disturbing was her older sister, Charlotte, whose attitude toward *Wuthering Heights* was profoundly ambivalent. One the one hand she wished to defend it from detractors who might suspect its author—her own Emily!—of being as "sombre, rude, brutal" as her book;[11] on the other hand she was painfully confronted by those very qualities in the character of Heathcliff, whom she loathed and yet evidently regarded as paradigmatic of the novel. "The worst of it is," she lamented to one correspondent, "some of his spirit seems breathed through the whole narrative in which he figures: it haunts every moore and glen, and beckons in every fir-tree of the Heights."[12] This is masculine Nature indeed!

Charlotte's penetrating and complex assessment of her sister's achievement is reflected in a remarkable passage in the "Editor's Preface" that she affixed to the 1850 edition of *Wuthering Heights,* two years after Emily's death. In this preface Heathcliff emerges as at once the story's leading spirit and the human embodiment of Father Nature—that is, of the harsh but alluring moors that provide the novel's setting. Although Charlotte recommends Nelly Dean and Edgar Linton to the reader's approval, she saw in Heathcliff—half unwittingly and surely unwillingly—both Emily's muse (Charlotte's own words are that Heathcliff is the "vision" of Emily's "meditations") and the larger realm of nature to which he stands as emblem or mediator.

Even the heath and cliff of Heathcliff's name figure in Charlotte's astonishingly suggestive evocation of her sister at work. In the passage to which I allude, Charlotte likens Emily to a sculptor (a male figure: clearly Charlotte did not identify the artist in her sister with her sister's femaleness) who finds "a granite block on a solitary moor" and, gazing on it, sees "how from the crag might be elicited a head, savage, swart, sinister; a form molded with at least one element of grandeur—power." With "no model but the vision of his meditations" this sculptor at last gives the crag "human shape; and there it stands, colossal, dark, and frowning." In this giant male figure is focused all of Charlotte's ambivalence concerning her sister's work. Emily's vision, hero, and novel all coalesce into a presence that on the one hand has the form of a human male and yet on the other is an element of nature—"half statue, half rock: in the former sense, terrible and goblin-like; in the latter, almost beautiful, for its colouring is of mellow grey, and moorland moss clothes it; and heath, with its blooming bells and balmy fragrance, grows faithfully close to the giant's foot." No other critic has so fully grasped the vast and at the same time disturbing implications of Emily's achievement in substituting the male for the traditionally female gender of nature and of the muse that mediates it.

Insofar as the male Romantic poet's muse is the projection of his temporal "being," that is of his female element as it partakes of earth and physical nature, the genders of artist and muse may be inverted without great distortion of meaning, however disturbing it may be to traditional habits of thought. This was the inversion that Charlotte saw in her sister's novel and reported in her preface. But those aspects of the Romantic muse that call on our earliest memories of infancy and that intimate the prospect of immortality through some reference to memories of the mother's womb or breast—those aspects of the muse are necessarily gender bound, and thus resist symmetrical inversion. A man's masculine identity depends on his having achieved successive divisions from his female origins in ways that a woman's female identity does not. If the male Romantic poet's female muse is his own female "perfected being" (his recollected glory, or antenatal paradise) projected outward in the form of a heart's sister through whom he may recover his own immortal being, so Emily's muse is her power of "doing" projected in male form—and this is very much the muse that we see her developing in her poetry. However, as we shall see, in her view the "doing" that the muse embodies is not "perfected doing." In Emily's case the imperfection may result partly from the fact of her mother's early death. For Emily language was indeed constructed over a loss, and quite specifically the loss of her mother. Emily's mother weaned her, replaced her with a new baby (Anne), grew painfully ill, and died—all by the time Emily was three. Little wonder that the realms of language and culture into which little Emily was then emerging are darkened by loss.

But the male muse (the element of "doing" projected outward) may present some problems and imperfections for any girl, not just for those whose mothers died when they were young. Winnicott, we recall, speaks of "doing" as following from "being." When this translates into the identity-experience of young women, the feeling that a male element has been derived from their being may seem less an enrichment than an impoverishment, a loss of wholeness through the splitting off of some "masculine" potency that had once been more fully their own. The psychologist Helene Deutsch noted that young girls often claim that they once had penises. And she recorded another fantasy that is closely related, and certainly significant for our understanding of Emily Brontë's Heathcliff—namely the claim frequently heard from young girls that they once had a little brother (often a twin) who died or was lost.[13] (Recall that Heathcliff replaces and takes the name of Catherine Earnshaw's dead little brother.) Deutsch's work does not suggest that such loss fantasies express a sense of impotence experienced by these girls; she recorded them rather as examples "of the girl's 'inner perception' of her own masculinity."

Until shortly before the time of her novel, Emily took joy in her " 'inner perception' of her own masculinity." She saw her male muse as a comforter, a welcome messenger from the realm of the dead mother, a source of visionary ecstasy and an inspirer of the poetry in which she secretly recorded her imaginative experience. But his very existence did presuppose that the "antenatal paradise" of united being and doing had been lost. And toward the end of her life, in her last poems and in her novel, she came to regard her male element principally in its separateness —not as a power to serve her, but as a "self" cut off from her in disastrous alienation. The Heathcliff of *Wuthering Heights* is no longer the sacred "God of Visions" of her poetry—though as muse figure he descends from that God.

Emily's Poetic Career

Although she wrote poetry from the age of eighteen or earlier, most of the poems for which Emily is most admired were written within the single year that preceded her writing of *Wuthering Heights,* that is between October 1844 and October 1845.[14] Then Charlotte discovered the secret notebooks in which Emily kept her poems and brought this phase of her sister's creative work to an end—or virtually to an end, for we must include in it the great poem "No coward soul is mine" which Emily wrote after she had already begun her novel.

The novel marks a decidedly new stage in Emily's creative life: it is her first work consciously directed to an audience and intended for publication. She seems to have approached this work with a powerful intensity of purpose, for it was apparently begun in November 1845, and it was completed by the following summer. Then, once the novel was done, she entered a third and final stage—a span of two and a half years of virtual silence, ending in death.

The medical cause of her death is not a matter of question: she had tuberculosis. But her mode of dying, her withdrawal, "stoicism," and refusal of medical attention, have led many students of the Brontës to think that she at least acquiesced to her disease. Close study of her evolving thought, however, has convinced me that she did more than acquiesce. It seems very clear that she actively embraced her death and also chose the artistic silence that preceded it.[15]

The grounds of that choice may be uncovered in her work, and help explain the three-stage movement of her career as I have described it. To begin with her poetry: we might think of this early writing as a means of survival. For one thing it provided a way of distracting herself from a weight of mourning that she felt unable to cope with by more conventional means; such distraction seems to have been at least part of the function of the whole complex theater of Gondal, though only the poems remain for us to judge by. Also, and increasingly, poetry provided Emily with a way of validating her intimations of immortality, her sense that time could not harm her because she was already in touch with eternity. This validation, achieved through entering the experiences of eternity into the records of time, was an especially important function of her "personal," or visionary poems. By the time of her novel, as we will see at the end of this chapter, the activity of writing no longer served the interests of eternity—or in other terms, of Emily's fidelity to the memory of her mother. After the novel, and especially after Charlotte revealed to her publishers that her sister Emily was "Ellis Bell," Emily apparently felt that she must die into silence.

During the years in which she wrote poetry, Emily built gradually a whole network of idea around the poetic muse, including ideas about life and death and their connection to the male and female elements in herself, her world, and her God. She could do this in poetry because poetry was by tradition capable of addressing issues of the spiritual and eternal; but also because such poetry, when she wrote it, was written solely for herself. Though the muse was male, he was derived from the mother-world and was thus an angel and a comforter. The poems he inspired might (for Emily's purposes) be called female speech, in being a mode of private introspection and retrospection contained within a "room" of Emily's own, shut away from the world of audience and the claims of community, and untainted by the motives of ambition that she attributed to the father-world. This network of ideas came to fruition in her final and greatest year of poetry, culminating in "No coward soul is mine." By reading a selection of those last, best poems as interconnected parts of a single, organic, matured system of thought, we may understand the final flowering of idea and imagery in which the muse took for Emily a most exalted spiritual role.

The remainder of this chapter will offer that reading, with attention to Emily's earlier work only as it helps clarify the direction from which her thought had come. Only eight poems will be quoted at length or analyzed in detail. Of these, six are from the great year of October 1844 to October 1845. One was written earlier ("Aye, there it is! It wakes tonight," dated 1841); it is included because it marks a crisis of discovery concerning the muse. And one, "No coward soul is mine," was written several months later (January 1846). Two are Gondal poems that nonetheless clearly depict Emily's own spiritual development or experience; the rest are directly personal and are drawn from her "personal" or non-Gondal notebook. Since with one exception the poems to be considered were all written within months of each other, and since all eight were part of the same rich flowering of thought, they will not be discussed in chronological order but rather grouped by relationships of imagery and idea.

We will be studying, then, the tenets of Emily's private theology and the systems of imagery that she developed to express it; but with frequent reminders, too, of the way her work echoes that of the Romantic poets on whom she was raised. We begin with the famous lament "Cold in the earth," then move to explore the concepts of the mother- and father-worlds ("Stars"); of the muse and his functions ("Aye, there it is" and "No coward soul"); of the tension within herself between worldly ambition and devoted fidelity ("O thy bright eyes must answer now" and "Enough of Thought, Philosopher"); and the commitment to her faith ("Death, that struck when I was most confiding"), which gave her the confidence to continue living and writing in the world ("Julian M. and A. G. Rochelle"). But this confidence was deeply shaken by Charlotte's discovery of Emily's secret work and Emily's own decision to let it be published. The present chapter ends by observing some of the effects of that discovery and decision, evident in the altered, published version of "Julian M. and A. G. Rochelle."

Rosina's Lament and the Wordsworthian Context

Emily's most famous poem offers a good place to begin. It demonstrates that the technique of doubling and repetition that critics have long recognized in *Wuthering Heights* had its roots in Emily's poetry, where it was grounded in her views concerning life and loss. And further, the poem suggests something of her debt to her Romantic predecessors—especially Wordsworth. It was, moreover, written right at the midpoint of her final, finest poetic year: dated March 3, 1845. Set in the world of Emily's Gondal fiction, the title indicates that this lament was supposed to have been spoken by the Gondal heroine Rosina Alcona to her long-dead beloved, the emperor Julius Brenzaida.

R. ALCONA TO J. BRENZAIDA

Cold in the earth, and the deep snow piled above thee!
Far, far removed, cold in the dreary grave!
Have I forgot, my Only Love, to love thee,
Severed at last by Time's all-wearing wave?

Now, when alone, do my thoughts no longer hover
Over the mountains on Angora's shore;
Resting their wings where heath and fern-leaves cover
That noble heart for ever, ever more?

Cold in the earth, and fifteen wild Decembers
From those brown hills have melted into spring—
Faithful indeed is the spirit that remembers
After such years of change and suffering!

Sweet Love of youth, forgive if I forget thee
While the World's tide is bearing me along:
Sterner desires and darker hopes beset me,
Hopes which obscure but cannot do thee wrong.

No other Sun has lightened up my heaven;
No other Star has ever shone for me:
All my life's bliss from they dear life was given—
All my life's bliss is in the grave with thee.

But when the days of golden dreams had perished
And even Despair was powerless to destroy,
Then did I learn how existence could be cherished,
Strengthened and fed without the aid of joy;

Then did I check the tears of useless passion,
Weaned my young soul from yearning after thine;
Sternly denied its burning wish to hasten
Down to that tomb already more than mine!

And even yet, I dare not let it languish,
Dare not indulge in Memory's rapturous pain;
Once drinking deep of that divinest anguish,
How could I seek the empty world again? (#182)

This poem's strengths lie in its incantatory rhythms and repetitions, and in the simplicity of its paradoxical argument. Like other passionate persons, the speaker has learned to exercise stern control over her wild desires in order to live passably in the world. But unlike those unsettling desires with which we are most familiar, her "burning wish" is "to hasten / Down" to the tomb. The poem opens by associating Julius' grave with what is cold, removed, and dreary—as we might expect; but by the end of the poem it is the living world that is empty and distant, whereas Julius' grave has become a center of burning desire, the locus of sun, stars, and bliss, a well of waters so potent that to drink of them is to indulge "rapturous pain" and know "divinest anguish." The orgasmic language suggests sexual longing; but here as elsewhere, when Emily's fictions hint at the time-honored metaphor by which reaching orgasm is "dying," they reverse the traditional emphasis. The force of the metaphor has generally been to dignify sexual experience (often ironically) by associating it with that supreme mystery which is death; but for Emily's speakers it is death itself that is sought with such reckless excitement and passionate specificity.

That this urgent lament speaks to a loss and desired reunion of Emily's own cannot, I think, be doubted. For one thing, the lament is surrounded by an entire network of poems expressing bereavement: it was for her a consuming topic. For another, the perspective and argument are throughout consistent with views Emily expressed elsewhere: the stoicism required of one who would live "without the aid of joy"; the emptiness of life in the world in contrast to a powerfully felt rival yearning for death; the frequently expressed value of loyalty to one who is departed, or to values that are in conflict with those of the living world. This speaker who "sternly denied" her soul's yearning after the departed is the creation of a poet who certainly understood the topic. But whereas Rosina longs for her dead lover, it is the dead Mrs. Brontë whom her daughter Emily remembers. We will see in a moment how the poem's imagery bears the traces of this haunting recollection.

The opening stanza of Rosina's lament defines the distance between living and dead. Separated as the living are from the dead, by earth and deep-piled snow, have they severed even the ties of memory? The questions of the first two stanzas are implicitly answered in the imagery of approach and thaw, as we "hover" attentively among spring-melting heath and fern leaves. The "burning wish" that impelled us here now seeks its own warm element in the sun, star, and bliss that lie in the grave. The beloved is not forgotten. "Faithful indeed is the spirit that remembers."

Stanzas 4 through 8 describe a process of unwilling adaptation to the world, and it is here that the imagery begins to bear a double burden: in Rosina's description of life without Julius we may hear the echoes of an infant's gradual submission to the rigors of life outside the womb. The speaker has been "borne" on the World's tide, beset by stern desires and dark hopes not really her own—the instinctive, unwilled impulse to survival. When the "days of golden dreams" perish, the bereaved one does not die also, even though she might wish to; she learns instead to be "cherished," "strengthened," and "fed without the aid of joy." She learns to "check" her tears, "wean" her yearnings, "deny" her wishes. This is an empty world indeed, whose repeated "sternness" recalls the "Stern Reason" of another of Emily's poems, a denouncer of dreams and a gloomy advocate of the values of time and mortality. Rosina's words build a whole network of *double entendre* that aligns her grief with the poet's own long history of divisions, losses, and sorrows—from birth and weaning up to the present widening gap between her living self and the dreamy memory of her origins and mother. Now, as the poem has brought the speaker closer to the departed and thawed the frozen ground that divides the living from the dead, the urge is powerful to close the gap entirely, to rush into the grave and drink deep of the melted snows of that lost paradise, to die out of poetry into an ecstatic silence that transcends both life and art.

The sense of a division or doubling pitched toward reunion extends even to the rhetoric and rhythms of the poem. We hear it in the coupled phrases ("Cold in the earth . . . cold in the dreary grave") and the doubled lines ("No other Sun . . . No other Star," "Then did I learn, . . . Then did I check") and words ("Far, far," "Love, to love," "ever, ever," "dare not . . . Dare not"), as well as in coupling patterns of a more mirrorlike symmetry ("Sterner desires . . . Sternly denied," "Time's wave . . . World's Tide"). At the same time the rhythms that open the poem as a slow-drummed dirge or death march ("Cold in the earth, and the deep snow piled above thee!") gather speed until in a massing of alliteration and internal rhyme they peak in the end to a rush of crisis (yearning, burning, down, dare, indulge, drink, deep, divinest).

The final closure that Rosina "Sternly denied," her rhetoric and prosody urgently impel. These opposing elements of denial and impulsion are poised in a tension that gives the reader the vivid sense of a structure strained just to the point of explosive but welcome collapse. The poem works like a time bomb set to destroy itself. The argument of this poem, like that of Wordsworth's "Ode: Intimations of Immortality from Recollections of Early Childhood," is a lament for lost glory. But unlike Emily, Wordsworth went on to claim an ultimate gain for the person who reaches maturity. In his familiar account, "Our birth is but a sleep and a forgetting: / . . . trailing clouds of glory do we come / From God Who is our home." For him as for Emily, our recollections of that homeland, shadowy though they be, are an enduring spiritual resource:

> . . .those first affections
> Those shadowy recollections . . .
> Are yet the fountain-light of all our day,
> Are yet a master-light of all our seeing;
> Uphold us, cherish, and have power to make
> Our noisy years seem moments in the being
> Of the eternal Silence. . . .
> Hence in a season of calm weather
> Though inland far we be,
> Our Souls have sight of that immortal sea
> Which brought us hither
> Can in a moment travel thither,
> And see the Children sport upon the shore,
> And hear the mighty waters rolling evermore.

His conclusion, however, was that although nothing can bring back that glory, still "We will grieve not, rather find / Strength in what remains behind." That strength seems to have meant, for him, the power to forge human connections in the face of death. Indeed his commitment to this view was so great that he came to define his vocation as poet by it: the poet is to sing "a song in which all human beings join with him," binding men and women together in community, as he wrote in his "Preface" to *Lyrical Ballads*. This was not Emily's conclusion, as we will see. But the Neoplatonism that Wordsworth employed to vivify his poetic argument was in such direct accord with Emily's thought that she expanded on it considerably. Her "Cold in the earth" goes well beyond what Wordsworth proposed concerning the power of "first affections";

for Emily they should be our final affections too, if we are faithful lovers. In a related, though minor, poem Emily depicts a girl-child "wiser" than her sire (counterpart of the boy-child who is Wordsworth's "best Philosopher") who comforts her father by asserting without question that the land from which we came, in being born, is the land to which we return in dying. Once there, we shall be reunited with all we have lost, and restored into Godhead:

> "I know there is a blessed shore
> Opening its ports for me and mine;
> And, gazing Time's wide waters o'er,
> I weary for that land divine,
>
> "Where we were born—where you and I
> Shall meet our dearest, when we die;
> From suffering and corruption free,
> Restored into the Deity." (#177)

These are the assurances of one who might well prefer death to life, silence to poetry. Wordsworth's poem may have permitted Emily's inference, but certainly neither pursued nor encouraged it.

And here we may begin to see some of the critical points at which Emily's thinking diverged from Wordsworth's, taking her toward death and away from the poetic ambitions that led him to pursue the great philosophical poem and father a new style of English poetry. The differences in doctrine seem to reflect among other things differences in their respective "recollections of early childhood." The clouds of glory that cling to the infant are for Wordsworth the lingering traces of the soul's knowledge of its own immensity, a knowledge that "upholds" and "cherishes" the adult. Emily likewise depended—increasingly so—on the memory of past "glory" for sustenance in the present. But whereas Wordsworth's confidence in his own spiritual power seems to have accompanied him at least into early maturity, focusing his poetic energies, Emily's suffered very early extinction. "Glory" was for her a condition barely remembered, certainly never retained: "Cut off from hope in early day / From power and glory cut away," she wrote when she was eighteen. According to Wordsworth, recalling his childhood later in life, "Nothing was more difficult . . . than to admit the notion of death as a state applicable to my own being."[16] Emily, by contrast, saw the application as only too obvious. Wordsworth tells us that as a child he was sometimes frightened by his vivid sense that the external world was really no more than a projection of his own inner being. "Many times while going to school have I grasped at a wall or tree to recall myself from this abyss of idealism to the reality." But Emily's young consciousness seems to have been born in the fear of its own extinction; the "idealism" that Wordsworth feared she achieved only near the end of her life, and when it came she did not feat it but welcomed it as furthering her readiness to die.

For Wordsworth the doomed "Lucy" of his Lucy poems served (like his sister Dorothy in "Tintern Abbey") as a kind of muse in that she is an inspiring embodiment of his former self, of the blessed childhood spirit and confidence which had slipped away from his in later years. Such losses force the mature poet to submit to "a new control," as Wordsworth phrased it in "Elegiac Stanzas" and explained it in "Ode to Duty." But what Wordsworth called "duty" and welcomed, Emily called "Stern Reason" and finally repelled as the mortal enemy of her vision and muse. Wordsworth and Emily agree that "A Power is gone, which nothing can restore" ("Elegiac Stanzas"), but where this recognition led Wordsworth toward community, bringing him to bid "farewell" to "the heart that lives alone, / Housed in a dream, at distance from the Kind!" we will see that it confirmed Emily's impulse toward isolation.

Rosina's "Sweet Love of youth" may be compared to Wordsworth's Lucy; both are versions of the Romantic muse in that they bear the traces of the poet's own original divinity, now lost in the world of yoke and custom. But to understand more fully the place of Emily's muse in her poetry, and in her view of herself as woman and artist, we must inquire more deeply into the whole issue of gender in Emily's thought. We will begin by observing how she mythologized her parents: the mother who left her daughter so early and the father who then brought her up in the world.

Mother- and Father-Worlds

To demonstrate how central to Emily's imagery were both her dead mother and the vigorous father who survived, let us turn to the poem "Stars," as Emily later titled it. Here the parents each take a role that is none the less recognizable for being realized in large mythic proportions. The night world of revery and dreams, of the unconscious or preconscious, of the "oceanic feeling" as Romain Rolland phrased it in his famous letter to Freud—all of these are dramatized by Emily through a tender evocation of herself as an infant nestled in her mother's arms, nursing at her breast ("I was at peace and drank your beams") and communing with her "bright eyes" (the stars) in a rapture of love and union. In turn the returning daylight world of ordinary human action, of rational consciousness, of bustling business, goal-oriented rivalry, ambition, and achievement—all of these are identified with masculinity and the father, whose consort is of course not the oceanic "undying Life" to which night and darkness have given the poet temporary visionary access, but the world of mortality (earth or nature) in which the poet is now living. In *The Psychoanalysis of Elation,* the analyst Bertram Lewin has demonstrated the relationship between ecstatic states and fantasies of return to the breast, and observed how "the breast is often condensed psychologically with a superego, a deathless one with which the ego identifies itself, so that it can participate in its immortality."[17] Correspondingly for Emily's speaker the nursing infant's dreamy communion with the mother's eyes offers divine refuge from the temporal world; she is loath to return to daylight and mortality, and as the stars fade with sunrise she calls after them.

STARS

Ah! why, because the dazzling sun
Restored my earth to joy
Have you departed every one,
And left a desert sky?

All through the night, your glorious eyes
Were gazing down in mine,
And with a full heart's thankful sighs
I blessed that watch divine!

I was at peace, and drank your beams
As they were life to me
And revelled in my changeful dreams
Like petrel on the sea.

Thought followed thought—star followed star
Through boundless regions on,
While one sweet influence, near and far,
Thrilled through and proved us one.

Why did the morning rise to break
So great, so pure a spell,
And scorch with fire the tranquil cheek
Where your cool radiance fell?

Blood-red he rose, and arrow straight
His fierce beams struck my brow:

The soul of Nature sprang elate,
But mine sank sad and low!

My lids closed down—yet through their veil
I saw him blazing still;
And bathe in gold the misty dale,
And flash upon the hill.

I turned me to the pillow then
To call back Night, and see
Your worlds of solemn light, again
Throb with my heart and me!

It would not do—the pillow glowed
And glowed both roof and floor,
And birds sang loudly in the wood,
And fresh winds shook the door.

The curtains waved, the wakened flies
Were murmuring round my room,
Imprisoned there, till I should rise
And give them leave to roam.

O Stars and Dreams and Gentle Night;
O Night and Stars return!
And hide me from the hostile light
That does not warm, but burn—

That drains the blood of suffering men;
Drinks tears, instead of dew:
Let me sleep through his blinding reign,
And only wake with you! (#184)

A great deal of research has been done in modern psychology on the role of eye contact between mother and infant, emphasizing the infant's intense gratification at seeing itself reflected approvingly in the mother's eyes during nursing, and taking that experience to be fundamental to the infant's development of a sense of its own reality and well-being. Building on this theoretical base, as well as on insights like Lewin's (quoted above), one recent study analyzes the varying ways that individuals perceive God. Noting that "eye contact in the context of feeding is the first indication of that exclusive human capacity to symbolize," this study finds that mother-infant mirroring "is the first direct experience the child has—very early in life—which is used in the formation of the God-representation."[18]

The joy of such mother-infant communion and the desolation of its loss both left their vivid marks on Emily's imagination. We may observe from her work how important the recollected communion was to her concept of divinity, and how deep was her desire for more contact with her mother's bosom, more experience of her embracing and approving love. Note that in the poem "Stars" the speaker's basic condition is one of separation from the mother. She is at present an earthling (she speaks of "my earth"), to whom the eternal mother-world is now accessible only under special circumstances which the speaker yearns to enhance ("Let me sleep"). To the soul prisoned in mortality, sweet communion with eternity comes only occasionally in moments of "pure . . . spell" that are all too vulnerable to the forces of the temporal, natural world.

Clearly, by the time of this poem Emily's primary attachment was to her dead mother. The stars are mothering lights, and unquestionably preferred to the masculine sun. But "Stars" is only one of several inter-related poems, all employing the imagery of sun and stars to define the values toward which Emily was working in the final years of her life. One learns a great deal from looking at "Stars" in the context of that larger progression.

Emily wrote "Cold in the earth," Rosina's lament for Julius, just a month before she wrote "Stars." And, in turn, just a few months before "Cold in the earth" she wrote a poem that provides crucial preconditions for that lament, first in that it offers the only evidence we have of an early affair between Rosina and Julius—making him in fact her "Sweet Love of *youth*" (my emphasis)—and second in that it voices Julius' doubts about Rosina, doubts that her lament would be designed to dispel. This preparatory poem Emily marked with two dates: the actual date of composition, alongside her own initials ("E.J.B., Nov. 11, 1844"), but also a second date and set of initials ("J.B., Sept., 1825"), indicating that the poem was supposed to have been written by Julius Brenzaida himself, years before. Julius is represented as having wondered, at that early time, whether Rosina's eyes did not reveal "Ambition" rather than love of him (imaged by the "tender star"). His thoughts had con-cluded:

> The tender star fades faint and wan
> Before Ambition's scorching sun.
> So deem I now—and Time will prove
> If I have wronged Rosina's love. (#178)

Other poems, in fact written earlier though not assigned to such an early period of the Gondal fiction, had already employed the same day/night imagery to address the topic of fidelity. In "Thou standest in the green-wood now" (#110), for example, the female speaker responds figuratively, but clearly in the negative, when asked if she has been faithful to her love:

> "I gazed upon the cloudless moon
> And loved her all the night
> Till morning came and ardent noon,
> Then I forgot her light—"

If the speaker there was Rosina, we may see that Julius' doubts about her loyalty were well founded. Indeed, a later poem, announcing King Julius' death (#151), explicitly mentions Rosina's "ambition" as an aspect of her interest in him.

But Julius had said that "Time will prove" Rosina's love, and in "Cold in the earth" Rosina offers that proof of time. If in those intervening years she has seemed to forget him, she says that it is only because to remember would have been suicidal (and remains so). And in proclaiming her loyalty she seizes on his own imagery to refute its figurative implications. How could the star of her love ever be effaced by the sun of her ambition when Julius himself has always been both sun and star to her?

> No other Sun has lightened up my heaven;
> No other Star has ever shone for me:
> All my life's bliss from thy dear life was given—
> All my life's bliss is in the grave with thee.

Now in "Stars" these images emerge from their Gondal wrappings and take on distinctly personal significance. Now Emily is asserting her own fidelity to the sweet love of her own youth.

In her seminal work on the Gondal poetry, Fannie Ratchford claimed "Stars" as part of the Gondal sequence, arguing that it records the heroine's irresistible attraction to Julius' blazing presence, "paling into invisibility all other loves and loyalties."[19] But such a reading—taking Julius as the sun—is simply out of the question here. The whole point of Emily's return in 1844 to the story of Rosina and Julius was to establish that Rosina, like her author, had been faithful after all. Since the point of "Stars" is that the speaker prefers the night world of stars to the daylight world of the sun, if anything it would have to be the stars that stand for Julius in this poem: "Let me . . . only wake with you!"

Other critics have seen the dazzling sun in this poem as a version of what I am calling Emily's muse—that is, as one of the inspiring masculine "visitants" who appear in so many of Emily's poems. But he is very much their opposite. He is associated not at all with the tender mother who died, but only with the ambitious and life-oriented father who survived her. Whereas darkness and dreams cradle Emily's speaker in maternal arms and evoke the longed-for oceanic feeling, daybreak marks the return of the rational, reducing the visionary or poetic spirit to mundane confinement under the despotic rule of the real. Although the word "ambition" itself does not appear in this poem, its connotations of zeal and bustle attach to the "dazzling sun," which Julius had already characterized as "scorching." Here again it scorches, an enemy to whatever is "tender." Some of the poem's best lines depict the poet's sense of having been searched out and hunted down by the inexorable energies of the daylight world. With his phallic weaponry and march of strongly accented syllables the sun is a cruelly efficient opponent of all that is visionary:

> Blood-red he rose, and arrow straight
> His fierce beams struck my brow:

Imprisoned like the powerless insects with whom she now identifies, the poet can only render her grim judgment on that scorching daylight power—it "drains . . . blood" and "Drinks tears." Inverting the conventional assumption that waking and sight are appropriate to daylight, she claims that for her they belong to the realm of the dark and stars. Daylight is "blinding"; she would prefer to sleep through it and wake only to the light of vision. This is another way of expressing Rosina's preference for the bliss of joining Julius in his grave over the stern alternative of imprisonment in the "desert" world. Thus Emily's hostile estimate of the virile father ("Blood-red he rose" and he "drains . . . blood") reflects her resentment of Patrick Brontë, not so much perhaps for surviving his wife's death as for implicitly calling on his daughter to wake and do the same.

Emily's view of the night and day powers are strikingly like Shelley's as he expressed them in his poem "The Triumph of Life." For Shelley too "the Sun sprang forth / Rejoicing in his splendour," waking "all things . . . of mortal mould" to "Rise as the Sun their father rose, to bear / Their portion of the toil which he of old / Took as his own and then imposed on them." Nor is Shelley's poet-speaker willing to rise and do the sunshine work of the father-world; rather he experiences "a strange trance," "a Vision" which the rest of Shelley's poem describes. Readers of Shelley will recall how mindless and destructive a force is "Life" as he presents it in his poem. Shelley died before he finished "The

Triumph of Life." For Emily, in a different way, the preference for night and vision was opening a lane to the land of the dead.

In sum, the whole competition between the motives of ambition and fidelity in Rosina's love parallels that between daylight and starlight for the poet's allegiance. The fundamental opposition couched in these pairs of concepts or images was expressed in every aspect of Emily's imaginative system, and was at bottom the opposition between the attractions of the father- and mother-worlds, between temporal life and the prospect of eternity beyond death.

The Male Muse as the Breath of God

But though Emily had certainly come to prefer darkness to daylight by the time she wrote "Stars," still her response to the waking world was complex. Vision might belong to the night, but writing about it calls on powers associated with the day. Not hostility, but rather a fine appreciation of life's energies makes possible such achievements as the poem itself. Notice the verbs—blaze, bathe, glow, flash, shook—and the way they invigorate the superbly rendered sounds and rhythms of the middle stanzas. Then in the ninth stanza a comparable wake-up effect is achieved by the rhythm: the heavy regularity of alternating stresses in the opening two lines is strained in the third, then explodes in a line of monosyllabic staccato: "And fresh winds shook the door."

For the poet-speaker that door-shaking masculine energy is unwelcome and threatening; she reminds us that such energies always have their brutal side, that they bring not just the birds and winds of morning, but also human suffering, blood, and tears. But for the poet-author that energy also gives life to her verse; though inexorably involved in the processes of time, and tainted by those processes, it is still as necessary to art as to life. This ambivalence toward creative energy Emily often focused on the power of the "life-giving wind," as she phrased it in one of her earliest extant poems (#5). That poem envisions a kind of apocalyptic prison break in which stormy winds sweep all creation free of its confinement in mortality, with man's spirit likewise "Bursting the fetters and breaking the bars."

The liberty depicted in #5 was brief. But the jubilant vision itself reminds us that although the wind was for Emily very much an instrument of the bustling father world, it could also be a figure for inspiration and an instrument of vision. It differs from the sun in being available to both the day and the night worlds—both literally (the wind blows day or night) and figuratively, in that it provides the vehicle of ecstatic release as well as the wake-up call of mundane morning. Indeed its energies are necessary to both vision and the practice of art, inspiring and inspiriting the poet's verse just as it links her mortal self with the immortal world beyond.

As a masculine "Breath of God" blowing to the artist from out of the mother-world, this wind is a version of Emily's muse.

But the muse's position was not always so exalted nor his presence so welcome. Emily's earliest poetic visions of the world "beyond" were more often terrifying than comforting. If the wind carried thoughts of her mother, it was the fact of her mother's departure rather than the memory of her tenderness that dominated Emily's visionary experience as recorded in the poems of 1836–1837. In a poem written when she was eighteen she looks back to see only the absence of mother love (the speaker never caused "A smile of joy, since I was born" and is "As friendless after eighteen years, / As lone as on my natal day"), and in that absence an enduring lack of self-worth, a repudiation of her conscious self:

> 'Twas grief enough to think mankind
> All hollow, servile, insincere;
> But worse to trust to my own mind
> And find the same corruption there. (#11)

Many poems of this early time give expression to a set of nightmare experiences that hint of Emily's youthful sense of alienation and loneliness amid dark visitations from some realm "beyond," the first hideous shapings of the muse to come. In one, a speaker tells how during a "night of storms" she "saw a shadowy thing" look down on her with an effect that is horrifyingly different from the "sweet influence" she will report in "Stars":

> My breath I could not draw, . . .
> But still my eyes with maddening gaze
> Were fixed upon its fearful face
> And its were fixed on me.

The figure seemed close by, yet is separated by the "gulph" of "death's eternity." The poem concludes:

> O bring not back again
> The horror of that hour
> When its lip opened . . .
> And heaven's lights shivered 'neath its power. (#12)

This spectral figure, coming from beyond the "gulph" of death, is itself the speaker of a second poem that Emily wrote on the same sheet of paper. The specter has observed a child praying to know its future fate, and chooses a doleful winter night for revealing it: "And now I'm come." In natural terms, the child hears the wind—"A fluttering blast that shakes the leaves"—but in visionary terms " 'tis the spectre's call." The terrified child wakes to learn that its life will be full of pain and losses. Yet the child's destiny is no different from that of every human being, as the spectral speaker itself makes grimly clear:

> Poor child, if spirits such as I
> Could weep o'er human misery,
> A tear might flow, aye, many a tear,
> To see the road that lies before,
> To see the sunshine disappear,
> And hear the stormy waters roar,
> Cut off from hope in early day,
> From power and glory cut away.
>
> But it is doomed, and morning's light
> Must image forth the scowl of night,
> And childhood's flower must waste its bloom
> Beneath the shadow of the tomb. (#14)

This account of life's progress parallels Wordsworth's in his Intimations Ode: the road traveled, the disappearing light, the lost power and glory, even the sound of distant waters breaking against the shore. But Emily's vision is far more dark and comfortless; and again, her journey takes her away from human community, not toward it.

Now at last the deeps of Emily's spirit that yielded her such anguish began to provide an antidote for it. The wind that was "the spectre's call" began gradually to bear messages not of death, but of transfiguration. This shift reached its climax in the summer of 1841, with the rejoicing poem "Aye, there it is! It wakes to-night." This poem is spoken by an unnamed observer who watches the visionary's changing face and expression as she is seized and swept by a wind that is in effect that "divine breath" or *hagion pneuma* which is translated "Holy Ghost" in the King James Bible. It is what I have been calling the Breath of God, familiar to readers of English Romantic poetry as a figure for creative inspiration.[20]

What the observer sees is that the visionary is experiencing a foretaste of immortality. The poem's second-person strategy is of course made necessary by the nature of the ecstasy, which has disconnected the visionary herself from all interest in language, earth, or audience. Such experience cannot be rendered firsthand. Instead we are offered an observer's account:

> Aye, there it is! It wakes to-night
> Sweet thoughts that will not die
> And feeling's fires flash all as bright
> As in the years gone by!
>
> And I can tell by thine altered cheek
> And by thy kindled gaze
> And by the words thou scarce dost speak,
> How wildly fancy plays.
>
> Yes, I could swear that glorious wind
> Has swept the world aside,
> Has dashed its memory from thy mind
> Like foam-bells from the tide—
>
> And thou art now a spirit pouring
> Thy presence into all—
> The essence of the Tempest's roaring
> And of the Tempest's fall—
>
> A universal influence
> From Thine own influence free;
> A principle of life, intense,
> Lost to mortality.
>
> Thus truly when that breast is cold
> Thy prisoned soul shall rise,
> The dungeon mingle with the mould—
> The captive with the skies. (#148)

The imprisoned spirit, held "captive" in so many of Emily's poems, has here achieved full sight of its land of liberty.

Like most of Emily's poetry (and virtually all of her best poetry) this poem focuses on death: on thoughts that "will not die," on the "world . . . swept aside," on the mingled "mould" of the final stanza. In fact if we consider carefully the poet's words and her second-person strategy, the speaker could as well be describing a death scene as a scene of visionary ecstasy. The true subject of this poem is transformation from a lesser to a higher condition—from imprisonment in death-entangled time and space to the freedom of universal power and being. From the perspective of those who remain behind, the transformed one may seem to have died; her departure is indeed a loss for those from whom she has departed. The phrase "lost to mortality" emphasizes this, for though it seems intended to be applied to the departer, the preposition points the other way: mortality is the loser, experiences the "loss." The visionary who "loses" mortality feels it only as an impediment swept aside, dashed away by the wind. It is as if Emily, having watched her mother die (or having imagined the moment when that maternal "breast" went "cold"), now read into the terrible event the signs of a reappointment in eternity. Separation may be endured, may even be fired with poignant sweetness, if the mother has not really "died" but rather transcended death to become the principle of life itself, her daughter's own true "home," the source of satisfactions first known at the breast or in the womb, but now perceived as recoverable through the agency of the muse.

Emily's visionary experiences are in effect reenactments of the precious moment when her imagination, trained in the paradoxes of Christian doctrine, learned to transform death into birth, or rebirth. The speaker of "Aye, there it is!" reports the telltale signs of visionary travel; we may see that they parallel the signs of death's approach—the altered cheek, the kindled gaze, the eager energy of a spirit being released from captivity. (We see all these signs again in the approach of Heathcliff's death in *Wuthering Heights*.) As visionary, Emily was striving to reenact for herself her mother's imagined "triumph," to hear in the "spectre's call" not the terrors of death, but an invitation to immortality. This poem's opening stanza connects present visionary experience with past "Sweet thoughts" that "will not die." And its closing stanza makes explicit the parallel between death (in the sense of dying into "Life") and vision: the flight of imagination is a version of the soul's flight to eternity. The pivotal four stanzas describing the transformation could be equally well spoken by one who is observing a death scene as by one who is observing visionary or "mystical" rapture, the experience of transcendence.[21]

When Charlotte revised this poem for publication after Emily had died, she made a number of changes in it, even adding an extra stanza of conclusion:

> Nature's deep being, thine shall hold,
> Her spirit all thy spirit fold,
>   Her breath absorb thy sighs.
> Mortal! though soon life's tale is told,
>   Who once lives, never dies!

Charlotte's changes not only break the rhythm and violate the imagery that Emily had established, but show that Charlotte either did not, or would not, understand her sister's meaning. In the original poem, the narrator makes clear that the woman observed as she undergoes this experience is not "absorbed," but rather transformed ("thou art now"). Freed of her individual consciousness ("thine own influence") she assimilates the visionary power or muse (the "essence" of the tempest) and becomes the universal mother ("principle of life") from whom he emanates. In the visionary's rapture, "doing" returns to its source in the ultimate "being" from which it sprang. Again, for Emily as for Winnicott, "After being—doing and being done to. But first, being."

Charlotte was perhaps led astray by her desire to bring her dead sister back into the natural world, or perhaps to make her sister's opinions sound more orthodox. But the experience Emily describes transcends nature and goes well beyond orthodoxy. As Charlotte interpreted her sister, the human spirit is subsumed into the "spirit" of nature. Whereas Emily tells us something quite different: in Emily's religion, dying nature, in being acted on and transformed by the power of Vision, is subsumed into the "principle of life." This is the faith that armed Emily from fear in "No coward soul is mine." Adjusting only Blake's terms of gender (which in his view merely reflected the constraints of fallen language anyway), Emily might have said of her origin: "The true Woman is the source, she being the Poetic Genius."[22]

Now we are in a position to understand more clearly the full range of Emily's ambivalence toward the fresh winds that shook her door in "Stars." As agents of the father, breaking into her private "room," they are allied with mortality—with the sunshine and birdsong of "my earth," but also with blood and tears, as the prisoned flies should remind us, recalling as they do the ancient *topos* of life's brevity. Such literal winds lead us not toward being, but away from it, into the processes of time and decay. This is the meaning of the often-quoted "Night-wind," which woos the poet like a muse, but is really a voice of earth and death after all, as is clear from the jolting *carpe diem* with which his song concludes: embrace earthly pleasures now, for

> ". . . when thy heart is laid at rest
> Beneath the church-yard stone
> I shall have time enough to mourn
> And thou to be alone." (#140)

But figurative winds (in contrast to literal ones) are agents of the immortal mother, visionary instruments that Emily variously addressed as "angle," "Guide," "messenger," "Comforter." Their function is to visit the poet and transport her home, sweeping and dashing mortal impediments aside, so that within the poet, as within her God, "doing" may return into its home in "being." The visionary "pours" her "presence into all" and the universal wide-embracing mother, having reclaimed her emanations, stands complete again. This reunited "Being and Breath" (which resides, in combination, both within the poet and beyond her) is the God Emily celebrates in what is probably her most quoted poem:

> No coward soul is mine
> No trembler in the world's storm-troubled sphere
> I see Heaven's glories shine
> And Faith shines equal arming me from Fear
>
> O God within my breast
> Almighty ever-present Deity
> Life, that in me hast rest
> As I Undying Life, have power in Thee
>
> Vain are the thousand creeds
> That move men's hearts, unutterably vain,
> Worthless as withered weeds
> Or idlest froth amid the boundless main
>
> To waken doubt in one
> Holding so fast by thy infinity
> So surely anchored on
> The steadfast rock of Immortality
>
> With wide-embracing love
> Thy spirit animates eternal years
> Pervades and broods above,
> Changes, sustains, dissolves, creates and rears
>
> Though Earth and moon were gone
> And suns and universes ceased to be
> And thou wert left alone
> Every Existence would exist in thee
>
> There is not room for Death
> Nor atom that his might could render void
> Since thou art Being and Breath
> And what thou art may never be destroyed. (#191)

The elements of "being" and "doing" are here distinguishable one from another in Emily's concept of deity—and by implication, the female is distinguishable from the male. But they are at the same time united, whole, One.

The female element is Being, also called "Undying Life," in whom "Every Existence would exist" even if the natural universe were gone. This element Emily says "in me hast rest," and clearly Emily "rests" in Her as well. More clearly even than before we can see how Emily's thought exemplifies Bertram Lewin's psychological view of the way memories of the breast condense with the idea of "a deathless one with whom the ego identifies itself, so that it can participate in its immortality." The male element, meanwhile, is Breath, also called the "spirit" that "animates . . . Pervades . . . broods . . . Changes, sustains, dissolves, creates and rears." This is the traditional *hagion pneuma* or Holy Ghost of Scripture.

A paradoxical reciprocity, yet identity, between the poet and the elements of her God is assumed throughout: God is both within Emily's breast and beyond her; as Catherine will say to Nelly, "there is, or should be, an existence of yours beyond you. What were the use of my creation if I were entirely contained here?" Emily and the female element of God abide in one another in their female essence. The male element, on the other hand, is the muse of her poetry. Emily says "I . . . have power in thee"—and in this case that power is the poet's vision and voice, her capacity to celebrate so eloquently her God's glories and her own answering faith.

Ambition Versus Fidelity: The Pull of Earth

This was Emily at the height of her visionary confidence. But she was not always so sure that her faith was right and her doubting reason wrong. And the busy world had its attractions. Like Wordsworth in the Intimations Ode, Emily often found "my earth," the father-world's consort, an engaging even if confining foster mother, a "homely Nurse," as Wordsworth said. Emily's carping reason reminded her, moreover, that earthly benefits were at least certain, whereas death might after all bring not greater life, but mere annihilation. The most that could be said for such a fearsome prospect was that it would bring rest from weary struggle and from the frustrating capriciousness and even occasional total absences of her visionary muse: "If any ruth can melt thee, / Come to me now!" (#138).

The appeal of earth and reason, coupled with doubts concerning what Keats called "the authenticity of the imagination," form the subject of much of Emily's mature poetic work. In one poem nature inquires directly of the poet, "Shall Earth no more inspire thee, / Thou lonely dreamer now?" (#147); and in another the poet expresses her filial tenderness toward the fostering but death-infested earth: "Ah mother, what shall comfort thee / In all this boundless misery?" (#149). In a third, she queries her own feelings and finds herself divided between her desire to leave worldly suffering for "calm Eternity" and her reluctance to relinquish her present life: "Alas! the countless links are strong / That bind us to our clay" (#155). In a fourth she calls on "Fancy . . . my Fairy love" to take her away from the "Grim world" and help her to imagine that "all the woe / Creation knows" is held here below, while those celestial worlds, the stars, roll on "in endless bliss through endless years"—but her posture is that of one who wishes the impossible (#157). Another praises and thanks "My Comforter," yet says that he teaches her nothing "strange or new," but rather rouses her own latent thoughts of comfort, brings her own hidden inner light "To gleam in open view" (#168). Finally, a poem titled "To Imagination" pits Reason and Truth against the comforts that Imagination brings:

> So hopeless is the world without,
> The world within I doubly prize;

but ends by admitting that although "I welcome thee, benignant power," still "I trust not to thy phantom bliss" (#174). With this poem "To Imagination" we reach the fall of 1844, the beginning of Emily's final, great poetic year. The following fall, in 1845, Charlotte was to discover and read her sister's notebooks, putting an unintended but effectual end to Emily's poetic career.

Let us now examine Emily's self-division as she dramatized it in two important poems of this final year. Each of the poems gives full expression to Emily's divided mind, even though both also demonstrate the clear direction of her leanings.

We have seen a confrontation long brewing between the two mighty powers of Emily's mental world, the gods of the "world within" and the "world without," the visionary and the sternly "reasonable" or "prudent." In the well-known poem "O thy bright eyes must answer now," she poses their conflict allegorically, through the figure of a trial. In a few months Rosina will tell Julius,

> Sweet love of youth, forgive if I forget thee
> While the world's tide is bearing me along:
> Sterner desires and darker hopes beset me,
> Hopes which obscure but cannot do thee wrong.

Now Emily herself must make similar excuses and fresh pledges to her "God of Visions," from whom she had sometime allowed herself to be distracted by worldly hopes.

The setting is a kind of celestial courtroom, and the poet has brought her God of Visions (deity of her "world within") to plead her case against Reason (deity of the "world without"), who is charging the poet with apostasy for having overthrown the worldly values she had once worshiped. The poet addresses her God of Visions before the trial, both to implore his aid in her defense and to assure him that whatever her past record, he can now count on her fidelity:

> O thy bright eyes must answer now,
> When Reason, with a scornful brow,
> Is mocking at my overthrow;
> O thy sweet tongue must plead for me
> And tell why I have chosen thee!
>
> Stern Reason is to judgment come
> Arrayed in all her forms of gloom:
> Wilt thou my advocate be dumb?
> No, radiant angel, speak and say
> Why I did cast the world away;
>
> Why I have persevered to shun
> The common paths that others run;
> And on a strange road journeyed on
> Heedless alike of Wealth and Power—
> Of Glory's wreath and Pleasure's flower.
>
> These once indeed seemed Beings divine,
> And they perchance heard vows of mine
> And saw my offerings on their shrine—
> But, careless gifts are seldom prized,
> And mine were worthily despised;
>
> So with a ready heart I swore
> To seek their altar-stone no more,
> And gave my spirit to adore
> Thee, ever present, phantom thing—
> My slave, my comrade, and my King!
>
> A slave because I rule thee still;
> Incline thee to my changeful will
> And make thy influence good or ill—

A comrade, for by day and night
Thou art my intimate delight—

My Darling Pain that wounds and sears
And wrings a blessing out from tears
By deadening me to real cares;
And yet, a king—though prudence well
Have taught thy subject to rebel.

And am I wrong to worship where
Faith cannot doubt nor Hope despair
Since my own soul can grant my prayer?
Speak, God of Visions, plead for me
And tell why I have chosen thee! (#176)

One critic argues that this poem expresses Emily's doubt about her power over language.[23] But Emily's real doubts here concern not her voice, but her loyalties. She is anxious about her ability to refute the arguments of her own "Reason." She sees that her commitment to vision is vulnerable to her rational doubts, and that from these doubts only vision itself can defend her. Emily does have a problem with language, but only in the sense that her own words keep betraying her ambivalence. Although she insists (quite vocally, after all, and with admirable rhetoric) that her allegiance is to vision, still her diction continually exposes her doubts. Her God of Visions she calls a "phantom thing" who deadens her to "real" cares; and even as her "King" he is subject to continuing rebellions instigated by her own "prudence," obviously an underground ally of Reason, the accuser. The conflict between faith and doubt is thus subtly both dramatized and enacted. It is all very well to turn from the emptiness, pain, and strife of reality to worship the visionary energy of one's own soul; but the question still echoes, "am I wrong?" In a mind as rigorous and forthright as Emily's, "Reason" will always require that the muse render account.

When Emily next returned to weigh the conflicting claims of reason and vision, she again chose a form that sharply dramatized, again without wholly resolving, the deep conflicts she was experiencing. "Enough of Thought, Philosopher" (#181) is one of Emily's most quoted poems, but also one of the most obscure and difficult. Whereas in "O thy bright eyes" the poet-speaker had dramatized her own divided condition by imagining herself placed between rival claimants for her allegiance, here there are two speakers, each representing an aspect of herself. One is the "Philosopher," whom I take to be again Emily's reason, her rational self —inevitably a materialist. The other is the "Seer," literally one who "sees"; in this case what the Seer sees is a powerful spiritual vision. This Seer perhaps derives her name from the "Seer blest!" of Wordsworth's Intimations Ode: the "Eye among the blind" that "readst the eternal deep, / Haunted forever by the eternal mind."

In "Enough of Thought, Philosopher," the Seer speaks first, urging the Philosopher to give over his "Unenlightened" thoughts and trying to rouse him from his depression. The Seer asks finally, "what sad refrain / Concludes thy musings once again?" And we are given the Philosopher's "refrain" verbatim:

> *"O for the time when I shall sleep*
> *Without identity,*
> *And never care how rain may steep*
> *Or snow may cover me!*
>
> *"No promised Heaven, these wild Desires*
> *Could all or half fulfill;*
> *No threatened Hell, with quenchless fires,*
> *Subdue this quenchless will!"*

"So said I," affirms the Philosopher; and he adds further that his views are not only unchanged, but unchangeable. They explain his longing for oblivion:

> —So said I, and still say the same;
> —Still to my Death will say—
> Three Gods within this little frame
> Are warring night and day.
>
> Heaven could not hold them all, and yet
> They are all held in me
> And must be mine till I forget
> My present entity.
>
> O for the time when in my breast
> Their struggles will be o'er;
> O for the day when I shall rest,
> And never suffer more!

To this confession of fragmentation, exhaustion, and despair, the Seer ("Haunted . . . by the eternal mind"!) responds with a stirring account of redemptive vision and of the resolution that visionary experience can provide:

> "I saw a Spirit standing, Man,
> Where thou dost stand—an hour ago;

And round his feet, three rivers ran
Of equal depth and equal flow—

"A golden stream, and one like blood,
And one like Sapphire, seemed to be,
But where they joined their triple flood
It tumbled to an inky sea.

"The Spirit bent his dazzling gaze
Down on that Ocean's gloomy night,
Then—kindling all with sudden blaze,
The glad deep sparkled wide and bright—
White as the sun; far, far more fair
Than the divided sources were!"

It would be needlessly reductive to argue for any one compelling source or meaning for this obscure and quite elemental vision. John Hewish has pointed to its biblical and Jungian associations.[24] But we should notice also those of Romantic poetry.

The influence of Wordsworth is joined by that of Coleridge. The inky sea and gloomy night ocean into which Emily's three rivers tumble recall, for example, the dark realm surrounding the sunny pleasure dome in "Kubla Khan," the "sunless sea" and "lifeless ocean" into which "Alph, the sacred river . . . sank in tumult." Similarly Emily's "Gods . . . warring day and night" recall Coleridge's "Ancestral voices, prophesying war"—which may itself be an allusion to Matthew 24:6, where the disciples are told "ye shall hear of wars and rumors of wars" before the Second Coming. The sunless inky sea, the lifeless ocean's gloomy night, the endlessly warring powers are all emblems of the mortal human condition for Emily as they were for Coleridge. Similarly, both poets seem to have regarded the experience of creative power as profoundly disruptive of ordinary life, deeply subversive of orthodox social and religious values.

But Emily's striking image of spiritual resolution, in which her three warring "gods" or colored rivers coalesce finally not in inkiness but in a kindling brilliance "White as the sun," recalls less Coleridge than Shelley, for it reformulates Shelley's powerful figure in "Adonais" of the relationship between the here and the beyond: "Life, like a dome of many-coloured glass, / Stains the white radiance of Eternity." For Emily, as for Shelley, the realm of colors is the fragmented realm of mutability.[25]

Like Shelley, a skeptic who had also known visionary wonder, Emily is torn between philosophic rationalism and her bright-eyed God of Visions. Significantly, she sees rationalism as polytheistic, reflecting the dis-integration or sense of inner dividedness experienced by one who struggles to quell by force of reason what D. H. Lawrence called the dark gods. As trapped and warring internal powers they can only demolish that which contains them. To the visionary, death does not mean the body's dissolution under the churchyard stone, but rather the bursting of the prisoner's chain, the release of infinite power and energy from its finite enclosure—in present terms, the freeing of those warring gods. In her conclusion to a French exercise written in Brussels on the topic of King Harold before the battle of Hastings, Emily had written that "Death alone can win victory over his arms; and Harold is ready to bow to her, because the touch of her hand is to the hero as the jailer who brings liberty is to the slave." Her teacher, M. Heger, did not like the final simile—indeed it is syntactically awkward—but the view contained in it should by now be familiar to us. Yet it stands in clear opposition to the Philosopher's view of death as annihilation, a view to which Emily apparently still feared she might succumb.

Who are the three "Gods" struggling within the Philosopher? Specific translation may be impossible; but as a warring threesome they offer a kind of infernal, repudiating parody of the mystery of the Christian Trinity. And beyond that, the Philospher's choice of metaphor assumes that his inner strife must be irresolvable. By contrast the Seer's three streams (no conflict required by this metaphor) can indeed coalesce to a single "deep," and of course they do so. When they are merely mingled, the gold, red, and blue rivers darken (as their colors would, in combination) to an "inky sea." But under the gaze of the Spirit their joint color kindles to achromatic white, the "color" of highest brilliance.

That the "glad deep" is "White as the sun" makes it by simile indistinguishable from the source of that spiritual light it may be thought to reflect—Shelley's "white radiance of Eternity." The Spirit's gaze and the confluent "sources" are thus by suggestive figure one monotheistic power: what Emily called "Undying Life." Like the speaker of "Kubla Khan," Emily's Seer may be thought to have drunk the milk of Paradise and known its heady power. But her moralizing Philospher had not; and this poem gives him, with his materialist's weariness of body and rationalist's despair of mind, the last word:

> —And even for that Spirit, Seer,
> I've watched and sought my lifetime long;

> Sought him in Heaven, Hell, Earth and Air,
> An endless search—and always wrong!

This is of course the wrong way to look: the Spirit is within, in the creative imagination. Such vision-blind philosophers will never be able to see anything but evil in life and annihilation in death:

> O let me die, that power and will
> Their cruel strife may close,
> And vanquished Good, victorious Ill
> Be lost in one repose. (#181)

No wonder the Seer calls the Philosopher "Man." The reference is less to gender than to kind: he is "mere man," mortal or natural man, space- and time-bound food for the worm.

And yet there may be issues of gender lurking here as well. Emily's relation with her male "Comforter" took its origin from her yearning after a departed mothering spirit, as visionary experience became a temporal analogue for full and final reunion beyond the world of time. Now perhaps we may see in the Philosopher a version of the father who remained behind, his blood-red vigor revealing its obverse side. Here the "Man" is depressed, even mourning; and he is consoled by a Seer, a female figure whose voice is part Emily's, part perhaps that of the deceased mother with whom Emily so deeply identified. Certainly this configuration of mourning man and consoling womanly girl is echoed in other poems. Take for example a Gondal poem of the same period. Dated November 6, 1844, it is set among "November's blasts"—the same blasts that next year will hold Lockwood overnight in the house of his reluctant host and landlord. This is the poem already mentioned in which a daughter "wiser than her sire" comforts her despondent father, who mourns his dead loved ones (#177). The daughter's arguments, even her cadences, recall Emily's earlier affirmations. The triumphant poem "Aye, there it is!" had concluded with the claim that at death "the prisoned soul shall rise":

> The dungeon mingle with the mould—
> The captive with the skies.

The wise daughter comforts her father in parallel (if clumsier) phrasing:

> Their dust is mingled with the sod;
> Their happy souls are gone to God!

"Well hast thou spoken, sweet, trustful child!" says her father, but he remains depressed. As with Wordsworth, it is children who best recall and retain "the might / Of heaven-born freedom."

Next year it will be the child in Catherine who remembers. The adult Catherine is destroyed in being torn between her primal fidelity to Heathcliff and her ambitious and socially quite reasonable attraction to the "handsome, and young, and cheerful, and rich" Edgar. In Nelly's suggestive words, Catherine's "ambition . . . led her to adopt a double character" (ch. 8). Emily's poems show that this "double character" was a matter of painful personal experience.

The Readiness Is All

Over the years this matter of fidelity, of self-dedication to memory, had become increasingly urgent for Emily. It focused tensions that had been building to the brink of a determined resolution, as we saw in the conclusion of Rosina's lament. "To remember" is to be ready to die; and Rosina now passionately remembers. I have already said that in writing about Rosina's dead lover, Emily was offering vows to her own lost "Beloved" who was in the immediate sense her comforting but evasive visionary muse; but that ultimately she was vowing fidelity to her mother, that originating home of both herself and her muse. "Heaven" or "home," as she calls the mother-world of her vision, is the "consecrated spot / Beloved in childhood's years" (#87). Its amniotic waters are the source of the "deep fountain" of memory "whose springing / Nor Absence nor Distance can quell" (#91).[26] The poem from which the image of the fountain of memory is taken must have had a special importance to Emily, for she used it to begin her notebook of personal poems. It opens with the call of the muse—"Loud without the wind was roaring"—and takes as its broad subject the recollection of past happiness, culminating in the optimistic prophecy that though life is "loaded with trouble and pain," still a time of reunion will come:

> . . . sometime the loved and the loving
> Will meet on the mountains again.

Thus this opening poem sets the terms for all the spiritual history contained in the pages that follow it, a history which—though uncertain, halting, and self-divided—was pointed surely toward the affirmations of "No coward soul is mine" and *Wuthering Heights*. Cut off from each other, "the loved and the loving" find the temporal world to be "empty" in Rosina's words, "a mighty stranger" in Catherine's. For both, reunion would make "death" the real life.

The commitment to a lost past that is affirmed in Rosina's lament is reaffirmed in the poem that follows it—"Death, that struck when I was most confiding" (#183). But this poem calls even more insistently for "death," and introduces a different system of imagery for talking about both death and reunion. Here again there linger memory traces of the infant at her mother's breast. But this time the primary imagery of the poem is drawn from sacred Scripture and not at all from sexual love.

The idea behind the imagery of "Death that struck" derives from the New Testament. Just after Jesus promised his apostles that he would send "the Comforter, which is the Holy Ghost" to "bring all things to your remembrance, whatsoever I have said unto you" (John 14:26), he defined his relation to them in a striking metaphor: "I am the vine and ye are the branches. . . . If a man abide not in me, he is cast forth as a branch, and is withered" (John 15:5). Shakespeare draws on the same figure in *King Lear* when Albany denounces Goneril's perfidious treatment of her father. Hers is a "nature which contemns its origin":

> She that herself will sliver and disbranch
> From her material sap, perforce must wither
> And come to deadly use. (IV, ii)[27]

This figure of the parent vine or tree whose offspring are branches that "wither" or "come to deadly use" when they "contemn" their origin had evidently occupied Emily's mind for some years. She seems to have associated "disbranching" with the sin of faithlessness or forgetting, as in the striking but obscure little poem "There let thy bleeding branch atone" (#142), in which the speaker evinces an angry impatience at being endlessly accused of sin, vowing that she remembers all too well the "early days" that she has apparently been reproached for forgetting. Now in "Death that struck when I was most confiding" Emily extends the botanical metaphor into a full allegory that draws on both its biblical and its Shakespearian implications: the relationship of vine to branch obtains both between God and creature, and between parent and child.

Emily's poem furthermore turns on a pun on death. Death is of two kinds, and they strike independently. The first might be called death of the spirit: what a Christian incurs in turning from Christ, what Goneril incurred in contemning her "origin." For Emily this death would result from pursuing ambition and violating her fidelity to her mother. It does not result from lesser sins, as the poem makes clear: so long as the branch remains undivided from its "fresh root," the ordinary kinds of "Sorrow," "Guilt," "grief," and "Sin" have at most a sort of seasonal power, just as winter soon gives way to returning spring.

The second kind of death is of the body—a literal disbranching, which is also the only "cure" possible for the spiritually disbranched. Once spiritually severed, the withered branch can recover its lost access to the sap of life only by a bodily severing by which it drops and returns to its source. There, just as the moldering body mingles with the bosom of earth from which it came, so the "dead" spirit nourishes and is nourished by eternity.[28] Emily's myth proposes in effect a female version of apocalypse, when all of nature will return to the "kindly bosom" of the eternal mother, the great first source, and once more receive the sap of life, just as Emily herself now asks to do.

> Death, that struck when I was most confiding
> In my certain Faith of Joy to be,
> Strike again, Time's withered branch dividing
> From the fresh root of Eternity!
>
> Leaves, upon Time's branch, were growing brightly,
> Full of sap and full of silver dew;
> Birds, beneath its shelter, gathered nightly;
> Daily, round its flowers, the wild bees flew.
>
> Sorrow passed and plucked the golden blossom,
> Guilt stripped off the foliage in its pride;
> But, within its parent's kindly bosom,
> Flowed forever Life's restoring tide.
>
> Little mourned I for the parted Gladness,
> For the vacant nest and silent song;
> Hope was there and laughed me out of sadness,
> Whispering, "Winter will not linger long."
>
> And behold, with tenfold increase blessing
> Spring adorned the beauty-burdened spray;
> Wind and rain and fervent heat caressing
> Lavished glory on its second May.
>
> High it rose; no wingèd grief could sweep it;
> Sin was scared to distance with its shine:
> Love and its own life had power to keep it
> From all wrong, from every blight but thine!
>
> Heartless Death, the young leaves droop and languish!
> Evening's gentle air may still restore—

No: the morning sunshine mocks my anguish—
Time for me must never blossom more!

Strike it down, that other boughs may flourish
Where that perished sapling used to be;
Thus, at least, its mouldering corpse will nourish
That from which it sprung—Eternity. (#183)

It is as if we only "live" so long as we suckle at the maternal breast; to remove our mouths from that source of living sap is to do wrong, or be wronged, in a way that only literal death can cure—so lethal is it to "contemn" one's "origin." As Cathy sobs to Heathcliff, "If I've done wrong, I'm dying for it" (ch. 15).

Indeed all Emily's systems of imagery, and all her best poems, were in 1844–1845 converging on this topic of her readiness to follow her muse back to their joint "origin" and die into "Undying Life." As early as 1838 she began a poem with this quite lovely incantation:

Fall, leaves, fall; die flowers, away;
Lengthen night and shorten day . . . (#79)

By 1839 hope for the future had been repeatedly dismissed, and "hope" itself had crossed over into the past, to be newly rooted in memory and the life of dreams (in #127). By April, 1840 (#135), the crossover was complete: "sunshine and awaking morn" were painting "no more golden visions" in the natural landscape. And just as the "light" Emily valued moved from day to night, it also moved from above to within, from the "sky" to "my soul." What this meant was that just as Emily was dissociating her experience of imaginative inspiration from the world of nature, so she was transforming the literal values of the natural world into figurative ones. Literal nature and the stern reason that asserted its primacy were for Emily aspects or correlates of the father—the world of ambition, but also of mortality, as the philosopher knew in "Enough of Thought, Philosopher." The earth that is death is his consort, her light and winds are instruments of his. On the other hand figurative nature is the realm of "Sweet thoughts that will not die," the realm of the wind as muse and the mother who is "A principle of life . . . Lost to mortality." The brightness associated with her is not scorching but healing, because it is inner brightness, spiritual rather than literal. What we see here, in short, is a process by which the external world is subjected to the will of the poet.[29]

To take Emily's use of the sun as our example, we may see that where the literal sun is her referent, as in the line "Ah! why, because the dazzling sun," its appearance is hostile and intrusive. It imposes its objective, literal presence, dispersing the poet's dream world and subverting her visionary powers. But when her reference is to the figurative, as in the poem "My Comforter," it is "Heaven's glorious sun" because it is an instrument of her imagination. In Emily's terms, the sun has departed the hopeless outer world to join the inner one she so much prefers, just as the wind that "shook the door," internalized and deified, is mother's messenger, the Holy Ghost. For Emily, to render the literal into the metaphoric was ultimately to reenact that first crucial imaginative transformation by which dying became visionary release into eternity. The result of this transformation was observed by the speaker of "Aye, there it is!" and confirmed in the calm assurance of "No coward soul is mind," whose speaker is ready for death because "what thou art may never be destroyed."

In the poem "Stars" we may see gathered into the dazzling sun of nature the entire range of values that Emily had been shedding over the preceding six years at least. Negative sun-words such as "scorch," "burn," and "Blood-red" are there clustered into association with ambition and the pull of the natural world. It is of course the literal sun that burns in the "desert sky" (#184) over a world that is "like a tomb, / A desert's naked shore" (#170); and that "desert sky" is in turn just one of the many variants of the "desolate desert" that young Emily had imagined as all that would remain after the cosmic prison break of #5:

> Darkness and glory rejoicingly blending, . . .
> Leaving a desolate desert behind.

Thus is the father—once the mother has died—an impotent creature really. However virile and productive he may appear, in his state of male separateness, of "doing" bereft of "being," he is a desolate desert of a man, a mere mourning philosopher. Like the God-alienated man of Jesus' metaphoric warning, he is a cast-off and withered branch because he no longer "abides" in God.

With steady purpose, then, Emily had over the years been gathering together the negative values of alienation, confinement, murderous energy, barrenness, and annihilating loss and attributing them to the outer world of stern reason, temporal nature, the harsh light of day. These values parallel the "yoke" and "custom" of Wordsworth's Intimations Ode, those "shades of the prison-house" that close around the growing child when his "vision splendid" fades into "the light of common day."

Correspondingly the positive values of comfort, reunion, and tranquility—Shelley's "antenatal dream" or the "Heaven" that Wordsworth said "lies about us in our infancy"—Emily rescued by internalizing and associating them with her ability to transform her mother's death into an imagined return to the power and glory from which she had in "early day" been "cut away." This is the place of childhood memories, of a glory and dream known then but rarely now (as with Wordsworth). It is the home from which the muse comes and in which the poet longs to abide once more. In this sense to pass into the "night" of death is really to be born again—but born, this time, not into the light of common day, but into the "glorious morn" of the spirit (#155). In such ways did Emily put Christian figure to her own use.

Six weeks after writing "Stars" Emily entered into her personal notebook the last poem (last except for "No coward soul") ever written there. This remarkable poem opens by exclaiming, "How beautiful the Earth is still" (#188, dated June 2, 1845), and depicts the poet's "readiness" as a condition of poised and happy stasis. All self-division or restlessness has now been externalized; it exists only in the world of others.

Certainly the domestic context in which this poem was written would have tested her convictions. It could hardly have been more unsettled and depressing. Charlotte was anguished and self-abasing over M. Heger's continued refusal to respond to her pleading letters: she was writing, "You will say once more that I am hysterical. . . . So be it Monsieur, . . . I submit to every sort of reproach. . . ." Anne was grimly depressed: she was to confide in her birthday note the following month: "I, for my part, cannot well be flatter or older in mind than I am now." Branwell was rioting in drunken hysteria. And finally, their father, Patrick, was going blind from cataracts. How, Emily's poem asks, does one keep up one's blissful spirits in such surroundings?

The answer is simple. Her "compeers" have seen the morning of their lives "melt in tears / To dull unlovely day" because they have foolishly pursued the pleasures of earthly existence, which are inevitably cloying and treacherous. She regards these "compeers" (by whom she would appear to mean her siblings, though she might, by a stretch, include her father) with contemptuous pity:

> Blest, had they died unproved and young
> Before their hearts were widly wrung,
> Poor slaves, subdued by passions strong,
> A weak and helpless prey!

By contrast she herself, taught by "A thoughtful Spirit," avoids such "fleeting treacheries." She repudiates all interest in the future insofar as it concerns matters of this world, and looks instead beyond the sands of life "To the enduring seas":

> "There cast my anchor of Desire
> Deep in unknown Eternity;
> Nor ever let my Spirit tire
> With looking for *What is to be.*"

Unweighted by earthly cares (they are the blazing, bustling father's business, not hers), she can take a child's simple pleasure in the here and now. The "thoughtful Spirit" is of course Emily's muse, her visionary imagination—the "God of Visions," the "true friend," and "thoughtful Comforter" she addressed so often in her poems. To this last-mentioned name she returns in the final lines, disclosing once more that the Comforter comes from the land beyond death:

> Glad comforter, will I not brave
> Unawed the darkness of the grave?
> Nay, smile to hear Death's billows rave,
> My Guide, sustained by thee?
> The more unjust seems present fate
> The more my spirit stands elate
> Strong in thy strength, to anticipate
> Rewarding Destiny! (#188)

"Fate is strong, but Love is stronger," she had just written in another poem. The present poem makes clear that the "Love" in question is to be recovered through the agency of her sustaining "Guide." It is the same love that Rosina sought in Julius' "tomb already more than mine." In one sense, of course, it is Maria Brontë's love.[30]

Visionary Narrative

Stasis, however, need not mean silence. Emily was still writing poetry, and clearly still enjoying it. But for this happy condition to continue, Emily evidently felt she must keep her poems absolutely private.

On October 9, 1845, Emily entered in her Gondal notebook her last "private" poem, that is, the last poem she ever wrote in the confidence that it was for her own eyes only. In her July birthday note Anne had observed that Emily was writing poetry, but only commented, "I wonder what it is about?" Although she mentions that Emily had read her some recent Gondal prose, she shows no expectation of having her curiosity indulged concerning the poetry. That it was not in Anne's character to insist, perhaps not even to voice her desire, is doubtless one of the reasons Emily retained her as a close companion. With Anne she could at once share what she wished and withhold without opposition.

This final "private" poem is for several reasons a very important work. First, it shows the poet's interest in rendering her visionary experience in narrative form; second, it offers the most lucid statement Emily has given us of what her visionary experience felt like; and third, she wrote two separate versions of the poem, with two different endings for the framing narrative. This curious circumstance allows us a unique perspective on the visionary experience that both versions contain. Finally—though this is a subject for a later chapter—after Emily's death Charlotte appropriated part of the poem and added yet a third ending of her own, which she attributed to Emily and published in her 1850 edition of her dead sisters' works. In that composite poem we may see the bridge by which Charlotte carried Emily's muse across into her own imagination, where, in transmuted form, he appears first in a late addition to *Shirley,* and then, fully evolved, at the center of *Villette.*

Emily entitled her original version of the poem "Julian M. and A. G. Rochelle" (#190)—two names that appear in no other extant Gondal materials and may have been invented specifically for this story. Emily's original version is the longest; critics have found it confusing because it is broken into two parts of uncertain relation to each other. A short opening section of twelve lines is spoken in the present tense by an unidentified speaker, possibly but not necessarily Julian; then the poem shifts abruptly into a second section (perhaps a flashback) of 140 lines, spoken in the past tense and certainly by Julian. The opening lines set a quiet scene and raise a question that the poem never explicitly answers. The setting is a silent house with a cheerful fire; looking out the window at the snows of winter the speaker trims a "little lamp . . . to be the Wanderer's guiding-star." The unanswered question concerns the "Wanderer." We are not told who he or she is, and if we are curious we are certainly in bad company:

> Frown, my haughty sire; chide, my angry dame;
> Set your slaves to spy, threaten me with shame:
> But neither sire nor dame, nor prying serf shall know
> What angel nightly tracks that waste of winter snow.

Then without transition (the next line is "In the dungeon crypts idly did I stray") the poem shifts to a time of past civil war in Gondal, and Julian tells the story of how he discovered his childhood playmate Rochelle in prison, rescued her, and won her love. Though the narrative connection between these two sections is unclear, the emotional content is quite consistent: the speaker in each section expresses contentment in a relationship that is at once secret, precious, and antisocial.

In this second section, "Lord Julian," "idly" touring the dungeons with the prison warder, pauses at the cell in which Rochelle is captive. Stirred by memory of "former days," he dismisses the warder and stays to converse with the prisoner. Rochelle's life history, as the poem briefly reveals it, again literalizes the progression depicted in Wordsworth's Immortality Ode, from the "joyous morn" of childhood to the prison house of maturity. Now, echoing the sentiments and even some words of "Death that struck when I was most confiding" (written just six months before), Rochelle says she longs only for death. Wearing the soft expression of an "unweaned child," she names the blow that having "been struck" has ended her desire to live: her parents have been killed. But she is sure that she has not long to suffer, and she describes the experience of visionary ecstasy that regularly takes her to the very borders of eternal release.

The passage that describes Rochelle's ecstatic flight must be quoted entire, so that we may see how fully Emily here summarized the key terms and images that I have been tracing throughout this chapter. Here in a few lines she gathers wind, stars, tenderness, darkness; the longing for feelings lost since childhood, the dread of future tears; the celestial realm internalized; the descent of peace onto the fretful spirit; the loss of consciousness and of all earth-awareness; the "music" (as in Wordsworth) of an eternal silence. And ushering all of this in is the messenger himself, who is at once an external beloved and the projection of the visionary's own "inward essence." All of these familiar elements are now fused into one dense anthem of desire:

> "A messenger of Hope comes every night to me,
> And offers, for short life, eternal liberty.
>
> "He comes with western winds, with evening's wandering airs,
> With that clear dusk of heaven that brings the thickest stars;
> Winds take a pensive tone, and stars a tender fire,
> And visions rise and change which kill me with desire—
>
> "Desire for nothing known in my maturer years
> When joy grew mad with awe at counting future tears;

When, if my spirit's sky was full of flashes warm,
I knew not whence they came, from sun or thunderstorm;

"But first a hush of peace, a soundless calm descends;
The struggle of distress and fierce impatience ends;
Mute music soothes my breast—unuttered harmony
That I could never dream till earth was lost to me.

"Then dawns the Invisible, the Unseen its truth reveals;
My outward sense is gone, my inward essence feels—
Its wings are almost free, its home, its harbour found;
Measuring the gulf it stoops and dares the final bound!"

The promised liberty, though tasted in these moments, has not yet been fully achieved. Checked in its daring, the "inward essence" has always been brought back down to its imprisonment in mortality. Yet however painful this strange mix of joy and torture may be to her, however moral or immoral it may appear to others, it is welcome to the eager visionary if it will only speed the end she longs for, an end described so vividly as to suggest (again, as with Rosina) an influx of frustrated sexual longing.

"Oh, dreadful is the check—intense the agony
When the ear begins to hear and the eye begins to see;
When the pulse begins to throb, the brain to think again,
The soul to feel the flesh and the flesh to feel the chain!

"Yet I would lose no sting, would wish no torture less;
The more that anguish racks the earlier it will bless;
And robed in fires of Hell, or bright with heavenly shine,
If it but herald Death, the vision is divine."

In sexual terms Emily reliteralizes the little death of orgasm ("kill . . . with desire") as death itself. In psychological terms she has convinced herself that death must not be feared; that it must be embraced because the integrated contentment of infancy, the "unsullied light" she longs for, will be recovered beyond the tomb. In sum, she locates her muse, her beloved source of creative energy, in an experience that approaches death as its limit and goal.

I have argued above that Emily's originating visionary experience occurred when she transformed her mother's death into a model of the visionary's release. (Rochelle's "unweaned" expression and dead parents are traces of that time of origin.) That Emily could now describe so vividly the ecstatic journey suggests how fully she felt herself prepared to undergo it, how ready she was to realize the ultimate implications of her theory of vision and leave forever the domain of her surviving earth-father, Patrick. Rather than comforting him as the girl "wiser than her sire" had comforted her father in #177, Emily was now poised to follow the lead of her "Glad comforter" and seek the "Rewarding Destiny" that would make her indeed "Lost to mortality." It seems that she no longer feared the churchyard stone.

But the narrative with which Emily surrounds this lucidly described visionary journey makes it clear that she did not yet feel compelled to die literally. She was ready to go, but could also wait contentedly until her time came. Life could still be "full of Happiness," as she had just claimed in the poem "How beautiful the Earth is still." Thus the original narrative of "Julian M. and A. G. Rochelle" does not end with Rochelle's ecstatic flight but pursues a different course. A sign of interest from Julian stirs answering interest in Rochelle after all: "Earth's hope was not so dead, heaven's home was not so dear."

Emily's poem, in other words, returns from vision to the world of time and narrative. It proves to be not death but Julian who releases Rochelle from her chains. He then secretly nurses her back to health, and —defying with "patient strength" his taunting kin and "the world's disdain"—wins at last her love. The poem ends where it began, in the contentment of a relationship that defies the world, but lives in it. This is the decision that Catherine did *not* make in *Wuthering Heights*—to marry Heathcliff and settle down in defiant privacy.

As suggested above, the opening twelve lines of the poem could be spoken by either Julian or Rochelle, so that in either case the other is the "angel" who nightly tracks the snow toward the silent house. Certainly the surrounding world of disapproving parents and servants is the same in both sections of the poem (and returns in Emily's novel). The unexplained connection between the nightly angel and Julian's love affair with Rochelle, that is between the poem's first and second sections, is in effect a narrative corollary of the privacy sought by the lovers, another expression of the poem's hostility to prying and spying altogether. As audience, we are among the excluded.

Strikingly, however, this poem does not align Rochelle's choice between death and life, between her "messenger" and the flesh-and-blood Julian, with the familiar opposition between fidelity and ambition. Rochelle's story is crucially different from Emily's earlier stories. This time there are two prison visitors, one immortal, one mortal; but they share a common valence in that both promise seclusion from the world. They offer parallel options to Rochelle, parallel kinds of release: one eternal, the other temporal. With either, ambition is renounced in favor of a "never-doubting love" that is calmly oblivious of the world's "contempt and calumny."

As we have seen, either of Rochelle's possible liberations entails a world-defying fidelity, and each brings seclusion from the world. This seclusion was the fictional correlative of Emily's own situation as she perceived it; it had long been the necessary precondition of her contentment and her work. However, the fact that in this poem Rochelle's two "lovers" are set in parallel rather than in opposition allows a quite new element to enter. The practice of poetic narrative was certainly not new, considering the Gondal stories. And the subject of this poem—release from imprisonment—was certainly not new to Emily's visionary poetry. But never before had visionary release meant anything but removal from the world of time. In this poem visionary experience is newly framed in a way that allows us to discern how Emily might transform Romantic "vision," essentially a timeless experience, into the kind of narrative that a novel might require. In this poem a temporal encounter is presented: Rochelle's lucid rendering of her journey heightens Julian's desire, which in turn brightens Rochelle, which leads him to break her chain, for which she embraces him. . . . Such serial steps, here sexual in their choreography, are possible with man-as-flesh in ways that they are not with a disembodied visionary messenger who can have only two steps to his dance: he can lift the poet over the "final bound" or he can return her to prison. And never before had even those two steps been described in terms as fleshly vivid as Rochelle makes them. Much less had they ever been incorporated into a story that reenacts them in the world of earth and time. Perhaps it really was a final release from the fear of death that at last allowed Emily to find a narrative analogue for her experience of visionary liberation—allowed her to tell it for the first time from the perspective of participant rather than spectator.

Of course for Emily to pursue such goals in her writing, the writing itself would have to be kept safe from the world, as free of earthly intrusion or motive as their author now felt herself to be. She seems to have assumed that her poems were as safe from spying and prying eyes as Julian's and Rochelle's love had been. Fidelity to her "angel" certainly required no less. But of course they were not safe. Fate and Charlotte together denied her the privilege of privacy, and gave instead a powerful new voice to the persuasions of ambition. Before we can consider Emily's second version of the story of Julian and Rochelle, we must listen to the sound of that powerful voice.

Enter Charlotte

Charlotte later described the moment of her great discovery:

> One day, in the autumn of 1845, I accidentally lighted on a MS. volume of verse in my sister Emily's handwriting. Of course, I was not surprised, knowing that she could and did write verse: I looked it over, and something more than surprise seized me, —a deep conviction that these were not common effusions, nor at all like the poetry women generally write. I thought them condensed and terse, vigorous and genuine. To my ear, they had also a peculiar music—wild, melancholy, and elevating.[31]

Charlotte does not indicate whether the volume she found was Emily's Gondal notebook or her personal one—perhaps both, if Emily kept them together. But whatever the original encroachment, Charlotte soon got access to the whole buried treasure, and like an eager archeologist dragged Emily's most sacred relics, the intimate record of her fidelity to the dead, out into the light of common day.

Predictably, Charlotte's triumph was Emily's nemesis. Emily first responded to her sister's intrusion with the rage of one threatened in her inmost being. Charlotte observed that "My sister Emily was not . . . one, on the recesses of whose mind and feelings, even those nearest and dearest could, with impunity, intrude unlicensed," and notes simply that "it took hours to reconcile her to the discovery I had made, and days to persuade her that such poems merited publication." Charlotte claimed that she "knew" that a mind like Emily's "could not be without some latent spark of honorable ambition." *Ambition!*—the very "scorching sun" from which Emily had been hiding all these years. And so the unwitting Charlotte "refused to be discouraged in my attempts to fan that spark to flame." The result was that Emily was indeed finally persuaded to join her sisters Charlotte and Anne in preparing and publishing a selection of their poems under the veiling pseudonyms of Currer, Acton, and Ellis Bell. But the cost was enormous: beset by her sister's and doubtless also by her own "darker hopes," Emily had once more got caught up in the world's tide, violating her sworn fidelity.[32] How enraged she was at her own behavior may be gauged by the energy with which she now repudiated her poetic work. As Charlotte lamented to a friend, once she had "wrung out" of Emily her "reluctant consent to have the 'rhymes' as they were contemptuously termed, published,"

Emily simply stopped alluding to them—"or when she does, it is with scorn."[33]

Emily did not allow Charlotte to publish "Julian M. and A. G. Rochelle" in its original narrative form. What appears in their joint volume is a highly truncated version of that poem, now entitled "The Prisoner, A Fragment." Gone are the opening twelve lines with their confident secrecy. This new version begins at the thirteenth line, "In the dungeon crypts idly did I stray," and continues almost without alteration through Rochelle's description of her visionary journey and reluctant return. In Emily's original version, this had introduced sixty more lines in which Rochelle's interest gradually turned back from death to life as Julian himself changed from jailer to liberator and the lovers retreated in defiant contentment, shielded from the hostile and prying world. But Emily's public version has four more lines only. As we read them we should keep in mind the description in "Aye, there it is!" of the departing visionary, whose appearance is imagined by a poet who had watched her dying mother. In "Aye, there it is!" the key signs of departure were the "altered cheek" and "kindled gaze" of her who is escaping the imprisonment of flesh. Now in the four final lines of "The Prisoner, A Fragment" those signs return. Rochelle, condemned to imprisonment, has just described her visionary journey and affirmed that "If it but herald Death, the vision is divine." Now with these following lines the poem ends:

> She ceased to speak, and we, unanswering turned to go—
> We had no further power to work the captive woe;
> Her cheek, her gleaming eye, declared that man had given
> A sentence unapproved, and overruled by Heaven.

What these lines mean for the narrative is that Julian remains a would-be jailer, whose idle wandering through the crypts is no better than a species of voyeurism. He is one more element of that hostile world from which Rochelle must escape through death, one more example of the "man" whose sentence of imprisonment "Heaven" must overrule. In the poem's closing, Mother reclaims her own.

What the altered lines mean for Emily is that she felt that her time had run out. Charlotte had always loved the father-world and prospered in its shine. But the effect on Emily was wholly different. The sun of ambition that gave life to Charlotte brought death to Emily when she was most confiding. Now death must "Strike again."

Wuthering Heights was apparently written in less than eight months.

Emily must have begun it almost immediately after Charlotte's discovery of the poems. This would have meant late November. Late, because Charlotte must have discovered the poems after November 18, when she wrote her final despairing letter to M. Heger. Yet the "November" of the novel's opening scenes is, given Emily's dating habits, a compelling clue to the month of the novel's inception. By January 1846 *Wuthering Heights* would have been well under way—the poem "No coward soul," which stands at the novel's root and center (and is echoed in its text) is dated January 2. By April Charlotte was already seeking a publisher; and by July 4 the work was ready to be sent off. We can understand how such an avalanche of work might result in a novel as meticulously ordered as *Wuthering Heights* if we recall how accustomed Emily was to the methods of prose narrative (in writing the novel she was using the familiar calendar of the Gondal chronicles) and how emotionally and intellectually prepared she was to give vent to the powerful insights that had already been gathering in her poetry before Charlotte intruded on it. That intrusion broke the dam, and Emily's novel poured forth.[34] *Wuthering Heights,* though set in the realistic social world of narrative discourse, takes as its conceptual center that abiding topic of Romantic poetry, the artist's engagement with her own creative energies. It delineates Emily's inner conflict between ambition and the love of her muse. In the later poems Rosina had vowed that the "tender star" of her love had not faded "Before Ambition's scorching sun" as Julius had feared it would, since Julius had always been both sun and star to her. In "No coward soul is mine" Emily expanded both that imagery and its implications in order to say (borrowing Rosina's terms) not just that the world is empty without Julius, but that Julius is in himself both the sun and stars that have joined him and also the world they have departed. There is nothing that is *not* Julius. Emily's beloved is existence itself. In the words of "No coward soul,"

> Though Earth and moon were gone
> And suns and universes ceased to be
> And thou wert left alone
> Every Existence would exist in thee[.]

This means that for one who holds Emily's faith there literally is not "room for Death." What looks like death is actually life. Death is the only fiction. Indeed in a sense death had become the writer of Emily's fiction. For her, the muse was no longer the divine breath inspiring the private devotions that might continue throughout an open-ended future of readiness, but was now become the very sign and emblem of her disbranched condition. Emily's religious convictions had never been surer; but she had broken faith with her Holy Ghost.

The issue is engaged most fully in *Wuthering Heights* itself, where it radiates from the famous passage that climaxes in Cathy's cry, "Nelly, I *am* Heathcliff!" Cathy is struggling to get Nelly to see why it would not be wrong to marry Edgar in order to benefit Heathcliff. To Nelly's objection that this is the worst of all the bad reasons Cathy has given for marrying Edgar, Cathy replies that this motive alone is not merely selfish —it is "for the sake of one who comprehends in his person my feelings to Edgar and myself." That is, Heathcliff comprehends in his person both Cathy's worldly ambition (her "feelings to Edgar" reflect the fact that Edgar "is handsome, and young, and cheerful, and rich," as Nelly observes, and will make Cathy "the greatest woman in the neighborhood") and what Cathy calls "myself," that inmost being and visionary capacity which Rochelle had called her "inward essence," and Heathcliff in more traditional vocabulary his "life" or "soul": "I *cannot* live without my life! I *cannot* live without my soul!" But what Emily understands, and her protagonist Cathy must learn, is that even if there is "an existence of yours beyond you" such that "if all else perished, and *he* remained, I should still continue to be; and, if all else remained, and he were annihilated, the Universe would turn to a mighty stranger. I should not seem part of it"—even if this "extended" self is the true self, it is still possible to turn from it, to violate the sanctity of one's union with it. In *Wuthering Heights* this violation, or infidelity—really it is an apostasy—consists in Cathy's turning from Heathcliff to marry Edgar. In Emily's own life it seems to have culminated in her permitting Charlotte to fan into flame her "latent spark" of ambition, persuading her to uncloak her inner being and sacrifice her God of Visions to publication and the public. This infidelity, this Rosina-like swerving from constancy to her Julius, Emily could now rectify only by a reaffirmed commitment, absolute and final. This commitment is voiced unequivocally in "No coward soul is mine."

But the inner history that climaxed in this moment and illuminates its implications was left to the novel to recount. This being the one work that Emily ever wrote for an audience in the world, it is appropriately pervaded by the masculine—"written" by Lockwood, dominated by Heathcliff. If it also represented any further capitulation on Emily's part to her "darker hopes," her ambition, it would at the same time redeem that failing by dramatizing the truth as she now saw it: "Time for me must never blossom more." Emily had lived long enough among polarities to understand both sides of most of the issues that concerned her life as an artist. She perfectly understood that from the perspective of her family—of people she loved very dearly and whose intentions toward her she knew to be generous—her coming withdrawal would seem incomprehensible. Perhaps her novel could speak to them as she herself had been unable to do.

TWO

Wuthering Heights

"Twenty years, I've been a waif for twenty years!"

So wails the ghostly child of Lockwood's dream. The time of the dream is given as late November 1801: Lockwood has just arrived in the North to take possession of his rental property, Thrushcross Grange, and has come on a visit to Wuthering Heights to chat with his neighbor and landlord, Heathcliff.

A snowstorm has forced Lockwood to stay the night in this most unpleasant household. Placed by the servant in what had been young Catherine Earnshaw's room, he retires to her boxlike enclosed oak bed, with its sliding panels on the front opening to the room, and its window in the back wall opening onto a fir tree and the snowy moors beyond. On the window ledge Catherine's name is scratched in various forms: her own, Catherine Earnshaw; and her two marriage possibilities, Linton and Heathcliff. Lockwood also discovers old books of hers stacked in the alcove, filled in their margins with diarylike scribblings that date from her childhood. Perusing these, Lockwood dozes off to dream that he stands accused of the ultimate sin (in Scripture this is blasphemy against the Holy Ghost: Matt. 12:31, 18:22), and is being cudgeled in a shower of noisy rappings. But when the noise wakes him, it proves to be only the fir tree rattling its dry cones against the windowpane. Recognizing this relatively innocuous source of the disturbance, he drops off again, this time however to an ever deeper level of nightmare. Again he hears the rapping, but in his dream he recalls the "real" cause of it, which he undertakes to stop. The window hasp having been soldered shut, in his dream he knocks through the glass "to seize the importunate branch: instead of which, my fingers closed on the fingers of a little, ice-cold hand!" This is the waif "Catherine Linton," as she identifies herself to him, begging "Let me in—let me in! . . . I'm come home, I'd lost my way on the moor!" "Terror made me cruel," Lockwood says; and in his effort to make the ghost-child release him, he "pulled its wrist on to the broken pane, and rubbed it to and fro till the blood ran down and soaked the bed-clothes: still it wailed 'Let me in!' and maintained its tenacious gripe, almost maddening me with fear." His yell of fright ends the nightmare, and brings Heathcliff rushing to the room.

Who is this ghost-child, and why does she appear? These questions, crucial to the very engendering of the book, the meticulous author answers with precision, threading all through her novel the lines that meet in this moment. To trace them, let us turn first to the novel's conclusion —specifically to Nelly's account of Heathcliff's death, offered to Lockwood on his brief return to the North in the fall of 1802.

At the time of Lockwood's dream in 1801, Heathcliff no longer slept in his and Catherine's childhood bed, the oak paneled one in which the servant placed Lockwood. The constant expectation of Catherine's presence, and constant disappointment, had long made that place a special torture for Heathcliff.[1] But in his final days he felt Catherine's spirit increasingly around him, and four nights before his death he returned to that room. He then dies in that childhood bed. When Nelly discovers his body she draws back the panels to find Heathcliff on his back, drenched with rain from the open window—the same window on which Lockwood had rubbed "to and fro" the ghost-waif's hand. Now Heathcliff's hand too is cut, in an action that echoes Lockwood's very words. Nelly recounts, "The lattice, flapping to and fro, had grazed one hand that rested on the sill"; but "no blood trickled from the broken skin . . . —he was dead and stark!" (pp. 410–11).

The dream-ghost had bled until its blood soaked the bedclothes. Now, at Heathcliff's death, the bedclothes drip only from the rain. That Heathcliff's broken skin does not bleed is medically a sign that he was already dead when wounded. He must have died in unhasping the lattice to let in Catherine's child-ghost, for at one level he himself was the "home" she sought, and reunion in that childhood bed was their common goal. Their wounds match because Heathcliff's wound is her wound, just as Catherine had told Nelly years before, "My great miseries in this world have been Heathcliff's miseries. . . . Nelly, I *am* Heathcliff" (p. 102). The ghost of Catherine had bled because with Heathcliff still living, her death was incomplete; his wound does not bleed because "they" —together—are really dead at last. The parallel wounds occur only five months apart in historical time: the first in November 1801 at Lockwood's first arrival, the second in mid-April, roughly five months before Lockwood's final return.[2] However, because the two events occur respectively at the novel's beginning and end, their joint effect is to form a frame, to emphasize that the narrative structure of the novel reflects not the order of chronological sequence (some forty-five years in sequential unfolding), but order of another kind.

The principle that orders Emily's fictional world is certainly not a "rational" one, despite the considerable realism of her fictional manner: it is that Catherine and Heathcliff derive from a single source that was divided long ago. They are not so much friends or lovers as they are male and female elements of a single being, fictional embodiments of the female artist and her male muse. To return to the language of Emily's poems, Heathcliff is Catherine's "Sweet love of youth" from whom "the World's tide" has borne her ever farther away, toward the obscuring hopes of worldly ambition. These hopes are figured in the novel by her attraction toward the rich and cultivated Lintons, and are consummated by her marriage to Edgar. In Catherine's self-division Emily depicted her own felt condition, with Heathcliff as her version of a "heart's brother." He is thus one of those familiar muses who—as with so many of the female muses of male Romantic poetry—enter as participating characters into the works that concern them, works whose deep subject is the artist's own experience of creative power. But in himself Heathcliff is no maternal messenger, no Holy Ghost. That sacred figure is not directly represented in *Wuthering Heights*.

Critics have long observed that the novel is organized by systems of doubling and repetition; but as J. Hillis Miller complains, "The reader is nowhere given access to the generative unity from which the pairs are derived." We never see, for example, "the moment in childhood when Cathy and Heathcliff slept in the same bed and were joined in a union which was prior to sexual differentiation." Indeed even when they slept in the same bed they were not truly united, for as Miller goes on to observe, their ultimate union must have been "prior to any sense of separate selfhood, prior even to language, figurative or conceptual, which might express that union. . . . This division has already occurred as soon as there is consciousness and the possibility of retrospective storytelling." The problem, it would seem, is in the genre of fiction itself. Miller concludes, "Storytelling is always after the fact, and it is always constructed over a loss. What is lost in *Wuthering Heights* is the 'origin' which would explain everything."[3]

But that "origin" is not lost in Emily's poetry. Memory, or fidelity to a past that has been lost but must not be forgotten, is an obsessive subject in her poetic work. In poems like "Stars," "Aye, there it is! it wakes to-night," and "No coward soul is mine" she renders with great poetic richness the treasured content of memory, the maternal "Being" that is the object of her faith, and even the holy "Breath" that returns her to its presence.

In a sense this remembered "origin" is not quite lost in the novel either, for (as earlier, in Rosina's lament) Emily points to it insistently through her very technique of doubling and repetition. Miller explains the significance of such repetition in the work of Virginia Woolf, of whom he writes: "The possibility that repetition in narrative is the representation of a transcendent spiritual realm of reconciliation and preservation, a realm of perpetual resurrection of the dead, is more straightforwardly proposed by Virginia Woolf than by most of her predecessors in English fiction."[4] But in the recognition and use of this technique Emily Brontë was the pioneer and Woolf the inheritor. Indeed Romantic poetry's focus on the transcendent realm was precisely what Emily carried over into Victorian fiction.

Still, Miller is right that in *Wuthering Heights* the treasured content of memory is not directly revealed. Fidelity to the past remains her subject, but since the great year of poetry her secret work had been exposed and her own fidelity violated. She had sinned against her Holy Ghost, and this is in fact the story the novel has to tell. Small wonder, then, that she is wary of further exposure. One reason for her reticence concerns her posture toward her audience: they are in effect already the receivers of stolen goods. She will not squander sacred gifts on the undeserving. But another reason concerns her attitude toward herself: she was now writing from the perspective of one whose spiritual history was closed. Death had "struck," and time for her "must never blossom more." Accordingly Heathcliff, the muse of her novel, is no visionary messenger guiding her to new heights. Like the ghost-child whose "home" he is, or shares, he is rather the fictionalized relic of something that has died in Emily herself, a rootless and restless fragment of her divided being, with whom she can be reconciled only beyond the world of time. Within the narrative, Lockwood's sin is that he "would lock" the ghost out of her "home" if he could; he would prevent the reconciliation of Catherine's sundered parts. From the author's perspective outside the narrative, however, the "sin" may consist in writing itself, if it does indeed lock out the "origin" over whose loss it is constructed. As writer, Emily had to protect that origin from profane eyes, yet also give it a home within her text.

To understand *Wuthering Heights* as the story of a fall from primal integrity, we should begin by observing that Heathcliff enters the novel as a substitute, a replacement for losses already incurred. First Catherine learns with furious resentment that her father had brought home a "gypsy brat" instead of the whip she had requested, indeed that her father "had lost her whip in attending on the stranger." Then the boy's status as displacing substitute is further emphasized by his being given the name of "a son who died in childhood."[5] Thus we see in him the very embodiment of loss: an unwanted stranger rather than a brother, much less an element of Catherine's own being. In a sense what Catherine called "more myself than I am" had already "died in childhood" before the story began. And of course further separation evolves from there, as she matures and drifts still farther away from Heathcliff.

The first half of Emily's novel depicts a struggle within Catherine between two opposing sets of claims, figured by the two claimants, Heathcliff and Edgar. With Emily's poetry in mind, we may recognize in these men respective embodiments of fidelity and ambition. Catherine's fidelity to Heathcliff is fidelity to memory, her past, her inner self, her origins;[6] her attraction to Edgar reflects her ambition for the future, for the world that lies outside and ahead. Ambition is at first the victor: Heathcliff gone, in effect driven off by Catherine's repudiation of him, Catherine seems to have forgotten him as she lives quietly married to Edgar. But then the repressed Heathcliff returns, not literally dead, but worse—dead to her. At his return, she begins to recognize what she has done. She has cut herself off from her source—"disbranched" herself, died a spiritual death. She has sinned against the Holy Ghost, and in so doing has spun off a ghost of her own, the wailing waif "Catherine Linton." Her sense of failed fidelity now awakened, it waxes stronger until she sees only one alternative: "Death, that struck when I was most confiding . . . / Strike again." Catherine's bodily death ends the first movement of the novel.

In the second half of the novel Heathcliff wanders the father-world without Catherine, a spectral force, cruel and ravening, loosed like the ghost-child and driven like her with a fierce yearning for "home." He is the Holy Ghost bereft of his holiness, doing cut off from being, a male muse indeed, but the muse of an ambitious novelist writing for the public, not of a sacred poet writing for the records of eternity. He and the wailing ghost-child share a restlessness that mirrors the restlessness of the Catherine who is the home they both long for, awaiting them beyond the grave. All three (Heathcliff, Catherine, and the wailing waif, the ghost of Catherine-as-child) converge at last when Heathcliff dies, unbleeding, in the original oak-paneled childhood bed.[7]

The Diminished Muse

We can see by now that Emily's poetry provided us with most of what we need in order to understand the novel's metaphysical substructure: chiefly the idea of woman's masculine element (the female artist's male muse) and her longing to reclaim him. The character Heathcliff is a diminished, human form of the divine spirit messenger who embodied the artist's creative energies and swept her back to her origins in the mother-world. In the figure of the ghost-child we see another aspect of that diminution. The "World's tide" has killed something in Emily/Catherine of which this child is a lingering ghost.

We recall Wordsworth's perception that "The Child is father of the Man," to which I added that for male poets the muse stands in for the mother, that she is at once the projection of the male poet's inner "paradise" and the human-formed paradigm of the vast female "being" that is his subject. Correspondingly we may say that for Emily the child is mother of the woman-poet, and that the Heathcliff who figures Emily's power of "doing" stands in for the father in being the human form of Father Nature. As he was the "heart's brother" of young Catherine, so the world he represents is as wild and savage as she was before she was "civilized" by Linton culture. The lost ghost-child "Catherine Linton" and Heathcliff are thus commentaries on one another, joint evidences of Catherine's loss of an original untamed integrity when Heathcliff really was "in my soul" (p. 197). As alienated elements of Catherine's being, the male muse and ghost-child both seek reunion with her beyond death. In the ordinary language of narrative, Heathcliff must "die" to achieve this end. But the ghostly waif's presence reminds us that from another point of view he was, like her, a specter from the outset. We might more properly say that he must be "laid." Nelly actually uses the term, in observing how the self-alienated Catherine "could neither lay nor control the spirit that served her."

On the other hand, within the fiction Catherine (like her creator, Emily) is a genuine mortal, a real person. But she is self-divided, and her division is depicted in the way she bears two different kinds of children. Her daughter Catherine is her mortal offspring, the child of her fleshly union with Edgar, who is himself both a member of and a very good representative of ordinary human society. The wailing waif (also a Catherine Linton) is in effect Catherine's spiritual offspring, painful evidence of her disbranching, her sin against the Holy Ghost, her temporal break with immortal Being. Heathcliff speaks of his own past and its progeny in similar terms. Observing the young Hareton, who uncannily resembles the first Catherine, Heathcliff sees in him "a personification of my youth, not a human being," "the ghost of my immortal love" (pp. 393–94).

As Catherine's masculine double and Emily's male muse, Heathcliff represents the final stage of evolution of the child Emily's special toy soldier "Parry," which she chose from among those that Patrick Brontë brought Branwell from Leeds in 1826. The point is noteworthy if we place it in the context of some of Freud's thinking in his essay on "The Uncanny." Citing the authority of Otto Rank to the effect that the idea of the double developed as a way of preserving the ego from extinction,[8] Freud goes on to remark that in dreams castration is frequently represented by a doubling or multiplication of the genital symbol. That is, what is "lost" is reproduced externally, in "doubled" or "projected" form. In Emily's case, lost "power"—the masculine element as she felt it to have been originally an integrated part of her own being, rather than an instrument of father-worldly action—is projected onto the doll Parry who will evolve into Heathcliff. Heathcliff is thus a double whose function all along was to record Emily's sense of lost power and at the same time to represent that power, to be a fictional embodiment of it. In this way what is lost (the "power and glory cut away") is preserved, yet its *loss* is at the same time recorded. Freud's idea prepares us for the view that writing is necessarily the recording of absence, but it also suggests that within Emily's fictions the technique of doubling and repetition preserves her power to create—to write the fiction of which Heathcliff, with all his limitations, is the muse.

But he is not in himself Catherine's "origin." Rather he and she share a common origin, and it is that, not Heathcliff himself, toward which Emily's doublings point. To help mark that origin while at the same time protecting it from profane eyes, Emily constructed an intricate pattern of clues surrounding the figure of Catherine's ghost.

The Ghost in the Mirror

By midnovel, as the derangement that precedes her death is near its height, Catherine is herself fully aware that if she is to recoup her losses she must travel a circular road, that in her case "home" was her childhood bed at Wuthering Heights, but also "my narrow home out yonder" (p. 156), i.e., the grave. These places are mirroring reflections of one another, both spiritually (being portals to the lost paradise, the

"Heaven which is our home" in Wordsworth), and physically, in the literal similarity Emily carefully establishes between Catherine's bed and her coffin. As children Catherine and Heathcliff had slept together in the oak bed with its sliding panels, and were not parted until after Mr. Earnshaw's death, when as Catherine explains "my misery arose from the separation that Hindley had ordered between me and Heathcliff—I was laid alone, for the first time" (p. 153). That separation, further widened in the ensuing years until it culminates in her marriage to Edgar and in the "alienation of intellect" that is her final state, is of course not curable in life. Catherine and Heathcliff can never again sleep, as unseparated children, in that paneled bed. But Heathcliff has prepared her coffin and his so that when he dies and is buried, the sexton (whom he has bribed to the purpose) can slide out the side panels so their dust may meet. As Heathcliff says, they can sleep "the last sleep" together, "my cheek frozen against hers" until they are finally "dissolved into earth" as one (p. 349).[9]

Their bodies, then, will merge at last. But what will become of their spirits, or souls, of which Catherine had said in her famous talk with Nelly, "Whatever our souls are made of, his and mine are the same" (p. 100)? The country folk say that their spirits walk, and have been seen together—"Heathcliff and a woman"—on the moors; Nelly, however, believes that "the dead are at peace" and Lockwood concurs, wondering "how any one could ever imagine unquiet slumbers for the sleepers in that quiet earth." But all such views are quite inadequate. Readers of Emily's poetry, and attentive readers of her novel, will recognize that the communion invoked by Catherine and Heathcliff goes as far in death beyond the peace of mingled dust as it had in life beyond the quickenings of sexuality, and equally that those troubled and passionate spirits did not plunge toward so radical a union in order to walk the moors together and peer in country windows.

In the same breath in which Catherine asserted to Nelly that Heathcliff's soul and hers were "the same," she said that she loved Heathcliff "because he's more myself than I am." This problem of "myself"—of what and where "myself" is—lies at the center of Catherine's story; indeed the entire novel circles around it, from the moment of Lockwood's encounter with the dream-waif to the very end, in the generational contrasts between reunion in death and union in marriage.

Appropriately the problem of "myself" is dramatized at the novel's center in a mirror scene that helps explain how Catherine's "ghost" was first generated, as well as why she should have appeared to Lockwood as a child, yet called herself "Linton," the name Catherine did not take on until she married Edgar. Catherine's derangement begins in a masochistic fury: "I'll try to break their hearts by breaking my own," she says of the feuding Heathcliff and Edgar (p. 143); and again in a rage at what she takes to be Edgar's complacency in the face of her self-willed illness, "If I were only sure it would kill him, I'd kill myself directly" (p. 149). But gradually the fit slips beyond masochistic spite into a kind of visionary hallucination. Nelly, annoyed with what she takes to be Catherine's play-acting, implies that Edgar has been happy among his books since the fight between him and Heathcliff that brought on the crisis in which Catherine locked herself in her room. "Among his books! And I dying!" cries Catherine, "does he know how I'm altered?" Staring at her reflection in a mirror on the opposite wall she asks, "Is that Catherine Linton?" and then adds a moment later, "I've been haunted, Nelly!" The verb "haunted" is set here as a signal: we are to watch its meaning gradually unfold.

To see what haunts Catherine we must begin by observing that she has been suffering a falling away of the child's experience of unconditional love: "How strange! I thought, though everybody hated and despised each other, they could not avoid loving me—and they have all turned to enemies in a few hours" (p. 149). Regressing, as if to reclaim for herself the experience of that childish confidence, she takes up what Nelly calls "baby-work"—pulling the feathers out of her pillow and ruminating over them. As Nelly steps about the room collecting the loose feathers, Catherine fantasizes how "fifty years hence" Nelly will be a withered hag "gathering elf-bolts to hurt our heifers," but adds—lest Nelly think that she is wandering in mind—that she really knows quite well where she is. "I'm conscious it's night, and there are two candles on the table making the black press shine like jet." But just as Lockwood's seeming rationality—he was sure that he knew, after his first dream, the source of the disturbing rapping in his second—signals not a return to the rational but a further drop into a deeper level of dream-vision, so Catherine's reach for rational evidence from within her regressive state yields evidence instead of the deepening of her uncanny insight. "There is no press in the room, and never was," Nelly tells her and us. But Catherine has again caught sight of her reflection in the mirror, and will not be dissuaded from the conviction that what she sees is a strange face looming out of the black press' shining surface. She thinks that she is back in her childhood room at Wuthering Heights where, as Lockwood has already told us, "The whole furniture consisted of a chair, a clothes-press, and a large oak case"—i.e., the paneled bed (p. 23). "Who is it!" Catherine demands, repeating the signaling verb: "Oh! Nelly, the room is haunted!" She is right, of course. Now when Nelly ingenuously responds, "It was *yourself,* Mrs. Linton; you knew it a while since," Catherine understands the truth, and gasps in recognition: "Myself." She recognizes the strange face as her own ghost's and sees that it is by "herself" that the room is haunted: "and the clock is striking twelve! It's true then; that's dreadful!" Nelly, not understanding Catherine's shock of recognition, but nonetheless alarmed for her sanity, tries to steal off to get Edgar when she is recalled by a piercing shriek—the analogue of Lockwood's yell. With this cry from the double depths of nightmare, Catherine, like Lockwood, finally "wakes."

What is this doubleness of condition such that Catherine can be haunted by her own ghost? Of what dead thing in her is this ghost the lingering evidence? Now awakened, Catherine recalls the unfolding process of her delirium, and in doing so provides an important part of Emily's exposition concerning the identity of that dead thing, an important insight into the ghost's meaning and its connection to Lockwood's wailing waif.[10]

"Oh dear! I thought I was at home," Catherine sighs, "I thought I was lying in my chamber at Wuthering Heights." She is quite analytic about her own case: "my brain got confused, and I screamed unconsciously. . . . I dread sleeping, my dreams appal me." By now it should be obvious that the dreams that appal her are closely connected with those that will appal Lockwood in 1802, as he lies in Catherine's chamber at Wuthering Heights. In this novel the world of dreams is evidently to some extent communal. Nelly is not inappropriately reluctant to become involved in it (p. 99). To Nelly's suggestion now that what Catherine needs is a "sound sleep," Catherine moans, "Oh, if I were but in my own bed in the old house! . . . And that wind sounding in the firs by the lattice." At her pleading Nelly opens the lattice for a few seconds, with the telling observation that now "our fiery Catherine was no better than a wailing child" (p. 152).

Again figurative speech cloaks deeper reality. Through Nelly's open window the ghostly, wailing "child" escapes; and it is those very "firs by the lattice" that reintroduce her, still "wailing," into Lockwood's dream: "Let me in!" The connections are drawn even more fully as Catherine goes on to describe to Nelly a terrifying experience she has been having repeatedly over the preceding days. What she describes is again a double-leveled shock of recognition, another version of her encounter with the fact of her own self-alienation.

Catherine recounts how when she locked herself in her room after the fight between Edgar and Heathcliff, she fell into a kind of fit. As she gradually "recovered sufficiently to see and hear" she experienced first "some great grief" and then, as she came fully to consciousness, that grief in turn was swallowed up in an even greater "paroxysm of despair" (p. 153). The fit itself she does not describe. But the recovery from it (the gradual, unwelcome return of sight and sound) echoes the pained return of Rochelle's "inward essence" from the borders of "its home, its harbour." We may guess that the fit was, like Rochelle's, a daring of final bounds: in this case, bounds that lie behind us, at the borders of our primal state. In the first level of return from her fit Catherine thought she was a child again, and that her surfacing consciousness had brought her up into the midst of some childhood sorrow. She thought she was "enclosed in the oak-panelled bed at home; and my heart ached with some great grief which, just waking, I could not recollect." As she struggles for the memory, it gradually clarifies: "I was a child; my father was just buried, and my misery arose from the separation that Hindley had ordered between me and Heathcliff. I was laid alone for the first time, and, rousing from a dismal doze"—the word "doze" is also used by Lockwood—"after a night of weeping, I lifted my hand to push the panels aside." This, then, is the first level of "reality" to which Catherine returns after her fit; as we know, there is a still more painful level of recognition to come; but let us pause over this level for a moment.

This first level to which Catherine has returned after her fit is the time following her father's funeral, the time recorded in the "diaries" discovered and read by Lockwood. The diaries begin as follows: "An awful Sunday! I wish my father were back again. Hindley is a detestable substitute—his conduct to Heathcliff is atrocious," and then they tell of her plan with Heathcliff to "appropriate the dairy woman's cloak, and have a scamper on the moors." This scamper—identifiable by the Sunday and the cloak—proves to be the occasion on which Catherine first encountered Thrushcross Grange. Bitten by their dog, she was kept there by the Lintons for "five weeks, till Christmas," during which time, in Nelly's words, her "self-respect" was raised by "fine clothes and flattery, which she took readily," so that she returned to Wuthering Heights no longer a "wild, hatless little savage" but "a very dignified person, with brown ringlets" (p. 65). The separation ordered by Hindley is being carried forward by Catherine's own hankerings after the Linton world and all it represents in the way of culture and society: these are the seductions of "Ambition"—of the "common paths that others run." In Rosina's words, "Sweet Love of youth, forgive if I forget thee / While the World's tide is bearing me along."

Lockwood, reading the diaries, correctly surmises that Catherine "ful-filled her project, for the next sentence took up another subject." Actually the subject it takes up is the next step in her separation from Heathcliff. Circumstances conspire to aid ambition: what the visit with the Lintons began is now further enforced at home. "How little did I dream that Hindley would ever make me cry so!" Catherine continues in this next scrap of diary. "Poor Heathcliff! Hindley calls him a vagabond, and won't let him sit with us, nor eat with us any more; and, he says, he and I must not play together, and threatens to turn him out of the house if we break his orders" (p. 27).

This, then, is the first level of "return"; these are the griefs of separation and loss over which Catherine thinks she has been weeping as, emerging from her "fit," she lifts her hand to push aside the panels of her childhood bed. But now the still worse reality confronts her. Instead of the familiar panels, her hand "struck the table-top! I swept it along the carpet, and then memory burst in—my late anguish was swallowed in a paroxysm of despair" (p. 153).[11] She is not after all the child Catherine weeping over her first stages of separation from Heathcliff. Infinitely worse: she is an adult woman, married to Edgar Linton, and violently torn between the two quarreling men as between two warring aspects of herself.

She cannot tell, she says to Nelly, "why I felt so wildly wretched—it must have been temporary derangement, for there is scarcely cause." In fact she fully understands the cause, as she demonstrates immediately, when she adds by way of explaining her wild wretchedness: "supposing at twelve years old"—her age at her father's death, when she and Heathcliff last slept together as children in the oak bed—"I had been wrenched from the Heights, and every early association, and my all in all, as Heathcliff was at that time, and been converted at a stroke into Mrs. Linton, the lady of Thrushcross Grange, and the wife of a stranger; an exile, and outcast, thenceforth, from what had been my world—You may fancy a glimpse of the abyss where I grovelled!" (p. 153) What she describes here are the two stages of her return from the "border"; together they form the "wrenched" condition of Lockwood's ghost-child, who is still a young girl and yet (at the same stroke) already a Linton. This is also a version of the condition of exile that Catherine had projected to Nelly in their famous exchange: if Heathcliff "were annihilated, the Universe would turn to a mighty stranger. I should not seem a part of it." Heathcliff has not of course been annihilated; but once Catherine became a Linton, Heathcliff was in effect annihilated for her. Unlike Rosina, Catherine has done her "Sweet Love of youth" real wrong, in marrying his rival. And now she finds that her "Sweet Love" has slipped from her grasp: "she could neither lay nor control it." In the terms of the poem "Death that struck when I was most confiding," Catherine has undergone the first death (of the spirit), and can now recover her loss only by undergoing the second (of the body).

The mirror scene concludes with Catherine wishing she were "a girl again, half savage," and then going to the window to look off toward Wuthering Heights. It is now that Catherine foresees that her journey "home" must pass through the churchyard graves. The little girl-ghost called up in her derangement, already "wrenched" from her "all in all," already the prospective Mrs. Linton, "the wife of a stranger," is here loosed once more to wander, lost, on the moors, to beg admission of Lockwood (who cuts her wrist), but to reach "home" at last only when she and Heathcliff (similarly wrist-cut) coalesce in death.

Division on Earth, Reunion in Heaven

But the waif heard by Lockwood had cried, "Twenty years, I've been a waif for twenty years!" whereas if we date back from Lockwood's dream in November 1801 to the time when Hindley ordered the twelve-year-old Catherine's separation from Heathcliff and she was first "laid alone," we get twenty-four years: those events occurred in October or November 1777, as Emily's meticulous and detailed system of dating makes clear. Nor does "twenty years" take us back to the date of the mirror scene and Catherine's derangement; the "ghost" of her lost self that she saw that midnight was already well established, and had been "haunting" her in her disturbed state for some time. The mirror scene occurred the night of January 13, 1784—the same night on which Heathcliff, loosed from Catherine's control and already embarked on his program of punishment and retribution, eloped with Isabella Linton.

Where, then, does the "twenty years" take us? We may suppose that the waif was merely speaking in general terms—rounding off the numbers. Yet it is always dangerous to underrate the significance of chronology in Emily's work. And chronology here is especially suggestive because if we take the "twenty years" literally we are returned to the three-year period that the narrative has left hidden, that is to a time between Heathcliff's sudden departure and Catherine's marriage to Edgar. We may surmise that the "twenty years" points to the time when Catherine betrayed her own heart by giving up thoughts of Heathcliff and actively focusing on becoming Mrs. Linton. Perhaps the narrative is silent about it, recording it only as lapse, because Emily found Catherine's infidelity—the betrayal of her own soul and heart—literally unspeakable.

But the "disbranchement" was less the result of some one moment than of a long process of estrangement. Nelly had recounted how after Catherine's first five-week stay at the Grange she had forborne to show her "rough side" in the Lintons' company, which led her "to adopt a double character." Catherine strove to keep separate the two halves of her character—the ambitious self that "imposed unwittingly" on the Lintons and enjoyed Edgar's admiration, and the other, primal self—"my all in all, as Heathcliff was at that time." Nelly observed that Catherine did not like Edgar to come to the Heights, that she "had evidently an objection to her two friends meeting at all" (p. 83). It was this desire to sustain both ends of a contradiction, to indulge ambition yet remain loyal to her first love, that prompted her suggestion to Nelly that if she married Edgar she could "aid Heathcliff to rise"—a self-deceiving notion, as Nelly is quick to point out. Yet Catherine clearly did know, in that famous scene, that marriage to Edgar would be a violation of fidelity—that is, of her true self. To Nelly's question "where is the obstacle?" Catherine responds, "in my soul, and in my heart." She would never even have considered the idea, she claims, if Hindley had not brought Heathcliff so low. Inadvertently attesting to the grip that ambition has gained on her spirit, she claims, "It would degrade me to marry Heathcliff, now" (p. 100). It is at this point—when "he heard Catherine say it would degrade her to marry him"—that Heathcliff departs. Returning three years later he will find the silent moment of fullest defection passed: the wild slip of a girl will have become "Mrs. Linton, the lady of Thrushcross Grange, and the wife of a stranger."

Thus, although Catherine had claimed that "every Linton on the face of the earth might melt into nothing"—like "the deep snow piled above thee"?—"before I could consent to forsake Heathcliff," in fact she did consent. Ill after his departure, she went to the Grange to convalesce a second time, with the result that Edgar's parents caught her fever and died. (There is something awesome about Catherine's virulence as parent killer; it is as if she were taking out on Edgar's parents, who tamed and civilized her, some rage against all the progenitors who had a hand in bringing her along on "the World's tide.") In any case her change of heart—which the "twenty years" places late the following fall—may be connected to the fact that with his parents dead Edgar's wife would indeed command first place in the neighborhood. In her ambition, Catherine must have veiled from herself the knowledge of her heart and soul: that as "Mrs. Linton" she would be an exile from her own world.

Alienation from Heathcliff occurs, then, through several steps—some the result of others' intervention, some the result of Catherine's own ambition and consequent adoption of a "double character." Still, the line was irrevocably crossed only when she committed herself to marriage with Edgar. As Heathcliff tells her on the day of her death, "you deserve this"; and his reproaches go to the heart of her defection. "*Why* did you despise me? *Why* did you betray your own heart, Cathy? . . . You loved me—then what *right* had you to leave me? What right—answer me—for the poor fancy you felt for Linton? Because misery, and degradation, and death, and nothing that God or Satan could inflict would have parted us, you, of your own will, did it." Unwittingly confirming the terms of Catherine's earlier infantile threat ("I'll try to break their hearts by breaking my own"), Heathcliff adds, "I have not broken your heart—*you* have broken it—and in breaking it, you have broken mine." Because he is "strong" he must live on, he knows; but "what kind of living will it be when you—oh God! would *you* like to live with your soul in the grave?" (p. 198). Catherine can only sob and ask him: "Let me alone. . . . If I've done wrong, I'm dying for it"; but as Heathcliff observes, he can forgive his own murderer, but not hers. Unluckily the two murderers are one.

Heathcliff's rhetorical distinction between murders—as if there were two—is the more grimly ironic for being set in a universe characterized throughout by an extraordinary wealth of doublings and divisions. Catherine is of course divided from Heathcliff by her own inner division, or "double character," but Heathcliff, too, is in a sense a double being. Angered at their last meeting by Heathcliff's attack on her "infernal selfishness" and by his unwillingness to comply with her call to "Come here and kneel down again!" Catherine comforts herself: "Well, never mind! That is not *my* Heathcliff. I shall love mine yet; and take him with me—he's in my soul." This is both true and not true: he is in her soul, yet also divided from her—"more myself than I am" yet not internal to her, not part of her present being, as the haunting waif-child also evidences. Catherine's monologue continues in terms familiar from Emily's poetry, terms that echo again Wordsworth's association of growing up with being enclosed in a prison house. "The thing that irks me most," says Catherine, "is this shattered prison, after all. I'm tired, tired of being enclosed here. I'm wearying to escape into that glorious world, and to be always there; not see it dimly through tears, and yearning for it through the walls of an aching heart; but really with it, and in it." Lest Nelly be pitying her, in her dying, she adds, "I shall be sorry for *you*. I shall be incomparably beyond and above you all" (p. 197).

Recalling these words the next day, after Catherine has died, Nelly sees in Catherine's peaceful corpse an "untroubled image of Divine rest" and feels sure that despite the wayward course of her life, "her spirit is at home with God!" But we know better: she cannot be "home" as long as Heathcliff remains alive and thus still divided from her, and Nelly's idea of "home" or heaven is surely not hers. As Catherine had observed to Nelly years before, "heaven did not seem to be my home"; and correspondingly, "I've no more business to marry Edgar Linton than I have to be in heaven." The heaven Catherine seeks is the same as Heathcliff's, and stands in full opposition to both Nelly's heaven and Edgar's marriage bed. So too when Heathcliff is dying years later he ignores Nelly's suggestion that he seek clerical advice—"any denomination, it does not matter," she says in an ecumenical spirit quite in keeping with the Brontë household—and that he learn the Bible's precepts and prepare himself for "its heaven." He is only pleased to be reminded to instruct her about the matter of his and Catherine's coffins, and assures Nelly that at his burial "No minister need come; . . . I tell you, I have nearly attained *my* heaven; and that of others is altogether unvalued and uncoveted by me." The day after next, he is dead.[12]

Although Heathcliff speaks as if his "heaven" were the grave—"I have my eyes on it—hardly three feet to sever me!" (p. 401)—the reunion in the grave, though desirable, is not sufficient. He must not only mingle their dust, but join Catherine in her "glorious world." We have already seen that his presence is required by Catherine if she is to reach that world. The suggestion is that her "ghost" has finally come to claim him with this end in view. Nelly recounts how over the last several days before Heathcliff's death his eyes had followed a moving specter, "an unearthly vision," in her words, "with such eager interest, that he stopped breathing, during half a minute together" (p. 404). "I won't rest till you are with me . . . I never will!" Catherine had warned Heathcliff (p. 154), and events prove her right. We learn later that the day of her funeral Heathcliff had dug up her coffin and was just "cracking about the screws" to open it when suddenly he heard a sigh and felt the warm breath of "some one above, close at the edge of the grave, and bending down. . . . I knew no living thing in flesh and blood was by—but as certainly as you perceive the approach to some substantial body in the dark, though it cannot be discerned, so certainly I felt that Cathy was there, not under me, but on the earth" (p. 350). She has beguiled him, he says, "with the spectre of a hope, through eighteen years"—that is, since he returned from his three years' absence (having "struggled only for you") and found her, first married but still caring for him, and then within six months dead, but still intimating her spectral presence. Alive or dead, her effect on him is much the same. "It was a strange way of killing, not by inches, but by fractions of hair-breadths" (p. 351). As Rochelle had said in Emily's poem, "A messenger of Hope comes every night to me" bringing visions that "kill me with desire." But as with Rochelle, though Heathcliff's "soul's bliss kills my body," it cannot satisfy itself (p. 408)—not, that is, this side of the final ecstasy. Therefore Rochelle and Heathcliff both welcome the very pains that expectation brings: in Rochelle's words, "The more that anguish racks the earlier it will bless."

Rochelle's story, as we know, eventually ends quite differently from Heathcliff's: "Earth's hope was not so dead," once her captor's love was offered her. But Heathcliff's beloved can no longer offer him love in this world—she lies cold in the earth, and all his "life's bliss is in the grave" with her. Heathcliff says that he can forgive his own murderer but not Catherine's; but Catherine, one might say, could forgive her own murderer but not the murderer of that first Heathcliff. Who was that murderer? What "killed" the original Heathcliff, her integrated "male element," the little "brother" who really was "in my soul"? This question the novel does not answer except by indirections such as the constant recurrence to a lost or longed-for "home" or "heaven," and the plethora of splittings and doublings that organize the novel from without (as narrative) and within (as fictional world). But we may see that Catherine's entry into time and the world was the moment of the first Heathcliff's "death," that in this sense his murder and her entry into mortality were one.

The split between Catherine and Heathcliff, and the reunion sought by them, pulses out from the novel's mysterious center in widening rings. Pivotal to its meaning are such clear doublings as the Catherine who looks in the mirror and the alien image she sees there; Catherine's buried corpse in the churchyard and her wandering, bleeding "ghost"; the Heathcliff in Catherine's soul and the one "beyond" her, whom finally she could "neither lay nor control"; the paneled bed and paneled coffins; the wrist wounds that begin and end the novel. Then there are more loosely suggestive symmetries such as the following: "It was the same room into which he had been ushered, as a guest, eighteen years before: the same moon shone through the window; and the same autumn landscape lay outside" (p. 346). These paired moments, occurring eighteen years apart, balance one of the final stages of Heathcliff's loss of Catherine against one of the first stages of his recovery of her. Specifically these are the two moments first of Heathcliff's return to the Grange when he found Catherine married to Edgar, since which time "she has disturbed me, night and day, through eighteen years—incessantly—remorselessly"; and second of his satisfied report (in the same setting) that "yesternight," after having dug up Catherine's coffin and bribed the sexton to arrange the sliding panel, he was "tranquil" at last: "I dreamt I was sleeping the last sleep by that sleeper, with my heart stopped, and my cheek frozen against hers" (p. 349).

Further doublings occur in the area of what one might call spiritual condition or psychological organization, for example in the already mentioned parallel between Catherine's double-descending disturbance and Lockwood's two dreams. The second, or lower level of disturbance into which Catherine descends in her mirror scene—first imagining Nelly as a withered hag "gathering elf-bolts," then proving that she really knows better, by pointing to a clothespress that turns out to be itself a product of hallucination—corresponds to Lockwood's second dream, where realistic explanation dissolves into the deeper horror of the ghost-child's appearance. As Catherine's lost girlhood travels interpsychically to appear in Lockwood's deeper level of dream, so the "upper" levels of their experiences pair off too, in Catherine's hostile hag and Lockwood's sin-denouncing Jabes. Both are figures of parent-gone-wrong: the hideous old woman who "is my hidden enemy. You witch!" (p. 157) and the accusatory Jabes, with his astonishing repertoire of sins.[13] In the generally parentless world of this novel, these are the spectral anti-parents, of whom the nuturing Nelly and grumbling Joseph are the more natural (but in their way no less menacing) human forms; appropriately both Nelly and Joseph support social and religious orthodoxy, and are unsympathetic to the amoral and irreligious values of Catherine and Heathcliff. As Nelly acknowledges, "I own I did not like her, after her infancy was past" (p. 82); and later, "My heart invariably cleaved to the master's [Edgar's], in preference to Catherine's side; with reason, I imagined, for he was kind, and trustful, and honorable: and she—she could not be called the *opposite,* yet she seemed to allow herself such wide latitude, that I had little faith in her principles, and still less sympathy for her feelings" (p. 132). Less generous than Nelly, but pursuing the same general ends, Joseph's loyalties are to a judgmental God and the traditional patriarchal social establishment. At Heathcliff's death Nelly thought for a moment that he would cut a caper of delight, but instead (the matter is too serious after all) "he fell on his knees, and raised his hands, and returned thanks that the lawful master and the ancient stock were restored to their rights" (p. 411).

We may thus see that the whole novel, insofar as it tells the story of

Catherine and Heathcliff, works like the poem "Cold in the earth," where a great gap is established only to be narrowed by a gathering rush toward closure in eternal embrace. The novel is constructed on an almost obsessive system of balance and contrast: the sociable Lintons and stalwart Earnshaws, the former of whom tend in their decadence toward the vapid and pettish and the latter toward abandoned brutality. These oppositions correspond within Catherine to the "ingenious cordiality" that she shows to the Lintons, and the "rough side" that she hides from them, the disjunction that leads her "to adopt a double character." Of course they correspond as well to the crimsom-carpeted Thrushcross Grange, with its gold-bordered ceilings and shimmering chandeliers, contrasted to the sturdy walls and exposed setting of Wuthering Heights. The very souls of their occupants are balanced in opposition: in Catherine's figurative language Edgar Linton's soul is made of something like frost and moonbeam, her own (as also Heathcliff's) of lightening and fire. At the peak of her rage because Edgar and Heathcliff have at last reached the point of full confrontation Catherine extends the same figure: to Edgar she cries "your veins are full of ice-water—but mine are boiling, and the sight of such chillness makes them dance" (p. 144).[14] Charles Percy Sanger's seminal essay on the structure of *Wuthering Heights*[15] was the first to demonstrate the rigorous formality of all these pairings and balancings: the striking symmetry of pedigree, the neat topographical balance, the rigorous calendar on which the story is based, and the accuracy of Emily's information in areas as diverse as botany and law. It all implies a concentration at once passionate and particular, a highly rational consciousness that balances the anarchic energies every reader feels in the book, and that warns us at the same time to be wary of dismissing any effect as accidental.

That there should be two separate Catherines in the first place (mother and daughter) suggests one kind of symmetry: a twice-told tale, whose two halves mirror and complement each other. Each Catherine occupies half the narrative, and they fulfill nearly opposite destinies. The first Catherine's story ends in derangement and death, her daughter's in love and the promise of new beginnings—as the novel closes she is to be married the following New Year's day. Each love story supplies a powerful critique of the other: each love is in a sense "selfless" and "redemptive," but the senses so differ as to be punning reversals of one another. One way to characterize the difference between the two kinds of love is to say that the daughter's is life centered and other related, the kind that is necessary to the survival and health of a society, knitting disparates into a unified fabric, as the Earnshaws and Lintons are to be knitted by the wedding on New Year's day. Education, cultivation, and reproduction are this love's values. By contrast the mother's love (and Heathcliff's) is what is termed solipsistic or narcissistic, directed backward in time, to the recovery of a primal, inner loss.[16]

In this novel Emily depicted a struggle of her own, the competition within herself between the values of "ambition" and "fidelity." The resulting study is penetrating and richly imagined, as one can see by observing how many other kinds of vocabulary could describe these polarities without distorting them. The novel offers, for example, a fine analysis of the more traditionally perceived opposition between isolation and community. At the book's opening the narrator Lockwood styles himself a lover of seclusion who has come north to this "perfect misanthropist's heaven" in order to escape "the stir of society," and whose interest in Heathcliff is initially aroused by what he considers a "sympathetic chord" touched by this "man who seemed more exaggeratedly reserved than myself."

In Lockwood this love of seclusion is of course mere posturing—and is very short-lived. His first intrusion into Heathcliff's company at Wuthering Heights ends with the words that conclude chapter 1: "It is astonishing how sociable I feel myself compared with him," a judgment he himself proves by repeating his visit the following day. He arrives to find the gate barred. "Wretched inmates!" he grumbles, "you deserve perpetual isolation from your species for your churlish inhospitality." So unpleasant is the reception that "I resolved to be cautious how I ventured under those rafters a third time" (p. 17). Nonetheless a third visit does occur—about six weeks later, by the calendar; but it occurs in the thirty-first of the novel's thirty-four chapters, after we have heard the entire history that brings us up to the narrative present. The purpose of this third visit, a chastened Lockwood tells us, is "to inform my landlord that I shall spend the next six months in London; and, if he likes, he may look out for another tenant to take the place (p. 361). "I'm of the busy world," he now knows, "and to its arms I must return" (p. 312). He is the very embodiment of father-wordly busy-ness.

His fourth and final visit to Wuthering Heights takes place the following year, after Heathcliff's death and Hareton's "cultivation" by the second Catherine. Having "invaded the neighborhood" unexpectedly on his way to visit a friend who has invited Lockwood to "devastate the moors" with him ("invade" and "devastate" are significant father-world verbs), he has decided impulsively to stay the night at the Grange before his lease runs out, and he walks again—seemingly an incurable visitor—to Wuthering Heights. To his surprise the intervening months have

brought major changes. Always before he had found "the jealous gate
. . . fastened" (p. 362), but now "I had neither to climb the gate nor to
knock—it yielded to my hand"; "both doors and lattices were open"
and from the garden comes "a fragrance of stocks and wall flowers."
With Heathcliff now dead, Wuthering Heights has been transformed,
and its inhabitants are no longer "wretched inmates" deserving "perpetual isolation." Instead the young people are to be married, after which
they will move to the more socially propitious Thrushcross Grange—
the novel's countering example of a genial and well-regulated home,
now the very microcosm of community, whose best values it will foster.
The values of "isolation," so threatening to survival and society, have
been encountered and overcome. At least for now.

Whatever the set of terms we choose to explicate its meaning, clearly
the novel works much the way visionary (Blake would say "prophetic")
poetry works. That is, it derives much of its power from the way it
renders figurative or metaphoric or mythic dimensions of human experience, working inward toward meanings that are psychological and
spiritual and at the same time outward toward ones that are public or
political.[17]

In the first Catherine we see a young woman self-divided between an
isolating fidelity to her relationship with the Heathcliff who is "always,
always in my mind . . . as my own being" (p. 102) and a sociable leaning
toward the Lintons, who represent to us, the audience, the values of
community, but to her little more than an opportunity to exercise ambition. Whatever force it is that Heathcliff represents, whether we mean
the Heathcliff Catherine said was "in my soul" or the external one she
could not "lay or control," that force is profoundly disruptive of family
and community life. It is for the second Catherine, accordingly, the
mordant power against which she must define herself and achieve her
meaning.

In the second half of the novel Heathcliff and the second Catherine are
released into independent life as the paired and opposed embodiments of
the first Catherine's bifurcated being. Literally born out of her mother's
death, Cathy personifies her mother's leaning toward the Lintons as it is
uncontaminated or uncompromised by those wild or savage qualities
that characterized the other half of her mother. The second Catherine is
less selfish than her mother, more capable of social feeling. Hers is
"ambition" civilized—the socially healthy will to personal success, domestic happiness, family connections. By the same token Heathcliff must
be not only her opposite but her enemy. The "abyss" at which the first
Catherine had groveled in her paroxysm of despair is inherited by him:

"take any form—drive me mad! only *do* not leave me in this abyss, where I cannot find you!" (p. 204). That "abyss" is in a way solipsism turned inside out, the condition of having no "being" at all, the experience of alienation through which the universe is turned to "a mighty Stranger" and one feels oneself no longer "a part of it." In the face of this universe-as-stranger, Heathcliff's balked yearning for his Catherine is transformed into a ruthless and demonic will to dominate and possess, an all-devouring rage that has been building since childhood, as Catherine pulled more and more away, and that after her death consumes his every energy. He never spares young Catherine because she is Catherine's daughter, for the very good reason—in thematic as well as psychological terms—that she is the product of Catherine's defection to the Linton world of domestic desires and conformity, literally the offspring of Catherine's social ambition.

After the first Catherine's death, then, her inner division lives on as two separate and conflicting characters; and in the rest of the novel each works out the logic of its own meaning. Young Catherine knits herself everywhere into human relationships, even with her pitiful cousin Linton, and as the novel ends is preparing to marry her other cousin, Hareton, and live happily ever after. By contrast the dehumanized Heathcliff is incapable of forming human ties. Heathcliff's very acquisitiveness is founded on alienation, as he furiously dominates, humiliates, punishes, and strives to ruin the world that had denied him Catherine. And then, as he senses her returning to fetch him, he relinquishes it all in favor of death. Perhaps, in the story of Heathcliff's survival after Catherine's death, we may hear Emily saying that her own essence had departed the world already, and that only her "disbranched" masculine energy remained to write this novel for publication—a hurt and angry muse indeed. "He" wrote this book with a furious intensity, as we know from the speed with which the book was finished, but also from the harshness of its style and story, which critics have complained of from Charlotte on down. But the real yearning of Emily's male muse was by now not for worldly glory (the bestseller list) but heavenly glory: to rejoin "life" and "soul" in the realm beyond death.

The Artist's Legacy

Emily repeatedly demonstrated the bankruptcy of any energy not directed toward its proper object: what profit to gain all the world if one loses one's own soul? Worldly power and possession were necessarily poor substitutes for Heathcliff's real object of desire, false food to his immortal hunger. But she clearly understood that if society is to survive, not everyone can recover antenatal wholeness. One might say that the special costs of that recovery are what the artist pays for all of us: she must leave the world behind, but leaves it richer for having passed through it. In one of Emily's most suggestive symbolic moments, we see that the bright-eyed visionary ("Oh thy bright eyes . . .") leaves brightened eyes behind her:

> [The young lovers Catherine and Hareton] lifted their eyes together, to encounter Mr. Heathcliff—perhaps you have never remarked that their eyes are precisely similar, and they are those of Catherine Earnshaw. The present Catherine has no other likeness to her. . . . With Hareton the resemblance is carried further: it is singular, at all times— then, it was particularly striking: because his senses were alert, and his mental faculties wakened to unwonted activity. (p. 392)

The living artist's turbulent presence is disruptive if not destructive to the dearest values of community; and for the artist herself, society's values can serve only to corrupt her from her purpose. But her passage through the community, though painful for everyone at the time, brings vitality, heightens life—even as she leaves life behind her.

It is instructive to contrast Emily's view of the artist as isolated, alienated, and asocial to Blake's view. He wished (with Moses and Milton) "that all the Lord's people were prophets," a species of spiritual populism that led him to transmute the Christian idea of Jesus' sacrifice, in which one man (who is also God) dies for the sins of all, into an idea in which all persons are God and "every kindness to another is a little Death / In the Divine Image."[18] Blake's point—rooted in the Christian doctrine of redemptive sacrifice, though he reinterprets its meaning—is that such acts of love open the path to eternity as no literal death could ever do (e.g., the crucifixion).

I see no evidence that Emily considered herself a Christian, even though she hinted obliquely that the Romantic artist's role is in certain respects like Christ's, in being sacrificial and redemptive. Rather, like Shelley and indeed like many others of her century, she adapted Christian modes of thought to her own independent purposes, finding in those modes analogues by which she might render intelligible the patterns of her own spiritual experience. There are hints in Emily's work that for her, as for Blake, human women are "female" and human men "male" only in their respective separateness from what is beyond gender: Being and Breath as One. At the same time, of course, it follows that insofar as

Emily was a woman born out of woman, her condition, in her longed-for reunion with her origins, would be at least metaphorically female. (It was metaphorically male, for Blake.) This difference may account for a further difference between the two writers. For Blake the self-forgetfulness of sexual consummation and unselfish love are temporal types of eternal reintegration; they are a first step on the journey toward what Blake variously called Liberty or Eternity. Emily, on the other hand, seems to have considered that sexual consummation (as a literal act) and even "unselfish" love of a more general kind were functions of "the World's tide," of the "common paths that others run," because they draw the artist from her inward-turned purpose: in other words human love will draw a woman artist away from origins, not back toward them. Only love of the muse, of her own energies projected as a male messenger from the mother-world, could take her toward her heaven.

These various differences between Blake and Emily are interrelated, and in part at least they are functions of the difference in gender. For the female writer, Heathcliff the muse has no real independent being; even as the human-formed embodiment of earth he is a function of the artist's perception. He leaves the novel as he entered it, an alienated element. He imparts no heritage of brightened eyes: that heritage is from Catherine, in her fleshly marriage to Edgar. Catherine herself need only recover her own female wholeness in returning to the "womb" (her bed and tomb) from where she pulls in Heathcliff and her child-ghost after her. By contrast a male artist like Blake or Wordsworth or Shelley must move outward and act on, or through, the female Other if he is to complete his journey to wholeness. His muse is a necessary instrument to the achievement of his goal, that Being upon which he must conceive his own immortality.

Still, Emily and her male Romantic forebears were certainly in agreement about one important spiritual truth: namely, that "acquisition" in the sense of material aggrandizement does not enlarge one's being. This truth Emily demonstrates not once, but repeatedly: first in the story of Catherine, who gains dominion over Thrushcross Grange and the position of first lady in the neighborhood at the price of groveling at the brink of nonbeing; then again in the story of Heathcliff, who first thinks to reclaim the stranger-universe through literal ownership (gaining title to all the Linton and Earnshaw properties), then finds restitution instead in "*my* heaven," whose deity is the dead Catherine—"senseless dust and ashes" in Nelly's limited perception—who stands, in turn, in some deep but unexplored relation to Heathcliff's "own black father" (p. 212), that is, to his own shadowy and ever-mysterious origins.

Indeed, for Heathcliff, to recover Catherine is to recover the entire universe (to make it not a "Stranger"). This is of course not the temporal universe of finance and real estate, but the eternal one where (quoting Blake) we become what we behold. As Heathcliff is preparing to die, he sees Catherine everywhere: "I cannot look down to this floor, but her features are shaped on the flags! In every cloud, in every tree—filling the air at night, and caught by glimpses in every object by day, I am surrounded with her image!" (p. 394). We should compare his words to Shelley's similar description in "Epipsychidion" of a world permeated by the presence of the being he loves:

> In solitudes
> Her voice came to me through the whispering woods,
> And from the fountains, and the odours deep
> Of flowers . . .
> And from the breezes whether low or loud,
> And from the rain of every passing cloud,
> And from the singing of the summer birds,
> And from all sounds, all silence.
>
> (ll. 200–209)

The ultimate "becoming" that will conclude such moments of "beholding" may look like death and dissolution to those who remain behind; but to Heathcliff it promises an eternal return. Emily makes the point implicitly in "Aye, there it is" and explicitly in "No coward soul," which is addressed not to the muse or messenger, but to the wholeness of being that is Divinity. The ideas that animate these poems lie also at the novel's narrative center and inform its visionary meaning. For Emily immortality is not a condition "beyond" in the sense that she must go outside her own being to achieve it. Rather it resides within her, as her own "inward essence." The "God within my breast" is her center—just as Catherine's plunge toward it is the novel's pivotal center. Both "centers" are ultimately inaccessible to language because it is precisely their loss that language records. Such union, or reunion, would obliterate language by annihilating our conventional distinctions between self and other, subject and object. Our intimations of that lost state give us the "oceanic feeling": what Wordsworth called the knowledge of "God-like hours." It is what Emily called "Love" (and opposed to "Fate," whose constraints are limited to the temporal world) in her paired poems #186 and #187. In this view of love she is akin to Shelley, who wrote of his epipsyche:

We shall become the same, we shall be one. . . .
One hope within two wills, one will beneath
Two overshadowing minds, one life, one death
One Heaven, one Hell, one immortality . . .
     ("Epipsychidion," ll. 573–86)

Here the "Spouse! Sister! Angel!" Shelley addresses is at once the literal Emilia Viviani, a pretty Italian girl, and the object onto which he has projected all his desire for the transcendent, all his spiritual yearning toward a divinity beyond the veil that men "call reality." In the terms of his essay "On Love," she represents "the ideal prototype of everything excellent or lovely that we are capable of conceiving as belonging to the nature of man." Yet as the ultimate object of love, she is no object at all, but the subject himself—his own being: "I *am* Emilia," he might have told Nelly.

Back to Biography

"Twenty years! I've been a waif for twenty years!" Within the fiction these words point us to the center of Catherine's defection; where would they take us if we followed them instead into Emily's own life? Uttered in the fictional month of November 1801, the words were actually written during or shortly after the month of November in 1845. Charlotte's intrusion into Emily's private world of poetry had already brought to crisis Emily's division of loyalties—between the world without and the world within, between her ambition and her fidelity to her God of Visions, between her attachment to family and through them to publication, recognition, the human community at large, and her ever-growing commitment to her own "messenger of Hope," her own "glad comforter." In permitting Charlotte to persuade her to join her sisters in the publication of their poems, Emily had in effect fallen into marriage with Edgar. Indeed there is more than one Charlotte-like element in Edgar's character: the predatory quality of his submissiveness, his ability to dominate through his very decency and reasonableness. Recall the way he responded to Nelly's warning about Catherine's waywardness: "The soft thing looked askance through the window—he possessed the power to depart, as much as a cat possesses the power to leave a mouse half killed, or a bird half eaten" (p. 89). In Brussels M. Heger had observed a relationship between Charlotte and Emily that he characterized to Mrs.

Gaskell years later: Emily "was egotistical and exacting compared to Charlotte, who was always unselfish; and in the anxiety of the elder [Charlotte] to make her younger sister contented, she allowed her to exercise a kind of unconscious tyranny over her."[19] Such tyrannies work both ways, Emily's depiction of Edgar suggests.

Catherine had been in November 1801 "a waif for twenty years"; if Emily—seated writing those words in 1845, and quite likely also in November—thought the same of herself, she would have had good reasons. A look at some of those reasons may help us guess at the origins in her psyche of the novel's argument. "Twenty years" would take us back to 1825 when her sisters had just died and the toy soldiers just arrived, when she herself was the age that Catherine and Heathcliff were at the novel's opening. It was on the calendars of those crucial childhood years (1826–1827) that Emily drew all her life for her Gondal fiction; those calendars again supplied, in transposed but still identifiable form, the basis for the careful chronology of *Wuthering Heights*.

The bond between death and art began in substitution: as Maria and Elizabeth had substituted for the dead mother, so the comforting Glasstown fantasies substituted for the sisters, whose successive deaths confirmed the primary loss by twice repeating it. Thus we can understand how Emily's own self-division into the child who loses (Emily was six when her sisters died) and the muse who replaces (she was seven when the toy soldiers arrived) would be repeatedly projected into her creative work, and would always arouse questions about her fidelity to the dead. It is of course in the nature of substitutes to be inadequate, and so evidently Emily perceived her young muse to be. (The first Catherine writes diaries only after Heathcliff has been driven from her. Like her author, it is *loss* that her writing records.) Whatever comfort Emily could derive from fantasy, clearly she would rather have kept her sisters and especially her mother. Among the French exercises Emily wrote in Brussels there survives one that is most striking in this connection. The general theme—a girl's letter home to her mother—may have been set by M. Heger, but the specific content of the letter would have been Emily's choice. What she imagines is a girl kept "solitary" by illness, excluded from the life around her. She longs to be home again, or to have her mother come to her: "I believe that your presence alone would cure me."[20] The plaintive tone, bordering on self-pity, is uncharacteristic of Emily; but the dramatic situation—illness in isolation and cure by reunion—is familiar indeed. The first is echoed in Catherine's "frightful isolation" among the Lintons (p. 187), the second in the reintegration that Catherine and Heathcliff seek beyond death. And of course it is the scenario of Emily's own approaching death.

Her creative "gift," however welcome in itself, could not fail to be a poor substitute for Emily's lost first happiness; but apparently it brought a further burden in being experienced by her as a dark and sullen power, which doubtless helps to account for her conceiving it as a masculine force in the first place, a male element or lost "brother," now "cut away" and drifting. From among the toy soldiers brought home by their father from Leeds, Emily had chosen a "grave-looking fellow" and identified herself with him. The event is strikingly paralleled in her novel by Mr. Earnshaw's return from Liverpool with little Heathcliff, "a gift of God, though it's dark almost as if it came from the devil." And outer appearance reflects inner nature: "from childhood he had a delight in dwelling on dark things, and entertaining odd fancies" (p. 394). So Emily also found her imagination, to judge from the violent and often brutal world of her writing.

Yet Emily seemed to have recognized equally that her own "gift" had a range of artistic dimensions—it expressed itself not only in writing, but also in drawing and music, at which she also excelled. A poem she wrote (#109) about the origins of musical talent takes us back to this same childhood period. A narrating voice asks the question: "Come hither, child—who gifted thee / With power to touch the string so well?" The child responds that when she was "six years old" and "had no one to love me," she was praying that she might die, when "Suddenly . . . / A sound of music reached my ear." It was "full of soul," and made her think at first that she was indeed dead already, that "Gabriel's self had come / To take me to my father's home." But not so. Instead it was a comforting visitation—an early visit of the muse—and the moment has left her with special power: "still the words and still the tone / Swell round my heart when all alone." The whole account offers a thinly veiled allegory of Emily's own recollected childhood despair at feeling that she had "no one to love me," and of her emotional recovery through her art. But the recovery was temporary. Alongside this poem, on the manuscript sheet, Emily added at some later time the further truth: "Alas that she would bid adieu / To all the hopes her childhood knew. / Hushed is the harp." If we ask what hushed the harp, we are asking what separated Catherine and Heathcliff, eventually what "murdered" the first Heathcliff; and we know from the novel that in Emily's judgment Catherine somehow did it herself, by betraying her "own heart" and even doing so of her "own will."

We traced in the preceding chapter Emily's growing repudiation of "the world," but saw her end in a willingness to wait: she was ready to die, but not impatient. This mood apparently changed when Charlotte stumbled onto her most private resource, her poetry, and dragged it out into "the hostile light / That does not warm, but burn" (#184). Already-divided Emily then watched herself actually participate in her own further self-alienation. At this crucial point, in the autumn of 1845, Emily did *not* muster every energy to eradicate the traces of intrusion and repel further advances. Instead she did two things. First, she cooperated, after a period of intense anger, in the sisters' publishing venture. This is to say that—in the terms of her fiction—she married Edgar Linton. And second, with one tremendous exception, she stopped writing poetry. The exception is of course "No coward soul is mine," which enunciates her final and most compelling commitment to the "Undying Life" toward which Catherine and Heathcliff yearn in yearning for each other. Then —as if summoning together everything she now knew about the relationship between herself and her muse on the one hand, and about the world and its values on the other—she wrote at tumultuous speed her novel for publication, giving that knowledge local habitation and a set of names, embedding it in the discordant and incongruous world of time and space. It was Emily's parting gift to her family and to the world she was preparing to leave, her last employment of the energies of ambition.

What Good Are Books?

Certainly it seems most ironic that one should declare one's dedication to solipsism and silence, one's repudiation of audience and community, of "doing" in all its worldly forms, by writing a book. The place of publication—of books—in Emily's final scheme of things (i.e., by 1845–1846) is clear from *Wuthering Heights;* and it is not a flattering one, from the perspective of the visionary.

Within the fiction, the book lovers are those who have least access to the sacred mother-world. Heathcliff himself "never reads," and destroys young Cathy's books when she is in his power. The first Catherine "hates a good book" and puts hers to service for her own writing—not a "legitimate purpose," in Lockwood's estimation (p. 24). The readers in *Wuthering Heights* are the Lintons, Nelly, and Lockwood, all partakers in their various ways of the values of patriarchal social community, fictional representatives of the audience toward whom the novel is directed.

Edgar Linton's library is his main place of resort, and it figures, in a way, his very hold on life. There he stays during Catherine's delirium: "Among his books!" she cries incredulously, when Nelly suggests (misleadingly) that his mind is on his reading rather than on his wife. But the library really is a comfort for Edgar. On the anniversaries of Catherine's death, he "invariably spent that day alone in the library" (p. 260), and it is to the library that he goes each day during "the brief period he could bear to sit up" (p. 322) as his own death approaches years later.

Edgar's sister Isabella reads for comfort in her hard days as Heathcliff's wife, and young Cathy inherits the Linton attachment to books. She and young Linton Heathcliff conduct their love intrigue by means of them, and later when she is in Heathcliff's power she, like Isabella, reads for comfort until Heathcliff takes her books away and destroys them. Most strikingly, the great wound in the social body created by the passion of Catherine and Heathcliff is healed through books, as young Cathy "civilizes" Hareton by teaching him to read.

When they first meet, Hareton cannot even spell out his ancestral name over the door. But Cathy's presence sparks his ambition; and though her contempt first causes him to renounce any interest in reading, with the later growth of her affection it rekindles and serves finally as the setting for their budding love. Nelly tells how the young lovers first reached an understanding bent over a book with "radiant countenances," and this is the posture in which Lockwood discovers them when he returns in 1802. Although, as Nelly says, "Earnshaw was not to be civilized with a wish," still with one of the young people "loving and desiring to esteem, and the other loving and desiring to be esteemed" (p. 384), civilization is around the corner.

Nelly, too, is a reader, as she tells Lockwood early on: "I have read more books than you would fancy. . . . You could not open a book in this library that I have not looked into, and got something out of also" (p. 78). When, after Zillah's departure, and shortly before his death, Heathcliff recalls Nelly to Wuthering Heights to serve as housekeeper, she "smuggled over a great number of books" for young Catherine (p. 375); in fact it is through one of these that Catherine makes her approach to Hareton and gains his heart.

And Lockwood indicates both his ties to the world of books and his own inner poverty in one economical outburst of sympathetic concern. Hearing from young Cathy that she has "no materials for writing, not even a book from which I might tear a leaf," he sputters "No books! . . . How do you contrive to live here without them? If I may take the liberty to inquire—Though provided with a large library, I'm frequently very dull at the Grange—take my books away, and I should be desperate!" (p. 364).

Books are directly associated with cultivation—in its figurative sense, as we have already seen, but also literally. Heathcliff is in Catherine's honest words "an unreclaimed creature, without refinement, without cultivation; an arid wilderness of furze and whinstone" (p. 126). Wuthering Heights, under his and Hindley's joint influence, becomes also an arid "wilderness" (p. 183). The young Hareton—heir to the past and link with the future—internalizes both that condition of wilderness and its potential for fertility and cultivation. Nelly comments, "I thought I could detect . . . lost amid a wilderness of weeds, to be sure, . . . evidence of a wealthy soil that might yield luxuriant crops under other and favorable circumstances" (p. 124). It is thus appropriate to both theme and imagery that Cathy's first act, after bringing him round with a book, should be to engage Hareton in helping her plant a garden. As she cultivates his soil so he cultivates hers. As the novel ends, the sexual and procreative applications of these values are soon to be fulfilled by their marriage. By contrast Heathcliff and the first Catherine are both procreators in the bare borderline sense: her pregnancy seems technical at best, and the product of Heathcliff's loins is a poor "puling chicken." Their generativity points inward, not outward.[21]

As an alien force that passes through the community and disturbs its calm, but that is eventually purged through the force of its own violent motion, Heathcliff embodies his creator's hostile and disruptive artistic power. No reader of books, he is metaphorically the energy that writes them. It apparently seemed to Emily that in a woman, at least, creative energy would necessarily prove inimical to social and family life. Although, in departing, it would leave these cultural values renewed, Emily seems to have considered the energy itself, the muse of her novel, as having something diabolical about it—"dark almost as if it came from the devil," in Mr. Earnshaw's prophetic words. Her sister Charlotte agreed, as we have seen.

Fully recognizing that the god of one religion is the demon of another, Emily was in the end wholly uninterested in any religion but her own. As she says in "No coward soul is mine," addressing the God within her breast:

> Vain are the thousand creeds
> That move men's hearts, unutterably vain,

> Worthless as withered weeds
> Or idlest froth amid the boundless main
>
> To waken doubt in one
> Holding so fast by thy infinity . . .

This was the point she had reached by the time she was writing her novel. Yet she did choose after all to give her vision a shape, to release her dark muse and write the book he so compellingly dominates.

Some Conclusions

We have seen from the novel that in Emily's judgment she had sinned against the Holy Ghost; she had betrayed her God of Visions and fallen prey to the seductions of ambition and "the world." Betrayal may have consisted in acceding to a desire for family approval; in nourishing some hope of recognition for her talents; or perhaps simply in desiring to live and write. As we saw from the poems, even her love of nature she came to see as misguided; even visionary poetry—the putting into words of "the Invisible, the Unseen"—would become under unscreened public scrutiny not only a falsification, but a violation of the sacred. The natural desire for family approval and love, for recognition of one's achievements, for sharing one's thoughts and hopes—this desire Emily did not judge as bad in itself, as her sympathetic story of the second Catherine makes clear. But she judged such desire to be dangerous for herself, wrong for her visionary "essence." Her own course must lie in gathering back the elements of her fragmented self; her direction must be taken not toward "doing" in the world of earth and audience, but toward "being," the world within. She must take visionary flight from the prison of mortality and seek recovery of antenatal solidarity with the beloved dead.

Freud observed that "sleep is a reactivation of intrauterine existence."[22] No wonder, then, that in Emily's vision bed and coffin coalesce, and that beyond their sliding panels lies the communal world of dreams. Again it is Shelley who asks directly: "Does the dark gate of death / Conduct to thy mysterious paradise, / O Sleep?"[23] And his answer was throughout his brief life increasingly affirmative, until at the climax of "Adonais," in words that eerily echo those of the marriage service, he cries "No more let Life divide what Death can join together."

One could say that for Emily *Wuthering Heights* is a monumental suicide note, embracing both a generous recognition of the values of the world she is leaving behind, and the most accessible account she could possibly offer of her reasons for leaving it. The book is an apology in the sense that it offers the argument that both her life and her death were worthy and right. In the fiction, the united houses of Linton and Earnshaw will be the stronger for having Catherine's vivid essence, now happily domesticated, surging through the veins of coming generations. But by the same token, the world will be better off, far better off, with Catherine herself gone from it. Self-divided, Catherine was at best an unwholesome presence. Even the "wondrously peaceful" life that she lived with Edgar before Heathcliff's return, though clearly approved by Nelly, was ominous: she had "seasons of gloom and silence" to which her husband responded with an anxious concern that betrayed an underlying awareness of her destructive potential. Her will was to be flouted in no particular, however minute. "There were no mutual concessions," Nelly observed; "and, for the space of half a year, the gunpowder lay as harmless as sand, because no fire came near to explode it" (p. 114).[24] But we must conclude from the result that this "peaceful" life could not have continued long. Catherine was already "haunted." It could be only a question of time until the repressed returned, until the ghost reappeared and disturbed the living, until the fire in Heathcliff's "soul" returned to ignite the powder in Catherine's.

Although, ultimately, Emily's reasons for leaving the world must remain inaccessible to any audience, they stand at the novel's hidden center, in the passion of Catherine and Heathcliff (and, in its obverse, in the silent moment when Catherine crossed the line into final defection). That silent and unknowable center is the truth to which "poetry" alone, in the Romantic sense of the word, might be thought to be capable of giving us access. Yet Emily devised another method—the counterpart of that irony by which she dedicated herself to silence and solipsism by writing a book. This method was to transmit her truth through the serial mediations of Nelly, who never pretends to understand it, and through Lockwood, who reconstructs for our benefit Nelly's account to him. Certainly we know him to be a man who misjudges virtually every circumstance he encounters ("Unhappy in your conjectures, sir!" observed my host"), and renders his few personal experiences into a mindless cant by which Emily parodies what she evidently regarded as the city sensibility—e.g., "I see now; you are the favoured possessor of the beneficent fairy" (p. 16). Lockwood's dream nonetheless indicates that he is implicated in that center of inexpressible experience far more deeply than he may suppose; and so, inevitably, are we all. The novel clearly proposes that we are all implicated in the artist's experience: hence the communality of the interpsychic depths of persons as spiritually distant from one another as Lockwood and the first Catherine. The deep, unspeakable, central truth of the novel, Emily implies, lies hidden in the heart of each of us, however eagerly we may ignore or deny it.

The insights of post-Freudian psychology have taught us to recognize that the awakening of consciousness in the child coincides with the child's taking on of a system of language that distances it from its own lived experience and assimilates it to the impersonal organization which is society. In this sense, the mere conceiving of an "I" is already a splitting off from the oceanic "One." In Jacques Lacan's well-known example, the infant who recognizes its own reflection in a mirror has already assented to all its future limitation. At that moment the infant is no longer everything, but rather *that* thing. It is "it." Or, to translate back into Emily's terms, some inner element, some little brother within, has died off into separate life; some part "more myself than I am" has been murdered, to reappear as a "he"—"*Heathcliff*"—whose fate it is to be driven further and further away from its divided source as that "source" grows up into the world and engages in the civil warfare depicted in "Enough of Thought, Philosopher."

Emily's poetry suggests that she would gladly have died, had she been sure death meant return to the true parents, the first home. But because she feared above all else that death—first faced in her mother's death— might mean mere annihilation, mere return to "mother Earth" in the brute physical sense, she undertook to invert the ordinary meanings of life and death, to elaborate what is essentially her private version of the Christian paradox that we die into eternal life. I have already suggested that Emily was in this effort indebted to Shelley, who also wished to purge the gold of confidence in immortality from any dross of church dogma, and to the Wordsworth of the Intimations Ode.

Blake's Eternity; Wordsworth's heaven that is our home; Coleridge's infinite I AM; Shelley's One Mind and antenatal dream; the Logos; the Oceanic; the undifferentiated unconscious: whatever we call this longed-for condition, clearly it was for Emily that presence whose absence or distortion is expressed in *Wuthering Heights* not as a fictional character, but rather through all the myriad splittings, mirrorings, divisions, and doublings that characterize both her fictional world (in the story) and her narrative structure—a structure of doublings and oppositions predicted in her great lament "Cold in the earth." The artist's alienation from society is a type of the muse's alienation from the artist, of lover from beloved, of living from dead, of the expressed from the imagined, of the

closed shape of a fiction or a fantasy from the great pool of the unconscious. This "pool" is in mythic terms the One into which Narcissus
plunges: being inexpressible ("the deep truth is imageless"), it is both
no-thing and all-things, the "O" that is zero but also total being, the
circle of reunion. So Emily saw the matter.[25]

Equally clearly she saw that though the artist may choose reintegration
with the sources of her art, the society from which she is thus alienated
has its own agenda which depends on the bonds of self with other (rather
than of self with self) — that widens the nets of kinship through love and
procreation, through culture and cultivation: the waking world of books,
gardens, libraries. To them the intrusion of the artist's disturbing force
will seem otherworldly and often unwelcome, uncanny or dreamlike
because its sources are the sources of dream. Momentarily imagining that
he is a seeker of isolation, Lockwood meets the ghost of the first Catherine's losses deep in a nightmare within nightmare; and having (during
the long convalescence that follows on this experience) heard Nelly
narrate her story, he gratefully returns to the arms of the busy world,
remembering his entire "residence in that locality" only as something
"dim and dreamy" (p. 369). As often observed, Lockwood is the reading
audience's representative in the text. Like him we "would lock" the
waiflike phantom of Catherine out of our dreams if we could, because
although we are willing to flirt with what Shelley calls the spirit of
solitude, we too are of the busy world, and wish — once we have completed this novel — to return to its arms. Accordingly the author who
conducted us in, through Lockwood, through Nelly, through Catherine's report of her derangement, even to the edge of the mysterious
center (the O), kindly conducts us back out. Our return takes us through
the increasingly familiar and reassuring characters and values of the
second half of the novel: through Catherine's daughter (born of her
body, but shaped and parented by Edgar and Nelly, and toyed with in
brief fantasy even by Lockwood), through the coming marriage that will
fulfill Nelly's desire ("The crown of all my wishes will be the union of
these two"), even to Lockwood's parting assurance that the earth has
closed forever over those "sleepers." We of the waking world are again
safe, and may replace the book on our shelves.

But a little reading is a dangerous thing, as Emily has already hinted,
through Lockwood's experience with Catherine's diaries. As young
Catherine and Hareton have inherited Catherine's eyes, we too must see,
through our encounter with Emily's art, certain visionary gleams —
provided we are capable of encountering her art at all. Emily's deprecation of Lockwood suggests that she was not optimistic about the audi-

ence her work might expect: his crude sensibility and foppish complacency show him to be locked pretty solidly in the prison of "common
day." Yet even he saw the wailing ghost.

In asking what brought Emily to choose the course she did—to prefer
death to life, silence to speech and art—we can really only speculate
from the evidence of her art. The tracks she left are few; there is much
we can never know. But although Emily's art reveals no historical
details, it is richly suggestive concerning her emotional or spiritual history, the biography of her imagination. In the peculiarly parentless world
of her novel, most of the mothering is done by Nelly Dean—the human-
ized embodiment of Wordsworth's "homely Nurse," the earth that does
all she can to make mankind "Forget the glories he hath known." And
sin-denouncing, patriarchal religion–spouting Joseph is the thoroughly
unattractive if somewhat comic father. We have already seen that deep
within us, or within what Emily regarded as the communal world of
dream, loom spectral presences that represent the forces of "society" and
"language." The spectral presences of Joseph as Jabes Branderham, whom
Lockwood in his first dream counterdenounces as "the sinner of the sin
no Christian need pardon," and of Nelly as Catherine's witchlike "enemy," in effect jointly guard their respective entryways to the interpsychic hallucinatory depths. And their presence there suggests that a
crucial relationship obtains between these terrible parent figures and
Catherine's waiflike wanderings. As already noted, the sin no Christian
need pardon is blasphemy against the Holy Ghost, the "Comforter"
whom Emily identified with her visionary power; and Jabes and the
"witch" are clearly the enemies of that. They are somehow responsible
for the murder of the dead brother, whom Heathcliff replaces. That dead
brother is in a sense the original Holy Ghost: Holy in his association with
the imagination, the God within; Ghost in his association with Emily's
memory or vision of happiness in the bosom of her long-dead mother.
In short, these parents are responsible for that primal separation in Catherine which Heathcliff himself attributes to her "own will." To shift (and
conflate) vocabularies, they are visionary embodiments of the social and
linguistic order into which Emily was born in accepting her identity as
"Emily." They represent the forces that effected that primal split between the unconscious "self" of immediate lived experience and the ego
which enters the systems of society through participation in language,
and, in entering those systems, gives up primary narcissism and learns
the facts of death. So much of Emily's experience in that social order was
fraught with pain that the "keepers" of it are foci of enormous rage: first
Catherine's rage that she can't both live in the world and retain Heath-

cliff, then Heathcliff's rage at the world that denied him Catherine. And rage breeds violence and cruelty, as Emily demonstrates with sublime self-knowledge.

Those spectral presences, then, are the spectral false parents—the murderous betrayers with whom Emily associated the irrecoverable "death" that is birth into separation, against whom Catherine avenged herself in killing off Edgar's parents. It was Emily's fear of mortality, the sense that as so many have died, she will surely die too, that made her turn from her foster mother Earth ("every phase of earthly joy / Will always fade and always cloy"; #188) and hold fast to the "infinity" of the God within her breast, since "what thou art may never be destroyed." This "infinity," as I have already suggested, would be the home of the "true" parents: both the father ("I thought that Gabriel's self had come / To take me to my father's home"); and the mother ("I believe that your presence alone would cure me"). But the mother most of all—as being precedes doing.

If Emily Brontë, writing *Wuthering Heights,* felt that she herself had been a waif for "twenty years," the implication would be that she made her definitive turn down the wrong road early in childhood—in the inauguration of that fantasy life that led at last to her becoming an artist, writing a novel for publication, telling the world the deep truth that is imageless and that yet may be pointed toward through a symmetrical narrative structure and a vortex of narrowingly concentric narrative rings. That novel completed, she need write no more, but could devote herself unreservedly to the commitment voiced in "No coward soul," and do what she felt she should have done at six—that is, die.

Although in September 1846 Emily did return to Gondal topics long enough to write one scathing and bitter poem, Charlotte reports that Emily mentioned her published poems rarely and only with scorn; she wrote no more at all until May 1846, when she stripped that one scathing poem down to its twenty-five-line essence as an invocation to apocalypse. The consolidation of evil is upon us, it suggests: time for the Second Coming.[26]

Charlotte—so much like Edgar in her virtuous and devoted assurance that she knew what was best for those she loved—had already invaded the sacred privacy of Emily's poems, fanned the flame of her ambition, called on all her tenderness toward her sisters to persuade her to venture into joint publication; in all these acts Emily cooperated, at least by giving her eventual consent. And her novel explained both the destructiveness of Charlotte's appeal to Emily for action and Emily's awareness of the human decency of her own willingness to respond—the importance of such response to the continuation of community. But the novel also made clear that Emily had reached her own final bound, and with one more push would pass it. That push seems to have been given, again by the unwitting Charlotte, in July of 1848, when, to her publishers in London, Charlotte thoughtlessly identified Emily as "Ellis Bell," the author of *Wuthering Heights*—a breach of confidence that Emily resented passionately and apparently never forgave. Instead she retreated behind an increasingly "harsh," "difficult" exterior, finally not even answering when spoken to. After Branwell's death in September this pattern of passive intransigence accelerated; refusing medical attention, Emily finally did cast her "anchor of Desire / Deep in unknown Eternity" and died in December, leaving the once more deeply bereaved Charlotte with only her sister's written words to linger over—to learn from them what she might.

THREE

Charlotte's Early Work

"He's moved the principle of life
   Through all I've written or sung or said . . ."

—#112, Charlotte Brontë[1]

It was as if the sisters had divided the parents between them. If Emily's imagination was bound up with the mother, Charlotte's was equally bound up with the father. Patrick Brontë stood at the center of Charlotte's life, and her yearning toward him was the source of lifelong problems for her, both as woman and as artist. For Charlotte as for Emily, the female infant is born out of the mother into the father-world; but unlike her sister, Charlotte desired that outer world. She seems to have had no wish to return to the womb or to follow her mother into death. Emily had figured her spirit's progress as a movement from female completeness into gender division and then (through death) back to female completeness; but for Charlotte, gender division was the root condition of all being. In her imagery the womb is a place of female isolation; it can offer temporary comfort and safety, as a cave in the sea, a dell in the forest. But if one were to remain there it would soon degenerate into a tomb. To experience anything at all—including rapture or beatitude—one must be born into the world; which meant, for Charlotte, that one must enter the father's stormy realm.

The world of Charlotte's imagination was altogether more physical and fleshly than Emily's, more hopefully engaged with the forces of time and society. Like her sister, Charlotte saw "Hope" as a female power, but for her this power took natural and personal forms. Charlotte's "Hope" had hair, shoulders, and bosom; she could raise an admonitory hand. And when she did, it was to encourage her daughter onward in life's journey. Like Emily, Charlotte often figured the world as a desert. But for Charlotte this was the desert of biblical story, a wilderness to be crossed in the company of the patriarchs on the way to the promised land. And for Charlotte the promised land, her spirit's true home, was not at all the heaven that lay about us in our infancy. Rather it was to be found in a man's embrace. Accordingly the food for which she hungered all her life she never figured as mother's milk, but as the nourishment of some paternal bounty, some version of father-food: in her own imagery it was manna from heaven, or (in her times of greatest deprivation) crumbs from the rich man's table.

The adolescent Charlotte's worship of her father was paralleled in her fiction by her heroines' worship of their hero; in her life as a young artist it was paralleled by her fervent submission to the power of fantasy. The muse who gave life to "all I've written or sung or said" was in those early years a despot who did not so much empower his author as dominate and submerge her. In fictional terms he was Zamorna, "the god" of "Our grand dream" (#112). Charlotte came to see that such worship was in all its forms neither virtuous nor healthy, tending as it did to both idolatry and a lethal self-submergence, and thus that her task as artist was closely entwined with her task as woman. She had to learn to imagine heroines who could critique their heroes and where appropriate resist the pull of passion, just as she had to learn to critique her own creative processes and resist the dizzying glamour of her dreamy "nether world" and its "god-like creatures." Gradually, and with great difficulty, she came to eschew the hot excesses of fantasy in favor of a cooler and more self-respecting treatment of that abiding topic in her work—herself in search of her father's love. This labor of liberation took many forms, and perhaps she never fully achieved her goal. But in her final novel, *Villette,* she did achieve a transformation for which she had been preparing all her life: a transformation both of her muse and of her own position as hungry woman. In the present chapter we will see how she laid the groundwork of that achievement, starting from the time of her early poems and stories (around 1830, when she was fourteen) and concluding with her discovery of Emily's notebooks in 1845.

The Central Dilemma

As a forceful, educated man and successfully published author, Patrick was the family model of intellectual vitality and creative achievement. As the father who survived the mother's death, he was also the one remaining source of approving parental love. Here lay Charlotte's life-long dilemma: she wanted on the one hand to be like Patrick a creative intellect, and on the other to be loved and accepted by him, gathered to his paternal bosom in all-enfolding tenderness. But as she understood her father's opinion on the subject, any woman who would succeed in winning paternal approval must be submissive and self-abnegating, as adoring and acquiescent as Charlotte seems to have imagined her mother had been. What hope could there be, then, for a young woman of spirit and ambition like herself? Moreover, the women Patrick had loved best, his wife and eldest daughter, both named Maria, had both died young — the first when Charlotte was five, the second when she was nine. Vulnerable women recur with obsessive regularity in Charlotte's early poetry and fiction under variations of the maternal name: Marian, Marina, Maria, Mary, Mina. All stand in the same relation to Charlotte's ubiquitous male hero. He is the charismatic king and lover, the embodiment of power and creative intelligence, the only source of love and even of life for these women who helplessly adore him. His godlike bosom is their home; torn from it they perish. Their one pleasure is in pleasing him by their beauty and their tactful but unceasing devotion; when they fail, their one consolation is that he will be sorry when they're dead.

Charlotte's first love story, written in 1830 when she was just turning fifteen, was entitled "Albion and Marina"[2] and set in the imaginary world that the four children had developed around their toy soldiers. We saw that Charlotte's special soldier had been named for Arthur Wellesley, first duke of Wellington, her father's hero and of course England's as well, but that increasingly it was the Iron Duke's two sons who moved to the center of Charlotte's stage. The elder son, Arthur, retained the glow of his father's heroism, as he was also his father's namesake; the younger Charles, whose name mirrored Charlotte's own, took on certain of her prickly personal characteristics. Arthur, as natural genius, was the poet. Charles, less elevated and vatic, was the prose writer. It is the more distant and elusive Arthur who becomes king of the fantasy land of Angria and object of the fanatical devotion of all those Marians and Marys and Minas.[3]

"Albion and Marina," purportedly written by Charles Wellesley in a fit of pique against his glamorous older brother, concerns a cast of characters familiar from other Angrian stories, although Charles has slightly disguised their names: Arthur himself is Albion, hero of Charlotte's father and fatherland; his fiancée Marian is here called Marina; and present also is the other female lead of Agnrian story, the bluestocking Zenobia, whose name, as the feminine of Zeus, suggests something of her daunting qualities.

But "Albion and Marina" is not quite an original story, for it takes its point of departure from one that Patrick Brontë had published twelve years before, when Charlotte was only a toddler. Patrick's story is entitled *Albion and Flora*,[4] and tells of a worthy young Englishman (Albion) who falls in love with and wins a blooming and virtuous young Irish woman (Flora). Patrick's loosely knit narrative allows for a good deal of improving commentary and instruction, including a patriotic digression on the duke of Wellington and his victory at Waterloo, which had occurred three years before the story was published. But the digression that should most give us pause—as it manifestly gave pause to Charlotte—concerns women of intellect. Talking with Flora's father and uncle, Albion observes:

> You have complimented the ladies on their beauty, sprightliness, and dexterity; don't you allow also that some of them excel in learning, and depth of intellect?

To this Flora's uncle replies that certainly there have been a few of this description; "but, in general, they were never the objects of my admiration, nor do I think that they could ever have inspired me with love." Albion pursues the question in terms that would have gratified a modern feminist, asking why so few of those "intellectual ladies" have ever been married: "Is it because they were too wise to have anything to do with our sex, or, that our sex being unwilling to be eclipsed, were afraid to have anything to do with them?" The uncle's answer, however, is considerably less gratifying, and Patrick allows him the last word.

> Why sir, . . . I allow, in the first place, that some of these intellectual ladies you allude to, have had eligible offers of marriage, and yet out of pure choice, remained single. But I do believe, that by far the greater part of them were incapable of inspiring the other sex with the *tender passion*. The chief reason, then, why in general they have remained single, is not because men feared them, but because they could not love them. The education of a female ought, most assuredly, to be competent, in order that she might enjoy herself, and be a fit companion for man. But, believe me, lovely, delicate, and sprightly woman, is not formed by nature, to pore over the musty pages of Grecian and Roman literature, or to plod through the windings of Mathematical Problems; nor has Providence assigned for her sphere of action, either the cabinet or the field. Her forte is softness, tenderness, and grace. And here she not only can solace, but conquer man. But when she endeavours to cope with him in strength of arm, or nerve of mind, she greatly mistakes her weapons, and is soon vanquished, or overlooked, and passed by.

So the topic ends in Patrick's story. But not in Charlotte's. Patrick had imagined a love story with two leading characters—Albion and Flora;

but in adapting her father's work Charlotte saw there must be a third as well, namely the intellectual woman who cannot be loved. She is the fiery bluestocking Zenobia, who enters Angrian fiction as the third point on that triangle whose other points are Arthur/Albion and Marian/Marina. Zenobia is modeled in meticulous detail on Patrick's "intellectual ladies": always learned in Grecian and Roman literature, always coping with man in nerve of mind and sometimes even in strength of arm. She is regal rather than delicate—and wholly incapable of inspiring "the *tender passion*."

Furthermore, Charlotte's "Albion and Marina" does not end in marriage. Instead, Albion, engaged to his beloved Marina, leaves her to travel with his father (a fictionalized duke of Wellington) to Glasstown, chief city of the Brontë children's first fantasy land. There Albion becomes "one of the greatest poets of the age." Much fêted by the best people, he meets "the most learned and noted woman in Glasstown," a woman as brilliant as "Mme. de Staël herself": it is of course Zenobia. In his admiration for her "majestic charms" Albion for a moment nearly forgets "the gentler ones" of his first love, who at that instant of his wavering appears to him in supernatural vision, repeating the words she had said on parting: "I shall be happy when you return." Albion—stricken with anxiety—notes the time of this vision and rushes at once back to England, where he finds Marina's house a deserted ruin and herself in the grave. She had died as her wraith had appeared before his eyes—the time midnight, June 18, 1815.

Charlotte chose a startlingly specific moment for Marina's death: it is the date of Wellington's victory at Waterloo, which Patrick had described with great dramatic flourish in his story. Albion's successes in poetry and in the parlor thus converge with his father's victory on the field (and Patrick's in publication) to suggest that in the economy of Albion's and Marina's relationship, his victory is her Waterloo.

For the purposes of analysis we should observe that in Charlotte's "Albion and Marina" there are really two stories. The first is Albion's, and it concerns the rivalry in his heart between a pair of strong and opposing values—the value of domestic happiness at home with gentle Marina, and the value of intellectual daring and achievement out in the larger world, characterized by the "majestic charms" of Zenobia. His dilemma is of course Charlotte's, and in this respect Albion figures Charlotte's own divided spirit. That is, she could emulate her father and lean toward Zenobia, or she could strive to please and be loved by him, and remain with Marina; but she could not do both. To be loved by Patrick she would have to cultivate "softness, tenderness, and grace." To pursue "nerve of mind," as Albion did in company with the intellectual Zenobia, kills the thing it loves and dooms all prospect of personal happiness.

On the other hand the second of those two stories, which is the women's, shows us that women suffer whether or not they inspire the tender passion. Marina, in whom Charlotte depicts her idea of Patrick's lovable woman, has been deserted by Albion in favor of intellectual pursuits in the larger world. Marina's lament is Charlotte's, longing for her father's attention:

> All my days were days of weeping;
>   Thoughts of grim despair were stirred;
> Time on leaden feet seemed creeping
>   Long heart-sickness, hope deferred
>   Cankered my heart.

Yet of course Zenobia, in whom Charlotte depicted her idea of Patrick's intellectual woman, inspires no love at all.

The neglected Marina can express her sense of outrage only by dying, a Pyhrric victory at best. But for many years it was the only victory Charlotte depicted for women who devote their lives to their hero, and she seems to have based her view on what she imagined to have been her mother's fate. Years later, in *Shirley,* we get a sense of Charlotte's most negative fantasies about her parents' marriage from the brief story of the rector Helstone's marriage to Caroline's aunt, Mary Cave:

> Nature never intended Mr. Helstone to make a very good husband. . . . He made no pretense of comprehending women, or comparing them with men; they were a different probably a very inferior order of existence; a wife could not be her husband's companion, much less his confidant, much less his stay. *His* wife, after a year or two, was of no great importance to him in any shape; and when she one day . . . took leave of him and of life, . . . he felt his bereavement—who shall say how little? Yet, perhaps, more than he seemed to feel it; for he was not a man from whom grief easily wrung tears.[5]

Charlotte's angry account of male aloofness tells little about her parents' actual marriage, but much about her own remembered girlhood rage at what she felt was Patrick's indifference to her. In her role as her mother's surrogate she clearly felt unloved, and as ambitious author—a Zenobia type—she was certain that she could not win his approval. How she felt about this latter fact may be inferred from the early poem "Reflections on the Fate of Neglected Genius" (#56), which asserts that "None can tell the bitter anguish / Of those lofty souls that languish" with their "sacred fire" "quenched by frowns" and "All their powers within them swelling, / Tortured by neglect to ire."

For the six or eight years after "Albion and Marina" Charlotte continued recording the deaths or self-submergences of her Marina-Marian-Mary-Minas and repeatedly depicted the bluestocking Zenobia, still unable to inspire "the *tender passion*," poring over Greek and Latin texts and coping with men in strength of mind and arm. But despite Charlotte's outrage and anguish at the neglect of her genius, and partly because she began to fear that it was a wicked gift, she identified herself primarily with her Marys.

Surviving the Storm

Charlotte saw in her personal life a pattern of repeated sinking and rising, shadowy submergence followed by triumphant resurfacing, and she invoked this pattern repeatedly in her fiction. She never ceased to fear that each submergence would be final, that she would be at last unable to arise; and she never ceased using her fictions as a medium for seeking a better, surer, more satisfying understanding of what "arising" might mean. What it had to mean eventually (she could be content with no less) was that she should achieve that seemingly impossible combination: the bounty of paternal love and at the same time success as an ambitious creative intellect. In short, to "be" as a woman and yet "do" as men do.

Charlotte's early writing is suffused with sinkings. Her Mary-women sink into the grave, into the sea, into the paternal bosom, into the bondage of a self-annihilating dependence on their hero Zamorna, just as Charlotte saw herself sinking into morbid depressions that she called "hypochondria," into a "necromantic" addiction to her fantasy life, into an idolatrous worship of "false gods"—of men who, like Patrick, accepted female adoration as their due but offered no sustenance in return. Buried in earth, sunk in ocean, fettered in sin, her lonely spark of spirit might consume her vitals in tormenting hellfire, or else simply smolder and die out, unseen. Either way she faced mere extinction.

This is where, for Charlotte, the figure of mother comes in. The mother cannot "save" her daughter, but she can provide a stay against disintegration. She can harbor her daughter temporarily in some womb-like cave or dell, encourage her with hope in her lonely depression, strengthen her virtue and accordingly her moral resistance to addiction and idolatry. This was the work of the moon-mother who urged Jane

Eyre to "flee temptation," and of the mother Nature who afterwards housed Jane, though roughly and briefly, in her fields and furrows. These mothers arise both within the daughter and above or beyond her, teaching her to care more for her own self and faith, and to depend less on unworthy men.

But for the daughter to arise fully from her sunken condition, a man must lift her up in his warm embrace. Just as a bad father pushes woman under, so a good father must raise her—both feed her with love and fire her with ambition. This good father Charlotte never found among mortal men, nor even depicted until after *Jane Eyre*. We will see that he is no Rochester. The first Rochester was already subtly sinking Jane even before the mock marriage, as many ominous signs emphasize; and after it she plunged to her nadir: "I came into deep waters; the floods overflowed me." With mother's help she survives to marry a Rochester who will not sink her; but neither can he lift her to new creative heights. In her last two novels Charlotte learned to create for herself—first tentatively and then in fully rounded form—the good father she needed. She did this by merging into a single fictional character both the nurturing paternal lover and the personification of her own genius, her own "male" power of doing, the talent lodged in her by God for the redemption of her life and work. Charlotte's good father turned out to be her version of the Holy Ghost—her muse in his fullest form. In *Shirley* he appears briefly as personified "Genius," in a passage added to the novel after a period of close study of her now-dead sister Emily's work. In *Villette* he is figured in Paul Emanuel.

I offer this spare outline now in order that we may better recognize Charlotte's underlying pattern of idea as we come upon it in its richly diverse expressions; for every fiction Charlotte wrote tells some part or some version of this story.

The sinking image occupied Charlotte's imagination from early childhood. We see it already implicit in the "n" that at fifteen she added to her dead mother's name, making Maria into the watery "Marina" in the story with which she secretly answered her father's *Albion and Flora*. Even the idea of Waterloo that Charlotte alluded to with such discreet suggestiveness in her dating of Marina's death contains its element of somber pun. In fact some of the origins of the special meaning that attached to drowning in Charlotte's imagination seem to lie in imagery employed by her father and to events suffered by her mother long before Charlotte was even born.

Back in 1812 Patrick Brontë, having received some mild rebuke in a letter from his young fiancée Maria Branwell, answered her with such a clamor of figurative storm language that the amused but startled Maria responded:

> I really know not what to make of the beginning of your last; the winds, waves, and rocks almost stunned me. I thought you were giving me the account of some terrible dream . . . having no idea that your lively imagination could make so much of the slight reproof conveyed in my last.[6]

Then she slightly—but suggestively—connected Patrick's storm imagery with a painful experience of her own: "I thought . . . you had had a presentiment of the fate of my poor box." With her wedding approaching, Maria had sent home to the south of England to have her "books, clothes, etc." shipped north to her. But at the time of this letter she had just learned that her bridal things had gone down among real "winds, waves, and rocks." Maria wrote:

> On Saturday evening about the time you were writing the description of your imaginary shipwreck, I was reading and feeling the effects of a real one, having then received a letter from my sister giving me an account of the vessel in which she had sent my box being stranded on the coast of Devonshire, in consequence of which the box was dashed to pieces with the violence of the sea, and all my little property, with the exception of a very few articles, swallowed up in the mighty deep.

Perhaps it seemed to Charlotte, hearing this story years later, that Patrick's figurative storm had somehow called up the literal one. Certainly in Charlotte's eyes her mother's fate as bride was foreshadowed in the fate of her bridal box.

Among the "very few" articles that survived were some magazines that contained a treasure of light reading. Charlotte later recalled how "they had crossed the sea, had suffered shipwreck and were discoloured with brine—I read them as a treat on holiday afternoons or by stealth when I should have been minding my lessons." But the magazines, too, Patrick eventually destroyed. "One black day my father burnt them because they contained foolish love stories."[7] In *Shirley* there is a pointed allusion to the shipwrecked magazines. Young Caroline has little to read in her uncle's parsonage household except for a few things remaining from her dead aunt:

> its collection of light literature was chiefly contained on a shelf which had belonged to her aunt Mary: some venerable Lady's Magazines, that had once performed a sea-voyage with their owner, and under-

gone a storm, and whose pages were stained with salt water . . . (p. 440)

Their presence on the parsonage shelves must have provided Charlotte with constantly visible signs of the emotional shipwreck that she attributed to the mother who had owned them. Yet that mother had sustaining powers too, even in her underwater world. The name "Mary Cave" that Charlotte gives her in *Shirley* anticipates in its imagery the maternal "cave in the sea" that will provide temporary respite for storm-tossed Lucy at her godmother's home in *Villette*.

Throughout Charlotte's early work the godlike powers of both storm and sunshine are regularly assigned to the character Zamorna, who is in this respect Patrick fictionalized. Certainly he can be a figure of solar brilliance:

Fire! Light! What have we here? Zamorna's self, blazing in the frontispiece like the sun on his own standard. . . . Keen, glorious being![8]

Yet when he is impassioned, he looks "like a sea-storm";[9] and these are the seas in which the various Marys and Marians and Minas "drown." In one of her poems Charlotte has Marian predict the figurative fate that awaited them all:

Ocean will be my tomb,
Sea-sand my pillow. (#84)[10]

In another, a Maria literally drowns herself when her "fierce and faithless love" deserts her:

For Far under the fairy sea
    Slumbers Maria placidly! (#115)

A comparable death is imagined for Zamorna's wife, Mary:

It would look well . . . to see her sinking
All in white raiment through the placid deep
From the pure limpid water never shrinking
Calmly subsiding to eternal sleep
Dreaming of him that's drowning her . . . (#116)

For all these Marys, Zamorna's bosom and the bosom of the sea are alike in offering refuge. But unlike the maternal womb, that kind of refuge dissolves female being rather than sustaining it. Its appeal is to woman's regressive hunger for the godlike father's love. Indeed, these Marys are all figuratively Zamorna's children. Even Mina, the most "active, energetic & accomplished" of them all, is infantilized in her relationship to him: "here she was as weak as a child."[11]

The imagery that associates our most powerful emotions with stormy seas that threaten us with drowning is of course familiar from religious and secular literature alike, and might have found an appropriate place in the Brontës' work on a number of grounds. Yet only one kind of woman drowns in Charlotte's fictions—the Mary kind, whose prototype was Charlotte's mother. And the waters she drowns in are the emotions aroused in and by one kind of man—which Charlotte saw as her father's kind. Still, even figurative storms are not all, of course, either love related or incitements to female regression. Nor did Charlotte Brontë imagine that they were. For her, as for Emily and the Romantic poets from whom both sisters learned so much, wind also figures inspiration, the "intellectual breeze" of creative thought. Yet for Charlotte even these forces empowered her paternal hero rather than herself. Already in 1829, the year before "Albion and Marina," she was describing her fictional hero as the author of verses about "the wild roaring of the ocean mingling with the tremendous voice of thunder when the flashing lightening gleams . . . over the face of the troubled waters"[12] and signing her poetry with his name rather than her own. Indeed, although Charlotte appears to have rendered the external world with its winds and weathers into metaphor still earlier and more easily than Emily did, there was this important difference between them: for young Charlotte, artistic sublimation did not bring that world under her control. Quite the reverse. In her case the whole universe of her experience, both outer and inner, belonged to the father-god whom she worshiped. Traces of his attributes linger in her work to the very end—in the way Jane Eyre's love for Rochester tosses her on an "unquiet sea, where billows of trouble rolled under surges of joy," and even in the way M. Paul fumes comically like a "bottled storm" in *Villette*. Not until near the end of her final novel did Charlotte engage her god directly and wrest from him the power to love and to write without fear.

Charlotte had imagined in Zenobia, however, a fearless intellectual woman. Why did she not try to explore through Zenobia her creative ambitions at least, if not her domestic ones? In certain respects she did. But even Zenobia cannot help loving Zamorna, and in pursuing him the "woman of intellect" behaves like any sinking Mary:

> Then will I serve thee all my after-days
> As thy poor handmaid, as thy humblest slave,

Happy to kiss the dust beneath thy tread,
To kneel submissive in thy lordly presence. (#59)

But even on her knees the intellectual woman cannot be loved, and her fate as woman scorned is even worse than that of the Marys. In "The Bridal," which reports Zamorna's marriage to Marian, we learn that the rejected Zenobia has turned into a disheveled witch, threatening Zamorna with a knife and prophesying that he will die a suicide if he continues to deny her. She has gone mad from being deprived of his love.[13] Elements of this crazed Zenobia will recur in Bertha Mason of *Jane Eyre*.

Still Zenobia did serve an important function in Charlotte's early struggles for achievement. This became possible when Charlotte's feelings about men were focused on her brother rather than her father, for there her creative goals were not in conflict with her domestic ones. Against Patrick's charisma, intellect might be useless. But not against Branwell's.

Charlotte had been home from school about a year when Branwell began making his funny and unflattering appearances in her work. In one story of 1833 ("The Green Dwarf") he appears as a carrot-haired fellow with "malicious black eyes" who rides a spring cart drawn by asses. In another ("The Secret") he briefly appears as "a broad carroty-locked man of a most pugnacious aspect" begging his employer for "largesse." In a more comprehensive caricature of 1834 he is satirized as P. B. Wiggins, recognizable again by his "bush of carroty hair" and an arrogance that leads him to expect to be honored one day as a musician greater than Bach, a poet greater than Byron, a painter greater than Claude Lorraine, from which state of earthly renown he will be at last "rapt to Heaven in a fiery chariot."[14]

This is very funny material. Yet when it was written, the family's hopes for Branwell were nearly as high as his own; and it was his sisters who were to pay the cost of those hopes. When the next year they all had to "divide, break up, separate,"[15] the reason was partly to give Branwell the opportunity to apply for study at the Royal Academy in London. In such a context one can understand Charlotte's sense of injustice and her indignation against the brother whose expectations she clearly thought were grounded in self-centered delusion.

Charlotte's association with Branwell allowed her to feel considerable moral triumph. But unfortunately it brought moral danger too. That danger is dramatized in the way Zenobia's moral being is affected by her marriage to Percy. Percy was Branwell's fictional self-representation, a former pirate (then aptly named Rogue) now become Zamorna's prime minister and political rival. His relationship to Zenobia is quite asexual and far from romantic, less a marriage than a structural alliance between independent and rather testy equals—a brother and sister, as it were. In some respects—e.g., in his "passionless yet perfect beauty"—there is certainly little of Branwell about Percy. But as transgressor of God's law and would-be regicide and implicit patricide, Percy's is the character Branwell attributed to himself and retained in Charlotte's fiction right through to her fullest and most devastating portrait in "Captain Henry Hastings" (1839).

Zenobia, married to this rebel, remains "the most learned woman of her age" and an able scholar of "ancient lore." But she grows in certain other respects more like her husband—more rebellious, more combative, even readier to "cope" with men in "strength of arm" as well as "nerve of mind," precisely as Patrick had warned women not to do. She is now a "grand form of feminine majesty" with "fire in her eye and command on her brow," who is not at all above using her handsome hands to curb the men who cross her: "She can spar, I verily believe, with her own husband, one of the best boxers on record." (Branwell's love of boxing is alluded to here.) Later one character even suggests to Zenobia that "Nature in your case mistook and placed a masculine soul in a feminine casket."

By 1834, when Charlotte was eighteen, she had clearly grown apprehensive about the unfeminine appetites that her alliance with Branwell released—possibly through her rivalry with him, certainly through her share in his rebellion against paternal authority, whether Zamorna's authority or Patrick Brontë's. For the first time Charlotte's narrator judges Zenobia not just socially—denigrating her femininity or sexual attractiveness—but morally. Was Charlotte herself seeking to subvert the father-god she worshiped? Apparently she feared so, for she imputes that desire to Zenobia. Though still "a noble creature both in mind and body, Percy's wife is now also full of the blackest defects: . . . a beautiful intellectual woman, but an infidel." Percy himself "embodies the most vivid ideas we can conceive of Lucifer, the rebellious archangel"; together he and Zenobia are types of Milton's incestuous pair, "Sin and Satan."[16]

Thus, although Charlotte was gradually bringing Branwell's masculine power under the control of comedy and gaining confidence in her rivalry with her one male sibling, paternal powers she still feared to oppose; rebellion against a father figure was implicitly rebellion against God. And this was Zenobia's sin. So in Charlotte's imagination Zenobia always remained an overreacher, the enduring model of intellectual woman as rebel and infidel—still unloved, and now no longer even morally defensible.

Old Testament, New Testament, and Charlotte's Testament

But the concept of "infidel" was a useful one. In the story "Mina Laury," written over the summer of 1834, Charlotte for the first time depicted Mina's slavish adoration as not just unhealthy for her, but actually profane. Mina is "the doomed slave of infatuation, devoted, stricken, absorbed in one idea, finding a kind of strange pleasure in bearing the burden and carrying the yoke of him whose fascinations fettered her so strongly"; her worship of Zamorna is a species of "Egyptian bondage" in which his "chains . . . are locked on every limb."[17] "Egyptian bondage"! From this Old Testament hint Charlotte now framed a fresh perspective on the entire imaginative enterprise by which her characters were playing out their roles as versions of Maria Brontë and her daughters on the one hand, and of Patrick and Branwell on the other. The biblical contraries of Egypt and the Promised Land provided, in their full typological significance, a newly liberating structure for the falling and rising pilgrimage of Charlotte's spirit. What if her stubborn impulse to rebel against the god who seemed so cruelly to diminish her was no sin after all, but a resistance to idolatry? What if her passionate love were to be redirected toward a worthier goal? Then might it not redeem rather than destroy her?

From their early copying of John Martin's modishly apocalyptic pictures, the Brontë children had associated Glasstown (or Verdopolis, as it came to be called in its upgraded French-Greek form) with "the cities of old: Ninevah and Babylon."[18] Now in October 1834, as Charlotte describes the departure of a portion of the Glasstown population on their way to settle their new kingdom, Angria, under the leadership of "King Adrian" (Zamorna of course), she adopts and adapts the language of Exodus. Her narrator, Zamorna's mildly sardonic younger brother Charles, speaks from the perspective of Egypt:

> The children of Israel are gone up from amongst us, and a mixed multitude went up with them, the flocks, and herds and very much *cattle*. They went by way of BAAL-ZEPHON and are camped in the wilderness of SIN. (I believe the original orthography is ZIN, but that signifies little). A pillar of a cloud went before them, a pillar of a cloud

by night and of fire by day (Is not that the just description of King Adrian, Angrians?) and in their departure they spoiled the Egyptians: they have not slain our first-born, but they have enticed them away, saying, cast your lot with us and we will do you good.[19]

The term "Zin," on which Charlotte has Charles pun here, in Hebrew means thorn or briar—familiar emblem of the troubles and limitations of the flesh. These are the emblematic associations of Thornfield in *Jane Eyre* and of Briarfield in *Shirley,* places of temptation and trial for Charlotte's heroines. But behind these associations lay the striking personal circumstance that Charlotte was herself born at Thornton (Thorn-town). It is with a glance at this name that she houses her narrator Charles at the "Thornton Hotel" in her story-land.[20]

By allusion, then, the "Egyptian bondage" in which Zamorna's women are held is the condition of all Charlotte's fantasy society, held spiritual captive by the luxurious "Babylon" of Verdopolis; and the departure of Zamorna and his followers becomes the Israelite flight toward the Promised Land. But—to pursue the typology—Angria is not the land of promise, Zamorna not even Moses, much less a true god. The world of Charlotte's juvenile imagination never moved beyond the stage of the wanderings in the desert ("the wilderness of SIN" in Charles' mocking phrase) and the worship of idols. Even when Mary is compared to Queen Esther supplicating for "the devoted Hebrews,"[21] the god she worships is emphatically not Jehovah but Zamorna: "My King, my Husband, my very Deity, smile at me once more. . . . Am I to eat the bread and drink the waters of bitterness, or blessed with the forgiving light of your countenance, am I to sleep in peace?"[22]

Still, Charlotte was exploring the fallen world of her fictions for possible avenues of release. In the context of the newly established Angria a character named Warner Howard Warner rises to prominence. He had been head of a clan in Angrian country before Zamorna and his followers settled there, and now becomes a kind of homegrown prophet who "warns" Zamorna of his sins and dangers. The clan he had headed was that of the Howards, Agars, and Warners. "Howard" is the story-name for Haworth, the village in which the Brontës actually lived; and "Warner" is a characterizing epithet. But the name "Agar" is the most arresting and suggestive, for it directs Old Testament wanderings toward New Testament salvation.

Agar is the New Testament name for Hagar, allegorically interpreted by St. Paul in Galatians 4:22–31 as the mother of the children of bondage, that is, of children born after the flesh. These are the children of

Jerusalem enslaved, contrasted by St. Paul with the freeborn children of the heavenly Jerusalem—the children of promise, born after the spirit. We find only children of bondage in Charlotte's juvenile world of fantasy, a "nether world" or "world below" in the young Brontës' significant phrases. But St. Paul's contrast between the children of this world and the next, though undeveloped in 1834, was already at work in Charlotte's imagination. It will be troublingly implicit in the different "masters" served by Jane and St. John at the conclusion of *Jane Eyre*. And it will define the structure of *Villette*.

Thus if the time before Charlotte's first stay at Roe Head was characterized by ambivalence concerning the divided possibilities offered her as a woman, the possibility of love on the one hand (Mary, etc.) and intellectual achievement on the other (Zenobia), the fiction she wrote during her three years at home working with Branwell focused on the costs, for a woman, of taking either course. She found that no element of her imaginative life was exempt from the sweeping imputation of sin and spiritual bondage: not intellectual and rebellious Zenobia, nor even the more dutiful and ladylike Marys. All were the children of Jerusalem enslaved. How then was their creator to be reborn as a child of promise? How was her imagination to be redeemed so that she might write a testament of woman's spiritual and creative liberation? These were the questions Charlotte faced in the early months of 1835. But her search for answers was roughly halted. Thrust out into the stormy world again, she now sank even deeper into bondage, wandered even farther into "the wilderness of SIN."

Charlotte left home for Roe Head the second time—now as teacher—in July of 1835 and worked there in stoic wretchedness until the summer of 1837, when Miss Wooler moved her school to Dewsbury Moor where Charlotte continued until May 1838. It was another case of sinking and rising. In her misery she first sank in reckless idolatry into the depths of her "bright darling dream," then began gradually trying to find means of self-rescue. Finally in the early months of 1838 she suffered what she called "hypochondria," and on a doctor's welcome advice returned home to Haworth.

The scattered scraps of Charlotte's writing that are referred to as the "Roe Head Journal"[23] reveal that even when she idolized her dream world she saw that its hold on her was morbid and disabling, that she was like Mina a "doomed slave of infatuation," though her god was now less the father who had sent her into this exile than the dreams that were providing the nourishment Patrick denied. Charlotte's beloved was now "my darling, my cherished-in-secret Imagination, the tender and the mighty," as she was later to phrase it in *The Professor*. This "darling" was certainly no redeemer.

During the Christmas holiday after her first term of teaching (December 1835), Charlotte wrote a long poem that editors have entitled "Retrospection" (#106). This poem both describes her "bright darling dream" and reflects her bondage to it. Its opening line gave Fannie Ratchford the title for her seminal study of the Brontë juvenilia: *The Brontës' Web of Childhood*.

> We wove a web in childhood
>   A web of sunny air
> We dug a spring in infancy
> Of water pure and fair
>
> We sowed in youth a mustard seed
> We cut an almond rod
> We are now grown up to riper age
> Are they withered in the sod[?]

This "web," "spring," "seed," and "rod" refer to the children's fantasy life, which has certainly not "withered," but burgeoned mightily. Most suggestively, their "dry unbudding almond-wand / Has touched eternity"—an allusion to Numbers 17, where God demonstrates that Aaron is His chosen priest. Charlotte's language here seems almost to suggest that the flowering of the young Brontës' art out of the deaths and losses of their childhood (the "shrivelled off-shoot" and "lone grave-mound") should be read as a divine sanctification of their "web":

> There came a second miracle
> Such as on Aaron's sceptre fell
> And sapless grew like life from heath
> Bud bloom & fruit in mingling wreath
> All twined the shrivelled off-shoot round
> As flowers lie on the lone grave-mound[.]

She does not pause to develop this latent concept of the sacred power of art to raise life out of death, but we should not forget it, as it gradually reemerges with important implications. For now she associates herself less with Aaron than with the sinning Israelites, as she sketches her growing infatuation with the "Dream":

> Oh! as thou swellest and as the scenes
> Cover this cold world's darkest features
> Stronger each change my spirit weans
> To bow before thy god-like creatures[.]

Returning to the school after that first holiday during which she had written "Retrospection," Charlotte records again her sense that for her the world of "reality" is deadly, that only her imagination sustains her. In a "Roe Head Journal" entry dated February 4, 1836, she expresses her sense of rescue and release by a biblical figure that is especially significant in view of her already established imagery: "I now, after a day of weary wandering, return to the ark which for me floats alone on the billows of this world's desolate and boundless deluge." It is of course the ark of her imagination. And her figure recalls that though the Israelite God drowns sinners, He rescues the faithful. Is she not after all one of these? Had her rod not blossomed like Aaron's? Now she continues to seek support from biblical analogue:

> It is strange I cannot get used to the ongoings that surround me. I fulfill my duties strictly and well. . . . [But] as God was not in the fire, nor the wind, nor the earthquake, so neither is my heart in the task, the theme, or the exercise. . . . the still small voice . . . comes to me at eventide, . . . like a breeze with a voice in it . . . ; it is that which takes up my spirit and engrosses all my living feelings . . .

What Charlotte is struggling to describe, this "breeze with a voice in it," is of course inspiration—potentially divine.

The whole moral spectrum is present by implication in "Retrospection": from the present certainty of being a "devoted, stricken" slave, to the glimpsed prospect of being God's chosen instrument. The same moral spectrum is implicit in #112, dated the month after "Retrospection." There the wind's "rush of sound" wakens "a hundred dreams" and "a thousand streams / Of poetry of thought." The muse of all this fantasy and poetry is of course the false god Zamorna, yet Charlotte's words echo one of the Bible's most powerful depictions of the experience of divine inspiration. This is Acts 2:2–4, where Christ's apostles heard "a sound from heaven as of a rushing mighty wind. . . . And they were all filled with the Holy Ghost, and began to speak . . . as the Spirit gave them utterance." This biblical scene was of central significance to the Brontës as to all those who use the wind as a figure for inspiration. Charlotte even chose the feast of Whitsuntide or Pentecost, which celebrates this moment, as the backdrop for her central, pivotal chapters in *Shirley*.

But for now the "still small voice" that came to Charlotte's ear came only from the "inaccessibly sacred beings" of her still sinful "world below."

And it came with a growing imperiousness. "I'm just going to write because I cannot help it," she opens a Roe Head Journal entry in which she describes herself writing with her eyes shut, in her tiny, wobbling "secret" hand. Here at Roe Head the wind "coming . . . with a rapid, gathering stormy swell" wakens not poetry but frustration. Her rage mounts against the oppressive routine of teaching: "Stupidity the atmosphere, school-books the employment, asses the society, what in all this is there to remind me of the divine silent unseen land of thought." Wracked by impatience with "those fat-headed oafs," she feels sweep over her "all the mighty phantasm that we had conjured from nothing . . . to a system strong as some religious creed. I felt as if I could have written gloriously. . . ."[24]

This mighty phantasm with its godlike force Charlotte would describe years later under the name of Creative Impulse in a vigorous comic passage in *Villette*.[25] But back in 1836 at Roe Head its power did not allow of comic treatment. Rather it began to grow frightening and oppressive. In one such case the dream "had acted on me like opium and was coiling about me a disturbed but fascinating spell" so "morbidly vivid" that Charlotte found to her shock that she could not dismiss it. It "remained pictured in my mind's eye with irksome and alarming distinctness. I grew frightened. . . . At last I became aware of a feeling like a heavy weight laid across me. . . . I wanted to speak, to rise—it was impossible. . . . the weight pressed me as if some huge animal had flung itself across me"[26]

Such fettering and frustration were not to be tolerated. And indeed when Charlotte recorded this frightening experience on October 14, 1836, she had already been at work for several months summoning forces to counteract the power of "phantasm." Surely relief would come to a child of bondage if she sought the aid of a child of promise. In May 1836 she had written her friend Ellen Nussey a letter of confession that may have bewildered Ellen, though its references are clear to us who know the secret of Charlotte's "infernal world." Her imagery—the fiery imagination, the water of life—should be kept in mind, for it will recur in her novels as part of their governing structure of idea.

> If you knew my thoughts; the dreams that absorb me; and the fiery imagination that at times eats me up and makes me feel Society as it is, wretchedly insipid, you would pity and I dare say despise me. But Ellen I know the treasures of the Bible I love and adore them I can *see* the Well of Life . . . ; but when I stoop down to drink of the pure waters they fly from my lips . . .[27]

For a time Charlotte seems to have hoped that Ellen's friendship would provide her with the love for which her "hot, tenacious heart" was starving, and release her from dependence on her dream.[28] Her lusts might be cured if she and Ellen could read the Bible together:

> if your lips and mine could at the same time drink the same draught from the same pure fountain of mercy, I hope, I trust, I might one day become better, far better, than my evil wandering thoughts, my corrupt heart, cold to the spirit, and warm to the flesh will now permit me to be. . . . my heart is a real hot bed for sinful thoughts . . .[29]

But by the spring of 1837 she had begun to fear that in turning to Ellen she had not so much freed herself from an old idolatry as fallen under the power of a new one. Bitterly saddened to learn that Ellen will be unable to pay a planned visit to her at Roe Head, she writes:

> Why are we to be divided? Surely, Ellen, it must be because we are in danger of loving each other too well—of losing sight of the *Creator* in idolatry of the *creature*.[30]

This is the situation in which Jane will find herself with Rochester as the time of the mock marriage approaches:

> My future husband was becoming to me my whole world; and more than the world: almost my hope of heaven. . . . I could not, in those days, see God for his creature: of whom I had made an idol.

Again in *Villette* the note is sounded by Miss Marchmont, who in telling Lucy of her long-dead fiancé Frank, observes.

> You see, I still think of Frank more than of God; and unless it be counted that in thus loving the creature so much, so long, as so exclusively, I have not at least blasphemed the Creator, small is my chance of salvation.

The direct reference in all of these cases is to Romans 1:25, in which we are told that God has given up those who "worshipped and served the Creature more than the Creator." And of course in the deeper background lies the first commandment issued to the Israelite wanderers in the desert, forbidding bowing to false gods. With or without Ellen, Charlotte was still in the desert, still insisting with weary fanaticism that her dreams were the "gods" of her "religion" (#137).

Charlotte knew that she had to have love to survive, and further, that the grip of dream was so tenacious because she was so lonely. In one interesting poem (#135) she suggests that if her own conscience—she calls it "that restless eye / Which haunts my solitude"—could only be embodied in someone outside herself, she could rouse herself from her depressed and enervated state. If the "eye" were near, she says,

> and if its beam
> Fell on me from a human brow
> I would awake from that wild dream
> Which spell-binds every talent now[.]

In such company her own "voice of Pride" might stir her to action, might bring her to break her "self-locked chain." This was of course the role she had unsuccessfully assigned to Ellen; eventually it would be triumphantly assigned to her muse.

For now Charlotte saw her need for love as a "religion" parallel to her "religion" of fantasy, both of them evidence of her sin against the First Commandment. One typical poem, whose first draft was written apparently in the same month as was #137, depicts a dying woman telling her priest that she has renounced his God for her beloved "Walter." "'Tis my religion thus to love," she asserts, and as she dies she calls to Walter as if to heaven: "I come! I come!" ("Apostasy," #192).

But since her heart had to adore, she could try again to improve its objects of adoration, to turn her heart away from Egypt and toward the Promised Land. She could imagine more worthy men, create more "reasonable" dreams. And this was the next course she chose. In June of 1837 she began drafting a poem later published as "The Letter" (#194) in which she depicts a woman absorbed in writing to her husband—no bewitching Zamorna, but rather a stern man whose "firm, determined face" reveals his "moral might." "Is he her God?" the poem asks, as if to emphasize the transition from the false to the true. The shift in erotic object is made explicit in another poem, which she eventually published under the title "Preference" (#186). It speaks the mind of a woman addressing a Zamorna-like man and contrasting him to his moral superior. To the immoral man the speaker confidently affirms: "I could not love thee," for "even by thine own confession / Thou art steeped in perfidy." His "rival" is the man she does love:

> There he sits—the first of men!
> Man of conscience—man of reason;
> Stern, perhaps, but ever just;
> Foe to falsehood, wrong, and treason,
> Honour's shield, and virtue's trust!

Lovers—and dreams—of such solid recommendation can surely secure Charlotte against some of her own fear of bondage and idolatry.

By her final year at Miss Wooler's Charlotte was taking a sharper and less wholly acquiescent look at Zamorna himself, and placing him in a world where the emotions, if not the plot and settings, were more realistically imagined and rendered. This shift had been in preparation during the whole time Charlotte had spent at Roe Head. Especially at first, the plotting had apparently been left largely to Branwell, who loved a good war. Accordingly Percy was permitted to succeed in overpowering his royal rival, whom he then sent into exile. Zamorna's planned revenge was to divorce his second wife, Percy's daughter Mary—an act that would certainly kill her and thus punish her father. These painful prospects were under consideration during Charlotte's period of religious self-accusation in her letters to her friend Ellen, and doubtless contributed to her depression. Certainly she conflated the personal and the fictional crises at some level of her mind; the prophetic Warner judges Zamorna in terms that reflect Charlotte's sense of her own condition: "I fear my lord, God will veil his face from you forever—remember, man may so tempt the Holy Spirit that it will finally leave us. . . ."[31]

But then somewhere in the early months of 1837 the plot was altered and Zamorna returned with Mary on his mind.[32] This return marks the beginning of a greater independence for Charlotte in her handling of Angrian story, and a corresponding shift in her writing away from simple melodrama and toward a more complex rendering of male-female emotional relationships. Certainly Mary still adores Zamorna, but she is now capable of a more natural sense of her wifely rights. And Charlotte's own attitude toward her hero reflects a corresponding gain in distance and judgment. Mary's former perverse dependency is now experienced only by the peasant-born Mina Laury, whose servant rank and mistress status might be thought to account somewhat more realistically for her devoted submission to her "lord" and "master," her willingness to accept his caresses "as a slave ought to take the caress of a sultan."[33] But Charlotte's narrator emphasizes the extent to which this gifted young woman has been dehumanized by her passion. "Miss Laury belonged to the Duke of Zamorna—She was indisputably his property as much as the Lodge of Rivaux or the stately woods of Hawkscliffe, & in that light she considered herself."[34] Even Mina admits her moral diminishment: her adoration of Zamorna "effaced everything else—I lost the power of properly discerning the difference between right & wrong." She thinks of him as her source of life; but what she dwells on, in describing her feelings for him, is not life but annihilation: "he superseded all things— all affections, all interests, all fears or hopes or principles—Unconnected with him my mind would be a blank—cold, dead, susceptible only of a sense of despair." In her love for Zamorna, Mina indeed "lost her identity—her very way of life was swallowed up in that of another." Such are the costs, counted with a new coolness, of any idolatry. As Lucy Snowe will instruct little Polly in *Villette,* "It is folly to think anybody perfect; . . . we should be friendly to all, and worship none."

Thus already in the period before her hypochondria Charlotte was beginning to reveal a new sense of judgmental perspective, both on her work and in it. With Angrian plot somewhat more in Charlotte's control, Mary begins to receive better treatment and Zamorna to be handled with irony and even deprecation. By the time of "Mina Laury" (January 1838) and "Henry Hastings" (1839), the once "inaccessibly sacred beings" of her imagination were beginning to seem thoroughly human and fallible. Very gradually Charlotte was learning to assert her own power of "doing," to liberate the inner energies through which she would eventually write her personal testament—the story of her own journey, as female creative artist, from bondage to salvation.

Hypochondria and Hope

Charlotte had not yet left her wilderness by 1838; and certainly no redeemer had yet come to rescue her with his love. But she was writing better than ever before—writing with a new independence and authority. Yet she still faced a grave difficulty, similar in some ways to what Emily faced in her conflict between "reason" and the values of physical life on the one hand, and "imagination" and the muse on the other. But Charlotte's position was all the more difficult because unlike Emily she did not find her imagination alone sufficiently liberating. She did not want to leave the world, but rather to live and love in it. And she wanted to work, surely not as a teacher of "fat-headed oafs" but as a respected creative writer.

Charlotte was able gradually to detach herself from her false gods and drowning Marys and so improve the quality of her work, partly thanks to a feat of imagination similar to Emily's but nearly opposite in its implications. Emily's feat had been to transform her mother's dying into a model of visionary release. Charlotte's was to see that although her mother had died, her supportive spirit survived in a figure Charlotte called "Hope," a woman-power who appears when her daughter is sinking into morbid depression, in danger of the submergence that Charlotte assumed her mother had suffered. This mother-power provides haven in time of need, courage in time of weakness. She is female "being" personified, the very capacity to survive.

During the months that followed her writing of "Mina Laury," Charlotte underwent at Miss Wooler's the "hypochondria" that enabled her to return home in May 1838.[35] Certainly she was thoroughly prepared for it—prepared to find in her collapse a grounding for recovery and achievement, in a way that would serve her as a model not only for the rest of her life but in all her fiction. A version of it appears in every novel. The actual hypochondria was of course a painful illness, yet like Jane Eyre's "unsounded depths of agony" that evoked the moon-mother at Thornfield, it brought Charlotte the maternal support she needed in order to move ahead. Similar measures bring similar results in both *Shirley,* where Caroline's critical illness brings the discovery of her lost mother, and *Villette,* where Lucy collapses to awaken in what seems a "cave in the sea"—actually the sanctuary of her godmother's home. In no case does this maternal support fulfill the ultimate needs of Charlotte's heroine; but it keeps her from sinking too far, supports her as she waits for the father-lover's saving embrace. And so for Charlotte herself, the female strength she was able to invoke at Miss Wooler's did not bring liberty to her spirit; it did not bring her to the Promised Land. But it rescued her from schoolroom bondage so that she could continue on her journey of creative work.

The disturbingly vivid scenes she had fantasized at Roe Head, the "heavy animal weight" that had held her down there, had shown how her adolescent muse could oppress with his sinful sexuality. But Charlotte had also learned at Miss Wooler's that one can drown in duty as surely as in any sexual waters. She and her talent might equally be swallowed by the mere work of survival in the father-world. One set of penciled lines from this period had asked plaintively whether "To toil to think to long to grieve" could be all the future held for her.[36] Another piece raises the same question far more powerfully; and this time it is not a Mary or Mina but rather the intellectual Zenobia herself who contemplates the prospect of annihilation. The scene opens with Zenobia meditating "how to save her pride and crush her feelings"—how, that is, to gird herself with the resources of female strength. But the great force levied against her is not sexual. Zenobia "feels unconsciously the power of—"; and with this expressive dash the prose breaks off and gives way to a remarkable poem, to my mind Charlotte's best. What it describes is the pull of depression. To sink into these lethal waters is to lose conscience and consciousness together, to let go of pride, courage, reason—

all that defines the ego and makes creative life possible. Inevitably it is to lose sight of "Hope."

> Look into thought & say what thou dost see
> Dive, be not fearful how dark the waves flow
> Sink through the surge & bring pearls up to me
> Deeper ay deeper, the fairest lie low
>
> I have dived I have sought them, but none have I found
> In the gloom that closed o'er me no ⟨form⟩ floated by
> As I sunk through the void depths so black & profound
> How dim died the sun & how far hung the sky
>
> What had I given to hear the soft sweep
> Of a breeze bearing life through the vast realm of death
> Thoughts wear untroubled & dreams were asleep
> The spirit lay dreadless & hopeless beneath[.] (#117)[37]

Here we see into the very depths of Charlotte's "hypochondria," her vision of being swallowed up in the father-world's mighty deep.

Return to her mother's solacing bosom was for Emily a return to her originating source; but for Charlotte the solacing parental bosom was the father's, and we have seen that it did not promise a recovery of lost being but rather threatened a self-dissolving plunge into depths that yield no pearls. Accordingly Charlotte reversed Emily's gender associations in other ways. Pride, ambition, reason—values that Emily associated with the father-world and increasingly abhorred—were for Charlotte maternal values, and crucial to woman's being, her survival. For Charlotte the sting of conscience, the voice of morality, the powerful will to religious improvement were means by which woman could sustain herself in "the world's storm-troubled sphere," could navigate the masculine waters that threaten to destroy women's hope. Thus the creeds that were "idlest froth amid the boundless main" to Emily provided bulwarks and beacons for Charlotte.

One of Charlotte's most curious poetic fragments (undated) picks up just these images and provides a superb example of the difference between her view and Emily's. It is an imitation of the conclusion of Shelley's "Adonais"—or rather it is a revision of both Shelley's words and his intention in that poem. In pencil, on the inside cover of her French grammar book, Charlotte had at some time begun an Angrian poem and then, in an apparent burst of repudiation, of revolt against this "Egyptian bondage," dropped it midline and turned to write angrily against the Angrian habit itself, arguing that the "sea-journey" of escapist fantasy is both immoral and annihilating. Such journeys take one (she is now sure) away from home, not toward it; they drive one off the shores of conscience and consciousness, and shroud the markers by which we measure our moral progress, tell right from wrong, remain true to ourselves. Shelley had argued in "Adonais" that the poet's journey to death, though difficult and fearful, is lit by transcendent promise: his own "spirit's bark," he wrote, is driven

> Far from the shore, far from the trembling throng
> Whose sails were never to the tempest given; . . .
> I am borne darkly, fearfully, afar;
> Whilst, burning through the inmost veil of Heaven,
> The soul of Adonais, like a star,
> Beacons from the abode where the Eternal are.
> ("Adonais," ll. 489–95)

And this had been Emily's view of the journey too—though she denied that she feared it. But Charlotte's reworking of Shelley makes clear how different were her views from his and Emily's. Repudiating her Angrian topic and all the childishness it implies, she vows, "I can speak no more of infancy," and then imagines her own version of Shelley's sea journey:

> I am further out on this sullen [sea]
> & Darker waves of its waters come
> Driving me faster from peace & home
> Never a beacon burns on the deep
> The fires are out & the watchers sleep[.]

Shelley welcomes death—"Die / If thou wouldst be with that which thou dost seek!"—and Adonais' soul is a beacon guiding the traveler to deity. But in Charlotte's experience of such journey the beacons are gone and woman is led by her delusive yearnings to an annihilation in which the spirit lies "dreadless and hopeless." As Mina knew, it leads away from "all interests, all fears or hopes or principles" to a "blank—cold, dead. . . ."

Charlotte's Shelleyan fragment concludes by detailing the horror of the journey as she saw it. Billows roll and seabirds scream, but worse by far is the spiritual condition that is figured by all this tumult:

> Ay the thoughts of an evil heart
> The croaks of a conscience not yet ⟨scar[r]ed⟩
> The visions that will not depart
> Are worse than all man has ⟨feared⟩

> On the most troubled sea that ever
> Made the strongest vessel quiver[.] (#122b)

Like Cowper in "The Castaway," Charlotte affirms that to sink in these seas is to be "whelmed in deeper gulfs" than those of any literal ocean.[38]

But we have seen that Charlotte did not drown. The deeper and stormier the father-world's waters, the stronger her woman's will to arise from them and reach toward salvation. We saw that by the winter of 1837–1838 Charlotte had subdued Zamorna, detached herself from the Marys, and was writing better than she ever had—but that she was still trapped at Miss Wooler's. One more plunge, the hypochondria itself, would set her free. We have just seen her estimate of the risks.

In an unfinished poem dated January 1838, just before the onset of her hypochondria, Charlotte tentatively explored her prospects. The fragment contains in inchoate form her whole drama of sinking and rising: the bad father's oppression, the maternal support, the prospect of redemption. Like an artist's preliminary pencil study, this fragment sketches ideas rather than developing them. But the outline it sketches was the central one of Charlotte's imagination. Indeed she introduces here a name that every Brontë reader will recognize.

The poem takes as its setting a forest dell whose leafy murmur Charlotte addresses as "The voice of Lowood" (#158b). Lowood is, of course, the fictional name Charlotte gave to the Cowan Bridge school in *Jane Eyre*—certainly a place of childhood depression or "hypochondria" for Charlotte. As her portrait of Brocklehurst makes clear, she believed it to have been governed under a devastating system of male oppression. Yet "mother" too was there, at least as Charlotte reconstructed the school in her novel. Hers is the caring figure of Maria Temple, who tries to help Helen and succeeds in helping Jane to survive until she can depart—not yet for "liberty," to be sure, but at least for "a new servitude" (Jane's phrase) at Thornfield. In the poem, acute loneliness characterizes the setting:

> The voice of Lowood speaks subdued
> In the deep shadowy solitude[.]

But Charlotte's speaker is "Inured to loneliness," and finds the spot not so much gloomy as restful, filled with the gentle "communing . . . / Of tree with tree, and gale with gale." Dells like this are always fetal settings for Charlotte, as we will see repeatedly in her later work. And her view of them is always highly ambivalent. They provide sanctuary, to be sure; but who wants to live forever hid away? This dell, however, is also a place where "dreams . . . dawn." And strikingly, for the first time these dreams are not necromantic but life giving. Their source is not infernal but heavenly. They express not Charlotte's bondage but her aspiration:

> And dreams will dawn like angel's bright
> From the long vista's tender light[.]

The remainder of the poem, until it breaks off at the twenty-ninth line, depicts Charlotte's own terrible loneliness. "Born for all kindness" and "Burning with love," she has no resources or outlet; "bereaved / Of human smiles and sympathy," she has no one to see her "passion swell," and is thus "doomed" to find release only in her "reverie"—that is, in the resources of her own imagination. But the poem has already suggested that the dreams imagination provides need not enchain her in Egyptian bondage, but may "dawn like angel's bright." And now, just as the poem trails off, she begins to develop that tantalizing thought. There has after all been "one," she says, whose fires have warmed her spirit:

> Yes one, by fiery glimpses oft
> The cloud enkindling changed to flame
> Then sun and balm immingling soft
> To melt the frozen winter came
> And even I have tasted joy
> Pure, bright from heaven without alloy[.]

Who or what is that "one" who brings joy "Pure, bright from heaven"? The poem does not say, although the final three lines suggest that the "one" is not some actual person, but a creation or power of her own:

> Yet strange it seems—that born to be
> A being all unchained and free
> With powers of bliss all self contained . . .

Here the poem stops. That her "powers of bliss" are "self-contained" suggests that this sunny, melting presence is Charlotte's first inkling that her own imagination might provide the liberating embrace she required, be felt as "enkindling" like Zamorna, but not fettering like him, in line with the morally improved heroes she had been writing about. Perhaps she was wondering if that "restless eye" of her own mind or conscience need be embodied in an actual "human brow" in order to awaken her "from that wild dream / Which spell-binds every talent." If not, the similarly redemptive "one" imagined now in "The voice of Lowood" could be some function of her own inner self—not her female element of being with its life-saving sanctuary and solacing hope, but what I have called her male element of doing. It may thus offer the first glimmer of the liberating muse to come. "The voice of Lowood" does not end optimistically. The words "Yet strange it seems" seem to point toward some coming paradox (born to be free, but . . .); and of course the poem is abandoned in any case.

But it is not the only poem of this period to hint that Charlotte was looking within herself for a savior, entertaining the possibility of imagining her own, inner redeemer. In her letters of 1836 to Ellen she had regarded her "fiery imagination" as an evil panderer to hot flesh and sinful thoughts. But now in a poem that opens "When thou sleepest," she goes so far as to call her flame a "holier fire," and to picture her restless longing as a longing for transcendency.

> Then thy spirit's waiting wings
>   Quivered, trembled, spread to fly . . .
> Oh! it longed for holier fire
>   Than this spark in earthly shrine
> O! it soared & higher higher
>   Sought to reach a home divine[.] (#128)

Again the imagery of wings and flight, of "a home divine," calls Emily to mind. But again the parallel in terminology only sharpens the contrast in idea. Like Emily, Charlotte wants to break free; but Charlotte's allies are Emily's enemies. "Reason" and "pride" are what can help "break / The chains" that bind Charlotte, because she is struggling to free herself not from the natural world but rather from an Egyptian bondage to her false father-god and from corollary addiction to the "long false dream" that "spell-binds every talent now." Her imagery is cumulative and insistent. Woman is "born to be / A being all unchained"; surely she need not submit passively to oppression. The mother in herself must give her not only the nourishment to keep her alive, but the moral strength to "break / The chains whose rust corrodes my heart." Her longing for "holier fire" (not the seductive heats of Angria, but the divine light of the Promised Land) is an assertion of this moral strength, as it also defines the new direction of Charlotte's goals.

In an untitled prose piece that editors have called "Farewell to Angria" and assigned to this period, Charlotte wrote of her affection for the places and persons of her childhood dream world, but concluded by saying that she was ready to leave behind its "burning clime" and flaming sunsets and turn to "a cooler region where the dawn breaks grey and sober & the coming day for a time at least is subdued in clouds."[39]

These clouds remain in Charlotte's work to the end, as a figure for the sobering hardships of reality. But now she sees the moony light of maternal "Hope" break through them, generating a mighty rainbow of promise.

The term "hope" had suffused the poems of the spring of 1837. One poem spoke of "hopes . . . with their rainbow wings" (#133); another of the "healing stream / Of hope and hope's fruition" (#145); another told how hope descends, "a golden guest" (#135). Others depicted the moon as a "golden lamp of hope" (#153), whose "radiant rising" would "fill / With hope divine the skies" (#150).[40]

It should be clear by now that the moony hope to whom Charlotte turned in her poems while at Miss Wooler's school, and which sustained her in her departing "hypochondria," was the progenitor of the supportive moon-mother figures in Charlotte's novels. But that moony hope also had a compelling literary progenitor of her own, and one intimately connected to Charlotte's view of herself as artist.

Back in 1830, just a month after writing "Albion and Marina," Charlotte composed a poem that she titled "The Violet" (#51). Her subject was a grand one: a history of great poets, culminating in her own (ostensibly more modest) talent. The extent of her actual modesty may perhaps be gauged by the fact that Charlotte took her title from the violet in Wordsworth's "She dwelt among untrodden ways," where the violet figures his dear Lucy who, though "fair as a star," went largely unappreciated because of her "half-hidden" place in the world. Certainly Charlotte felt that she knew firsthand the feelings of one "whom there were none to praise / And very few to love." (Her poem "Reflections on the Fate of Neglected Genius" was written in the same month as "The Violet.") But although "The Violet" alludes to Wordsworth, the body of the poem is modeled not on any work of his, but rather on Thomas Gray's "The Progress of Poesy."

Like Gray, Charlotte considers the long sweep of poetic history in order to place her individual talent in that august tradition. Turning first to "those who in long ages past / Attuned the muse's shell," she makes her way, as Gray did, from Homer and the Greek dramatists through Virgil and Tasso to the poets of England. And here we find the source of Gray's special fascination for her: she quotes the generating image directly from her source. Recounting how Nature favored Shakespeare and withheld none of her secrets from him, Gray wrote:

> To Him the mighty Mother did unveil
> Her aweful face. . . .

To Charlotte this image was irresistible, and she seized it whole, for use in her own poem:

> Nature unveil thy awful face
> To me a poet's pow'r impart
> Though humble be my destined place[.]

The prayer is heard:

> It reached the "Mighty Mothers" ear
> She saw me where I lowly stood[.]

But what had been for Gray merely a poetic figure gripped Charlotte's imagination with the force of revelation. Gray moves on, unruffled, to consider Milton and Dryden, and finally himself. But Charlotte, unwilling to depart the "Mighty Mother," devotes forty-four lines to evoking a full vision of the goddess. First Charlotte describes the voices of wind and river; then a moonlike light illumines the air; and finally there appears "A shape more beauteous than the morn":

> A womans form the vision wore
> Her lofty forehead touched the sky
> Her crown, a rugged mountain hoar
> Where plume-like trees waved solemnly[.]

Her belt is a river; moon and stars bind her hair; and she smiles in an "attitude of heavenly grace" beneath a bright rainbow arch. This, then, is "Nature," and having made this ceremonious personal appearance, she speaks, granting Charlotte's "high request," though in terms appropriate to the humble standing of the recipient: not the laurel but the "lowly violet" shall form Charlotte's wreath.[41]

The request granted, the "glorious deity / Then passed in dazzling light away" and Charlotte is left to do as she has been told. It is here that we encounter the echo of Wordsworth's "violet by a mossy stone / Half hidden"—a reminder that even as imparter of poetic power, a mother's places are "half-hid," fetal ones. Charlotte recounts:

> I plucked the violet where it grew
> Beside a stone, green moss amid
> Its lovely leaflets bright with dew
> Like modest worth half seen half hid[.]

The connection in Charlotte's mind between herself and Wordsworth's Lucy will provide, years later, one of the several grounds for Charlotte's choice of her heroine's name in *Villette*.

That this divine mothering figure is allied in Charlotte's mind with the bright rainbow and moon figures of hope, and in turn with morality and self-respect, is clear from her many future appearances. Let me here note only two: the first in a brief French exercise entitled "L'Espérance" and the second in a more fully and suggestively developed scene in *The Professor*. The French essay assures us that "there exists in the heavens a power divine, the attentive companion of religion and virtue." This power helps us through life, guides us to port in times of storm: "Faith and Charity call her sister—her name is Hope."[42] Important here is not only Hope's help amid storm, but also her ties to religion and virtue as sources of female strength.

But Hope's role in relation to Charlotte's break from domination by her fantasy gets full-dress allegorical treatment in *The Professor*. In her "Farewell to Angria" Charlotte had decided to turn from the flaming sunset world of Angria to a "cooler region" where the "dawn breaks . . . subdued in clouds." In *The Professor* William Crimsworth, having just re-discovered his lost love, Frances, walks home thinking of the time when they can marry. (How the male William embodies the female Charlotte will be discussed in my chapter 4, below.) As he walks, he travels a double course. At one level he is moving literally from west to east like the Israelites of Exodus traveling toward the Promised Land, and his journey recalls theirs. But he is also enacting Charlotte's figurative passage from the hot enslavement of Angrian fantasy toward the cooler, clouded land of realism, freedom and hope. In leaving "the west behind," with its "crimson" sunset sky, William, like Charlotte, is leaving behind an old bondage. "Stepping . . . eastward" he faces hardship —the "vast bank of clouds" alluded to in "Farewell to Angria." But since east is also the direction of liberty, to be sought with the virtuous determination that Charlotte's inner mother always did support, William sees a vision of "Hope." By daylight what he sees among the clouds is "a perfect rainbow—high, wide, vivid." But that night in his dreams the rainbow takes on all the symbolic associations that Charlotte had by now attached to her "Mighty Mother." Beneath the rainbow in William's dream churn those dangerous waters that suggest hypochondria and drowning. But within the bow shines the divinity who promises aid to those who struggle. William writes:

I at last feel asleep; and then in a dream were re-produced the setting-sun, the bank of clouds, the mighty rainbow. I stood, methought, on a terrace. . . . [He cannot clearly make out what is below him] but hearing an endless dash of waves, I believed it to be the sea; . . . A spark of gold glistened on the line between water and air, floated up, approached, enlarged, changed . . . under the arch of the rainbow; . . . a large star shone with still lustre on an angel's forehead; . . . and a voice in my heart whispered: "Hope smiles on Effort!"[43]

The Promised Land toward which William journeys is a steady job and marriage to Frances. Charlotte's Promised Land is a liberated condition in which she could both be loved and do creative work in the world.

Charlotte's hypochondria at Miss Wooler's school did not, then, drown her. Instead, she kept up her hope and did finally get home. If we may read from the way this pattern is reiterated in her novels, Charlotte's illness, though certainly painful, served somehow to put her back in touch with the mother in herself. This "mother" helped break her bonds of morbidity and urged her toward more constructive and "realistic" creativity. The father's breast excites, endangers, infantilizes. But the mother advises hard work and strenuous virtue because these sustain the ego, promoting pride, reason, the power to create from strength rather than from the helpless need that we hear in the Roe Head cry, "I'm just going to write because I cannot help it." This inner mother preserved the creative liberty of Charlotte the artist and—as we will see in the next section—was preserved by that artist from opprobrium and death.

The Hot Heart Hides in Ice

"Captain Henry Hastings" (1839) was Charlotte's first attempt at fictional autobiography, and as such it is an immensely revealing personal testament. But before she was ready to write it she had to evolve one more strategy for dealing with the "hot, tenacious heart" that seemed to be the source of so much of her trouble. She had come to believe that if her inner fires were really to survive—neither burning her up in loveless loneliness nor being quenched themselves in the "void depths" of reckless adoration—then they must be hid behind a shield of cautious reserve. The purity of her passionate feelings seemed to depend on their being permitted neither expression nor fulfillment. She knew too well that to indulge them was to become enslaved by them; even to acknowledge them was to be in danger of having them imposed on. Given the world woman must live in, coolness is wisdom. This austere view is the origin of Lucy's snow in *Villette*—the work that was Charlotte's final draft of her personal testament.

In her poem "Preference" (#186), Charlotte's speaker had wondered if the smiling false lover imagined her "coldness" toward him to be "But a mask of frozen seeming, / Hiding secret fires from view." She had assured him that this was not the case: "Dream not that I strive to smother / Fires that inly burn for thee." But the method itself, the idea of hiding secret fires under a "mask of frozen seeming," Charlotte came to think was not a bad idea.

In July of 1838, two months after leaving Miss Wooler's on the advice of her doctor, Charlotte was making the preliminary sketch of a new type of heroine—neither a Zenobia nor a Mary, but rather a character who combined elements of both: Mary's submissive manner, Zenobia's intellectual power, and their shared capacity for strong feeling. The result was a somewhat idealized version of Charlotte herself, placed in the Angrian setting. This character she called "Miss West."[44]

The choice of name was significant, for West was Angrian code for Ireland, land of Patrick Brontë and the hot Irish temper inherited by the young Brontës. Zamorna, Mary, and Mina are all "Westerns," burning with "Western fire"—a "fervour almost wild & rude / My fathers gave me to inherit," as Charlotte phrased it in one of her poems (#133). The connections among West, Ireland, and the Brontë heritage of fiery passion are made repeatedly in Charlotte's early stories. They even account for the surname of Jane Eyre. The Brontë children owned a copy of Du Fresnay's *Geography for Youth*, which still remains in the Brontë Parsonage Museum in Haworth. It explains that the name *Ireland* is "derived from the Irish word *Hiere*, which signifies west, for this is the most western country of Europe."[45] Miss West is thus in several ways the progenitor of Jane Eyre, for the *Eyre* of Jane's name is an alternate spelling of Hiere or Eire—that is, Ireland. Critics who have found in the name Eyre such puns as *air, heir,* or *ire* may not be wrong; but in Charlotte's own mind the name's principle association was with her father's native land.[46]

Du Fresnay's geography also offers a definition of the Irish "temper,"[47] a definition that has been carefully copied out in a child's hand in pencil on a blank leaf at the back of the book. The Irish, it tells us, "are bold and courageous, haughty, quick-witted, . . . full of resentment, and violent in all their affections." Such are the "Westerns" of Charlotte's fiction.

This Miss West, a governess in the sumptuous Lonsdale household, is admired for her perfect governess bearing, her self-effacing decorum and tact. But she is a study in protective duplicity; beneath her submissive exterior beats a fiery "Irish" heart. "It is not in Society that the real character is revealed more especially when truth is so veiled by the shadow of habitual and studied reserve as it was in the present instance."

Even in the privacy of her room, "freed from disguise & restraint," she retains enough of her mask to make it seem as if her quiet aspect "could never be broken or kindled by any feeling of undue warmth," and that she had "no quick acute sensations to be wounded." Miss West knows that despite her care, her disguise of "frozen automaton" might be penetrated, that someone might guess at "those sudden, flashing fits of excitement which she could not always control." But there is no danger that the shallowly handsome Lonsdale girls will see through her, or know how low is her estimate of their vapid little passions. To them she never "betrayed the scorn that often swelled at her heart."

Miss West reappears as Elizabeth in "Captain Henry Hastings."[48] Miss West had seemed a "little dusk figure" beside the Lonsdale girls; now Elizabeth Hastings provides a "dim dusk foil" to the statuesque Jane Moore, yet, like Miss West, is far superior to her employer in intellect and spirit.

In the Hastings family the Brontës are represented under the barest disguise. Branwell is Henry Hastings, a dissolute and cowardly "Cain-like wanderer with a price upon his blood." Repudiated by his father ("an exceedingly obstinate, passionate man" is the characterization of Patrick), Henry's only friend is his loyal and talented sister Elizabeth, in whom Charlotte portrays herself.[49]

"Captain Henry Hastings" has frequently been cited as evidence that Charlotte sympathized with her brother Branwell, even in his disgrace, because in the novella we are told that though Henry is in fact "a Monster," "his sister did not think a pin the worse of him for all his Dishonour. . . . Natural affection is never rooted out."[50] But it is after all Charlotte who ascribes to Henry this monstrous character: he is not only foolishly arrogant—which Branwell may really have been—but a "murderer, an outlaw—a deserter & a traitor, mutinous & selfish & accursedly malignant." No one can help such a miserable creature, not even Elizabeth; nor does he deserve help. In fact this portrait is far more consistent with the hostility that Charlotte had felt toward Branwell since at least 1833 than with the "Natural affection" attributed to Elizabeth. Henry finally saves his own neck by informing on his friends, and departs ignominiously from the story. Elizabeth's loyalty to him is clearly not evidence of his worth but of her virtue.

In her valiant effort to help her brother, however, Elizabeth has fallen in love with a young nobleman who has been, significantly, one of her brother's chief pursuers. This Sir William Percy has seen through her mask of quiet efficiency to the unique powers of mind and imagination that lie hid within, and he is attracted to her. By way of courting, he walks with her one day to a country graveyard where he seats her upon a gravestone whose history takes us back to the abandoned-woman theme. In answer to Elizabeth's questions, William explains that this is the grave of one Rosamund Wellesley, a cousin of Zamorna's—a woman who, we learn, was beautiful like the Marys and Marinas but specifically "clever" and "sensitive" as well. Zamorna had been Rosamund's guardian and tutor, and had violated her. As William rather sardonically recounts, he "Guarded her with a vengeance and tutored her till she could construe the Art of Love at any rate." But in time "Shame and Horror" at her illicit love worked her into a delirium and she died, possibly a suicide. Elizabeth observes that since on occasion Zamorna visits her grave, it must mean that "he remembered her after she was dead." But William is no more impressed than Charlotte now seems to be by this old-style Pyrrhic victory, and says irreverently, "Oh! and that's sufficient consolation! as the Duke of Zamorna is a very fine, proud God incarnate I suppose. G–d d—n!" To which Elizabeth replies ingenuously, "The Duke of Zamorna is a sort of scoundrel from all that I ever heard of him. . . ." From "Albion and Marina" we've come a long way: Arthur is now a scoundrel, his love mere sordid womanizing; and Rosamund has died not just in hopeless devotion or the hollow expectation that at least he'll be sorry when she's dead, but rather in something near an assertive moral act. A victim of his charisma, she has nonetheless shown herself to be in some measure a woman of spirit. On her gravestone is carved the word "Resurgam"—"I shall arise."

And so she does, in effect, through Elizabeth. For literally as William and she sit on Rosamund's gravestone, William proposes to Elizabeth that *she* be *his* mistress. She has admitted that she adores him, and he counts on her "very ardent, very imaginative temperament" to help his cause. Indeed the conflict is severe: she is torn in "silent agony" between "passionate love" on the one hand and a "secret triumph" in her own rectitude on the other. But rectitude wins; and she disappears into the moonlit night saying, "Goodbye, I suppose, for ever!"—leaving William where always before the women had been left, in the churchyard among graves.[51]

It is important to recognize how this has been done. As Charlotte has taken to her self-representation some of the Zenobic qualities of intellectual power and creative gift, so she was also imagining more clearly an alternative source of parental love and approval. Her mother was dead; but might she not also arise? As Elizabeth arises from Rosamund's grave and departs her seductive lover, she resurrects within her own spirit a whole history of buried women, from Rosamund back through her fictional forebears to her source in Charlotte's sisters and mother. In Elizabeth, Charlotte has for the first time imagined a woman who shares all her own ardent yearnings, but who nonetheless resists the death-tending passion and continues on her way alone. The intellectual woman need not be unloved; she need only give up her lover. Moral rectitude may have been the weapon of Elizabeth's resistance, but it is surely not the true cause for which she struggles. That cause is survival. There is no reason, for example, why in this story William could not simply have proposed marriage rather than dishonorable union. He proposes an unacceptable union because the fiction requires a ground for righteous refusal, for the decisive departure that allows woman to escape male power.

Indeed the history of buried women that lies behind Rosamund's tomb suggests no moral distinctions: some like Mary were moral wives, some like Mina amoral mistresses who had "lost the power . . . of discerning the difference between right and wrong." But as women their fates were all the same; they had lost their identity, their "very life was swallowed up in that of another."[52] Enslaved and fettered, worshiping a false god, they had been swept into a common grave from which they now arise, resurrected by the moon-illumined action of a woman who loves passionately but refuses to relinquish her identity as the price of love. No longer need Patrick be sorry that his wife is dead. Through her daughter she has arisen to become identified with Hope and the female disciplines of courage and virtue. Resurgam!

Because the Hastings family is so transparently a fictional representation of the Brontë family, the details of its economy reveal much about Charlotte's attitude toward her brother and father. Henry's behavior in murdering his superior officer, and the hints that he "went near to become a regicide,"[53] reminds us that Charlotte attributed to her brother a patricidal impulse as one element of his generally destructive character. Though she calls Henry a "Cain-like wanderer" (p. 202), the man Henry kills is not some fraternal equal, an Abel, but "Adams," his superior officer—that is, our first father, and here the figure of paternal authority. Henry murdered Adams directly after having been told bluntly by his king, Zamorna himself, "you're a lost, worn-out broken-up scoundrel" (p. 213), a judgment the more painful because its truth could not be denied. It is hard not to feel that Charlotte's aggression against Branwell, exercised this way in her fiction ("How are the mighty fallen!" concludes her section on his dishonorable fate), gave her rare satisfaction even as it must have released again some of her rage against Patrick as "false god."[54]

Charlotte's angry impulses are thus doubly effected here—first in making the brother such a scoundrel, second in expressing through him the desire to kill the father. The only trace of these feelings in Elizabeth lies in the circumstance that the man she falls in love with, Sir William, is one of the leaders of the pack pursuing Henry, whom they "hunted down in blood at last," in William's own contented phrase (p. 222). Charlotte/Elizabeth can thus both have her aggression (Adam killed, Cain caught), yet repudiate association with it—among other ways, by refusing the love offer of William, who as Henry's captor stands last in this line of assault. To submit to William's advances would be among other things to become complicit in that male industry of death, and at the same time (as we are reminded by the presence of Rosamund Welles-ley's tomb) to lose one's own identity. "I shall arise"—but only by keeping the men at a distance, and letting them destroy themselves and one another. They are as dangerous—as morbid, indeed—as fantasy itself.

This, then, is the function of the chill casing that Charlotte was now erecting around her heroines' hot hearts. By smothering "intense emotions . . . under the diffidence of prudence & a skilful address" one prevents their "bursting forth like lava" (p. 220). It is scorn and pride—"which, after all, gave the little woman the power of valuing to their full extent her own acute perceptions and mental gifts" (p. 223)—that form the protective barrier; and we have already seen how heavily hope depends on pride.

Charlotte's depiction of Elizabeth is immensely instructive if we wish to understand how Charlotte saw herself, how she understood her powers and dangers, in the period before Brussels. Her self-estimate is a cheerful one: Elizabeth shows "the activity of an emmet," is "brisk as a bee"—terms that suggest both Charlotte's self-conscious awareness of her tiny stature and her determination to think as well of it as possible. And Elizabeth's powers of intellect and spirit are as we have already seen considerable. She has "address & lady-manners," is much admired by her pupils and their wealthy and powerful families, and soon runs a school of her own. This is of course Charlotte's wishful thinking, but all within the realm of only slightly inflated possibility.

Still, Elizabeth's superior intellect has one drawback: except for Sir William, "she had not met with a single individual equal to herself in mind, & therefore not one whom she could love" (p. 243), and here we see Charlotte's estimate of her problem, of that aspect of her character that is fraught with danger for herself. The analysis she provides of Elizabeth's "burning" desire for love is striking in that Charlotte directly associates it with Elizabeth's being cut off from the love of her brother and father. From her brother she is cut off by his degradation; more telling is that she has herself "forsaken" her father. We are told that she has turned against her father out of loyalty to her brother (read: she shared her brother's rebelliousness?) and the retaining of this distance has now become a matter of "Pride" (p. 244)—that significant term of resistance in the cause of female survival. As Charlotte yearned for her dream and Mina for her "lord," so Elizabeth yearns by day for her father (the "lonely old man in Angria") and by evening for Sir William with his "quick hawk's eye." Her shift in object is really, of course, only a shift from father to father figure, as that "hawk's eye" reveals. That eye is Zamorna's; it will return in Rochester. Its origin was in Patrick, as Charlotte saw him.[55]

In her state of ungratified desire, Elizabeth composes a song whose key words summarize Charlotte's view of her own "morbid propensity for castle-building" (p. 246). Elizabeth's images are Charlotte's, returned to in seemingly compulsive repetition. Fantasizing about Sir William, Elizabeth struggles to break the "dreamy spell." She is "chained" by her dreams; they hold her in a "trance." But even as she vows to "leave her visions / And seek life's arousing stir," she laments that her "kindled soul" may never tell its love (p. 245). In fact of course Charlotte does at last grant Elizabeth the opportunity to tell her love—"I adore you"— but only to rise above it, leaving William among the graves that would have claimed her had she remained.

While she was at work on "Captain Henry Hastings," Charlotte received and refused her first offer of marriage—a businesslike proposal from one of Ellen's brothers, the Reverend Henry Nussey. Her letters of refusal to him, and of explanation to Ellen, reveal once more both her self-estimate and the style of her romantic desires. Complacently she assures Henry of her inappropriateness for him: he should have a mild, pious wife, one whose character is not "too marked, ardent, and original." Herself he would find "romantic and eccentric" as well as "satirical and severe."[56] To Ellen she adds that she could never marry a man for whom she did not feel "adoration" (the word recalls Elizabeth's "I adore you," written at just this time). Such an easy first experience in refusing male blandishment must have been pleasantly reassuring.

Despite her talk to Ellen of "adoration," Charlotte was now no longer slave to visions of a Mina-like love—or at least she was resisting them with all her powers of Pride. In "Caroline Vernon," written right after "Captain Henry Hastings," she dissects her own sexual and romantic fantasizing in a study of young Caroline's infatuation for the much older

Zamorna, whose ward she is. Here as elsewhere, the choice of the name "Caroline," being like "Charlotte" a variation of "Charles," points to the special closeness between character and author.[57] But these days Zamorna is "a man vicious like other men" (p. 323); he is "selfish Zamorna," with "too little of the moral Greatheart in his nature" (p. 352). (St. John Rivers and Paul Emanuel will be the two "Greathearts" in Charlotte's fiction.) Near the climax of the seduction scene, Zamorna takes Caroline in his arms with a gesture whose history we know; it is the irresistible fathering gesture; "there was something protecting & sheltering about it as though he were calling her home" (p. 352). No Elizabeth Hastings, Caroline is completely overcome: "in a mind like Miss Vernon's, Conscience was feeble opposed to passion" (p. 354). And he spirits her off to "a little retreat" aptly named "Scar House" (p. 353). Its significance, and Charlotte's judgment on that significance, are unequivocal: recognizable from "Captain Henry Hastings," Scar House was once the "retreat," and its churchyard is now the grave, of Rosamund Wellesley.

It was in keeping with these rather austere estimates of the power of sexual love that Charlotte advised her friend Ellen the following year (1840) against excessive love of a husband. A woman must be able to respect her mate, but "as to intense *passion,* I am convinced that is no desirable feeling. . . ."[58] The intense passion of her own Irish heritage Charlotte had earlier condemned in a sweep of purple prose written during this period of enforced chilling; it offers a vivid account of the destiny of those "western Aristocracy" who indulge their feelings:

> They rushed with more of uncontrolled impulse into those vortices which the passions open in society, and excited a moment by the rapid reel of the waters, were presently engulfed at the centre and dragged down to darkness—hurled by boiling eddies upon flinty rocks where at last the shark death found and devoured them.[59]

The frosty surface built to protect and hide inner fires, the determination to live an active life in the world rather than to drown in erotic dreams—these had brought Charlotte considerable successes by the end of the 1830s. She received and rejected a second proposal of marriage—a sudden declaration from a young Irish curate she had barely met. The inappropriateness of both of her first two suitors led her to judge herself "certainly doomed to be an old maid." But this she claimed to have long expected: "Never mind. I made up my mind to that fate ever since I was twelve years old"—that is to say, more or less since puberty.[60] The loves of her life had been her father and her dreams: like Elizabeth Hastings she was trying to turn her back on both, and finding the liberation exhilarating if painful.

At this time the Brontë sisters were struggling to think of ways by which they might establish a school of their own. Their efforts as governesses and schoolteachers had been most unpleasant. But it would be quite another matter if the sisters could be together and control their own project. It was with a view to furthering this possibility that Charlotte and Emily departed for the Pensionnat Heger in Brussels in February 1842. There Charlotte might hope to release her inner energies without danger to her identity. She would fly, not drown, in this stimulating new element:

> Such a strong wish for wings . . .—such an urgent thirst to see—to know—to learn—something internal seemed to expand boldly for a minute—

The moment of Hope proves to be brief:

> then all collapsed and I despaired . . .—these rebellious and absurd emotions . . . I quelled . . . in five minutes.[61]

But we have seen that Charlotte had learned to follow collapse with hope and energy; and within six months of having "despaired" of reaching what she called her "promised land," she and Emily were there.

The Life Test: Brussels and After

The story of Charlotte's passionate adoration of her older, married teacher, Constantin Heger, is too familiar to need much repeating. Let me merely observe its place among the patterns we have been tracing. For their first nine-month stay in Brussels from which they returned in November 1842 at the death of their Aunt Branwell, Charlotte and Emily had one another's companionship; and Charlotte, at least, thoroughly enjoyed the somewhat childish pleasures of being "a schoolgirl, a complete schoolgirl." But from the first there were signs of danger to her identity, implicit in her pleasure in that schoolgirl role. The Mary in her makeup was stirring back to life. She likes "to submit to authority instead of exercising it," Charlotte writes Ellen; when M. Heger "is very ferocious with me I cry; that sets all things straight." The Belgian girls she begins to stigmatize with the very terms by which she had dismissed the heavily handsome Angrian beauties—they are "cold, selfish, animal, and inferior . . . and their principles are rotten to the core." These signals of self-isolation, infantilism, return to the terms of fantasy, were nonetheless merely signals during Charlotte's first stay.

But with Emily gone the second year, Charlotte's self-protective structures collapsed. Her theme could no longer be "I shall arise." Rather it had become again "I shall sink." And sink she did, in dizzying plunge. Within three months of her return to Brussels she had worked herself into a state of almost complete isolation and dependency. She could discern among the people of the school "only one or two who deserve anything like regard": these were the Hegers, and of these two Charlotte soon lost one, for she felt that Madame had turned against her in jealous dislike. Then even Monsieur, influenced by Madame (as Charlotte felt), seemed to express at least tentative disapproval. As for the rest, "I don't hate them—hatred would be too warm a feeling." In short her whole world was narrowed once again so as to focus on the bosom of one man, whose acceptance or rejection was emotional life or death to her. Outer life was at a stop—"easeful, stagnant, silent." Her letters no longer praise the joys of growth and new discovery. Most telling of all, she has fallen back into the old bondage: "It is a curious metaphysical fact that always in the evening when I am in the great dormitory alone . . . I always recur as fanatically as ever to the old ideas, the old faces, and the old scenes in the world below."[62]

Brussels, anticipated as the Promised Land, has turned out to be another Egypt, with M. Heger as the false god in whom are subsumed all the old idolatries. Marian had died when "the sunshine of those eyes which had been her idolatry" was withdrawn from her; Mary had sacreligiously begged her husband to bless her "with the forgiving light of your countenance"; now Charlotte identifies her own condition by the same biblical echo in her report of Heger's supposed disapproval: "he has . . . withdrawn the light of his countenance."[63] Interestingly it was Charlotte's increasing self-isolation that by her own account evoked these signs of disapproval from her "master."

Emily Brontë and Mary Taylor both recognized the state of hypochondria into which Charlotte had sunk. Emily's trenchant (and early) observation concerning her sister's condition suggests no suspicion that Heger might be causing the problem: clearly she saw it more as a familiar pattern in Charlotte herself. "If you would go over for half a year," Emily suggested dryly to Ellen Nussey, "perhaps you might be able to bring her back with you, otherwise she might vegetate there till the age of Methuselah for mere lack of courage to face the voyage."[64] Charlotte's own letters, and such evidence as her French *devoirs* provide,[65] suggest that her self-diagnosis at the time was that she missed family and home.

Mary Taylor would not have had reason to think of Heger as a contributing cause unless Charlotte told her he was,[66] yet she clearly saw Charlotte's morbid stagnation and wrote her from Germany a letter that essentially commanded her home.

This command—the voice of a "mother"?—Charlotte finally obeyed. Significantly she departed with considerable confidence in M. Heger's continuing friendship for her. To Ellen she wrote shortly after returning:

> I think, however long I live, I shall not forget what the parting with M. Heger cost me; it grieved me so much to grieve him, who has been so true, kind, and disinterested a friend.[67]

The four letters that survive of those Charlotte wrote to M. Heger over the next two years make painful reading. Almost at once she seems to have presumed on his friendship with a show of feeling that she later acknowledged was inappropriate *("peu raisonnable")*—but the letter in which this excess occurred does not survive, so we may not judge it for ourselves. What do survive are four subsequent letters attesting to her increasingly frantic need and final bitterness, as Monsieur ceased answering her at all.

The first of these letters, dated July 14, 1844, is determinedly vigorous and cheerful. The second, dated October 24, 1844, is brief—she had just learned of an opportunity to send a letter with a friend who can also bring back an answer: be it ever so brief, her "master" must report on his health and that of his family and school. The third, dated January 8, 1845, expresses anger and hurt. It begins by observing that her friend has returned and brought no word from him: how has she deserved this? Heger may disapprove of her for having "black thoughts," but she is dying of emotional starvation: "If my master withdraws his friendship from me entirely I shall be altogether without hope." The poor, she says in humble analogy, ask only "crumbs" of the "rich man's table"; refused even these, they die of hunger.

Her final letter, dated November 18, 1845, refers to an intervening one of May, which has not survived. Possibly M. Heger also wrote briefly to her at that time, if this is the meaning of her comment that "Your last letter was stay and prop to me—nourishment to me for half a year." If he were separated from one of his children, wouldn't he want news, she suggestively asks. She recognizes her bondage and has struggled against it: "It's humiliating—not to be able to master one's own thoughts, to be slave to a regret, a memory, slave to a dominant and fixed idea that tyrannizes over the spirit." But the fact remains that for her, her master's letters are "life." Without them, she withers away *("je déperis")*.

It was at this moment that Charlotte lighted on Emily's notebook of poems; Hope's rainbow blazed over the dark waters; the indomitable woman in Charlotte surfaced again. Resurgam!

Yet recovery was less the function of chance circumstance than this account might suggest. Charlotte certainly recognized her own symptoms of hypochondria and she knew the prescription for cure. The collapse in Brussels and afterwards had perhaps been her worst, the one in which fantasy was most deeply rooted in the ground of external reality: Heger was a real man, with real feelings and failings. But the isolation in Brussels, the morbid and enervating dependency on unrealizable dreams, the idolatrous worship of a false god—a god who swallows up the votary, or leaves her to sink into nonbeing—all of these Charlotte had experienced before, and had repeatedly depicted. And from the depths of hypochondria she had emerged before, with brother-father-lover–repudiating energy. Though she had now sunk again, she would arise stronger than ever. One might even suspect that she provoked Heger with her letter *"peu raisonnable"* into the restraint and silence that were necessary to his fulfilling the role of false god who must be thrown down. That he apparently acted his role all too well was certainly anguishing for Charlotte, but it also fueled the rage, the sense of injustice, that she seemed to require in order to marshal her mother-power and loosen her bonds.

Her gradual reemergence into life and strength is recorded in a series of poems undated, but certainly begun in Brussels and ending near the time of her discovery of Emily's poems. Their immediate subject is her relationship to Heger; but the emotional substance, the diction, the imagery, even the plot—the familiar sinking and rising—are woven of strands that wind back into her very earliest work.

The first of these poems, written in a Brussels exercise book, Charlotte employed with only slight revision as Frances' poem in *The Professor*. It is significant as expressing Charlotte's fantasy of what she would have wished for from M. Heger in the best of all possible worlds.[68] As always, what Charlotte wants is both paternal love and the "laurel-wreath." But she had believed at least since 1830 that these two were mutually contradictory for a woman, and so they prove also for the "Jane" of this poem. No sooner has she won the laurel than she must give up the tender relationship:

> The strong pulse of Ambition struck
>   In every vein I owned;
> At the same instant, bleeding broke
>   A secret, inward wound.

This is the wound of loss—the pain of the parting that is necessary to female survival, as in Elizabeth Hastings' "Goodbye, I suppose, for ever!"[69] In the poem from *The Professor* Jane's anguished "master" embraces her, invokes God's guardianship over "my foster-child," and tells her that "when deceived, repulsed, opprest" she must "Come home to me again!" Thus the fantasy expressed by the poem is that of achieved laurels coupled with an offer of love that is flattering but will be courageously foregone.

But Charlotte's own situation differed from those of Elizabeth Hastings and the Jane of this poem in two crucial ways. First, Charlotte had in fact achieved no special "laurel." M. Heger appears indeed to have discouraged as impractical any hopes she might have had of becoming a writer. Second, Heger had offered no proposition that she could ringingly reject; there were letters to be written and received, and reasonable expectations of other kinds. The Hegers had even spoken of sending their children to the Brontë sisters' school, should they succeed in establishing one. The tight logic of gain and loss, of achieved ambition and relinquished love, was in this case worked out in art before it was worked out in life.

Then Charlotte's offending letter brought the silence that activated the next step in Charlotte's progress: in face of Heger's silence she was forced to call on her own energies and denounce her former idol as a false god.

> Idolater I kneeled to an idol cut in rock!
>   I might have slashed my flesh and drawn my heart's
>   best blood,
> The granite God had felt no tenderness no shock
>   My Baal had nor seen nor heard nor understood.
>
> . . . Now Heaven heal the wound . . . (#210)

The granite God, the Baal alluded to here, is of course Heger refusing her starving appeals for "crumbs" from his rich table. But the striking image recurs in *Villette*, where it is applied not to the Heger character (M. Paul), but to "Creative Impulse," a deity which, like Heger and his prototypes,

> would not hear when appealed to . . . but would stand, all
> cold, all indurated, all granite, a dark Baal with carven lips and
> blank eye-balls, and breast like the stone face of a tomb.

This is an embedded recollection of the enchaining "mighty phantasm"
of the Roe Head years, from whom Charlotte was turning in her search
for her true muse, the inner "Genius" that would not enslave her energies, but feed, liberate, and redeem them.

The next poem in this sequence of recovery repeats one stanza and
some of the argument of the much earlier poem "Reason," but places the
speaker's thoughts in a dramatic context that distances them from Charlotte's own voice: this poem she published in 1846 under the title "Frances"—
the name she would shortly give to her heroine in *The Professor*. The
poem asks: how can one "forever" keep to the mask strategy employed
by such earlier heroines as Miss West and Elizabeth Hastings—"With
outward calm mask inward strife"? To Frances, the entire outer universe
seems like a granite God—dumb, deaf, and blind—so that all life seems
to be confined to the single dark "cell" of her own mind. She is in effect
"diving into thought," and she asks whether when she dies there will
only be such nothingness as the poem "Diving" had envisioned: "the
blank of lost identity? / Erasure of both pain and bliss?" But then the
"mother" appears: perhaps one may after all find "hope." On this cue
the poem expands to consider the complex possibilities of hope. The
hope of being loved was mere "thin illusion"; her "lover" has grown
careless and cool, and gone "self-contained and calm, away." She must
seek a different kind of hope. "Though lightning-struck, I must live on,"
she concludes, in imagery that looks forward to *Jane Eyre*. Instead of
dwelling on her misery, she will look ahead. In her adaptation of Shelley's "Adonais" Charlotte had imagined herself drifting off into dark
waters where "Never a beacon burns on the deep." But now, as she
repudiates thoughts of "death" and seeks life again, the missing beacon
returns: "I see a nearer beacon gleaming / Over dejection's sea of gloom"
and that "beacon" is the confidence that "I yet have innate force"—it is
"Pride," the internal ally of the beaming goddess "Hope." She will
permit no more delusive dreams: "Of God alone, and self-reliance, / I
ask for solace," and on this rising note the poem ends. *God alone, and
self-reliance*: these are the twin solaces that will finally be accorded to
Lucy Snowe.

The final poem of this series is an astonishing three-part revenge
melodrama published in 1846 under the title "Gilbert" (#185). It provides the fullest and most explicit statement of the drowning woman

theme in all Charlotte's work. An angry indictment of M. Heger, it attributes to him gross misbehavior of a kind for which no known evidence exists, but the thought of which evidently gave Charlotte comfort. In this poem betrayed woman gets even at last.[70]

In part 1—"The Garden," set recognizably in the Pensionnat Heger in Brussels—Gilbert enjoys, even more than Zamorna had, "the triumph of a selfish heart." Complacently he savors the memory of his unnamed admirer's devotion:

> . . . 'She loved me more than life;
>   And truly it was sweet
> To see so fair a woman kneel,
>   In bondage, at my feet.'

The adored man is here explicitly responsible for woman's bondage, her tendency to helpless worship. Although "I knew myself no perfect man / Nor as she deemed divine," still when her vigorous imagination imputed to him perfections that he did not have, and "sanctified" his "sensual frame of flesh," he willingly took advantage of her error—and of herself:

> . . . like a god did I descend
>   At last, to meet her love;
> And, like a god, I then withdrew
>   To my own heaven above.

But as Gilbert thinks these mean things, revealing his selfish arrogance and hard heart, he is briefly but palpably shaken by a "nervous thought," so intense that it shakes even the tree against which he is leaning. Appalled but unrepentant, he hurries back into the house.

Part 2, "The Parlor," pictures Gilbert some time later, at ease indoors, surrounded by his handsome wife and happy children. Suddenly what had been in part 1 a mere nervous jolt takes on the weight and complexity of a sustained visionary experience, such that "His fireside chair shakes with the start / That shook the garden tree," and he feels himself engulfed by churning seawater, amid which there floats before his eyes a shape familiar from so many of Charlotte's juvenile poems and stories:

> A woman drowned—sunk in the deep,
>   On a long wave reclining;
> The circling water's crystal sweep
>   Like glass, her shape enshrining[.]

Her dead face still bearing its expression of anguish, the body floats "So near, he could have touched the spray" of her pillow. Then, as inexplicably as it had come, the vision departs among turbid strands of seaweed and broken timber. "All was gone—gone like a mist," and Gilbert is once more amid his family. But the man is without ruth. By no means sorry the woman is dead, he is instead quite relieved. Dead, she cannot betray him. His reputation will be safe, his compromising behavior in having caused such woe will be hidden.

This lady-killer is too churlish, then, even to feel guilty. But part 3, "The Welcome Home," enforces the penalty that his conscience had declined. For ten years Gilbert has been enjoying increasing worldly success; but one night when he returns home late, expecting the embrace of his family, he is instead greeted at the door by an avenging phantom —a woman clad in white, with hollow eyes and seaweed in her hair.

> Lo! water from her dripping dress
> Runs on the streaming floor . . .

Charlotte had several thoughts about the conclusion. In one manuscript version Gilbert's "tide of life" simply "stopped," and he was found dead in the morning.[71] But in the version she finally printed, he kills himself, as the rejection-crazed Zenobia had once predicted Zamorna would do.

> And thus died, by a shameful death,
> A wise and worldly man,
> Who never drew but selfish breath
> Since first his life began.

This poem must have given Charlotte a good deal of satisfaction, its revenge is so naked and the terms of it so fully appropriate to her own imaginative system. Apparently it freed her—or marked the occasion of her freeing herself. For one thing, the Maria who drowned herself in the "fairy sea" of 1836 (#115) has finally turned her rage outward onto her "faithless love" and slaughtered the brute—or better yet, got him to slaughter himself. As in "Captain Henry Hastings," Charlotte lets the men do their own bloody business. No need to kill the woman-drowning father; let him do the job himself.

The punitive last portion of "Gilbert" is worked out in its several versions in a German notebook. This notebook Charlotte now put to a telling set of uses: the "Gilbert" drafts are followed by a rather polished draft of the poem that she later inserted in *The Professor*. That poem provides a kind of emotional synopsis of the novel in which it will be placed. This draft of the "Professor" poem is then followed by a series of hints and notes, embracing material that will surface in each of her later novels. Among these are names that appear in *The Professor* (Lucia,

Yorke) and in *Jane Eyre* (Gateshead, Eliza, Georgiana, even a "Mr. R."); then there is mention of "Coriolanus," title of a chapter of *Shirley;* and even figures who will appear in *Villette* (Pauline and "R. C. Priest"). At this moment Charlotte's energies are reaching vigorously outward and forward.

Thus the discovery of Emily's poems, though it certainly shaped the immediate direction of Charlotte's energies, had already been thoroughly prepared for. With the discovery itself, Charlotte sprang forward into renewed life.

✺ FOUR

The Professor, Jane Eyre, Shirley

"Of all things, herself seemed to herself the centre . . . , a spark of soul, emitted inadvertent from the great creative source, and now burning un-marked to waste in the heart of a black hollow. She asked, was she thus to burn out and perish, her living light doing no good, never seen, never needed, —a star in an else starless firmament, —which nor shepherd, nor wanderer, nor sage, nor priest, tracked as a guide, or read as a prophecy?"

—from *Shirley,* "La Premiere Femme Savante"

The Professor: Sex Roles and Gender

Charlotte's work with her sisters in getting out their joint volume of poems still left her time to undertake her first novel specifically conceived and intended for publication— *The Professor.* In her "Author's Preface" Charlotte characterized the progress of her thoughts on literary method: "I had got over any such taste as I might once have had for ornamental and redundant composition, and come to prefer what was plain and homely." Her work would now stick close to the unadorned realities of life—pursue no more Angrian sunsets, worship no more false gods.

But the novel nonetheless mixes fantasy with fact in suggestive and revealing ways. Its immediate topic was Charlotte's Brussels experience, but with a twist: for Charlotte here casts herself in a double role.[1] She is both halves of the couple whose love story the novel tells: both William Crimsworth and Frances Henri. William is a young Englishman who goes to teach English in Brussels at a school whose male and female divisions are directed by a M. Pelet and Mlle. Reuter. At the school William falls in love with a young pupil-teacher, Frances Henri, and, despite the jealous interventions of Mlle. Reuter (a fictionalized Mme. Heger), he eventually marries her. Together they run a successful school and finally return to England, where they have a son and live in a vine-covered cottage retreat.

William Crimsworth is lineal descendent of the Sir William who propositioned Elizabeth Hastings, and retains something of the edgy arrogance inherited from their joint forefather, Charles Wellesley, Charlotte's earliest mouthpiece and by extension still her narrator in this novel. But he now expands to include also certain elements of M. Heger, in being Frances' beloved "master" who fulfills Charlotte's wishful fantasy of being loved by her Belgian teacher. This "master" does not send away his gifted pupil, but rather repudiates all connection with her rival, Mlle. Reuter, seeks out the bereaved Frances at the grave of the aunt who had been a mother to her, and—in a marked new development for Charlotte—takes her to his heart forever.

Frances, in turn, descends from Miss West and Elizabeth Hastings. Miss West had been a "little dusk figure" beside her showy pupils; Elizabeth Hastings was a "dim dusk foil" to hers. As humble lace mender Frances Henri is at first an even more downtrodden and shadowy figure than they; but like them she harbors brilliant inner fires, and under William's encouraging support her fires kindle and flash even more than Miss West's or Elizabeth's had done.

The novel opens in a thinly disguised Angrian setting, with characters recognizable even by name: the brothers Edward and William Crimsworth are the old Edward and William Percy. Even the Angrian Percy's minion Timothy Steighton is present in this novel as Edward Crimsworth's minion of the same name; and William's odd friend, the hostile yet protective truth teller Hunsden Yorke Hunsden, descends from the prophetic Warner Howard Warner of Angria. (Hunsden and Warner, and later Mr. Yorke of *Shirley,* are all modeled to some extent on Mary Taylor's father, whose family business at the Hunsworth Mills contributed to the names of both Hunsden and Crimsworth.)

The grinding oppression under which William struggles in the opening chapters loosely parallels Charlotte's hard years as teacher and governess, when the sense that she was doing her duty was her only real-life pleasure. As if in reference to this autobiographical period, Crimsworth is said to appear "weary, solitary, kept-down—like some desolate tutor or governess";[2] he even compares his situation to that of the Israelites enslaved in Egypt. But William's departure for Brussels and his job at the Pensionnat are drawn far more literally from Charlotte's life, with details changed only as necessary to account for the shift in gender. Doubtless partly because he is male and must incorporate elements of M. Heger, William is never a student in Brussels, as Charlotte herself had been; he is teacher only, and the role of pupil is assigned to Frances.

Ever since childhood Charlotte had been interested in exploring the implications of gender reversal—not only in assuming as author a male persona, but also in assigning character and role within her fictions. Charlotte seems to have been probing the problem of how gender relates to fate: must it always be the women who are swallowed up? Could Zamorna, with all his dangerous glamour, take female form? Before going any farther into *The Professor,* we must glance briefly at the history of Charlotte's interest in this question. Its issues are central to all her mature work.

To the early love story of Zamorna and his first wife, Marian, Charlotte attached a curious plot complication whose main purpose seems to have been to test the boundaries of gender. In "The Secret,"[3] written in November 1833, we learn that there had been a childhood engagement between Marian and a third Percy brother, Henry, whom Charlotte apparently invented for this purpose. Marian and young Henry had not been in love; their engagement was rather the result of youthful friendship and the dying wishes of their mothers. Accordingly, when Henry was drowned at sea three years later in the wreck of *The Mermaid* (a ship commanded by the same Steighton who appears in *The Professor*), Marian felt regret at his death, but no deep loss. And soon thereafter she fell passionately in love for the first and only time of her life—or course with Zamorna. Just as plans for their marriage were going forward, however, Marian was told that her youthful fiancé was not dead after all, and the marriage was held up until Henry's wraith appeared supernaturally, assured her that he really was dead, and released her from all obligation. Of the several wraiths to appear in Charlotte's stories after "Albion and Marina," Henry's most nearly prefigures that of the drowned woman in "Gilbert" (like hers, Henry's rises "wet and dripping" from the sea). But Henry's message is helpful rather than vengeful: "fear not that I shall return. Death and the waters of a vast deep chain me to my place; be happy and think of your first love no more." To be sure, Henry had no grounds for vengeance: Marian had neither seduced nor abandoned him. She did not even meet Zamorna until well after *The Mermaid* had gone down with her young betrothed. Still, Marian's new attachment bears implicitly on Henry's fate; and her metaphoric destiny (ocean tomb and sea-sand pillow) mirrors his literal one.

Charlotte finished "The Secret" in 1833; but apparently she felt that she had not yet finished exploring the implications of Henry's story, for in 1834 she returned to the topic in a long poem entitled "Stanzas on the Fate of Henry Percy" (#95).[4] In this new, expanded version, Marian is still not explicitly responsible for Henry's death. But her passion for Zamorna is now directly implicated, and the narrator assures Henry that she will suffer just as he has:

> . . . thy love, so strong, so unreturned,
>   Shall be avenged, on earth her time is brief
> The radiant Form, for whom, her spirit burned
>   Shall smile awhile then leave her bowed with grief[.]

Near the end of the poem Charlotte shifts her meter to signal a shift in narrative perspective. Henry is now dead, and the speaker addresses us rather than him: Henry "never from that vision woke," we are told; "coral banks" now "pillow" his head, and "tangled seaweeds wet with brine / Are garlanding his hair." Although "how he died no tongue can tell," still "dark . . . rumors" suggest that Percy, Henry's "awful father!" may have had Steighton kill the boy. Meanwhile Henry's rival in love, the successful Zamorna, basks in public adulation. In familiar figure, he is a wild and stormy but "enkindling" power.

Marian is in this poem less an independent agent than a middle figure caught between the two men. As she is swept by "passion's waves of conflict" in her love of Zamorna, Henry in turn drowns loving her. But the critical point has been established: men as well as women may drown in love. And this point is reinforced by the water imagery that consistently links love with death. Marian's eyes shine "like mirrored stars that glassed in dark waves lie"; her love for Henry disappears in the "rapid burning tide / That flows" from Zamorna's eyes. And of course the implications of stormy and engulfing water are literalized in Henry's drowning. The narrative hints that it was the sight of Marian's defection that really killed Henry: having once envisioned her burning for the "radiant form" of Zamorna, Henry "never from that vision woke." But Percy too may have had a hand in it. A father figure's treachery would be for Charlotte an entirely consistent element of the emotional blow of loss.

That Henry's ship is called *The Mermaid* is a point of central significance to this issue of gender inversion. As early as 1830 Charlotte had written in a poem titled "A Serenade" (#57) of the dangerous mermaid whose "still, sad music"—not "of humanity," as in Wordsworth, but of inhumanity—lures sailors to their death:

> It is the maiden of the sea, that sings within her cell . . .
> And when her, monstrous form is seen swift-gliding o'er the
>   deep
> The Blood within the sailors veins, in frozen streams doth
>   creep[.]

This same mermaid is still a topic in *Shirley*, when Shirley and Caroline, planning a voyage, imagine encountering some mermaid with a "preternatural lure in its wily glance." "Were we men," Shirley observes, "we should spring at the sign, the cold billow would be dared for the sake of the colder enchantress; . . . Temptress terror! monstrous likeness of ourselves!" Caroline objects that the mermaid is "not like us: we are neither temptresses, nor terrors, nor monsters"; but Shirley reminds her that "Some of our kind, it is said, are all three. There are men who ascribe to 'woman,' in general, such attributes."[5] In her lethal attractiveness the mermaid is Charlotte's version of a female Zamorna; this is her meaning in Henry Percy's story, where *The Mermaid* bears Henry to his love death. But her added association in *Shirley* with the gentle Caroline, whose hair is "long as a mermaid's" (p. 112) and whose face is in the mermaid "style" (p. 276), suggests that Charlotte thought that any woman, even the least offensive, might have some mermaid characteristics.

The mermaid as dangerous siren stands for men's fear-induced misapprehension of women; Charlotte has Shirley assert that even "the acutest men are often under an illusion about women . . . they misapprehend them, both for good and evil: their good woman is a queer thing, half doll, half angel; their bad woman almost always a fiend" (p. 395). But mermaids also represent a certain truth about women. Women provide within their own bodies the amniotic sea that we all left behind in being born. The man who is lured to his death by a mermaid is in effect lured by woman-as-mother, in whom reside both the ocean of his origins and the life-long model of all his objects of sexual desire. His watery plunge, and the consequent loss of masculine separateness that he undergoes in responding to the mermaid's seductive appeal, is the male analogue of the infantilization and loss of identity that Charlotte feared from the submerging embrace of the false father.

We may pursue the parallel even further. As the male God redeems man from eternal death in the great "mother" whose dangers the mermaid emblemizes, so for Charlotte the female Divinity—Hope, the moon-mother, etc.—helps woman defend herself from the seductive father. Recall Zamorna's siren call to Caroline Vernon: "he knew how to give a tone, an accent . . .which should produce ample effect . . . — there was something protecting & sheltering about it as though he were calling her home." He is calling her in fact to his fatherly bosom and her doom. "When Zamorna kissed her & said in that voice of fatal sweetness . . . 'Will you go with me,' " Caroline, lacking a mothering conscience, is as lost as any succumbing sailor at sea.[6]

This dark version of the family romance is dramatized at least twice in *The Professor*. Just after William has wooed and won his cherished pupil, he falls briefly but helplessly prey to "hypochondria." As Charlotte associated woman's experience of hypochondria with being folded in the submerging bosom of an infantilizing father-lover, so William's hypochondria is personified as a woman who takes him "to her death-cold bosom" and holds him "with arms of bone." Though no mermaid, this figure is symbolically related: a "sorceress," she draws William to the brink of death's "black, sullen river." Because what she embodies is Charlotte's fear that the sexual plunge taken in marriage may be fatal, William rightly sees his hypochondria as the rival of his love: "I repulsed her as one would a dreaded and ghastly concubine coming to embitter a husband's heart towards his young bride." It may be that she frightens rather than attracts William partly because (though a man) he has already seen and been strengthened by the goddess Hope.

In another startling image Frances too encounters the pull of a love that is crossed with death. Having just agreed to marry her beloved "maître," she pauses in rapt contentment: "as stirless in her happiness as a mouse in its terror" (p. 224). What terrifies her, of course, is the possibility that she has gained her heart's desire at the price of being swallowed up. She weeps at the approach of her wedding; more ominously, perhaps, she shows herself after it "as docile as a well-trained child" (p. 247). It is her attendant capacity for "firmness"—chiefly shown in her insistence on retaining her professional occupation—that saves her from a Mary's fate.

Charlotte's interest in gender inversions, her awareness that both sexes may be seduced as well as seducing, helps explain why in *The Professor* she appropriates the roles of both male and female protagonists. She was struggling to imagine a sexual relationship in which both members might prosper; in which, because both are versions of herself, neither need be a "siren" luring the other to doom. As William is Charlotte's persona, a version of the voice she had been using for years, so the name "Frances" too emphasizes the ambiguities of gender—especially so since the M. Pelet who marries Frances' rival, Mlle. Reuter, is named "François" (p. 110). And Frances Henri's surname is of course a link back to Henry Percy. Although in her effort to make William convincingly masculine Charlotte attributed to him characteristics that are traditional in her domineering males—overbearing aloofness, touches of sadism— she studied the characteristics from the inside, providing motivation, exploring, as if it were her own, the need or desire out of which such behavior might arise. William flings open the classroom door and strides in masterfully just the way M. Paul will. But William offers a practical reason: "I had found that in entering with aplomb . . . consisted the grand secret of assuring immediate silence" (p. 118). He takes on the hard and indifferent character of "a rigid pillar of stone" not because it is innate to him as it will be to Brocklehurst, but in response to Mlle. Reuter's behavior: "Servility creates despotism" (p. 129).

Several critics have remarked on the feminine imagery that attaches to William. Not only is he "kept down like some desolate tutor or governess," a detail from Charlotte's own experience, but there are several slips into gender-inappropriate metaphor, as when Hunsden remarks that "Any woman, sinking her shaft deep enough, will at last reach a fathomless spring of sensibility in thy breast, Crimsworth" (p. 93), or when Mlle. Reuter's addresses to him are couched in the figurative language of male seduction or rape: "her finger, essaying, proving every atom of the casket—touched its secret spring, and for a moment—the lid sprung open, she laid her hand on the jewel within . . ." (p. 105).

In *The Professor* Charlotte's pattern of sinking and rising is experienced by both William and Frances. Frances' experience is given in two versions: it is encapsulated in the poem ostensibly written by Frances, said to be "not exactly the writer's own experience," but suggested by "portions of that experience" (p. 217), and it is recounted in the plot. The poem was actually, of course, Charlotte's own wish-fulfilling fantasy, composed on leaving Brussels and later published among her poems under the title "Master and Pupil" (#205). In the poem the young speaker "Jane" falls ill at a school closely modeled on the Pensionnat Heger; but when visited at her bed by her beloved Professor, who places his hand on hers "with gentle stress" and says "God—she *must* revive!" she feels "The sense of Hope" begin its "healing work." Then as she convalesces the Professor continues to show a tender solicitude for her, and when at the end of the poem she must depart, he urges his "foster child" to "come home to me again." Thus as Jane sinks, her Professor is a mothering figure bringing hope (another gender inversion, of course, and as such it looks forward to the healing role of Caroline's mother in *Shirley*), even as he also offers the fatherly "home" that Charlotte's heroines have been learning to refuse in the interests of survival and achievement.

The other version of Frances' rising is an alternate wish fulfillment. She sinks in having lost all who love her: her aunt has died, her rival has dismissed her from the job that gave access to her Master, whom she expects never to see again. In her despair, she retreats to the fetal harbor of the graveyard "nook" where her aunt lies buried. There William discovers her and raises her into the sunshine of love, work, and a happy marriage.

This time Charlotte's old opposition between love and achievement is partly resolved by the fact that William is less a "father" than a male version of the author. But it is resolved only partly; for Frances is the *female* version of the author, and Frances splits in two after her marriage. "I seemed to possess two wives," marvels William. The first is the achieving "Madame the Directress" of their school, "a stately and elegant woman, bearing much anxious thought on her large brow," but the second—a lovable, adoring little pupil—takes her place at six o'clock. "I then came home, for my home was my heaven—ever at that hour, as I entered our private sitting-room—the lady-directress vanished from before my eyes, and Frances Henri, my own little lace-mender, was magically restored to my arms; much disappointed she would have been if her master had not been as constant to the tryste as herself" (pp. 251–52). Frances is in fact Charlotte's first heroine to keep alive both her sexuality and her intellectual ambition. The cost is high—a compartmentalization that verges on dissolution. But the gain is crucial too.

William's experience of sinking and rising provides the novel's basic story line. He is first rather attracted to Mlle. Reuter but then meets the far worthier Frances and begins to take joy in her—the first real joy he has known in life. But suddenly she disappears; and William compares his loss and prospect of recovery with that greatest falling and rising, death and resurrection. Then he finds Frances in the graveyard nook, recognizes their mutual love, and sees the goddess "Hope." Here complications enter, in the form of additional variations on the theme of collapse and recovery. These variations seem necessary not to the plot but to the author, allowing her to recur to favorite themes.

The first of these variations is William's odd encounter with hypochondria, which we have discussed already. But more curious by far is William's relationship with his friend Hunsden, who now returns to the story. Hunsden is another ambiguous parent figure—hostile and teasing, but ultimately supportive. Though modeled in part on Mary Taylor's father, Hunsden is (like his handwriting) "neither masculine nor exactly feminine" (p. 192). As observed earlier, his Angrian original was the religious and prophetic Warner Howard Warner, who had actually been called a hermaphrodite. Hunsden's return to the story is initiated by a compressed allusion to the Old and New Testament themes of Egyptian bondage and Christian salvation. He warns of his approaching visit with a letter in which he teasingly imagines William "sitting like a black-haired, tawny-skinned, long-nosed Iraselite by the flesh-pots of Egypt," and tells his friend to be ready for him: "Be on the look-out, for you know neither the day nor hour when your ——— (I don't wish to blaspheme, so I'll leave a blank) cometh" (p. 193). The unspoken "Redeemer" is part Hunsden himself, part the gift that he brings—a portrait of William's mother, which William has longed for but never hoped to possess, and which Hunsden makes him "pay" for through a species of humiliating teasing. Here, as throughout the novel, Hunsden is characterized by a strange perversity, evident here in both the near-blasphemy and the combination of kindness with cruelty. But perhaps this perversity, too, may be explained as a function of Charlotte's experiments with gender. The hero and heroine of *The Professor* are both explicitly parentless. Hunsden seems meant to fulfill the roles of a mother who supports and urges forward and a masculinely tough and satiric father. Thus he catapults William somewhat roughly out of the Egyptian slavery of Edward's millworks (like a masculine mother) and later descends on him bearing his mother's portrait, as a "Redeemer" (like a female father). In all of this Hunsden is not a very successful creation, but Charlotte's conception of him was certainly ambitious.

We can see the way William and Frances each reflect Charlotte's view of her own self and history. William represents Charlotte not only in that he is the oppressed "slave" of his brother, and then a teacher in the Pensionnat schoolroom; but also in his physical similarity to his sadly sensitive dead mother, in his susceptibility to hypochondria, in his vision of the goddess "Hope." In short, even though William is a man, he speaks from Charlotte's experience, both inner and outer.[7]

Frances, meanwhile, has Charlotte's gender as well as her small stature and delicate features; she is literally banished (as Charlotte had felt figuratively banished) by a powerful rival for her "master's" heart (Zoriade Reuter is an unflattering portrait of Zoë Parent, M. Heger's wife). Frances' difficulties in achieving authority as a teacher were evidently Charlotte's; she offers her "master" the "charms" that Charlotte felt she could offer Heger—"application, love of knowledge, natural capacity, docility, truthfulness, gratefulness" (p. 120)—and, like Charlotte, she differs from the Belgian girls in being "of a race less gifted with fulness of flesh and plenitude of blood, less jocund, material, unthinking" (p. 122). Like Charlotte, Frances knows the power of her intellectual gift. Though she does not respond in words to her teacher's praise, her "radiance" and "frank and flashing glance" communicate the self-confidence of genius, something Charlotte herself must often have felt: "Do you think I am myself a stranger to myself? What you tell me in terms so qualified, I have known fully from a child" (p. 137). And, as Charlotte had regarded Belgium so Frances regards England as "the promised land." Like Charlotte, "a little affection, ever so little, pleased her better than all the panegyrics in the world" (p. 147). Like Charlotte she feared for her eyesight (p. 191). And finally, the fact that Frances has no real home, but lives in "Rue Notre Dame aux Neiges" (the Street of Our Lady of the Snows), looks forward to the virginal Lucy Snowe into whom Frances will develop in Charlotte's final novel.

But the mutual growth of love between Frances and her "master"; their rediscovery of one another, after cruelly imposed separation, at a "mother's" grave; the calm courtship, happy marriage, successful joint careers—all of these are the stuff of Charlotte's wishful fantasy, even though muted to the terms of what she imagined to be workaday marital realism.[8]

The marriage of William and Frances is thus at one level a model of the marriage Charlotte dreamed she might have had with Heger, had Fate only arranged things differently. But at a deeper level—the level of her profoundest hopes and fears—this is no marriage at all, but rather a metaphor for the union of elements within Charlotte herself, of her male narrator and female self-representation. The way is prepared for Jane Eyre, the first of Charlotte's heroines to write her own life.

Jane Eyre: Marriage and the Missionary

By taking this new step of making her female self-representation the author of her own narrative, Charlotte was bound to raise more sharply than ever before the question of the muse. How was Charlotte now to express her muse? How represent within the narrative her relationship to her own artistic vocation? The answer was: with deep ambivalence. That ambivalence leaves its mark on the shape of the novel, and especially on its last chapters.

Readers have long differed about the success of *Jane Eyre's* ending. The following balanced pair of critical judgments demonstrate the problem.

In a perceptive essay entitled "Jane Eyre: The Temptations of a Motherless Woman,"[9] Adrienne Rich sees Jane's marriage to Rochester as a moral and aesthetic triumph. It is "not a patriarchal marriage in the sense of a marriage that stunts and diminishes the woman; but a continuation of this woman's creation of herself." In an equally perceptive essay entitled "The Brontës, or, Myth Domesticated,"[10] Richard Chase sees the novel's conclusion instead as a collapse of the sexual and intellectual vitality of the book into maudlin domestic stasis; "a relatively mild and ordinary marriage is made after the spirit of the masculine universe is controlled or extinguished." To translate back into the terms of Charlotte's life-long dilemma, Adrienne Rich is celebrating the success of the woman who needed Patrick's love: she has gotten it, and on her own terms. No perishing Mary or Mina, Jane can affirm: "I am my husband's life as fully as he is mine."[11] This is indeed a triumph of the female imagination, both in the historical context of the 1840s and even more poignantly in the personal context of Charlotte's own experience. But Richard Chase is right, too, in recognizing that something has been lost. Not only has the masculine Rochester been fettered like the caged eagle to which Jane compares him, but Jane too has radically narrowed the range of her ambitions. Where is the girl who had longed at Lowood for "Liberty, Excitement, Enjoyment," knowing "that the real world was wide, and that a varied field of hopes and fears, of sensations and excitements, awaited those who had courage to go forth into its expanse" (p. 100)? Where is the young woman who had at Thornfield "longed for a power of vision which might . . . reach the busy world, towns, regions full of life" (p. 132)? Where is the visionary artist who could capture in paint the landscape of her author's own creative imagination—the woman drowned, the Evening Star, the polar visage of death? This dynamic spirit was the "wild, free thing" (p. 405) that Rochester had earlier failed to capture. What he gets, however, and what Jane too gets, is something whose tone is quite different. All Jane's insight, excitement, and ambition now come to focus on the single point of her marriage: a happy marriage, as Adrienne Rich has said, but nonetheless one in which both members are rather quenched and muted. Not only Rochester is tamed; Jane too has lost the soaring energy that Richard Chase called "masculine" and whose departure he decried.

The energy is gone at the end because Charlotte's muse is gone. Forced (as she felt) to choose between a mate and a muse, between being loved by Patrick and being like him, in this novel Charlotte emphatically chooses the mate, the love. And the muse suffers accordingly. The muse and his call—which Charlotte now saw as a call to celibate commitment, to a necessarily loveless priesthood of art—must be repudiated by this heroine and her author. But the rebuffed muse takes his revenge on the novel's ending. To understand how he does this, why the ending stirs such contradictory responses, we must race several threads of Jane Eyre's plot back to their origins in Charlotte's earlier work.

We saw how at fourteen Charlotte depicted in "Albion and Marina" her own dilemma of wanting to be loved by her father yet also to be ambitious and accomplished like him. In that story Albion was torn between the values of domestic happiness at home with Marina and independent achievement out in the larger world, characterized by the "majestic charms" of Zenobia. The structural elements of this early story Charlotte retained in *Jane Eyre,* keeping them remarkably intact—but with two great transformations: first, the sex roles have been reversed; and second, the "Marina" of the novel is not dead at the end, only somewhat deadened.

The "Albion and Marina" framework enters *Jane Eyre* in midnovel, right after the interrupted false marriage. Jane and Rochester are avowed lovers, but Jane takes Albion's role and departs from a grieving Rochester to seek her way alone in the world. Moor House is not the fantasy land of Glasstown, but it does have its wish-fulfilling capacities, for there Jane comes into her own: finds a congenial family (in contrasting parallel to the Reeds), receives a large inheritance, and becomes, as she says, "an independent woman" (p. 556). St. John Rivers stands in the Zenobia spot, tempting Jane away from her first love and toward a competing ambition. As she wavers, Jane receives a supernatural call, and like Albion notes the time and acts on it instantly. Albion had found on his return not the joy of reunion but a "desolate and ruined apartment" and his beloved in the grave. Says Jane returning to Thornfield, "I looked with timorous joy towards a stately house: I saw a blackened ruin." The switch in sex roles that this parallel reveals is oddly underscored in the text of *Jane Eyre* itself. Presumably to prepare the reader for the shock of Thornfield's ruin and at the same time to build the suspense, Jane introduces her revelation with a digression that recalls the original story and gender roles which the novel has revised in retelling. Jane is seeking Rochester at Thornfield, but finds it demolished and empty. She describes her tender expectation and then the shock of horror that succeeds it.[12]

> A lover finds his mistress asleep on a mossy bank; he wishes to catch a glimpse of her fair face without waking her. He steals softly over the grass, careful to make no sound; . . . now his eyes anticipate the vision of beauty. . . . But . . . how he starts! How he calls aloud a name. . . . He thought his love slept sweetly: he finds she is stone-dead.
>
> I looked with timorous joy towards a stately house: I saw a blackened ruin. (pp. 542–43)

Jane's first thought is that Rochester may be, like Marina, in the grave— "My eye involuntarily wandered to the grey church tower"—but he is not, though as he later tells her he "was forced to pass through the valley of the shadow of death" (p. 571). Rather, "one eye was knocked out, and one hand so crushed that Mr. Carter, the surgeon, had to amputate it directly" (p. 549). This is the biblical punishment for adultery; as many critics have noted, it amounts to symbolic castration.

How had Charlotte brought her original vision of the relative male and female conditions to this astonishing reversal? For Charlotte's early heroines the need for paternal love had to take precedence over any intellectual ambition, because their survival depended on it. The abandoned Marias could only die; even Zenobia was driven mad by Zamorna's rejection. But by the time of "Captain Henry Hastings," written in 1839 when she was turning twenty-three, Charlotte had strikingly strengthened her emotional position. She had recovered a new source of love in the mother figure "Hope," a moon and rainbow goddess evolved from Gray's vision of the "Mighty Mother" nature. And she had seen through her "genius" brother well enough to skewer him as the hangdog Henry Hastings. Now she could picture herself in the role of Henry's sister Elizabeth who literally arose amid maternal moonlight—"Resurgam"—from Rosamund Wellesley's grave to say goodbye to her lover and go her way free and alone. With this act Elizabeth both symbolically resurrected her feminine forebears (the human dimension of "mother") and became herself a model for future heroines, an early version of Jane Eyre repudiating the dishonorable proposals of the man she adored but to whom she would not surrender her integrity.

Elizabeth's assertive act is curiously encoded directly within *Jane Eyre*. Readers of the novel will recall that in the character of Helen Burns Charlotte depicted her mothering eldest sister Maria, whose death from an illness contracted at the Cowan Bridge school marked a nadir in young Charlotte's life. To Jane's masochistic assertion that "to gain some real affection " from one she loved, she would "willingly submit to have the bone of my arm broken, or to let a bull toss me, or to stand behind a kicking horse, and let it dash its hoofs at my chest" (all striking images of the destructive power of male sexuality), Helen mildly returns, "Hush, Jane! you think too much of the love of human beings" (pp. 80–81) and recommends instead the love of God. Acknowledging that her own father will not miss her when she is gone, Helen asserts that we have in heaven another and better "mighty home" (p. 67) presided over by a loving "Universal parent" (p. 96). Soon after, she dies in Jane's arms, a victim of Brocklehurst's oppression. The narrative of her story concludes:

> Her grave is in Brocklebridge churchyard: for fifteen years after her death, it was only covered by a grassy mound; but now a grey marble

tablet marks the spot, inscribed with her name, and the word "Resurgam." (p. 97).

Presumably Jane herself supplied the marker. But its significance lies in the fact that it is Charlotte's own self-coded reminder of what she had already accomplished imaginatively, through her fiction, when in arising from Rosamund's grave and departing from her human lover, Elizabeth raised and redeemed the spirit of Maria Brontë, prototype of all Charlotte's fictional women who had "died of love."

The results of that resurrection permeate *Jane Eyre* and help account for Jane's successes. To begin with, we can now understand the ambiguous gender and meaning of Jane's visionary visitor in the red room scene at Gateshead. Ostensibly the child fears the ghost of her uncle; but the vision she imagines has more the attributes of a remembered mother:

> I wiped my tears . . . , fearful lest any sign of violent grief might waken a preternatural voice to comfort me, or elicit from the gloom some haloed face, bending over me with strange pity.

Seeing a light gleam on her wall, Jane imagines it the "hearald of some coming vision from another world" and swoons to a "rushing of wings" (p. 15). Jane's collapse is painful, of course; but its practical result is to get her removed to Lowood, and on her way in life. Mother has risen—and helped.

At its next appearance the vision's gender, relationship, and purpose are made utterly explicit. As the grief-frozen Jane is struggling to convince herself to leave Rochester after the attempted false marriage, she sleeps and has a dream:

> I dreamt I lay in the red-room at Gateshead; . . . The light that long ago had struck me into syncope, recalled in this vision, seemed glidingly to mount the wall. . . . the gleam was such as the moon imparts to vapours she is about to sever. I watched her come. . . . She broke forth as never moon yet burst from cloud: . . . then, not a moon, but a white human form shone in the azure, inclining a glorious brow earthward. . . . It spoke to my spirit: immeasurably distant was the tone, yet so near, it whispered in my heart—
> "My daughter, flee temptation!"
> "Mother, I will." (p. 407)

In departing, Jane is both an Elizabeth Hastings leaving William behind among the graves of women who have succumbed to male blandishments, and an Albion leaving (in Rochester) an anxious and abandoned

Marina. "He would feel himself forsaken; his love rejected," muses Jane at the door; "he would suffer; perhaps grow desperate. I thought of this too . . . and glided on" (pp. 408–9).

The story of Albion and Marina shows us that Rochester's maiming is in effect a commuted death sentence. Indeed in a sense one Rochester has died, and another taken his place. The earlier Rochester would have proved to be another Zamorna, whose love is doubly threatening. First, it fetters: as Jane tells us, echoing the Marys and Minas before her, Rochester's influence "took my feelings from my own power and fettered them in his" (p. 218). And then it carries always the covert threat of being withdrawn, with fatal results for the woman. Jane remarks later as she looks back on the wisdom of her escape, "oh, yes, he would have loved me well for a while . . ." (p. 459). Over this Zamorna type Jane has triumphed, with mother's help, by exchanging roles and leaving him behind to die the death of Marina.

The Rochester Jane marries is in that sense a different man: Zamorna shorn of his power to endanger women is no longer really a Zamorna, but rather the male equivalent of Jane herself insofar as she is a loyal, loving, intelligent companion. He is now pretty much bereft of his dazzling sexual magnetism, but at the same time he will never depart. Their life together could almost be that of contented father and daughter. In fact their union has been arranged and blessed by mother herself—a curious circumstance that I shall return to in a moment.

But first we should observe a third factor enabling Charlotte to depict the astonishing role reversal of *Jane Eyre*. The brother conquered, the father's power offset by the redeemed mother's encouraging presence: these hard-won achievements of Charlotte's imagination were important. But it also matters that the novel was begun under remarkable emotional conditions, and further, that even these emotional conditions have a history in Charlotte's fictional imaginings.

In a story that Charlotte wrote shortly after "Captain Henry Hastings," she had a character named Louisa Vernon (one of Zamorna's mistresses, the Angrian forbear of Céline Varens, little Adèle's mother), imagine a way to "take down" Zamorna:

O, I wish something would happen—that I could get a better hold of him. I wish he would fall desperately sick in this house—or shoot himself by accident so that he would be obliged to stay here & let me nurse him. It would take down his pride if he were so weak that he could do nothing for himself—& then, if I did everything for him, he would be thankful. . . .[13]

This is of course precisely Rochester's condition when Jane returns to him. But more important, as Charlotte's imagination was preparing the ground for *Jane Eyre*, Patrick himself was for the first time in Charlotte's life also in precisely this helpless condition—with Charlotte his care-taker. As if by divine sanction, Charlotte's fantasy had been realized. This circumstance seems to have suggested to Charlotte that her heroines need no longer be celibate (or even self-divided) to survive. The fictional idea that had been so strikingly realized in fact might now return to find new use in fiction.

The background was this: for several years Patrick had been suffering from cataracts, and by the summer of 1846 was nearly blind. It was Charlotte who insisted that he undergo surgery and made the practical arrangements for it. As she put it, "I was obliged to be very decided in the matter."[14] She accompanied the anxious old man to Manchester, sat by him during the entire operation (performed, of course, without anesthetic), and was his companion and support during the long and difficult period of recovery.

On the very day of Patrick's surgery *The Professor* was returned to Charlotte with a publisher's rejection letter. Undaunted, she continued sending it out. But far more significantly, she also began *Jane Eyre*. The heroine of this new novel was to experience what Charlotte herself was now tasting—the sweetness of being needed and thanked by her "master." Jane Eyre would be another Miss West—a daughter of Ireland like Charlotte, and as poor and homely and parentless as Charlotte had felt herself to be. Reviled and restricted by unworthy relatives she would nonetheless survive and make her way into the heart of the hero—that stern, dominating model of paternal manhood. But here the roles would shift: instead of being left by him to sink, she would leave him and rise. She would evade his dangerous grip just as it seemed to close on her, and depart to experience surprising successes in the wider world. Only then —vastly strengthened even as her hero was vastly weakened—would she renounce that wider world and return to his embrace, to nurse him in his helplessness and enjoy his grateful love.

This conclusion clearly satisfied Charlotte's sexual and domestic am-bitions, her desire to see her self-representing heroine fully "be" as a woman, unequivocally and forever beloved. Accordingly the same ma-ternal powers that had insisted Jane "flee temptation" and leave the dangerous Rochester exert a force almost magical in calling her back to marry the maimed one. In the scene in which Jane is tempted to marry St. John and join in his missionary calling, she entreats of Heaven, "Shew me, shew me the path!" But it is no masculine "Heaven" that answers her. Rather her prayers are answered by mother: "the room was full of moonlight" when suddenly "I heard a voice somewhere cry—'Jane! Jane! Jane!'" This was "the work of nature," Jane assures us; "She was roused, and did—no miracle—but her best" (p. 535–36).

In a sense St. John Rivers is John Reed in a new guise, that is to say a brother figure, a version of Branwell purged of all his vices except the will to domination by which in earlier years he had sought to make Charlotte an adjunct to his own presumed "genius." Charlotte had successfully resisted him then, as we have seen, and she resists him now. But Charlotte's imagery reveals that St. John's appeal is also paternal. Like the first Rochester, St. John poses the same threat of annihilation that faced Zamorna's women. All of these men threaten to swallow up woman's "very being." As Jane says of St. John, "I was tempted to cease struggling with him—to rush down the torrent of his will into the gulf of his existence, and there lose my own" (p. 534). St. John is in no way associated with the father Charlotte wanted to be loved by. But as a figure for the father Charlotte wanted to be like, St. John is a version of the male muse.

Female being is the direct concern of mother-power, which had long been counseling Charlotte's heroines to "arise," to assert "*I* care for myself" (p. 404), to avoid the ego-obliterating waters.[15] Now mother carries Rochester's cry across England to reach Jane's ears because Rochester no longer threatens her being, whereas St. John emphatically does, in trying to substitute "vocation" for domestic happiness. Like Albion she rushes back home—to find Rochester not dead like Marina, but providentially damaged.

The hungers and hopes of so many years, and the fictional vehicles that had for so long conveyed them, all converge in this novel of woman's domestic victory. Yet amid all that satisfaction the unresolved countertheme of intellectual ambition obtrudes itself disquietingly.[16] In terms of the old story of Albion and Marina, this countertheme was expressed by Albion's attraction to Zenobia and the Glasstown literati. The traces of this competing desire may be detected in *Jane Eyre,* but the desire itself has been strenuously diverted and repressed. Both Zenobia and the male muse take strangely distorted forms in this novel.

Let us look first at what remains here of the old Zenobia. Bertha Mason is certainly no artist or intellectual, but the Brontë scholar Fanny Ratchford demonstrated years ago how in Charlotte's fictions Bertha descends from Zenobia,[17] and we can extend the similarities. Bertha's mad rage, like Zenobia's, is that of the woman scorned. Rochester has married her, but as he confides to Jane, "I never loved, I never esteemed,

I did not even know her" (p. 389). As Jane's anger burned against Aunt Reed for forcing her to "do without one bit of love or kindness" (p. 39), so does Bertha's burn against the husband who slighted her (and whose attempted marriage trick was in effect slighting Jane). Thus when Jane is threatened, Bertha's anger is eerily supported by the "woman-power" of moonlight. The night Bertha tries to burn Rochester in his bed he has as yet no sexual plans for Jane; accordingly no moon-mother is needed, and Jane saves Rochester from danger. But the night of Bertha's attack on Mason is different. In his gypsy disguise Rochester has begun his teasing game with Jane, and that night Jane is wakened by the "glorious gaze" of the moon to hear the effects of Bertha's fury: the moon "was beautiful, but too solemn: I half rose, and stretched my arm to draw the curtain. Good God! What a cry!" (p. 258). The night on which Rochester proposes bigamous marriage to Jane and receives her innocent assent with an "accent and look of exultation savage" (p. 321), the moon retreats behind clouds from which not Bertha herself, but "a livid, vivid spark" of lightening leaps out and splits the horse chestnut where they have been sitting (p. 322). As Jane looks at its cloven trunk later, just before the mock marriage, and imagines that its "unsundered" base is an example of faithful sympathy, the moon's appearance shining through the fissure of the tree is a comment on Jane's confusion: "her disk was blood-red and half overcast: she seemed to throw on me one bewildered, dreary glance, and buried herself again instantly in the deep drift of cloud" (p. 349). And of course Bertha also tears Jane's wedding veil—an act less of jealousy than of motherly warning, to judge by the fact that she leaves Jane herself untouched, and that Jane's own subconscious has just been yielding dreams of Rochester as retreating father.

That the magnificent Zenobia should end in Charlotte's fiction as a bloated animal suggests how very grim is Charlotte's estimate of the fate of the woman of intellect forced to live unloved. She might indeed go "mad from solitary confinement"—an experience so spiritually disabling as to render the sufferer, like "Nebuchadnezzar, the imperial hypochondriac," a mere crouching and groaning beast.[18] In a way it is really Zenobia's revenge when Bertha tames Rochester by setting the blaze that puts out *his* fire.[19]

Bertha's fiery departure from the novel signals a complex set of changes. First, of course, it frees Rochester to marry Jane. His question on Jane's return, "I suppose I should now entertain none but fatherly feelings for you: do you think so?" (p. 557) is rhetorically pointed, planted in order to be explicitly denied both by Jane and by the supernatural powers that have clustered about her throughout the book and have now summoned her for her happy ending. Second, in setting the fire that maims Rochester, Bertha fulfills literally Jane's own earlier, figurative act. For Jane herself had observed that in leaving him "I had injured—wounded—. . . my master" (p. 410). That "wound" had been the generic wound of separation, analogous to the "secret, inward wound" that the earlier Jane had received in Charlotte's poem from *The Professor.* Jane Eyre knows that in separating herself from the man she loves she wounds herself as well as him, that it will plunge her into "unsounded depths of agony." But even as Jane contemplates those depths, her "conscience" addresses her directly and rather brutally: "you shall tear yourself away; none shall help you: you shall, yourself, pluck out your right eye; yourself cut off your right hand" (p. 379). In Jane's case this mutilation is only metaphoric; but Rochester will have to endure it literally in Bertha's fire.

Third and most important, but also most troubling, Bertha's death signals the end of the "wild free thing" in Jane, that quality of spirit that M. Paul will recognize and foster in Lucy Snowe—the "wild and intense, dangerous, sudden, and flaming." This is not to say that Jane is powerless or even weakened at the novel's end. Far from it. In getting her man Jane does not split into two "wives" as Frances had done, and the man she loves will surely be faithful to this woman who is now the light of his life. Most significant of all, Jane survives to tell her tale—and tells it with marvelous vigor. But the "wild, free" Jane is now domesticated; she went out with Bertha's fires, as surely as intellectual Zenobia did.

The novel's final words do not belong to Jane, but rather to St. John Rivers, who (with Jane safely married) speaks no longer as moral bully but rather as apostle of God. This fictional embodiment of Charlotte's muse, of her restless creative imagination, had to be depicted as harsh and cold that he might not challenge the primacy of Rochester, the paternal lover whom Charlotte now at last felt safe in allotting her heroine. Yet as aspirant, rover, poet, and priest, St. John very much figures the father Charlotte wanted to be like. He is the writer as apostle, serving that Master of all masters, the Word. The point is crucial; let me explain.

Other critics have remarked how St. John carries forward themes started by Helen Burns, specifically Helen's deprecation of the ties of the flesh, of human love compared to divine. And they have had trouble reconciling this connection between the two characters, especially in view of Charlotte's obvious admiration for Helen and hostility to St. John. The fact is that Charlotte was in heavy battle with her muse over the ending of this novel: he was pulling her where she didn't want to go

—a muse in rebellion, much as Blake said Milton's had been. For as Rochester embodies Charlotte's longing for human love, St. John embodies her vaulting ambition to be an apostle of art, her restless yearnings for spiritual liberty and intellectual excitement, for the "wild, free" energy of the artist on her way to her promised land.

We should observe, for example, that St. John knows real poetry when he sees it, and that poetry marks a special bond between him and Jane, indeed between him and his creator, Charlotte. Bringing Jane a copy of Scott's "Marmion," he elicits a response from her that recalls the image of Aaron's rod in Charlotte's poem "Retrospection." Then, as now, Charlotte implicitly connected the priest's or missionary's calling with the mission of the artist, the redemptive power of God with that of Genius: "I know poetry is not dead, nor genius lost; . . . Powerful angels, safe in heaven! . . . they not only live, but reign, and redeem" (p. 473). Like Charlotte and the young Jane, St. John burned "for the more active life"—

> for the exciting toils of a literary career—. . . yes, the heart of a politician, of a soldier, of a votary of glory, a lover of renown, a luster after power, beat under my curate's surplice. (p. 462)

St. John has just summarized everything Emily Brontë meant by "ambition" and was urgent to avoid. The effect is to dramatize the difference between the sisters' perspectives; for St. John's ambition here is Charlotte's own. "Curate's surplice" aside, his could be the voice of Charlotte's "genius" speaking:

> my powers heard a call from heaven to rise, gather their full strength, spread their wings and mount beyond ken. God had an errand for me; to bear which afar, to deliver it well, skill and strength, courage and eloquence, the best qualifications of soldier, statesman and orator, were all needed. (p. 462)

Though St. John's is ultimately the call of God and Charlotte's the call of art, this is the very language in which Charlotte regularly couched her sense of vocation. In Glasstown with Zenobia, Albion's mind had been roused by literature to "eaglelike flights into higher regions." Charlotte herself had felt "such a strong wish for wings," as she had phrased it in a letter to her friend Mary Taylor some years before, "such an urgent thirst to see—to know—to learn—something internal seemed to expand boldly." And Jane, too, had used the same figure, hinting at the way fiction can substitute (as it did for Charlotte) for real adventure:

> The restlessness was in my nature; . . . Then my sole relief was . . . to
> let my heart be heaved by the exultant movement which . . . expanded
> it with life; and, best of all, to open my inward ear to a tale that was
> never ended—a tale my imagination created, and narrated continu-
> ously . . . (p. 132)

This restless desire for experience Albion had expressed by traveling to
Glasstown, becoming a great poet, and nearly forgetting Marina. Given
the force of such longings, it is not surprising that Jane should remark of
St. John: "he was of the material from which nature hews her heroes.
. . . Well may he eschew the calm of domestic life; . . . there his faculties
stagnate" (p. 502).

It is for this heroic calling that St. John gives up marriage to Rosamond Oliver—"The Rose of the World" (p. 479)—preferring to strike
out boldly toward "the true, eternal Paradise" (p. 469).[20] In Jane he
recognizes a fit companion for his journey. But though St. John was
prepared to give up the hope of romantic love and domestic happiness in
pursuit of a "higher" ambition, that is not what Charlotte wants for her
heroine, and she casts it in grim mold, makes St. John and his invitation
harsh, chilling, to be rejected.

St. John is chilling because as Bertha personifies the hot heart, so he is
the ice—sexual repression personified. And Jane need not accept that ice,
as Charlotte's earlier heroines had been forced to do for the sake of
survival. But once Jane's marriage is accomplished, her domestic happiness assured, St. John may safely re-enter the story, his character no
longer ominous, but admirable. Now not harsh or chilling, "His is the
exaction of the apostle, who speaks but for Christ" (p. 578) in calling for
the sexual self-denial that Charlotte had rejected for her fictional heroine
but apparently believed bitterly necessary to her authorial self.[21]

This is why the muse can exact the price that he does. The energy has
all gone to St. John's corner, and it follows him out of the book. A
telling index to Charlotte's at least subliminal awareness of the implications of her choice lies in the complex of puns concerning the domestic
and the divine that clusters about the novel's ending. As St. John had
appealed to her with the force of the call to St. Paul from Macedonia,
Jane had insisted, "I was no apostle. . . . I have no vocation" (p. 514).
But Charlotte herself did have a powerful sense of vocation, and increasingly she was thinking of it in apostolic terms. Thus although we are
certainly expected to approve of Jane's happiness with her maimed "master," we are not allowed to forget that St. John's Master is Christ. St.
John is "the servant of an infallible master" and he wonders "that all

round me do not burn to enlist under the same banner" (p. 513). In fact in all the book only Helen so "burns." The novel concludes by quoting the penultimate verse of Revelation—"Surely I come quickly. Amen. Even so come, Lord Jesus!"—whose author was of course also a St. John.

Both personally and through quotation St. John gets the last word. Moreover his family name, Rivers, derives its significance from the same closing biblical chapter (Revelation 22:1): "And he shewed me a pure river of water of life, clear as crystal, proceeding out of the throne of God." We shall see that the river of the water of life becomes a crucial figure in Charlotte's last work, where it stands in healing contrast to earthly waters.

How do we know that Charlotte had a struggle with her muse over the ending of *Jane Eyre,* willing Jane's marriage in defiance of her muse? How do we know that St. John indeed bears the weight I have given him, in effect carrying off the spirit of Jane—her fiery poetic genius— and leaving only her mortal husk in the company of Rochester? Partly I think we can see it in the novel itself, for example in the role of Helen Burns, who connects the woman who "will arise" with the redemptive values of our "mighty home," the province of those "Powerful angels," Poetry and Genius. Charlotte's juvenilia contrasted the flesh and the spirit, the children of bondage and the children of light. Now Helen Burns' reading of *Rasselas* should remind us of Dr. Johnson's conclusion there: that the "choice of life" is really the "choice of eternity."

In Charlotte's last two novels, the muse who finally solved her dilemma arose out of just the kind of religious perspective and biblical imagery that Helen and St. John here introduce. That perspective and imagery return in the story of Eva's marriage to "Genius," told in the striking little essay "La Première Femme Savante" of *Shirley;* and then most fully in *Villette,* in the love between Lucy and Paul Emanuel.

Shirley: Men and Mothers

It was surely in part the stunning success of *Jane Eyre* that emboldened Charlotte to undertake in her next novel a topic less overtly personal, more ambitiously "public" in its theme. She had been writing for years about woman's inner needs and dangers. Now she would confront some of the broader social problems. The mission of *Shirley* was to relate the condition of women as a class to the larger conditions of class society in England, to show how human waste and misunderstanding corrode both sexual happiness and social welfare, to demonstrate that the human spirit in everyone needs food as much as the body does. Of restless women and workers alike it is true that "starving folk cannot be satisfied or settled folk."[22]

But even in this proto-feminist book Charlotte seems to have been prepared to attribute "genius" rather to the male than to the female: men have it, women marry it. Charlotte's system of double heroines allowed her to explore a double range of woman's needs and potential, divided along the lines of her own long-standing dilemma of domestic as opposed to intellectual success. But although the two heroines Caroline and Shirley embody the opposing poles of this dilemma, as women they share a common fate; each achieves her goal not so much in herself as in her marriage. Submissive and contemplative Caroline seeks in a man the stern and practical qualities that she really needs to develop in herself, and finds them in Robert Moore, the mill owner, who loves her in his way but must secure his financial position before indulging any romantic inclinations. The more freewheeling Shirley displaces her ambitions in just the same way. Charlotte gives her a frank and flashing character, clearly meant to be as awesome as it is admirable. But for her husband Shirley requires "a *master*. . . . A man I shall feel it impossible not to love, and very possible to fear" (p. 627). She finds him in the learned and intelligent Louis Moore who as her literal "master"—the tutor of her youth—carries forward Charlotte's long tradition of love between "Master and Pupil."

In Caroline we follow the course of woman as she is socially reticent and financially dependent, without a mother to serve as model or a father to feed the hungers of her young heart. She longs for a job in life—some occupation for her energies, some "place in the world," a requirement that for her is finally and fully met in the happy ending of marriage. By far her greatest hunger is for human parenting, which she expresses in the poignant dream

> that her mother might come some happy day, and send for her to her presence—look upon her fondly with loving eyes, and say to her tenderly, in a sweet voice, "Caroline, my child. I have a home for you: you shall live with me. All the love you have needed, and not tasted, from infancy, I have saved for you carefully. Come! it shall cherish you now." (p. 362)

Consistent with this parental need is her silently consuming love of Robert Moore, the authoritative man of business, who desires a comfortable "home,"[23] but is at the same time proud and rather hard. As Shirley observes, "Prince is on his brow, and ruler in his bearing" (p. 632). It turns out that Caroline's job in life will be to humanize him by her tactful influence; she will be the angel in his house.[24] But she must first nearly die in an illness modeled on the hypochondria of Charlotte's earlier stories, and be rescued by her mother; and like Rochester, Robert must undergo the rough taking down so complacently imagined by Louisa Vernon. In Robert's case this is the bullet wound that puts him, "not dead, but much hurt" (p. 636), under the care of the intimidating Mrs. Horsfall: "she taught him docility in a trice" (p. 644). From there the happy marriage of Robert and Caroline is a short and easy step; and the family circle is made complete by the fact that Caroline's newly discovered mother will live with them, making up what seems to have been Charlotte's ideal threesome.

Through Shirley, on the other hand, we are asked to imagine what it might be like if a young woman of wealth and spirit were to experience the social freedom regularly accorded to young men of her status. Charlotte is careful to assure the reader of Shirley's essential propriety—her innate dignity and delicacy of feeling vouch for that—but in other respects Shirley is allowed to cavort on the very borders of female respectability. She administers her estate with unladylike authority and decision. As owner of the mill, she is Robert's business superior, though Charlotte is quick to emphasize that Robert will be no one's "subject," that his bearing expresses "no servility, hardly homage." She takes a lead in planning the financing of local poor relief; she bodily expells a rude curate from her garden; she "fraternizes" (her own word) with none of the local ladies (p. 233); she can handle a gun without fear, and is happy to earn the epithet "Captain Keeldar."

Mrs. Gaskell says that Charlotte told her that Shirley was modeled in part on Emily (who was nicknamed "The Major"), and so she may well have been. But both Caroline and Shirley are in important ways projections of Charlotte herself.[25] Caroline is Charlotte's social self, a trenchant but preferably silent observer; she embodies Charlotte's longings for a loving human mother and a caring but dominant fatherlike husband. As the sexual hero, Robert is Rochester demythologized, his "hard dog" (p. 287) edges and masculine energies given functional historical-economic explanations; even the event of his taming (the bullet wound) is given the realistic context of the Luddite uprisings. Shirley on the other hand is Charlotte's buoyant and self-assured inner spirit, the one that Frances Henri had briefly revealed in her "frank and flashing glance," but whose bright and easy grace as a real, functioning woman Charlotte probably had no model for. Certainly Shirley is often hard to believe. Correspondingly Louis, as Shirley's "master," is barely a character at all: rather he is the persistent shadow of Charlotte's old yearnings after the intellectual leadership and concerned kindness that M. Heger appears to have shown her during the best moments of their relationship.

Shirley is a less successful creation than her "sister" Caroline, probably partly because of the conditions under which Charlotte wrote about her. The novel was written during a time of devastating losses. Branwell died in September 1848 when *Shirley* was hardly a third done, before the character Shirley had even been introduced. Then Emily sickened, and died in December; and Anne died the following May. Hard indeed to write convincingly of the graceful and fearless from under such a weight of grief; yet the book was done and in the publishers' hands by September, as the year of deaths came full circle.

But the format of the novel suggests that Charlotte would have had problems making Shirley convincing under even the best of circumstances. Despite its title, the book is really organized around Caroline, whom, as I have already suggested, Charlotte had good reason to know from the inside out. When I say "organized around," I mean it quite literally: the book is drawn to a rigorous symmetrical scheme, planned, presumably, before the writing even began. (It seems a strange irony that so many readers have found it structurally disorganized.) There are thirty-six chapters, plus a brief thirty-seventh "Winding-Up." Half of thirty-six is eighteen.[26] The eighteenth chapter, the book's midpoint, is suggestively entitled "Which the Genteel Reader is Recommended to Skip, Low Persons being Here Introduced." The "Low Persons" are of two kinds, women and workers: this is the crucial chapter that knits together the book's two thematic strands, that of class and that of gender. Around this pivotal central chapter, which the "Genteel Reader" (a vowel beyond "gentle reader") is sardonically invited to skip, the book breaks into concentric rings organized by multiples of six. The sixth chapter, "Coriolanus," establishes Robert's unbending character; the thirtieth chapter (sixth from the end), "The Shot," recounts its predictable result. The twelfth chapter, "Shirley and Caroline," sets the theme of women's bonding in relation to their love of men; this theme comes to crisis in the twenty-fourth chapter, "Valley of the Shadow of Death" (twelfth from the end). These two chapters, the twelfth and twenty-fourth, are also the opening chapters of volumes 2 and 3.

The book's third theme, that of the loneliness of female genius, seems to have been a late addition, as it is given special treatment in late additions to the novel. I will return to consider this matter separately.

My point just now is that Charlotte appears to have planned *Shirley* according to a complex set of parallels and symmetries. Each of the paired heroines reaches toward her appropriate "mother" in the central eighteenth chapter, set against the background of Pentecost, which celebrates the descent of the Holy Ghost. Here is where Caroline is inspired with longing for her lost human mother and Shirley has her powerful vision of her spiritual mother, the "woman-Titan" Nature, whom Charlotte modeled closely on the Mighty Mother of "The Violet." And of course the plot draws to its close with another symmetry, as figurative sisters marry literal brothers in a resounding double wedding.

But despite its title and all these balanced pairings, the novel is shaped much more around Caroline than around Shirley. And this is so not in some technical sense, such as that Shirley enters the novel late; but rather in that Charlotte focused the interest of the novel, as she wrote it, much more on the domestic themes associated with Caroline than on the visionary themes assigned to Shirley. Like *Jane Eyre, Shirley* addresses Charlotte's passionate need for love more successfully than it does her intellectual ambitions. Though Shirley figures woman as she is strong, vital, and free, and thus points toward Charlotte's creative being, she is not herself a practicing artist or intellectual. Charlotte offers Shirley's "indolence" as her excuse for not being a creative writer. Had she a little more acquisitiveness, Charlotte suggests, Shirley might write down the productions of her imagination "and thus possess what she was enabled to create"—the rest of the sentence, later lined out and omitted, continues "by the power of the mighty Genius Inspiration." But it is Louis who does the writing, such as it is. As his unconvincing "journal" is our only evidence of his genius, the case for him is weak. Still, Louis figures the "muse" insofar as he embodies the values of art and creativity. He is in this respect St. John Rivers made warm, wholesome, and attractive, though even less than St. John is he a projection of Charlotte's own artistic spirit: he is too poorly perceived for that. If we return to the terms of Charlotte's early dilemma—whether to be loved by Patrick or to be like him—we must conclude that for both Shirley and Caroline the choice is to be loved. It is consistent with this need that the book is laced with vigorously presented examples of the problems women face when they are not loved: the fate of the "old maid," the need for respectable work.

But if women need men, they also need each other; and this is why the issue of "mothers" lies at the center of the central chapter. Caroline's and Shirley's respective "mothers" were meant to cover by implication the whole range of women's need for mothering. Mrs. Pryor is without question Charlotte's fantasy of what her own mother, Maria Brontë, might have been like, could she suddenly have been magically restored. Her suggestive assumed name echoes both *prior* (i.e., the original mother) and *prayer* (in answer to which she has returned). And from half-hidden cues we find her to be even more self-referentially part of the personal Brontë story, in that her maiden name is revealed to have been Agnes Grey (pp. 424, 495), the name Anne Brontë had chosen for the autobiographical heroine of her first novel.[27] The husband James Helstone who had caused Mrs. Pryor such suffering had "died" in the fiction; but his function as a figure for Patrick Brontë, and father surrogate for Caroline, is taken over by his brother, Reverend Matthewson Helstone. The name Helstone is of course like Pryor a descriptive, and in this case a judgmental, one. Reverend Helstone bears Patrick's reputed likeness to Wellington, the so-called Iron Duke,[28] and treated his wife (now long dead) with a callous neglect that appears to echo a charge Charlotte lodged in her heart against her own father.

Shirley's "mother," on the other hand, is not at all so fully developed or so complexly woven into the book. Rather she remains what Caroline calls her, a "vague and visionary" figure. She is the direct descendent of the Mighty Mother, as already mentioned; close relative of the rainbow figure in *The Professor;* of the Evening Star and moon-mother in *Jane Eyre;* and so on. But whereas in "The Violet" she had been herself the source of genius, the imparter of poetic power, now in *Shirley* she is "Jehovah's daughter," female analogue not of God or the Savior, but of Adam. Thus she is not a source of creation, but a result of it; not a goddess, but a creature. Although in Shirley's view the first woman was a Titan, whose breast yielded the rebellious Prometheus and ultimately the Messiah, not even Shirley thinks of woman as quite man's equal. Earlier she had said that good men are "the lords of creation. . . . the first of created things." "Nothing ever charms me more than when I meet my superior—one who makes me sincerely feel that he is my superior." Now she acknowledges that although it would be "glorious to look up," she finds herself disappointed in the quality of most actual men. When she is "religiously inclined," unfortunately "There are but false gods to adore." It is Louis' function to be worthy of Shirley's religious inclinations; and the final chapters detail his success in taming her to her devotional role. But for all that, he remains at best an Old Testament Abraham to her Hagar. When Caroline remarks to Robert that "Shirley is no more free than was Hagar, " he returns, "and who, pray, is the Abraham; the hero of a patriarch who has achieved such a conquest?" Though all of Charlotte's normative characters approve of Shirley's marriage to Louis, there is something slightly ominous in this evocation of Angrian wilderness wandering. Pleased at her friend's happy devotion, Caroline observes with satisfaction: "Shirley is a bondswoman." But few readers have shared her satisfaction. Moreover, Charlotte was well aware that Hagar is the mother of the children of bondage, born after the flesh, not of the children of promise, born after the spirit. Where are those latter children in this book? What mother have they?

A Late Addition: "The First Bluestocking"

At the last moment Charlotte did provide the children of promise with a spiritual "mother" of their own. She is a new character named Eva, a visionary creature that Charlotte added near the end of her novel, in an essay purportedly written by Shirley years before when she was a schoolgirl—an essay modeled on those that Charlotte and Emily wrote for M. Heger in Brussels. Like those essays, Shirley's was supposedly written originally in French, though for the purposes of this English novel it is recalled and translated verbatim by Shirley's admiring teacher Louis. The essay was titled in French "La Première Femme Savante," which Charlotte translates "The First Bluestocking."

To understand both the genesis of Shirley's essay and its meaning, we must recall that in the fall of 1850, following the deaths of Emily and Anne, Charlotte was rereading her sisters' papers with the prospect of editing their literary remains. She found the work bitterly painful; in the case of Emily's papers this was so not only because they stirred her grief but also because they forced her to face much that troubled her in her sister's thought. We have seen that she recognized with unmatched clarity the meaning of Heathcliff in *Wuthering Heights*. She softened the novel as much as she could, both by excusing Emily in her "Editor's Preface" (creative power is not always in the author's control, she explained) and by actually altering details of the text. With the poems, however, she went still further—not only revising with an even freer hand, but also making substantial additions that she then attributed to Emily, perhaps even adding entire poems to the canon. E. W. Hatfield, in his standard edition of Emily's poetry, assigned no number to the poem "Often rebuked, yet always back returning" because he considered that it was not one of Emily's own poems, but rather written by Charlotte as part of her effort to excuse or explain her sister.[29] Certainly Charlotte did add an extra stanza to "Aye, there it is! It wakes to-night." And to Emily's opening twelve lines of "Julian M. and A. G. Rochelle" Charlotte added her own ending, attributing the whole to Emily. This ending that Charlotte added now requires our attention; it helps explain why Charlotte returned to add "The First Bluestocking" to her nearly finished novel, and in important ways it sets the terms for *Villette*.

Emily's opening twelve lines had described a secret vigil. In a warm, silent house "One, alone" is awake and watching, trimming a lamp "to be the Wanderer's guiding-star." Emily's twelve lines end with the watcher taunting the household:

> Frown, my haughty sire; chide, my angry dame;
> Set your slaves to spy, threaten me with shame:
> But neither sire nor dame, nor prying serf shall know
> What angel nightly tracks that waste of winter snow.

To Emily's twelve lines, Charlotte now added the following eight more, creating in effect a new poem:

> What I love shall come like visitant of air,
> Safe in secret power from lurking human snare;
> Who loves me, no word of mine shall e'er betray,
> Though for faith unstained my life must forfeit pay.
>
> Burn, then, little lamp; glimmer straight and clear—
> Hush! a rustling wing stirs, methinks, the air:
> He for whom I wait, thus ever comes to me;
> Strange Power! I trust thy might; trust thou my constancy.

Several elements here are very unlike Emily, and all tend to a literalizing of the relationship between speaker and angel: the intimate reciprocity of feeling ("What I love," "Who loves me"); the bodily bulk of the angel (his "rustling wing stirs . . . the air"); the whole atmosphere of romantic assignation ("He . . . thus ever comes to me"). Yet there are elements equally foreign to Charlotte as we have known her, all suggesting that this lover and his love are figurative or symbolic after all: the odd mix of pronouns hints of some difficulty in identifying the visitor ("What," "Who," "He," "Thou"), who seems in any case less a person than an effect ("Strange Power," "secret power"). It is as if Charlotte had tried, in these lines, to merge with her dead sister, to transform Emily's vision of the muse as a godlike power, an angel messenger, into something Charlotte herself could approve and use. It would be a way, perhaps, of keeping a part of Emily alive.

Until now Charlotte's "visitants of air" had all been female, goddess-like projections of the strong mother-will in herself, of her own female powers of pride and hope. But in this final confrontation with Emily's work Charlotte seems to have been struck by the possibilities that the male visitant provides. There remained inevitable differences between the sisters' views. For Emily deity was female. The maleness of her angelic messenger evidenced Emily's distance from that deity, whom the messenger's very presence made Emily long to rejoin (really re-become, resume). But Charlotte's God was male, as we have seen: not some strength within herself, like the mother, but a power beyond her, like the father. For Charlotte, then, the male visitant would be some aspect of God Himself—his Son, perhaps, or the Holy Ghost. Might she not construe Emily's visitor, too, in some such way, especially as Emily (echoing the New Testament) had called him her "comforter"?

Emily had titled her original poem by the names of its chief characters, Julian and Rochelle; then, revising it for publication, she had given it the dour title "The Prisoner, A Fragment." But Charlotte's new version she called "The Visionary." By means of it she bridged the gap between Emily's and her own beliefs concerning the source of creative power. As she attributed to Emily eight lines of poetry that she herself had written out of her new insight into Emily's thought, so in *Shirley* she attributed her narrative rendering of this same understanding to the "visionary" Shirley in whom she had already tried to portray elements of her sister.

Perhaps Charlotte was especially attracted to Emily's idea of the descending masculine "power" because she herself had come to feel that no actual human lover could remain entirely outside "the wilderness of SIN" —a judgment implicit in the fact that Shirley compares even Louis to "a god of Egypt: a great sand-buried stone head" (p. 707). And certainly part of the attraction lay in Charlotte's conviction that human love would not come to her. Charlotte had hinted at both of these views in earlier poems, and now reemphasized them in this passage and in several others that she added late to *Shirley*.[30]

Accordingly when she turned this time to the Bible for a text that she could apply to her own case, she selected not the passage in Acts 2:2–4 in which the Holy Ghost descends as a wind of inspiration (though she retains hints of this image), but rather the more personalized, even sexualized, passage from Genesis 6 which tells how the daughters of men were taken to wife by "the sons of God." Having invoked this curious passage she was wise enough to refrain from trying to interpret its biblical meaning and concentrated instead on the way it could contribute to her own mythology, newly expanded by her insight into Emily's.[31]

In orthodox Christian doctrine there is of course only one Son of God, who as a member of the Trinity is mystically One with the Father and the Holy Ghost. In her parable Charlotte is tactfully evasive as to doctrinal specifics (Eva "had her religion: all tribes held some creed"). But by a rich texture of biblical allusion she conflates Father, Son, and Holy Ghost into one "Seraph, on earth, named Genius" who descends to claim and redeem the lonely and parentless "Eva."

As "Comforter," the seraph Genius is the Holy Ghost, at whose approach Eva appropriately echoes the words the Virgin Mary spoke at the annunciation: "Lord! behold thine handmaid!" As "True Dayspring from on high!" he is the Messiah (Luke 1:78), whose promise, "Surely I come quickly," along with the answer, "Even so, come, Lord Jesus" that concludes both Revelation and *Jane Eyre* are now echoed together in Eva's cry "Lord, come quickly!" And as the "Presence, invisible, but mighty" that invites her to "Enter my arms; repose thus," and then gathers her "like a lamb to the fold, " he is the adored but disappointing temporal father now transmuted into the eternal Father—Him in whom total power is joined forever with total love. Together, these allusions associate "Genius" with all three members of the trinity. So envisioned, Genius is of course God, the ultimate muse: and as the classical muses had their fountains of Helicon, so Genius offers Eva "a living draught from heaven"—alluding, of course, to the "pure river of water of life . . . proceeding out of the throne of God" (Revelation 22:1). This is— again—the heavenly "river" from which St. John Rivers derives his name in *Jane Eyre*.

All her life Charlotte had been assembling the pieces of what had by now developed into a kind of personal theology. She pressed the Protestant habit of individual interpretation into special service, using biblical allusion to give heightened texture and enlarged dimension to her personal experience. The waters out of which we are born and into which we die may be nearly universal in their symbolic suggestiveness, as expressed in the opening verses of Genesis and in the practice of baptism, where one is "reborn" into salvation through the water of life. But for Charlotte the implications of water imagery focused, as we have seen, not on the state of woman as she is yet unborn in her mother's womb, but rather on her danger of slipping back into a state that is fetal in its mindless infantilism; in Charlotte's experience this resulted from her tendency toward self-submergence in her love of what her experience brought her to feel were unworthy men. This condition of passivity and bondage paralleled in her imagination the Old Testament captivity of the Israelites in Egypt and their worship of false gods in the wilderness—all of which, according to the New Testament interpretation of St. Paul, in turn figures the condition of fallen humanity unredeemed by Christ: the children of bondage as opposed to the children of promise. The latter are born of Jerusalem above, "which is the mother of us all" (Galatians 4:26) and which is, in Revelation, the "bride of the Lamb."

Thus the Old Testament quest for the Promised Land and the New Testament quest for salvation in Christ were for Charlotte types of woman's struggle to liberate herself from a devotion that is a deadly bondage, and to search after a worthy love, one that nourishes and redeems her and infuses her with life. Put another way, it figures Charlotte's personal effort to detach herself from a father whom she considered charismatic but killingly cold and to replace him in her imagination with an accepting and all-supportive one. The former love is regressive, submerging, infantilizing; love of that kind she imaged as a swallowing sea—as in "The Fate of Henry Percy," "Diving," "Gilbert," and the first of the three pictures that Jane Eyre showed Rochester, where the "swollen sea" has nearly submerged a woman's "drowned corpse." The latter is redemptive, and raises her up.

We have seen that for Charlotte women may be rescued from regression by their mothers, that is by the redeeming "mother" in themselves. But this same "mother" is also a source of woman's vengeance. It is she who as moon-mother sends Jane away from Thornfield and then as Bertha exacts the price of adultery from Rochester. It is again she who suffuses the room with light as Jane hears Rochester's eerie call. It is she who as moon stares with "strange red glower" at Robert and Yorke over Rushedge, in *Shirley*, as each confesses his misapprehensions and mistreatments of women, her "scowl" and "menace" anticipating, almost summoning, the shot that fells Robert. She even operates comically through energetic Mrs. Horsfall.

But although this female power can aid woman to survive, can help her evade the clutches of men when they are unworthy or oppressive, and can subdue male power, even punish violators, still she is not herself the goal that woman seeks. Never since "The Violet" has Mother been the source of what Charlotte's heroines require. Mrs. Pryor's mother-love sustains Caroline when she is dying of loneliness; but for happiness it is marriage to Robert that she needs. The mother can give woman her first —her mortal—birth; she can lead woman out of temptation and deliver her from evil; Moses, indeed, might have been a woman.[32] But the Promised Land itself, the kingdom and the power and the glory— these belong to God, and for Charlotte God is thoroughly male.

I suspect that the Shirley-Louis story, as Charlotte first envisioned it, was meant to offer a truly alternative view of woman's power and potential, that there was to be another at least partial gender reversal, in which the old Zamorna charisma belonged to Shirley. Relics of this prospect survive in Louis' perception that Shirley "must be curbed": this would be the function of the dog bite that brings Shirley to her knees, asking Louis' help. And another relic glimmers most interestingly in Louis' little "fable of Semele reversed," as he calls it. Semele was the mortal who was destroyed by the sight of Jove in the majesty of his godhead. Louis imagines the inversion: a priest of Juno, in love with "the idol he serves," prays to the goddess to smile on him in person. Answering his prayer, she appears to him in her sanctuary at night, in a burst of sudden blinding light: "an insufferable glory burning terribly between the pillars." At dawn the people find "the shrine is shivered," the priest gone: in his place, at the foot of the goddess' statue, "piled ashes lie pale" (pp. 597–98). But the power of female sexuality here so vividly evoked ("glory . . . between the pillars") seems quite foreign to the Shirley who actually emerges in the novel, despite Charlotte's repeated emphasis on her extraordinary flair and "originality" (p. 619), and her qualities as "lioness," "leopard," or "Pantheress!" who "gnaws her chain," pining after "virgin freedom" (pp. 697, 705, 718).

Possibly the deaths of Charlotte's sisters, which intervened between the conception of *Shirley* and its execution, so humbled Charlotte's confidence in her own energies, so daunted her by dealing her such a powerful blow just as her creative powers seemed at their height, that she could no longer honestly envision female deity, nor as a consequence portray it.

Or perhaps the Mighty Mother had been always too much a mere theoretical construct, created more from need than from experience. For whatever reason, when Charlotte returned to volume 2 after Emily's death, she shifted emphasis as she wrote; the effect was to reemphasize both the potentially godlike qualities of the male sex and the masculinity of God. Her late additions to the manuscript confirm this trend and supplement it, as in the late-added discussion of men and marriage in volume 2, where Shirley vows that good men are "the lords of creation." Also in that passage the young women discuss Cowper's "The Castaway," the poem Mary Taylor said all the Brontës had appropriated and made almost their own.

Caroline's odd assertion that Cowper "was not made to be loved by woman" appears to derive from Charlotte's assent, at last, to the view that certain types of creative persons—like Patrick's "woman of intellect" who became Charlotte's Zenobia—really are incapable of inspiring sexual love. Charlotte's figurative language suggests that the power of genius itself drives love away. Caroline remarks that Cowper, writing his poem, "was under an impulse strong as that of the wind which drove the ship"—a familiar use of the romantic metaphor by which the wind is a figure for inspiration; but then Charlotte had Caroline add the striking observation that those who might wish to love Cowper are driven off by that same creative wind, "forced away . . . as the crew were borne away from their drowning comrade by 'the furious blast.' " Charlotte does not make explicit the connection she has implied; but she clearly did fear that she was herself one of these persons whose genius drove away *"the tender passion"* and left her to drown in loveless isolation. Caroline adds, "And what I say of Cowper, I should say of Rousseau. . . . And if there were any female Cowpers and Rousseaus, I should assert the same of them" (p. 255).

Such a one Zenobia had been, and so Charlotte saw herself as she had already asserted in her poem "Reason": "Alas! there are those who should not love; / I to this dreary band belong." The failure to be lovable Charlotte seems to have associated with a neurotic morbidity that she increasingly recognized in herself. Caroline says that personally she does not like characters of "the Rousseau order." Despite their "divine sparks," she says, "taken altogether" they are "unnatural, unhealthy, repulsive." Shirley declares herself more tolerant—as she can afford to be. But I think Caroline's estimate was Charlotte's self-estimate. It is clear from her depiction of Lucy in *Villette* that she was reaching a pretty firm assessment of her own morbid qualities. She wrote her publisher concerning Lucy, "I consider that she *is* both morbid and weak at times; . . . anybody living her life would necessarily become morbid. It was no impetus of healthy feeling which urged her to the confessional, for instance; it was the semi-delirium of solitary grief and sickness."[33] That trip to the confessional was Charlotte's own: the cited instance of Lucy's morbidity, painful autobiography.[34] By the time she was concluding *Shirley,* then, Charlotte had come to feel that the Shirley-Louis story did not adequately render her views on the relationship of creative woman to creative Genius. For one thing, she was now crushingly sure that no human "master's" love would ever come to herself. For another, though Shirley was a fine critic she was no creator; though Louis was a sensitive and demanding teacher, he was no creative spirit, no "Strange Power!" And finally, the woman of intellect Zenobia had burnt out. Somehow the theme of Charlotte's own soaring ambition had disappeared with her. It was in answer to the need to replace her, to bring her back into the fiction and give her Charlotte's version of Emily's "angel" to love her, that Charlotte had Shirley inscribe her into the last-minute French *devoir.*

The Eva who results from this effort is not Milton's cook, to be sure;

but neither is she Shirley's woman-Titan. Rather she is a composite of all
of Charlotte's heroines insofar as they are versions of her own inner self.
The original Zenobia she cannot be, because that Zenobia could not
inspire *"the tender passion";* and without some "one" to feel that passion
for her heroines, and by extension for herself, Charlotte had come to
think that neither they nor she could live. To be an unloved woman of
intellect was, we saw, to die of one's own flame. But Eva's ties to the
Zenobia idea are implicit in the essay's French title: "La Première Femme
Savante"—the first woman of intellect, which Charlotte translated "The
First Bluestocking." Zenobia really was the first bluestocking to appear
in Charlotte's work: Charles Wellesley had called Zenobia a bluestocking
in his introduction to "Albion and Marina." The difference is that whereas
Zenobia was unlovable, Eva is loved by a "visitant of air." Zenobia was
childless; but Eva can mother the children of promise, born after the
spirit. As Bertha, Zenobia "took down" the overweening Rochester to
make him a safe husband for Jane; but Eva is the beloved of Genius
himself. Eva replaces not Jane, but (in another gender reversal) St. John,
the apostle whose "master" is God. "Amen; even so come, Lord Jesus!"

Accordingly the story of Eva's origins is a mythically rendered story
of Charlotte's own history, needs, and inner condition, as Charlotte
herself had long conceived and understood them and regularly conveyed
them in her work. In "a forest valley" Eva lives "a child bereaved of
both parents. None cares for this child," except Nature herself, who
"nurses her, and becomes to her a mother." The womblike "forest
valley" is Eva's place of fetal solitude, in which her "modest worth" is
"half hid," as she had said of the violet borrowed from Wordsworth's
Lucy poem. This valley, a "black hollow" in which Eva's "spark of soul"
was "burning unmarked to waste, " recalls the "deep shadowy solitude"
of "The Voice of Lowood" (#158). There she had described the same
forest setting:

> Unhonoured, little thought of now
>   I come to rest my weary head
> Where leafy branch and ivied bough
>   Their canopy of calm will spread

—and the same wasted potential. "Have many lived as I have lived?" she
had asked in that poem:

> Born all for kindness yet b[e]reaved
>   Of human smiles and sympathy. . .
> Burning with love yet forced to sigh
>   That none will mark that passion swell[.]

In "The Voice of Lowood" she had affirmed that "one, by fiery glimpses" did indeed come to deliver her, to enkindle her cloud and melt her "frozen winter." But she had been evasive as to who that "one" might be—some inner power or something external to herself—beyond the hint that "even I have tasted joy / Pure, bright from heaven."

In *Jane Eyre* there had of course been a Lowood too, again specifically located in a "forest-dell" (p. 89). There, despite Brocklehurst's oppressive efforts, Jane had been warmed by Helen Burns and nourished by Maria Temple, and had survived to move on to Thornfield and Rochester's fiery glimpses. But this is not yet deliverance, not yet salvation; it is not in the power of the thorny wilderness to foster "joy / Pure, bright from heaven." So when the false marriage is called off, "frozen winter" returns:

> Jane Eyre, who had been an ardent, expectant woman—almost a bride —was a cold, solitary girl again. . . . A Christmas frost had come at midsummer: a white December storm had whirled over June. . . . My hopes were all dead—struck with a subtle doom, such as, in one night, fell on all the first-born in the land of Egypt. (pp. 373–74).

"The floods overflowed me," says Jane, quoting Psalms: she has been at one defathered and nearly drowned. Her dreams had warned her that both the woman and the child in her would be soon bereft of the man-father, and indeed she is now left with "no relative but the universal mother, Nature" (p. 412) who sustains her (though barely) in her hour of need. Cold, hidden, lonely, but with a stubborn fire still burning at "life's source"[35]—this is the condition of woman waiting for the enkindling man, for a "contact" that "strikes the fire from you that is in you," in Rochester's prophetic words. As Caroline Helstone's experience indicates, mother-love can go far toward warming and comforting the needy child in us. But the same experience also shows that mother-love is a first step only.

The forest dell's association with cloistered womanhood is emphasized in its next appearance, which occurs in *Shirley* when Caroline and Shirley propose an outing together, to "Nunnwood." This reminiscence of Lowood carries forward the imagery of sylvan isolation: the girls' excursion is to take them to "a dell; a deep, hollow cup, lined with turf" and ringed with leafy trees. We have here still the symbolic scenery of Wordsworth's half-hidden violet, but the shift in name from Lowood to Nunnwood emphasizes the celibacy of the place, a point made explicit in the text: in the bottom of the dell which is the object of their excursion "lie the ruins of a nunnery." Appropriately the girls discuss the question of whether it would be preferable to go on this excursion with or without the company of men, and agree at once that on this outing, to go without is better. In the presence of men "We forget Nature" and in turn "Nature forgets us; . . . conceals her face" (we should recall that in "The Violet" the "mighty Mother" is asked to unveil her face) "and withdraws the peaceful joy with which, if we had been content to worship her only, she would have filled our hearts." What women get in exchange, men being present, is "more elation and more anxiety: an excitement that steals the hours away fast, and a trouble that ruffles their course" (pp. 237–39): in short, stormy weather, troubled seas.

The "deep forest dell" is an analogue of the "cave in the sea." Both are images of fetal life, a kind of unborn state in which woman is protected by "mother" (e.g., Helen Burns and Maria Temple at Lowood, Lucy's godmother Louisa Bretton in Villette). In this protective womb, woman can be nourished and kept alive; but it remains a condition of potential only. There her "flame" is kept low, her value "half-hidden from the eye," her mental and spiritual capacities necessarily shadowy, enfolded. In Charlotte's theologically trained imagination, we have our mortal birth from woman's womb, but the rebirth that was for her creative and intellectual life, and ultimately spiritual salvation, requires the agency of the Father. Just as false gods thrust us back into the waters of infantilism and mortality, the true God alone can pluck us from them.

This un(re)born condition is Eva's, then, as she first appears in Shirley's *devoir*. The setting is that of Lowood and Nunnwood—"A forest valley, with . . . profundity of shade, formed by tree crowding on tree," in which people dwell "in alleys so thick branched and over-arched, they are neither heard nor seen." Eva's spiritual state is the fetal one described above: she is "a small forgotten atom of life, a spark of soul, emitted inadvertent from the great creative source. . . . She asked, was she thus to burn out and perish, her living light doing no good, never seen, never needed—a star in an else starless firmament . . . ?" This allusion is again to Wordsworth's Lucy, "Fair as a star when only one / Is shining in the sky." But Eva is no more content to remain unborn than the young poet Charlotte or her heroine Jane Eyre had been. The *devoir* continues:

> Could this be, she demanded, when the flame of her intelligence burned so vivid; . . . when something within her stirred disquieted, and restlessly asserted a God-given strength for which it insisted she should find exercise?

Out of this restless yearning she cries at last, "Guidance—help—comfort—come!" and is answered by a sound "like a storm whispering" (even here the male retains his stormy characteristic)—it is "a Son of God" calling her name:

"Eva!"
"Lord!" she cried, "behold they handmaid!". . .
"I come: a Comforter!"
"Lord, come quickly!" (pp. 550–52)

And so the biblical resonances assemble.

As God made humanity in his image, so this "Son of God . . . feels himself in the portion of life" that stirs and burns in Eva. The "flame of her intelligence" is a spark from his flame; and Eva's savior has come to "reclaim his own" in a vast, gathering embrace. At last, then, Charlotte can have it both ways, can satisfy through the agency of one unifying figure both her sexual-domestic and her creative-intellectual longings. As to the sexual: the beloved "master," paternal and charismatic, is here a *true* God and thus worthy of worship; truly loving and eternally faithful not because crippled or curbed, but because divine. His is the "mighty home" that Helen Burns had envisioned, of which Jane's eventual safe and contented home at the "retired and hidden" Ferndean is at best a muted, secular version. As to the creative: at last Charlotte's intellectual vitality need be thought of as neither wicked nor isolating. It is neither a source of spiritual bondage nor a wind that blows love away. She has been redeemed from the wanderings of the wilderness; unlike Moses, she can not only see, but actually reach the promised land. The dangerous and despotic "fiery imagination" about which young Charlotte had confessed to her friend Ellen Nussey (1836); the "sparks of fire" and the flame of "intense emtions" that threatened to burst "like lava" through the "veil of reserve and propriety" in Elizabeth Hastings (1839); the "frank and flashing glance" through which Frances Henri fleetingly expressed "her sense of her powers" (1846); the fire of ambition that made Jane Eyre's heart restless and "expanded it with life," that made her in Rochester's eyes a "savage, beautiful creature," and that through the agency of Bertha finally devoured all of Thornfield and part of Rochester (1847); this inner fire, purified and redeemed, is now projected outward into male form and personified as a "Son of God," at once the source of Charlotte's own genius and the external embodiment of it. Unloved Zenobia has burnt herself to ashes; as woman maddened by loneliness she has departed the story. But as the embodiment of intellectual strength she has finally been integrated into the fires of Charlotte's own spirit.

This had not yet happened when Charlotte wrote *Jane Eyre*. Helen Burns had pointedly offered the redemptive reading of these spiritual fires in observing that the "spark of spirit . . . —the impalpable principle of life and thought" is the gift of "the Creator to inspire the creature"; and she had predicted that "whence it came it will return." But Charlotte was not willing to turn her book over to this vision. In her driving need to let Jane have her Rochester, and have him happily ever after, right here in this world, Charlotte had turned herself and her heroine away from the insight she attributed to Helen, embodying it instead in the provocatively named St. John Rivers, a man whose energies she had to respect, but whose appeal she condemned as inhuman. The ambitions of St. John were, however, Charlotte's own ambitions insofar as they extended beyond the domestic sphere—beyond contentment at Ferndean —and demanded the full scope of intellectual and spiritual liberation that she associated with the burning presence of God as the source of creative genius.

When Rosamond Oliver—St. John's "earthly angel"—departs from him, Charlotte says that he "would have given the world to follow." But he is no wilderness wanderer, no pursuer of false gods: for happiness with Rosamond "he would not give one chance of Heaven; . . . one hope of the true, eternal Paradise." And here is where Charlotte reveals her deep ambivalence, what I have called her struggle with her muse over the ending of that book: "Besides, he could not bound all that he had in his nature—the rover, the aspirant, the poet, the priest—in the limits of a single passion. He could not—he would not—renounce his wild field of mission warfare for the parlours and the peace of Vale Hall." These words could be describing Jane Eyre, at her hottest; certainly they speak for a part of Charlotte.

In the Eva *devoir,* then, the "master" who so excited the desire of Mary, Mina, Frances, Jane, and Shirley is elevated into a version of the divine Master, who promised St. John, "Surely I come quickly!" Lover and muse are united in the person of divinity. The Marys have arisen— Resurgam!—and though in the person of Eva they must sustain "the agony of the passage," they will be at last "redeemed" and "crowned . . . with the crown of Immortality."

This was not of course the first time the connection had been made in Charlotte's mind between male sexual object and female creative gift: it was there in the sunny Zamorna who was early associated with Apollo. But only with the unnamed "one" whose "fiery glimpses" bring joy from Heaven in "The Voice of Lowood" did the pairing begin to bring creative life to *woman*. Most significantly, the love of such a "one" is not sexual but celibate: the "bridal-hour of Genius and Humanity" with which the story of Eva climaxes is modeled on the marriage of the lamb and his bride in Revelation, which though spoken in the language of sexual love, in fact figures the mystical union in eternity of Creator and Creation, of God and his Church. The analogue of this union, among earthly institutions, is the symbolic "marriage" of virgin nun to Christ. Hence Charlotte's acute interest in the subject of nuns and nunneries, an interest that dates at least from the time when she was beginning to dethrone Zamorna and to teach her heroines to say no. "Captain Henry Hastings" did not end with Elizabeth's rejection of Henry, but with a domestic scene in which among other things Zamorna accused Mary of wanting to enter a convent, "some sacred retreat where the follies of carnal affection might beset you no more."[36] Well might a weary Mary want such peace; that peace is of course precisely the attraction of "Nunnwood" to Caroline and Shirley.

At the end of Shirley, the "sisters" both marry human husbands, just as did Frances Henri and Jane Eyre and Maria Temple and (despite the virginal implications of their names) Diana and Mary Rivers. In the Eva devoir for the first time a heroine is swept away not by a man whom in the kindness or blindness of her love she had elevated to godhead, but by a god indeed. She is, in effect, a nun to art. Moreover, as the "chosen bride" of divinity ("Thou only in this land"), she is fully the equal of any mortal man; indeed she represents humanity at its very highest, humanity as it is redeemable and redeemed by "Genius."

Perhaps, as I have suggested, Charlotte's severe personal losses contributed to her inability to embody both themes—of woman's love and woman's genius—in the human love story of master and pupil. After Emily's death the possibilities of happiness in this world must have seemed bleaker than ever before, and the need even more absolute to look for fulfillment in the realm of spirit rather than of flesh—as Emily had done through her Romantic mysticism. Charlotte's long-felt need to improve the moral quality of the gods of her imagination—and by extension the quality of her imagination itself—also contributed to Charlotte's shift away from the natural toward the transcendent world. This was the function of the passage in Jane Eyre in which St. John affirmed that "poetry" and "genius" are "Powerful angels, safe in heaven!" where they triumph over Mammon and mediocrity, and from where they will "assert their existence, their presence, their liberty and strength again one day." Even now they not only live, but "reign and redeem."

It is in keeping with this view that Shirley faces down her uncle

Sympson over the subject of marriage values. Shirley, who as a girl "used to catch fire like tinder" on the subject of poetry, claims enthusiastically, "Oh! Uncle, there is nothing really valuable in this world, there is nothing glorious in the world to come, that is not poetry!" But she knows that her uncle will never understand her. "Your gods are not my gods," she avers: "Your god, sir, is the World." His god, like the deity worshipped in Bunyan's Vanity Fair and Thackeray's *Vanity Fair* (both texts were admired by Charlotte), governs the realms of money and power, of marriages made for position or profit. All that surrounds this god "hastens to decay: all declines and degenerates under his sceptre. *Your* god," Shirley concludes resoundingly, "is a masked Death" (p. 634).

This is to place "poetry," and the love of poetry, and the values and desires and fiery energies that are connected with it, in the company of divinity, heaven, redemption, eternity; in glorious opposition to Mammon and mediocrity, to all who raise idols and worship false gods in the wilderness, and struggle for pitiful straws of power in the fallen world of Death. It is to equate art with the Messiah.

But could such a vision—certainly familiar enough in Romantic poetry—ever be incorporated into a novel? Could its figures survive the imposition of realistic settings, local habitations, human names? The Eva allegory has struck many critics as a weak spot in *Shirley:* overwrought in language, sentimental in concept, eccentric to the principal movements of the book in which it figures. Charlotte, too, was apparently dissatisfied, though perhaps not on the same grounds. How little eccentric it was to the progress of Charlotte's thought, I hope I have shown. But to her gifts as a novelist it was clearly inadequate. To render its themes in novel form was the work of Charlotte's final masterpiece, *Villette*.

♌ FIVE

Villette, Exiled in Egypt

"O come O come Emmanuel
And ransom captive Israel
That mourns in lonely exile here
Until the Son of God appear."

—thirteenth-century hymn
(1st stanza)

Charlotte's final novel is astonishing for its art in fusing past concerns with present ones, for the mastery with which the author collects the themes and images that we have seen evolve out of the deepest layers of her mind and history, and brings them to bear on the events of her immediate life. The plot—an inspired expansion of the Eva *devoir*—draws on elements that have a history of more than twenty years in the life of Charlotte's imagination, dating at least from 1830. The setting is again the Brussels of 1842–1843; M. and Mme. Heger are again present, along with other elements of less significance deriving from that critical time ten years before. But much of the book's heightened power, the sense of nervous immediacy it conveys, derives from its effectiveness as a vehicle for discharging the pressures that built to bursting within Charlotte over the years 1849 to 1852, when *Villette* was conceived and written.

Charlotte claimed that reality should not dictate in art, but only suggest; and so in her work it had always done. The immediate reality that suggested this novel was Charlotte's experience with two of her publishers—the charming George Smith, of Smith, Elder, and Company, who made it all too clear to Charlotte that he could never love a plain woman, and his colleague James Taylor, a "horribly intelligent, quick, searching, sagacious" man who did love Charlotte, but from whom she recoiled in instinctive aversion. From this double experience she reaped a renewed conviction that passionate human love, fully reciprocated, was never to be hers. It might be that her very creative gift, her genius as a writer, prevented it: this had, recall, been her speculation concerning Cowper and Rousseau. But the allegory of Eva and Genius had recharged her search for an alternative avenue for passion, with personified "Genius" itself as her reciprocating object. It was this alternative, complexly interwoven with the realities of her experience with Smith and Taylor (and beyond them, with Heger and Patrick), that she developed in her final novel.

Contemporary reviewers on the whole liked *Villette;* they found it a work of great "power," worthy of the author of *Jane Eyre* and *Shirley,* though painful, even morbid, as neither of the earlier novels had been. And indeed despite its many comic elements the book does seem ruthlessly consistent in one key area of authorial policy: as Brontë wrote her publisher, "I am not leniently disposed towards Miss Frost"—her earlier name for Lucy Snowe; "from the beginning I never meant to appoint her lines in pleasant places."[1] Certainly she did not do so: alone in the world almost from the time we meet her, Lucy is for most of the novel a stranger in a strange land, learning twice to reach out for love, and bowing twice to loss.

The doubleness of that experience was an aesthetic problem for some reviewers. For example, *The Spectator* for February 12, 1853, observed that "of plot, strictly taken as a series of coherent events all leading to a common result, there is none." For others it was a problem more nearly moral: Harriet Martineau noted that Lucy "leaves the reader under the uncomfortable impression of her having either entertained a double love, or allowed one to supersede another without notification of the transition."[2] Thackeray, in a private letter, was more blunt: "it amuses me to read the author's naive confession of being in love with 2 men at the same time."[3] Charlotte's "confession," however, was in fact far from naive: she knew exactly what she was doing, and fully understood that "the spirit of romance"—as she wrote her publishers—would have indicated a course very different from the one she took; "it would have fashioned a paramount hero" and "kept faithfully with him." The "transfer of interest" that occurs, she explains, even if unwelcome to readers, was "in a sense, compulsory upon the writer."[4]

What, we may ask, could be the sources of such a "compulsion"? Why should two plots (in effect) be necessary to the telling of this story? Why in any case did Brontë remove her heroine all the way to a foreign city—Villette in the novel, Brussels in reality—to fall in love with one childhood acquaintance, Dr. John Graham Bretton, only to have him happily marry another childhood acquaintance, Paulina Mary Home de Bassompierre? Surely they might all have stayed comfortably in England for that. Students of the Brontës have generally assumed that the reason the novel must be set abroad and move, in its love interest, from the first "hero" (Bretton) to a second (M. Paul), was that Charlotte needed to portray again, in Paul, her beloved M. Heger. And they have argued that once she decided to give up trying to publish *The Professor,* a decision she finally reached in February 1851, some months before she began writing *Villette,* she was freed to incorporate its materials into this new novel and could not resist doing so. But if Charlotte's intention had been from the outset to review and to revise yet again in fiction the course of her love of Heger, why should Dr. John so dominate the first half of the story? And why should her imagination, from the time she first began experimenting with the scenes and ideas that eventually evolved into this novel, have hovered with such fascination over the rather vapid figure of Paulina, his eventual mate?

These questions may be answered in several different ways, each interesting in its own right and all significant, in their implications and interconnections, to the student of the Brontës and of Romantic literature. One answer is biographical: in a moment we will trace its course through Charlotte's letters of the period from 1849 to 1852. A second might be called aesthetic: she was interested in establishing and exploring two conflicting systems of value, that of the philistine materialist, who may be good or bad as a moral being, but is surely lacking in any visionary capacity; and that of the creative artist, who may be crotchety, morbid, and neurotic (or worse), but is nonetheless gifted with unique powers of spirit and imagination. A third answer is fundamentally religious. Charlotte saw the opposition between the pull of the physical world and the pull of genius (and of her own will to survival) as types of the Old Testament opposition between Israel in bondage, bowing to idols, and Israel in search of the promised land, worshiping the true God. As already observed, this opposition was in turn interpreted by St. Paul in the New Testament as the opposition between those who are fallen and those who are redeemed through Christ: between the "children of flesh" and the "children of promise" (Romans 9:8). Working from this structure of oppositions, Charlotte dramatized through Lucy's story the redemption of her imagination.[5] From its early, fallen condition, its death-tending worship of false gods, of sexuality and the flesh, it rises to an eternally life-giving worship of God the Father, the source of her own creative genius and also its mighty analogue and original. In psychological terms, the divine Father at last slakes Charlotte's thirst for love and approval, a thing that her human father, Patrick, had never been able to do.

The Biographical Background

To understand the creative achievement of Charlotte's final novel, one must know in some detail the biographical context out of which it grew. What Charlotte did was shape intolerably painful personal experience into a flesh that clothes the bare bones of idea that she had advanced in the Eva essay.

Villette was written at a time when Charlotte had to look beyond her own household for all her support and companionship. Her sisters dead, her father fast aging, she found for a time in her publishers at Cornhill in London some relief from her isolation. With the kindly Mr. Williams, who had been the first to recognize the potential of this new young writer and to respond encouragingly, Charlotte had shared her anxiety and grief in letters during the terrible year of deaths. But now, in a series of brief visits to London, she was getting to know George Smith better too, and finding him a generous and stimulating friend. Dr. John and his mother Louisa Bretton are fictional portraits of Smith and his mother, as both Brontë and Smith later explicitly acknowledged. And although M. Paul exhibits important characteristics of M. Heger, he has his immediate imaginative basis in Charlotte's encounter with another member of the Cornhill firm: James Taylor. An irritable and despotic little man whose red hair reminded her of Branwell's, he cut quite a swathe through Charlotte's barren life: he courted her with unwelcome forcefulness, apparently showed himself jealous of her vain attachment to Smith, and was in 1851 suddenly dispatched by the firm to India for five years, leaving a troubled and bewildered Charlotte to puzzle out the meaning of what she had learned about herself from all this and to place the new lesson into the context of her thought as it had been developing over the years. *Villette* is the result.

That in Lucy Charlotte was representing her perception of herself is by now, I hope, clear beyond dispute. Critics have argued that she distanced herself from her heroine, even that she did not like her. Possibly. But the very qualities of emotional disengagement and morbidity that are thought to evidence her distance from her heroine are qualities Charlotte attributed to herself: Lucy Snowe *is* the hot heart hid in ice. Writing to George Smith, Charlotte both exhibits and mocks the ironic tone and emotional caution that as novelist she was even then assigning to the young Lucy: "Of course I am not in the least looking forward to going to London," Charlotte writes, "no: I am very sedulously cool and nonchalant—Moreover—I am not going to be glad to see anybody there; *gladness* is an exaggeration of sentiment one does not permit oneself; to be *pleased* is quite enough . . . with pleasure of a faint tepid kind —and to a stinted penurious amount." This is the Lucy who surveyed with so cool an eye the passionate reception given her father by Polly: "I, Lucy Snowe, was calm." And although in this letter Charlotte's manner is playful, her letter to Mrs. Smith a week or so later shows how little playful were her grounds for frosty caution: "I will not say much about being glad to see you all. Long ago, when I was a little girl, I received a somewhat sharp lesson on the duty of being glad in peace and quietness—in fear and moderation; this lesson did me good, and has never been forgotten."[6] Such lessons are dramatized for us in the opening chapters, where the already painfully educated Lucy watches young Polly learn them.

In her biography, Gérin postulates that Charlotte began conceiving of *Villette* in the winter of 1849–1850, during her visit to London, when she stayed with the Smiths for the first time. Several fragments relating to the novel's opening scenes date from that time. And certainly the novel does draw on the experience of that visit, along with the subsequent visit of June and July; for all during that time Charlotte was caught in deep struggle between the conflicting powers of "Imagination" (hope) and "the rude Real" (despair) concerning her feelings for George Smith. This struggle did not end until at least the summer or fall of 1851, after a third visit. That fall brought stormy times to Charlotte's spirit, as we shall see. But careful review of the period leading up to 1852 when she was actively writing suggests a later date than the one Gérin proposes for Charlotte's arrival at her overall plan. She first began to see her way into her new work in the spring of 1851, but its overall shape certainly did not become clear until the fall of 1851. Once she saw that shape, she felt able to predict that the novel might be ready by the following autumn. Her estimate was remarkably accurate: during the summer of 1852 she found herself enabled at last to write, and she sent off her final volume on November 20, 1852. One may trace the steps of Charlotte's preparation and enablement quite precisely, and they reveal a great deal about the novel's meaning and importance to her.

Emily had died in December of 1848, causing Charlotte the most bitter grief of her adult life—not excluding even her shattering disappointment in Heger. But within two months after Emily's death she had copied out the first volume of *Shirley* and was initiating an entirely new stage in her relationship with the outside world. In a letter dated February 1, 1849, she offered Mr. Williams what was for her an astonishing suggestion: "I will tell you what I want to do; it is to show you the first volume of my MS." Never before had she shared work in progress with anyone but her sisters. Now, however, she was perforce widening her circle, though cautiously. Three days later, obviously having received vigorous encouragement from her publishers, she sends the manuscript on its way with words that usher James Taylor into her life: "Your mention of Mr. Taylor suggests to me that possibly you and Mr. Smith might wish him to share the little secret of the Ms.—that exclusion might seem invidious. . . . If so—admit him to the confidence by all means—he is attached to the firm and will no doubt keep its secrets. I shall be glad of another censor—and if a severe one, so much the better, provided he is also just."

It may be significant that when she did receive criticisms from all three, she responded first to Taylor—who seems also to have taken on himself the job of selecting the contents of a packet of books loaned to her at the same time—and only the day afterward to Williams and Smith, together, in a letter addressed to Williams. It may also be significant that the date of her letter to Taylor—it is in effect the date of the opening of their acquaintance—was Thursday, March 1, which will become a significant day in *Villette:* "M. Paul's fête fell on the first of March and a Thursday."[7] Her letter itself shows no special sense of anticipated relationship, though it does end "With a sincere expression of my esteem for the candor by which your critique is distinguished." And to Williams she confesses, "Mr. Taylor is quite right about the bad taste of the opening apostrophe—that I had already condemned in my own mind."[8] It is the one criticism from them all that she assents to. But her next letters are only to Williams; they chiefly concern Anne's failing health and ultimate death (May 28) and do not mention Taylor, unless he is included in the "two or three friends in Cornhill to whom I owe much kindness, and whose expectations I would earnestly wish not to disappoint."[9]

Home again after burying Anne at Scarborough, Charlotte wrote Williams on June 25 a letter that suggests her readiness to return to writing, and her painful reasons for it: she absolutely requires the escape that work provides. A month later she expands on the point: "The fact is, my work is my best companion—hereafter I look for no great earthly comfort except what congenial occupation can give—For society—long seclusion has in great measure unfitted me—I doubt whether I should enjoy it if I might have it. Sometimes I think I should, and I thirst for it —but at other times I doubt my capability of pleasing or deriving pleasure. The prisoner in solitary confinement—the toad in the block of marble—all in time shape themselves to their lot."[10] This toad was presently being used in *Shirley,* but the thirst and the prisoner are figures she would return to in *Villette.* Between now and then bitter experience was to demonstrate that congenial society she most surely did enjoy, desire, and need—but was apparently not to have.

Arrangements were made for Taylor to pick up the completed manuscript of *Shirley* on September 8, 1849, as he returned south from a holiday in his native Scotland. What Charlotte thought of him then there is no evidence to tell; what he thought of her may be inferred from his subsequent eager attentions to her.

But when she came to London in December she found the Smiths warm, comfortable, and attractive, and staying in their home a pleasure despite her shyness; whereas Taylor's advances sent her flying for emotional cover. "Mr. Taylor—the little man—has again shown his parts," she writes Ellen; "of him I have not yet come to a clear decision; abilities he has, for he rules the firm . . . he keeps 40 young men under strict control of his iron will. His young superior," i.e., George Smith, "likes him, which, to speak truth is more than I do at present; in fact, I suspect he is of the Helstone order of men—rigid, despotic, and self-willed. He tries to be very kind and even to express sympathy sometimes, but he does not manage it. He has a determined, dreadful nose in the middle of his face which when poked into my countenance cuts into my soul like iron. Still he is horribly intelligent, quick, searching, sagacious, and with a memory of relentless tenacity. To turn to Williams after him, or to Smith himself, is to turn from granite to easy down or warm fur."[11] As Gérin observes, "The fact was that James Taylor was falling in love with Charlotte, in the masterful, domineering manner of her own heroes."[12] But whatever the case in art, in life she found herself more offended than fascinated. In part, no doubt, she sensed in Taylor too many of the qualities that in Branwell and Patrick had always worked to her detriment: she feared that to accede to him would be to invite being swallowed up again, though this time certainly not from the violence of her own passion. To judge from her imagery, his very sexuality was repellent to her: the granite, the dreadful poking nose, she found alarming. She turned in relief to warm fur. Smith's less aggressive manner was clearly less threatening; and also Smith, unlike Taylor, might be approached and defined through his female connections. "I like him better even as a son and brother than as a man of business," she confided to Ellen in the same letter. For the remainder of this visit a well-timed attack of rheumatic fever kept Taylor out of Charlotte's way. Smith, on the other hand, she was getting to know in just the circumstances most likely to make him appealing. These attitudes toward the two men are the same as Lucy's in the first volume and a half of *Villette:* there Dr. John and his mother are kindly but not really intimate friends, and Paul is no more than an annoying provocateur. In Lucy's own words, summarizing her early view of Paul: "Once—unknown, and unloved, I held him harsh and strange; the low stature, the wiry make, the angles, the darkness, the manner, displeased me" (p. 710). Such was Taylor for Charlotte. Unfortunately, such he was also to remain.

From May 30 to June 25 Charlotte visited in London again, during which time she covered at least a portion of the emotional ground recorded in the second volume of *Villette*. Gérin speculates that during this month in London Charlotte "snubbed" Taylor, apparently for having shown himself jealous of her growing attraction to Smith.[13] Such speculation is certainly supported by the scenes in the novel where M. Paul haunts Lucy's exchanges with Dr. John, intimating that they are unworthy of her and that she might better direct her civilities to himself. Without question Lucy's gradual reassessment of John Bretton's character, and her recognition that he would never love her, echo Charlotte's recognitions concerning Smith as they began to take shape this summer of 1850.

One event of this visit stands out for the richness of its influence on Charlotte's thinking both about herself and, eventually, about her novel. On June 12 Thackeray held a dinner honoring Charlotte at his home—a party to which everyone came expecting to lionize the author of *Jane Eyre*. The event was, however, a social disaster. One of Thackeray's daughters later described its demise: "It was a gloomy and silent evening. Everyone waited for the brilliant conversation which never began at all. . . . The room looked very dark, the lamp began to smoke a little, the conversation grew dimmer and more dim, the ladies sat round still expectant, my father was too much perturbed by the gloom and the silence to be able to cope with it at all."[14] The evening dramatized to Charlotte not only her lack of social grace, but also the fact of her physical plainness. Another guest that evening, noting that there was "just then a fashion for wearing a plait of hair across the head," observed that Charlotte, "a timid little woman with a firm mouth," had too little hair to form such a plait "so therefore wore a very obvious crown of brown silk."[15]

Charlotte's poignant awareness of her defects, both physical and social, account for the free hand with which she dispenses the corresponding graces to Polly in *Villette*. That they were not qualities to be disdained as superficial we may know from the contrast Charlotte insisted on between Ginevra, whose beauty really is only a matter of "material charm" (p. 447), and Paulina, whose animation and delicacy in conversation are the pride of her father, but whom all admire as well for her lovely features and the telling "brown shadow and bounteous flow of her hair" (p. 266). Polly embodies the Lucy—that is, the Charlotte—that might have been, the lovely woman she wished she were, and thought she might have been had her ardent nature been nourished, and had it taken compatible physical form. As the name Lucy Snowe suggests, Lucy's is a fiery soul encased in the snows of a repression taught by bitter experience. Like Miss West and Elizabeth Hastings before her, she had learned to mask her inner truth with impenetrable chill: "in catalepsy and a dead trance I studiously held the quick of my nature" (p. 152). The same "ice of pride" (p. 379) protects Polly, but it lets her inner light shine through. Her real "charm," we are told, did not "lie in complexion . . . nor in outline," but rather "in a subdued glow from the soul outward." What has frozen to hardness in Lucy is merely polish in Polly, who is "a lamp chastely lucent"—the pun on Lucy is there, half-hid—"guarding from extinction, yet not hiding from worship, a flame vital and vestal" (p. 395). Such might Charlotte have wished for herself that evening at Thackeray's, for she was realizing with increasing clarity that these charms would be necessary to any woman who would win the love of a man like George Smith. Accordingly they were those with which she shortly endowed the heroine who was to win the love of Dr. John. Returning in the carriage from Thackeray's party that night, Charlotte acted on an impulse which might be read as the first stirring in her mind of the future relative roles of Lucy and Paulina. Smith describes the moment in his memoir: "One of Mr. Thackeray's guests was Miss Adelaid Procter, and those who remember that lady's charming personality will not be surprised to learn that I was greatly attracted to her. During our drive home I was seated opposite to Miss Brontë, and I was startled by her leaning forward, putting her hands on my knees, and saying 'She would make you a very nice wife.' 'Whom do you mean?' I replied. 'Oh! you know whom I mean,' she said, and we relapsed into silence."[16] During this silence the novelist, one suspects, was already at work.

Charlotte said that her own "lack of all pretension to beauty etc." was a perfect safeguard against there ever being any misunderstanding between herself and Smith concerning the "meaning" of their friendship,[17] and she was perfectly correct. As Smith admitted years later to Mrs. Humphrey Ward, "I was never the least bit in love with Charlotte

Brontë. I am afraid that the confession will not raise me in your opinion, but the truth is, I never could have loved any woman who had not some charm or grace of person, and Charlotte Brontë had none—I liked her and was interested in her, and I admired her—especially when she was in Yorkshire and I was in London. I never was coxcomb enough to suppose that she was in love with me. But I believe that my mother was at one time rather alarmed." His mother had indeed not favored a trip that George and his sister were planning with Charlotte to Scotland; but at his insistence she changed her mind, even urging Charlotte, too, to comply. "His mother is master of the house, but he is master of his mother," as Charlotte observed dryly at the time.[18] Smith was aware of the pain that her plainness caused Charlotte. "I believe she would have given all her genius and all her fame to have been beautiful," he opined —somewhat naively, given Charlotte's fiery ambitions. "Perhaps few women ever existed more anxious to be pretty than she, or more angrily conscious of the circumstances that she was not pretty."[19]

There does seem a note of masculine presumption is all this. Yet there is insight too, as we may gather from Charlotte's depiction of Lucy's feelings on the subject of beauty. Addressing M. Paul in one of their last moments together, Lucy asks, "Ah! I am not pleasant to look at—?" explaining to the reader, "I could not help saying this; the words came unbidden: I never remember the time when I had not a haunting dread of what might be the degree of my outward deficiency; this dread pressed me at the moment with special force." So she again urges the question: "the point had its vital import for me. He stopped, and gave me a short, strong answer—an answer which silenced, subdued, yet profoundly satisfied. Ever after that, I knew what I was for *him;* and what I might be for the rest of the world, I ceased painfully to care" (pp. 698–99). Tellingly, Charlotte does not imagine for us the satisfying words themselves, but only summarizes their happy effect.

The brief Scottish tour that ended this London visit was delightful for Charlotte, a final moment of pleasure before the dark fall and winter, the second anniversary of Emily's illness and death, when she undertook to edit her sisters' works and so lived again among constantly wounding memories. As she confessed to her friend Ellen at the time, "The reading over of papers, the renewal of remembrances brought back the pang of bereavement, and occasioned a depression of spirits well-nigh intolerable."[20] Among other painful things, she was now forced to the clearer understanding of Emily's thought, of the meaning of her art, that she was shortly to reveal in her "Preface" to *Wuthering Heights* (see my chapter 1, above).

A letter from Taylor in September came as a pleasant surprise and initiated a continuing correspondence during these fall and winter months. The letters to Taylor are certainly impersonal, compared to those she wrote Smith and Williams. With Smith she is playful; with Williams she is intimate in a rather daughterly way. But with Taylor her tone is austere: her topics are literary, intellectual, or religious, almost exclusively. One of these letters[21] is especially interesting for the analysis she offers of the character of Dr. Thomas Arnold, then famous as headmaster of Rugby. She had just been reading his *Life,* on loan from Cornhill, and Taylor had apparently requested her opinion. Dr. Arnold's character she perceived and described in terms that she would later use to describe M. Paul's. Perhaps her study of Arnold provides a link between the fictional M. Paul and the actual James Taylor, to whom her letter was addressed. "Dr. Arnold," she wrote, "was not quite saintly; his greatness was cast in a mortal mould; he was a little severe—almost a little hard; he was vehement and somewhat oppugnant. . . . Exacting he might have been . . . and a little hasty, stern, and positive, those were his sole faults." Arnold's faults sound like M. Paul's, and so do his virtues: "Where can we find justice, firmness, independence, earnestness, sincerity, fuller and purer than in him?" And here Charlotte adds a paragraph that, had Taylor known how to hear it, he might have turned to account in his wooing. Certainly the qualities here praised are central to the shift in Lucy's feelings for Paul. "But this is not all, and I am glad of it. Besides high intellect and stainless rectitude, his letters and his life attest his possession of the most true-hearted affection. Without this, however we might admire, we could not love him, but with it I think we love him much. A hundred such men, fifty, nay ten or five such righteous men might save any country, might victoriously champion any cause." Might win any woman's heart?

Dr. Arnold's destiny in life was not, however, the model for Paul's; rather it was more nearly a model for John Bretton's. Concerning Arnold her letter continues: "I was struck, too, by the almost unbroken happiness of his life . . . owing partly to a singular exemption from those deep and bitter griefs which most human beings are called on to endure. . . . God's blessing seems to have accompanied him from the cradle to the grave." These sentiments are echoed in the chapter that closes the story of Paulina's marriage to Dr. John: "I *do* believe there are some human beings so born, so reared, so guided from a soft cradle to a calm and late grave, that no excessive suffering penetrates their lot, and no tempestuous blackness overcasts their journey. And often, these are not pampered, selfish beings, but Nature's elect, harmonious and benign; men and women mild with charity, kind agents of God's kind attributes" (p. 632). By tempestuous blackness was Charlotte's own journey just now greatly overcast, however, as she worked her way through the materials of her sisters' published and unpublished papers, suffering the shocks of both memory and, in Emily's case, painful new insight.

By January 1851 Charlotte felt called on—and able—to define her feelings for both Smith and Taylor, or at least those feelings she knew she must cultivate for the sake of her peace of mind. Ellen had apparently offered the flattering suggestion that in Smith's attentions to Charlotte there was an "undercurrent" that implied "fixed intentions" of a roman-tic sort. "Dear Nell—" writes the unoffended Charlotte, "your last letter but one made me smile. I think you draw great conclusions from small inferences. I think those 'fixed intentions' you fancy—are imaginary—I think the 'undercurrent' amounts simply to this—a kind of natural liking and sense of something congenial. Were there no vast barrier of age, fortune &c."—were she, in short, a Paulina—"there is perhaps enough personal regard to make things possible which now are impossible. . . . but other reasons regulate matrimony—reasons of convenience, of con-nection, of money." She does not mention beauty. "Meantime I am content to have him as a friend—and pray God to continue to me the common-sense to look on one so young, so rising and so hopeful in no other light." But the emotions Charlotte must contend with are far more unruly than is Ellen's friendly imagination. Smith was now proposing another trip, this time to the Rhine; but this time Charlotte was firm in her refusal. Her letter to Ellen reveals her growing awareness that Smith did not understand the world of her feelings. "That hint about the Rhine disturbs me; I am not made of stone—and what is mere excitement to him—is fever to me." Such obtuseness makes him, like Dr. John, de-spite good intentions a painful friend to have. But Charlotte like Lucy cultivates the discipline to endure: "Goodbye, dear Nell, Heaven grant us both some quiet wisdom—and strength not merely to bear the trial of pain—but to resist the lure of pleasure when it comes in such a shape as our better judgment disapproves." Of such resolutions—often con-firmed and unflinchingly enforced—are the frosts and snows of the spirit made.

But if Smith must be acknowledged to be out of reach, perhaps Taylor need not be. In another letter to Ellen, written ten days after the one just quoted, Charlotte responds a little irritably to more persistent teasing about Smith, and about the fitness of romance between successful author and handsome publisher. "You are to say no more about 'Jupiter' and 'Venus,' what do you mean by such heathen trash? . . . my common-sense laughs it to scorn." Her common sense has apparently been at work not only negatively, but also positively. She is apparently thinking, however cautiously, of the now rather lengthy attachment of "the little man" Taylor, whose attentions had once, at least, been offered with "vehement ardour." Despite sustained rejection, Taylor had persevered; perhaps he deserved better treatment from her? He had for a time sent her regular copies of *The Athenaeum,* but had then withdrawn them, leading her to assume that the paper "was gone to the tomb of the Capulets," that repository of dead lovers. But no: it had then "reappeared with an explanation that he had feared its regular transmission might rather annoy than gratify. . . . This little Taylor," she had concluded with satisfaction, "is deficient neither in spirit nor sense."

So now in January 1851 when the "heathen trash" must be scorned, Charlotte finds herself returning in her thoughts to Taylor, and suggesting tentatively that "The idea of the 'little man' shocks me less—it would be a more likely match if 'matches' were at all in question, which *they are not."* But the vein of her letter contradicts her own emphasis: "He still sends his little newspaper—and the other day there came a letter of a bulk, volume, pith, judgment and knowledge, worthy to have been the product of a giant. You may laugh as much and as wickedly as you please—but the fact is there is a quiet constancy about this, my diminutive and red-haired friend, which adds a foot to his stature—turns his sandy locks dark, and altogether dignifies him a good deal in my estimation. However, I am not bothered by much vehement ardour—there is the nicest distance and respect preserved now, which makes matters very comfortable. This is all nonsense—Nell—and so you will understand it."[22]

But Charlotte's mind this winter was probably less occupied by her heart than by her pen: she was finding herself unable to begin work on a fourth novel. A scheme to unearth the often-rejected first novel, *The Professor,* was not encouraged, her publishers apparently trying both to reassure her that they were not impatient—that she should take her time —and also to indicate that she really should undertake some fresh topic. Smith apparently suggested that another visit to London might refresh her spirits, but Charlotte's answer is both playful and revealing. "I don't deserve to go to London: nobody merits a change or a treat less. I secretly think, on the contrary, I ought to be put in prison, and kept on bread and water in solitary confinement—without even a letter from Cornhill —till I have written a book. One of the two things would certainly result from such a mode of treatment pursued for twelve months; either I should come out at the end of that time with a 3 vol. MS. in my hand, or else with a condition of intellect that would exempt me ever after from literary efforts and expectations."[23] Meanwhile her own barometer was falling. A letter on February 11 to Taylor says that she has found the defense of atheism in "Miss Martineau's and Mr. Atkinson's new work, 'Letters on the Nature and Development of Man'" too disturbing to consider in any "impartial spirit" or "collected mood." She finds this life far too grim to admit any doubt of a better one to come. In a letter written on February 26 to Ellen she seems enervated almost to stasis. And a note dated March 8 to George Smith does not even get mailed.

Then suddenly, into this confluence of literary, romantic, and religious depression, George Smith unwittingly drops a double bombshell. Charlotte's quiet note of March 8—still unsent on March 11 when she excitedly snatched it up again—now continues: "The preceding was written before I received yours; a few more lines must now be added." And what she adds reveals the nature of the first explosion. Her publisher has made some innocent remark about how she must not use her friends at Cornhill as subjects in her next novel—having in mind, no doubt, the numbers of portraits drawn recognizably from life in *Jane Eyre* and *Shirley*. Charlotte almost whoops:

> Do you know that the first part of your note is most dangerously suggestive? What a rich field of subject you point out in your allusion to Cornhill, &c.—a field at which I myself should only have ventured to glance like the serpent at Paradise; but when Adam himself opens the gates and shows the way in, what can the honest snake do but bend its crest in token of gratitude and glide rejoicingly through the aperture?

Then she backs off a little: "But no! don't be alarmed. You are all safe from Currer Bell." Still, the temptation to speculate on the possibilities is irresistible:

> Were it possible that I could take you all fearlessly, like so many abstractions, or historical characters that had been dust a hundred years, could handle, analyse, delineate you, without danger of the picture being recognized either by yourselves or others, I should think my material abundant and rich. This, however, is no more possible than that the Nurse should give the child the moon out of the sky. So —I repeat—you are *very* safe.

In fact, of course, he had never been less safe. Perhaps the moon Charlotte alludes to here was a first glimpse of mothering Hope. Certainly her response shows the momentary flash of hope's light.

The second bombshell of Smith's note proved no less explosive, though somewhat slower of effect. For, apparently in the context of telling about the firm's expansion and growth, he announced that James Taylor would be voyaging shortly to India to take charge of expanded business there. Charlotte's letter comments at some length on the general matter of expanding trade, but limits her response to the particular news about Taylor to a one-sentence paragraph: "I hope Mr. Taylor will bear the voyage and change of climate well."[24]

She might recall that it was now two years since she had first met Taylor: two years since their correspondence opened with her letter of Thursday, March 1, 1849. He had cared for her that long, she had taken his "quiet constancy" almost for granted, had even been struggling to locate and honor those qualities in him that might make "the idea of 'the little man' " less "shocking." But now he was leaving with unpredictable suddenness, and word of it had come not even from himself. Her response is—characteristically—to numb herself, to bank up a little more snow against the pain. Ten days later she returned in the mail to Cornhill the books and papers Taylor had lent her, and followed them the next day with a letter to Taylor, noting coolly that she will not comment at length on an article to which he had directed her attention since "if I rightly understood a brief paragraph in Mr. Smith's last note, you are on the eve of quitting England for India." Her letter concludes: "I do not know when you go, nor whether your absence is likely to be permanent or only for a time; whichever it be, accept my best wishes for your happiness, and my farewell, if I should not again have the opportunity of addressing you."[25]

By March 24 she at last received a letter from Taylor himself, who had apparently all this time been absent in Scotland, unaware that Smith had announced the planned trip, or that Charlotte had responded to it. His letter seems to have suggested that the decision to go was the result of a crisis through which he had passed. If Charlotte understood him to mean that the crisis had reference to herself, her response does not show it. Still, his letter had asked if he might visit her father and herself on his return from Scotland, and that request she can hardly have thought to be without significance. "May your decision in the crisis through which you have gone result in the best effect on your happiness and welfare; and indeed, guided as you are by the wish to do right and a high sense of duty, I trust it cannot be otherwise. The change of climate is all I fear; but Providence will overrule this too for the best—in Him you can believe and on Him rely."[26] Indeed her letters to Taylor throughout their correspondence indicate that strong religious conviction is one of the bonds between them—a fact that might contribute to his appropriateness as partial model for Paul Emanuel. In this particular case, however, it is hard to tell how much of Charlotte's firm acquiescence to Providence is a way of masking pain (another loss to her whose resources of affection are already so severely narrowed) and to what extent it merely indicates emotional caution (no wish to encourage unfounded hopes).

Meanwhile George Smith has been a continuing disappointment. Mrs. Gaskell had written Charlotte apparently around March 20, and when Charlotte had delayed answering the letter for some days, had written Smith to inquire about her friend's health. Hearing of the inquiry, Charlotte comments daily that she cannot guess what report Smith could have given of herself, as "he had not heard from me for some time"—the point being, of course, that she had not heard from him.[27] But Mrs. Gaskell's inquiry stirred Smith to get back in touch with Charlotte, who responds a little coolly to his polite letter: "I am in very reasonable good health, thank you, and always in as good spirits as I can manage to be."

Her letters of this period show how much she feels the need of a comfort she cannot find. Perhaps in line with this need, she takes the occasion of a letter to Smith to state firmly—almost ostentatiously—her regard for Mr. Taylor: "I believe he is a good man, firm-principled, right-minded, and reliable. . . . To be appreciated he must be known. In him the kernel is not without its husk; and you must have time and opportunity to penetrate beneath the outside, to get inured to the *manner* before you even understand the man. So I think at least."[28] This would seem to be her way of going on record—not only for the benefit of Smith (between whom and Taylor Charlotte increasingly suspected some bad feeling), but also in the hope that her words would reach Taylor and act as a sort of apology. And finally, perhaps, it was meant to serve as a physic for herself, in preparation for Taylor's impending visit. She had turned away from him too quickly before, perhaps responding to the husk only. Now she must try to discern the kernel within, to see if Taylor were not indeed a man she might learn to love.

Five days later the critical encounter was over. No comfort had come of it after all. To Ellen she wrote: "Mr. Taylor has been and is gone; things are just as they were. I only know in addition to the slight information I possessed before, that this Indian undertaking is necessary to the continued prosperity of the firm of Smith, Elder, & Co., and that he, Taylor, alone was pronounced to possess the power and means to carry it out successfully—that mercantile honour, combined with his own sense of duty, obliged him to accept the post of honour and of danger to which he has been appointed, that he goes with great personal reluctance, and that he contemplates an absence of five years."[29]

Much of this voyage—its mode of announcement, the disinterested sacrifice required in the service of others' money, the journey's duration and destination—finds its place, though modified as to detail, at the climax of *Villette*. M. Paul's voyage, too, is announced by a third party and left long unexplained to the anxious Lucy: "He is preparing for a long voyage. A very sudden and urgent summons of duty calls him to a great distance. He has decided to leave Europe for an indefinite time. Perhaps he may tell you more himself" (p. 636). This announcement comes similarly just as the friendship between Lucy and M. Paul has been ripening into something that provides her with the first real emotional support she has had in Labassecour—perhaps in her life. M. Paul's voyage is not to India but to the West Indies, and will be for three rather than five years—though Lucy, like Charlotte, has to wait a long time before receiving even this information. Similarly, in *Villette* "the business which called him abroad related to a friend's interests, not his own: I thought as much" (p. 638). Summarizing the origin and object of M. Paul's journey, Lucy concludes: "Its alpha is Mammon, and its origin Interest." Mme. Beck, Père Silas, and Mme. Walravens all had monetary reasons for nursing the West Indian project. "But the distance was great, and the climate hazardous. The competent and upright agent wanted, must be a devoted man." "Paul, if he liked, could make the best and faithfullest steward: so the three self-seekers banded and beset the one unselfish. They reasoned, they appealed, they implored; on his mercy they cast themselves, into his hands they confidingly thrust their interests" (pp. 668–69). This is a more colorful rendering of the claims made on Taylor: the firm's needs, the unique qualities of the man chosen, the sense of duty that must overcome personal reluctance. For the "Mammon" of *Villette* we may perhaps substitute the god blamed in Charlotte's letter to Taylor: "doubtless 'business' is a Moloch which demands such sacrifices."[30]

By the time these events occur in *Villette,* however, Lucy is in love with M. Paul; whereas Charlotte was certainly not in love with Taylor. "He looked much thinner and older," she reported to Ellen after the visit. "I saw him very near and once through my glass. . . . He is not ugly, but very peculiar; the lines in his face show an inflexibility, and I must add, a hardness of character which do not attract. As he stood near me, as he looked at me in his keen way, it was all I could do to stand my ground tranquilly and steadily, and not to recoil as before. It is no use to say anything if I am not candid—I avow then, that on this occasion, predisposed as I was to regard him very favorably—his manners and his personal presence scarcely pleased me more than at the first interview," when she certainly *had* recoiled. "He gave me a book at parting, requesting in his brief way, that I would keep it for his sake, and adding hastily, 'I shall hope to hear from you in India—your letters have been, and will be a greater refreshment than you can think or I can tell.' "[31]

Charlotte was not in love with Taylor, but she had counted heavily on his love for her, on the possibility of learning to reciprocate such a feeling from one whose principles, intellect, and constancy she had come to respect. To Ellen she confides:

> "And so he is gone, and stern and abrupt little man as he is—too often jarring as are his manners—his absence and the exclusion of his idea from my mind—leave me certainly with less support and in deeper solitude than before. . . . He seemed throughout quite as excited and nervous as when I first saw him. I feel that in his way he has a regard for me; a regard which I cannot bring myself entirely to reciprocate in kind, and yet its withdrawal leaves a painful blank."

Glumly she concludes, "Something at my heart aches and gnaws drearily, but I must cultivate fortitude."[32]

Four days later she returns again to the subject. "Certainly I shall not soon forget last Friday—and *never,* I think, the evening and night succeeding that morning and afternoon." Mr. Brontë had been ill during the evening, and though he grew enough better to doze off early in the night, the warning had not been lost on Charlotte. If he should die, where on earth could she turn in her loneliness? "I came down to the dining room with a sense of weight, fear and desolation hard to express and harder to endure." Ellen had apparently tried to console Charlotte with the thought that after his return Taylor might still be available to her. "You speak to me in soft consolatory accents, but I hold far sterner language to myself, dear Nell. An absence of five years—a dividing expanse of three oceans—the wide difference between a man's active career and a woman's passive existence—these things are almost equivalent to an eternal separation." Yet Charlotte has not talked herself into a love she did not feel, for as she points out, "there is another thing which forms a barrier more difficult to pass than any of these. Would Mr. T— and I ever suit? could I ever feel for him enough love to accept of him as a husband? Friendship—gratitude—esteem I have—but each moment he came near me—and that I could see his eyes fastened on me—my veins ran ice."

Now this would seem to be the root of the problem. When had Charlotte ever loved a man who was available to her? M. Heger had been married, and thus her adoration was certain never to face the test of reality. None of her other suitors had interested her in the least. Smith, she had come to see even as she grew to like him more and more, was never going to fall in love with *her*. But Taylor was a man whose character and abilities could not be easily dismissed, whose constancy had been proven: and yet her veins "ran ice." She describes her response with striking self-insight. "Now that he is away I feel far more gently toward him—it is only close by that I grow rigid . . . which nothing softens but his retreat and a perfect subduing of his manner."[33] The very excitement in him which was gratifying as a sign of his regard seems to have been at the same time threatening, an aspect of the "manner" which must be "subdued." One recalls her earlier alarm at his dreadful poking nose, her dislike of his "vehement ardour." And yet the loss of his attention is desolating; she finds even her father's ill health a welcome relief, in that it keeps her thoughts off "other matters—which have become complete bitterness and ashes—for I do assure you—dear Nell —not to deceive either you or myself, a more entire crumbling away of a seeming foundation of support and prospect of hope—than that which I allude to—can scarcely be realized."[34]

Apparently she could endure neither to accept the man nor to let him go; but of the two, acceptance was the more unendurable. The bare possibility of seeing him after all one more time stirs her "bitterness and ashes" into quite a flame. She was planning a visit to London in the first week of June; in what Charlotte termed a "quiet little note" Taylor asked if she might come in time to see him once more before his departure? By no means! To Ellen she explains her position in language mountingly hostile to "the little man," as if renewed opportunity alone were enough to freeze her to the bone: "I am sure he has estimable and sterling qualities, but with every disposition and with every wish, with every intention even, to look on him in the most favorable point of view at his last visit, it was impossible to me in my inward heart, to think of him as one that might one day be acceptable as a husband." Her vehemence on the point increases. "It would sound harsh were I to tell even *you* of the estimate I felt compelled to form respecting him; dear Nell, I looked for something of the gentleman—something of the *natural* gentleman; you know I can dispense with acquired polish, and for looks, I know myself too well to think that I have any right to be exacting on that point. I could not find one gleam, I could not see one passing glimpse, of true good-breeding; it is hard to say, but it is true. In mind too"—this of the man whose intellect she had so often praised—"though clever, he is second-rate; thoroughly second-rate. One does not like to say these things, but one had better be honest. Were I to marry him, my heart would bleed in pain and humiliation; I could not, *could* not look up to him."[35] Can Taylor's "quiet little note" have aroused all this animus? The prospect of having the opportunity to call her own emotional bluff, to exchange her "bitterness and ashes" for something more nourishing: perhaps that prospect in itself was so intolerable as to require a resurgence of hostility to fend it off. Or it may have been that the contrast of Taylor to Smith was not to be borne. For although she really knew very well that Smith could never be hers, that seems still to have been a knowledge more easily avowed than embraced. For her to accept it fully would require one more trip to London and its ensuing "reaction"—the title of the corollary chapter in *Villette*. It is the chapter that prepares, in Lucy's anguished heart, the way for Paul.

But one troubling element in Charlotte's feelings about Smith and Taylor does not find its way into the novel, or rather it takes curiously altered form. Taylor's visit seemed to increase her sense that all was not right between him and Smith. To Ellen she noted: "In his conversation he seemed studiously to avoid reference to Mr. Smith individually— speaking always of the 'house,'—the 'firm.'" And even in her later letter, so generally hostile to Taylor, she concedes: "There is still a want of plain, mutual understanding in this business, and there is sadness and pain in more ways than one." She appears to have suspected Smith of selfish or jealous feelings toward Taylor.

In *Villette* Dr. John is certainly capable of selfishness; but it is Mme. Beck, not Dr. John, who is jealous of Lucy's and M. Paul's relationship, who strives to keep them apart, and sends M. Paul off on his dangerous voyage with the dog-in-the-manger wish that he may never return alive to claim Lucy for his wife. Can Charlotte have nursed, however much against her own best knowledge, the shadow of a hope that Smith's sending Taylor out of the way reflected some jealousy over Taylor's regard for herself? It is perhaps worth noticing that Smith's business capacities, his ability to restrain feeling into the service of practicality, are also characteristics assigned to Mme. Beck rather than to Dr. John. And if one is to see the Cornhill "house" anywhere in the book, it is shadowed negatively in the jealous circle of "Malevola," of whom M. Paul is a straying member. (Charlotte had joked about Cornhill as a kind of Catholic cabal in October 1850.) In such an interpretation Williams, with his paternal gentleness, approximates the well-meaning Père Silas, just as certain of Smith's less attractive qualities are reflected in Mme.

Beck. (Of course the primary model for Mme. Beck is Mme. Heger; my point here is merely that in certain respects her posture toward Paul parallels Smith's toward Taylor.) Mme. Walravens, the leader of this "secret junta" (p. 666), has a status all her own, as I will show later on.

If Charlotte nursed such a hope as that I have suggested, it did not survive long. And even at the time she seems to have felt that her inability to respond to Taylor would leave her an "old maid"; indeed she already thought she had the inclinations of one. The letter so hostile to Taylor is signed "With kind regards to all, I am, dear Nell, your middle-aged friend, C. Brontë."

The story of her remaining relationship to Taylor is quickly told. On May 5 she wrote Ellen that a long letter from Williams "speaks of Mr. T —with much respect and regret—and says he will be greatly missed by many friends." Perhaps more unpredictably, her own father apparently took Taylor's side as well. "I discover with some surprise that Papa has taken a decided liking to Mr. Taylor. . . . When I alleged that he was 'no gentleman'—he seemed out of patience with me for the objection. . . . I believe he thinks a prospective union, deferred for 5 years, with such a decorous reliable personage would be a very proper and advisable affair —However I ask no questions and he asks me none, and if he did, I should have nothing to tell him."

But if Williams'—and even more Patrick's—championing gave Charlotte pause, it made no difference in the long run. Except for a couple of letters, "the little man" had permanently left her life.

She did not face this truth immediately, but she did actively contribute to it. Her next letter to Taylor was her last, and it happens to have survived. Taylor had apparently complained of the lack of intellectual companionship in Bombay, and of his missing friends at home—perhaps a veiled compliment to her, and certainly a remark that might have been taken as encouraging Charlotte to consider herself capable of helping to fill that void. But she studiously avoids such a reading: "It would seem to me a matter of great regret that the society at Bombay should be so deficient in all intellectual attraction. Perhaps, however, your occupations will so far absorb your thoughts as to prevent them from dwelling painfully on this circumstance." Certainly few men would be encouraged to pursue any flattering hopes in the face of such studied disinterest. Her closing paragraph, moreover, is nearly insulting: "I had myself ceased to expect a letter from you. On taking leave at Haworth you said something about writing from India, but I doubted at the time whether it was not one of those forms of speech which politeness dictates; and as time passed, and I did not hear from you, I became confirmed in this view of the subject. With every good wish for your welfare,—I am, yours sincerely, C. Brontë.[36] If we recall her own account of Taylor's apparently rather tender words—"your letters *have* been, and *will* be a greater refreshment than you can think or I can tell' "—we must wonder at Charlotte's revision of the occasion. I have already suggested that his availability itself seems to have worked against him, his "vehement ardour," his very standing near her and looking at her in his "keen way." She complains consistently of his "hardness": he is like "granite," he has a "hard nature," she doubts his capacity for "kindness." And yet there runs a corresponding current of admiration for him, a suggestion that the manner is not the man, that the husk belies the kernel. This ambivalence seems to have been paralleled in Charlotte's own posture toward him: on the surface, and in her direct encounters, she bristles and rejects, but in her heart she hungers for the love she cannot accept. Even her almost insulting last paragraph might be read as a kind of lover's reproach: why didn't you write sooner? I was hurt by your delay.

But Taylor apparently did not read it so, for he appears never to have answered this letter. On February 24, 1852, Charlotte notes without comment to Ellen that "the Indian mail brought me nothing." Some days later she expresses gratitude to Ellen for not discussing the matter with Miss Wooler: "Now—less than ever—does it seem to me a matter open to discussion. I hear nothing." With surprising understatement she admits that the uneasiness she feels "is not the uneasiness of confirmed and fixed regard—but that anxiety which is inseparable from a state of absolute uncertainly about a somewhat momentous matter." Perhaps indeed the best termination would be "lasting estrangement and unbroken silence," she admits; "yet a good deal of pain has been and must be gone through in that case." Her letter concludes with a postscript alluding once more to her sense that the relationship has had some malevolent force undermining it, that it has cooled not merely as the result of her own coolness, but from some more sinister, external chill: "Understand —that in whatever I have said above—I was not fishing for pity or sympathy—I hardly pity myself. Only I wish that in all matters in this world there was fair and open dealing—and no underhand work."[37]

But three days later she is back again, dwelling on her sense of disappointment and loss. "I have not a word of news to tell you—Many Mails have come in from India since I was at Brookroyd—and always when the day came around—(I know it now) expectation would be on the alert—but disappointment knocked her down. I have not heard a syllable—and cannot think of making inquiries at Cornhill."[38] To her friend Laetitia Wheelwright she summarizes the experience of these months—

though of course with no reference to Taylor—in words strikingly echoed in *Villette:* "Some long, stormy days and nights there were when I felt such a craving for support and companionship as I cannot express. . . . It was a time I shall never forget."[39] On April 22 she is so disoriented as to write Ellen, "I have forgotten whether the 22nd is your birthday or mine; whichever it be, I wish you many happy returns." (In fact Charlotte's had been the day before: April 21.) More than two months later she wearily concludes to Ellen, "You ask about India. Let us dismiss the subject in a few words and not recur to it. All is silent as the grave. Cornhill is silent too. There has been bitter disappointment there at my having no work ready for this season. We must not rely upon our fellow-creatures, only upon ourselves, and on Him who is above both us and them."[40]

This condition of loneliness and depression is the familiar fetal huddle most recently and fully described in the Eva *devoir* of *Shirley*. Out of such a "black hollow" Charlotte now believed her stricken spirit could be rescued only by the power of the true god who as Genius had brought "Guidance—help—comfort" to Eva. August, September, and October wring from Charlotte cries of loneliness and desolation, but somehow out of the darkness help has begun to come. Again Charlotte has begun to rise from the grave: Resurgam! At last the novel is going forward.

On October 30 she is able to send the first two volumes of *Villette* to Cornhill; on November 20, the third and last. On January 11, 1853, she reported—presumably still on the basis of information from Smith, as this letter was dated from Smith's home in London—that "Mr. T" is "said to be getting on well in India. . . ." It was the last time Taylor's name would occur in Charlotte's letters. She no longer needed him. Greatly transmuted, he had already rendered full service to her art.

The First Man Is of the Earth, Earthy

Commentators on *Villette* have consistently assumed that the model for M. Paul was Constantin Heger, and so he obviously was in some respects: the foreign setting, the details of the school, Lucy's relationship to Paul both as student and teacher, and many of Paul's qualities of appearance, manner, and history recall Heger. Heger's brother-in-law, like Paul's brother, was a pianist. Heger's wife, like Mme. Beck, was mistress of the girls' school, and in Charlotte's view was jealous, secretly observant, and manipulative in many of the same ways. Her name is even the source of a mischievous wordplay: for Mme. Heger's maiden name had been *Parent,* and the maiden name of her counterpart, Mme. Beck, is *Kind*—German for *child.*

But it is also important to remember that biographers have regularly drawn much of their information about Heger and his wife, and about Charlotte's attitude toward them, from her novels, so that Gérin, for example, describes qualities of Heger's character by quoting directly from *Villette;* inevitably the effect is circular. Moreover, in the novel Paul is referred to repeatedly as "the little man," which was Charlotte's term for Taylor; and her terms for Paul's rough manner—"stern, dogmatic, hasty, imperious" (p. 584)—are paralleled in Charlotte's letters by the terms she uses to describe Taylor—"rigid, despotic, self-willed," "stern and abrupt," and so on. What distinguishes Paul from Taylor is, of course, that the kernel beneath his husk is so fully revealed, and shown to be so rich with the tender warmth that Charlotte found missing in Taylor, though present in Heger. What distinguishes Paul from Heger is that he is unmarried, that he loves Lucy, and that he departs, in the end, on a journey to serve others' financial gain.

But most important, though Charlotte is drawing on the past for her knowledge of what it feels like to adore—certainly she loved Heger passionately and did not love Tayler at all—she is without question drawing on the present for embodiments of her now fully ripened vision of the New Testament contrast between the "flesh" and the "promise" (see Romans 9:8); between the stormy experience of sexual longing and the peaceful beatitude of fulfilled desire; between the wilderness of wandering and the redeeming embrace of God. The former is figured by Lucy's life in Villette, and its attractions are summarized in her encounters with the handsome, worldly, sociable, but ultimately shallow man whom she cannot help loving but knows she can never attract (George Smith as Dr. John Graham Bretton). The latter is summarized in Paul Emanuel—Charlotte's fantasy of what it might be like to penetrate the husk of a man like Taylor, a superficially harsh and unattractive man who nonetheless loved her, and to find revealed in his kernel everything she had always longed for, the "god" of her passionate desires.

Charlotte well knew that no man on earth could provide her with such happiness: no more so Taylor than Heger; and certainly not Patrick himself. But it was not beyond the reach of her own muse—of that "Comforter" who was at once the source and product of her own imagination. This point may be slyly implicit in Lucy's use of the term "humanity" in summing up her final feelings for the M. Paul who had at first so displeased her: "Now, penetrated with his influence, and living by his affection, having his worth by intellect, and his goodness by heart

—I preferred him before all humanity" (p. 710). Dr. John is an example of "humanity"—and quite a good example too. But M. Paul is far more: he is Charlotte's muse, her "darling . . . cherished-in-secret, Imagination, the tender and the mighty."[41]

As such, M. Paul personifies the power Charlotte compared to "a breeze with a voice in it" in her Roe Head Journal. As such he fulfills the implications of "Genius," Eva's lover in *Shirley*. "Genius" was also a still small voice permeating the atmosphere: "that voice, soft, but all pervading, vibrated through her heart like music." So too for Lucy: "M. Paul talked to me. His voice was so modulated that it mixed harmonious with the silver whisper, the gush, the musical sigh, in which light breeze, fountain, and foliage intoned their lulling vesper" (p. 705). Genius gathered Eva to his bosom "like a lamb in the fold," just as in *Villette* Paul Emanuel "gathered me near his heart." Eva's Genius had chosen "Thou only in this land." Paul asks Lucy, "Be my dearest, first on earth." Genius brought "a living draught from heaven"; Paul's plenteous and loving letters are "living water that refreshed." Eva saw in the descent of Genius a "revelation": "The dark hint, the obscure whisper, which have haunted me from childhood, are interpreted. Thou art He I sought." So is Paul what Lucy had sought—fulfilling God's promise to "call . . . her beloved, which was not beloved" (Romans 9:25). In response to Lucy's moment of "utmost mutiny" (rebellion was the sin of Zenobia, and of Charlotte herself as a creative "woman of intellect"), Paul "reserved one deep spell of peace." He is "the Comforter, which is the Holy Ghost, whom the Father will send in my name," whose deep spell of peace is divine: "Peace I leave with you, my peace I give unto you: not as the world givest, give I unto you" (John 14:26–27).

In Dr. John and M. Paul, then, the contrasts of the book are summarized: *"The first man is of the earth, earthy: the second man is the Lord from heaven"* (1 Corinthians 15:47).

Unlike Emanuel, the fiery physician of souls, Dr. John, the materialist, is a physician of bodies, and a good one, though necessarily limited. Since his function is to incorporate the seductive values of the secular world, let me begin my analysis of Charlotte's presentation of that world with an analysis of his role in it.

In loving Dr. John, Lucy accedes to the seductions of "the world," and Charlotte knows that they are powerful, by no means easily dismissed. But they are deeply treacherous too. Dr. John gives "as the world giveth," with a careless generosity quite capable of failing just when one needs it most. In Lucy's seven-week period of despairing loneliness she receives from him "no word . . . not a visit, not a token."

Bitterly she recalls her degradation of spirit at that time: "I suppose animals kept in cages, and so scantily fed as to be always upon the verge of famine, await their food as I awaited a letter" (pp. 383–84). By contrast Paul "wrote as he gave and as he loved, in full-handed, full-hearted plentitude. . . . he would give neither a stone, nor an excuse — neither a scorpion, nor a disappointment" (p. 713). The allusion here is to the familiar passage in Luke — "ask and it shall be given" — which is in fact centered on the issue of proper fathering. "If a son shall ask bread of any of you that is a father, will he give him a stone? . . . Or if he shall ask an egg, will he offer him a scorpion? If ye, then, being evil, know how to give good gifts to your children: how much more shall your heavenly Father give the Holy Spirit to them that ask it?" (Luke 11:11–13).

Charlotte outlines for us with a careful hand both Dr. John's attractions and his limitations. When we first meet him, he is a blue-eyed, golden-haired, "handsome, faithless-looking youth" (p. 20) whose childhood home in Bretton, with its green pastures and still waters, is a type of the earthly paradise of the Twenty-Third Psalm, to which Brontë alludes through a quotation from *Pilgrim's Progress*. When Lucy next encounters him (years later) she does not recognize him, but his behavior to her is wholly consistent. She has just arrived in the night at the station in Villette, and appearing out of the dark he kindly helps her locate her trunk. She likes and trusts him immediately: "He might be a lord, for anything I knew: nature had made him good enough for a prince, I thought," and she then adds, with an irony available to Lucy the narrator but not Lucy the young character: "I should almost as soon have thought of distrusting the Bible." Following him briefly, as he undertakes to direct her to an inn, she adds, "I believe I would have followed that frank tread, through continual night, to the world's end" (pp. 84–85). But he is a false redeemer, and she loses her way in the dark city almost at once.

By the time she has seen him several times attending patients at the Pensionnat, she has reached at least unconsciously a juster estimate of his trustworthiness. Absorbed in his own interests he does not even notice her existence, but she is keenly attentive to his, and watching him with his tawny hair gleaming in the sunshine she notes significantly:

> I was driven to compare his beamy head in my thoughts to that of the "golden image" which Nebuchadnezzar the king had set up — (p. 136)

—a comparison that both implies his status as a false god[42] and also subtly locates the moral geography of the story, for Nebuchadnezzar had raised his golden image "in the plain of Dura, in the province of Babylon" (Daniel 2:1). *Dura* means *town,* as of course *Villette* does too. And Babylon is the spiritual progenitor of Labassecour; it is the "world" as captor, holding the eternal spirit in fleshly bondage.

This vision of Dr. John as the golden image that Nebuchadnezzar commanded the "people, nations, and languages" to worship, brings Lucy at once to the (presently unacknowledged) further recognition that he is the same person she had earlier known as Graham Bretton: "an idea new, sudden, and startling, riveted my attention with an overmastering strength and power of attraction" (p. 136). Her expression of shocked recognition catches his eye and he questions her; but she retreats instead back into the anonymity that at this point in the story she consistently prefers—hiding her discovery even from the reader, at least for now.

For a time Lucy's mind is full of questions of love: does the school's capable mistress, Mme. Beck, perhaps love Dr. John? Does Rosine the portress? Seeing that he is infatuated with someone at the school, Lucy comes to realize that his object is the shallow coquette Ginevra Fanshawe. Lucy is aghast at his taste, but feeling that Dr. John is an incomparably more worthy suitor than the frivolous and feeble de Hamal whom Ginevra unaccountably prefers, she urges him not to despair: "Who should hope, if not you?" (p. 212).

In the world of *Villette* no one could be in fact more justified in hoping that Dr. John, for as he embodies this world's gifts, he also receives them. In this he is Lucy's opposite. She is fatally out of step with the world and all its values, as the novel repeatedly demonstrates, and in her honesty she well knows that its lucky representative will never show much deep concern for her. For Lucy "Fate was of stone, and Hope a false idol—blind, bloodless, and of granite core" (p. 224);[43] whereas Dr. John "was the aspirant to woo Destiny herself, and to win from her stone eye-balls a beam almost loving" (p. 253). Because he has none of the transcendence that Paul will show—"Expect refinements of perception, miracles of intuition, and realize disappointment" (p. 271)—Dr. John can do little for Lucy. No mate for her spirit, he cannot even be an adequate physician for her body. His greatest power is to offer kindness, though toward her it must be the utterly impersonal kindness of abundant nature:

> I learned in time that this benignity . . . belonged in no shape to me:
> . . . he imparted it, as the ripe fruit rewards with sweetness the rifling
> bee; he diffused it about him, as sweet plants shed their perfume. (pp.
> 524–25)

In her starved state, even his ambiguous kindness is a great gift, a crumb from the rich man's table; but its effect in context is rather to expose the poverty of her condition than to lift her out of it. As narrator, Lucy enforces the implications:

> I have been told since, that Dr. Bretton was not nearly so perfect as I thought him: . . . I don't know: he was as good to me as the well is to the parched wayfarer—as the sun to the shivering jailbird. (p. 354)

As wayfarer, as jailbird, Lucy feels glad to snatch whatever is offered. But so deprived is she that a momentary loss of a letter Dr. John has kindly sent her reduces her to a "grovelling, groping, monomaniac" (p. 353). And so little does Dr. John understand the true proportions of her need that he is willing to tease her about the letter, to seize it and hide it from her:

> Curious, characteristic manoeuvre! . . . He had hidden it in his waist-coat pocket. If my trouble had wrought with a whit less stress and reality, I doubt whether he would ever have acknowledged or restored it. Tears of temperature one degree cooler than those I shed would only have amused Dr. John. (pp. 354–55)

If Lucy even then considered Dr. John "perfect," she surely does not allow us to do so. Recognizing that her nervous problems stem from "long-continued mental conflict," Dr. John prescribes "happiness." But as Lucy observes, it is hollow mockery to be told to *"cultivate* happiness." Happiness is no "potato, to be planted in mould, and tilled with man-ure." Rather, as she significantly phrases it, "Happiness is a glory shining far down upon us out of Heaven" (p. 358).

Heaven, however, is not at all Dr. John's vantage point. When his benevolence is aroused, he is helpful; but he regards Lucy "scientifically in the light of a patient" (p. 364). Correspondingly he insists that her experiences with the ghostly "nun" are "all optical illusion—nervous malady, and so on." Lucy is not convinced, knowing that she has in fact seen something: "but I dared not contradict: doctors are so self-opinion-ated, so immovable in their dry, materialist views" (p. 368). As she recognizes from his response to the performance of the actress Vashti, "His heart had no chord for enthusiasm." It is appropriately at that performance that he meets Paulina and initiates the seven weeks of neglect so agonizing to Lucy.

These seven weeks raise Dr. John to yet one more height of happiness and success, however, as he courts the lovely Paulina: "Dr. John, throughout his whole life, was a man of luck—a man of success. And why? . . . no tyrant-passion dragged him back; no enthusiasms, no foibles encumbered his way" (p. 457). We have seen that such a man will not at all understand Lucy: "I realized his entire misapprehension of my character and nature. He wanted always to give me a role not mine." And the reason is that he shapes his experience to meet his own desires; despite his "natural benevolence," as Lucy keeps calling it, he is ultimately a selfish man. "He did not at all guess what I felt," Lucy comments at a moment particularly painful to herself; "he did not read my eyes, or face, or gestures; though, I doubt not, all spoke. Leaning towards me coaxingly, he said, softly, '*Do* content me, Lucy' " (p. 455).

This selfishness is, of course, at the very root of Dr. John's success: it is the mark of his worldliness, for he judges as the world judges. Lucy had wondered to herself about his fluctuating kindnesses to her; had she been better "placed," would he not have been more consistently attentive? Addressing Dr. John in her own mind, she wonders:

> Had Lucy been intrinsically the same, but possessing the additional advantages of wealth and station, would your manner to her, your value for her have been quite what they actually were? (p. 452)

Like Mme. Beck, he has a certain manipulative capability, "a harmonizing property of tongue and eye" (p. 356); and like her he knows how to value rank and money. Accordingly, while Dr. John truly admires the "pearl of great price" that is Paulina herself, his ultimate (if unwitting) attachment is to its valuable "setting":

> The pearl he admired was in itself of great price and truest purity, but he was not the man who, in appreciating the gem, could forget its setting. Had he seen Paulina with the same youth, beauty, and grace, but on foot, alone, unguarded, and in simple attire, a dependent worker, a demi-grisette, he would have thought her a pretty little creature, . . . but it required other than this to conquer him as he was now vanquished. . . .

Lucy concludes:

> There was about Dr. John all the man of the world; to satisfy himself did not suffice; society must approve—the world must admire what he did, or he counted his measures false and futile. In his victrix he required all that was here visible—the imprint of high cultivation, . . . the adjuncts that Fashion decrees, Wealth purchases, and Taste adjusts. . . . (p. 536)

Seeing these qualities united in the person of Paulina, he goes after them with a will: "mettle and purpose were roused in him fully," and also, of course, successfully. In one chapter more, he and Paulina will be engaged, married, and dismissed to live happily ever after.

Lucy has not by any means stopped loving Dr. John; there are strong indications that she loves him right to the end of the book. But at midnovel (from the time of the Vashti performance) she learns to give him up; she endures the seven weeks of torture, foresees his coming union with Paulina, faces the death of her own hope, buries her letters from him—"I meant also to bury a grief"—and recognizes that "if life be a war, it seemed my destiny to conduct it single-handed" (pp. 424–25). Biographically this point parallels the point at which Charlotte relinquished hope of happiness with either Smith *or* Taylor, as natural men, and began to rely not on "our fellow-creatures" but "only upon ourselves, and on Him who is above both us and them"—that is, on her own Genius, manifestation within her of "God with us," the deliverer Emanuel. From here on in the novel, the pace of Lucy's relationship with M. Paul quickens into vibrant life.

Charlotte was aware that her readers would expect Lucy finally to marry Dr. John, but she was emphatic in rejecting such a dénouement. Dr. John is not meant for the likes of Lucy, she wrote her publisher:

> He is a 'curled darling' of Nature and of Fortune, and must draw a prize in life's lottery. His wife must be young, rich, pretty; he must be made very happy indeed.[44]

But after having finished and sent off the last volume she found herself still dissatisfied with her delineation of his pretty 'prize':

> I greatly apprehend . . . that the weakest character in the book is the one I aimed at making the most beautiful; and, if this be the case, the fault lies in its wanting the germ of the *real*—in its being purely imaginary I felt that this character lacked substance; I fear that the reader will feel the same. Union with it resembles too much the fate of Ixion, who was mated with a cloud. The childhood of Paulina is, however, I think, pretty well imagined, but her . . .[45]

—and here the letter is provokingly torn off, to resume on a different topic. But who is this cloudy paragon, whose fate it is to receive the worldly treasures denied to Lucy—and to Charlotte? What is her role in this drama of redemption?

A Mate for the Man of Earth

Readers have generally agreed that the childhood of Paulina is well imagined, and indeed the vigor of Polly's presence in the opening chapters has tempted one critic to think that she, rather than Lucy, must have been initially intended as the novel's heroine.[46] But Polly is no such thing. She is the best the world has to offer—the best Charlotte could imagine as growing in any way out of the root of herself; and as such she is a proper mate for the first man, of the earth, earthy. They are the "romantic couple" in a novel determined to look beyond romance, determined to transmute literary cliché into a form at once more elevated and more honest, to exchange fantasy for the deeper truth of something that might be called creative religious vision.

What the early chapters do establish is the close association between Lucy and Polly, amounting almost to split identity: both born into this world, Polly is headed to an earthly fulfillment, Lucy—after great pain —to a divine one. It is the old distinction that *Jane Eyre* had attributed to St. John Rivers, between the sensual "elysium" of marriage to Rosamond on the one hand, and on the other, the "true, eternal Paradise" preferred by "the aspirant, the poet, the priest." Indeed in what appears to be a rejected draft of an early scene intended for *Villette,* the child who will come to be called Polly is named Rosa, surely an allusion to those earlier Roses of the World, Rosamond Oliver and Rosamund Wellesley.[47]

The difference between Lucy and Polly when we meet them lies in the fact that fourteen-year-old Lucy has already been schooled by life to withdraw from the powerful emotions that seven-year-old Polly still feels but is in process of learning to repress. Lucy obviously knows what it is to ache and long for something beloved, and not to have it. Seeing Polly calling for her "Papa" at prayer like "some precocious fanatic or untimely saint," Lucy's flame is stirred within her snowy exterior, and she finds that her own responsive thoughts "ran risk of being hardly more rational and healthy than that child's mind must have been" (p. 15). What Polly experiences that Lucy does not is the contentment, after all that aching prayer, of having her wishes come true.

Charlotte makes clear that Lucy's response to the reunion of Polly and her father is not the impassiveness she pretends, but pained chagrin.[48] When Polly's father departs again, and Polly cries after him with "a sort of 'Why hast thou forsaken me' " agony, Lucy reports "I, Lucy Snowe, was calm." Yet it is Lucy herself who supplies the words that connect

Polly's agony with the crucifixion, for Lucy understands the cost of coping with such experience. (And behind Lucy, of course, is the Charlotte who had all her life written about woman deserted by the withdrawing father-god.) What Lucy perceives Polly achieving is what she has herself fully achieved:

> The little creature, thus left unharrassed, did for herself what none other could do—contended with an intolerable feeling; and, ere long, in some degree, repressed it. . . . She grew more passive afterwards. (p. 28)

Lucy's "snow" is the effect of just such costly repression and enforced passivity. The difference between Polly and Lucy—and it is all the difference in the world, by the time the two young women are grown—is that Polly actually does have a loving and protective father who may be counted on to reclaim, cherish, and guard her. Their very name is "Home." Lucy, by contrast, has none of this, until Paul at last takes her "home" in his "one deep spell of peace."

Polly and Lucy are alike, then, in that both are by nature passionately loving, deeply feeling women in a world that consistently rewards shallowness and self-interest. Such devotion, such depth of feeling as they are capable of is in this world normally the province of only the fanatic or saint, whose mind is from the secular perspective neither rational nor healthy. The child Polly gives her heart with the dangerous and excessive selflessness of all of Charlotte's early Mary heroines:

> One would have thought the child had no mind or life of her own, but must necessarily live, move, and have her being in another: now that her father was taken from her, she nestled to Graham, and seemed to feel by his feelings: to exist in his existence. (p. 32)

The allusion is to St. Paul's words concerning God the Father in Acts 17:28: "In him we live, and move, and have our being." But Lucy has her author's hard-won (if inconsistently applied) knowledge about false gods, and tries to caution Polly against inappropriate adoration:

> Wise people say it is folly to think anybody perfect; and as to likes and dislikes, we should be friendly to all, and worship none.

This is good advice, but not easy for either girl to follow. When Polly asks, "Are you a wise person?" Lucy can only answer, "I mean to try to be so." She knows, as Charlotte knew, that for herself the effort is requisite to survival, and she wonders concerning the vulnerable Polly:

> How will she get through this world, or battle with this life? How will she bear the shocks and repulses, the humiliations and desolations, which books, and my own reason tell me are prepared for all flesh? (pp. 44–45)

How Indeed? For Polly, the novel provides a simple answer: she will never again really have to face any "shocks and repulses."

Paulina at seventeen has not lost the child's capacities of heart and spirit, but they no longer threaten her happiness. One of Polly's distinguishing activities as a seven-year-old was her needlework, a tiny "shred of a handkerchief" she was hemming as a keepsake for the Papa in whom she then "lived . . . and had her being." But as she worked, the great needle continually swerved out of control in her small hands, leaving "a track of minute red dots" from her pricked fingers on the white cloth (p. 14). This is a telling emblem of her vulnerability and her willingness to sacrifice for the men she loves. But when Lucy re-encounters Polly ten years later, the emblem has been transformed in both substance and meaning. Now wealthy and cherished, she stands radiant in a gown of "white, sprinkled slightly with drops of scarlet" (p. 394); Polly herself has become the "keepsake," and the "red dots," no longer the marks of blood sacrifice, have become decorations to set off her beauty.

From this point on, Polly functions less as a character in her own right than as a kind of experimental control, evidence of what Lucy might have been had she not been so constantly embattled, had she experienced neither the privileges nor the pain of being singled out for suffering in worldly matters, exaltation in matters divine. If, as Gaskell attests, Charlotte intended Shirley to represent what Emily "would have been, had she been placed in health and prosperity," Paulina is Charlotte's comparable projection for herself.[49] We have already seen that she is Lucy's counterpart in that she shares Lucy's identifying figure, the snow-encircled flame; the distance between them is ironically underscored by the fact that whereas Lucy nearly dies of the cold, for Polly "that gentle hoar-frost of yours, surrounding so much pure, fine flame, is a priceless privilege of nature" (p. 545).

When Polly as a child parted from Graham to rejoin her father, she was "trembling like a leaf" but "exercising self-command" (p. 45). This self-command must take its toll on charm and beauty, as Lucy later observes to her friend:

> As a child I feared for you; . . . under harshness, or neglect, neither your outward nor your inward self would have ripened to what they now are. Much pain, much fear, much struggle would have troubled

the very lines of your features, broken their regularity, . . . you would
have lost in health and cheerfulness, in grace and sweetness. (p. 545)

The alternative experience has of course been Lucy's own (as it was
Charlotte's), and with the predicted result. As we saw Charlotte explain,
in effect defending her own character along with Lucy's, Lucy *"is* both
morbid and weak at times; . . . anybody living her life would necessarily
become morbid." Both Polly and Lucy have "sinew" and "stamina" (p.
450), but only Polly has beauty and grace, which are nourished by wealth
and station, by the protection of a loving parent, by the gifts of fate.

Polly was not sent away to school because the one time her father
tried it, he found at once that he could not bear to be parted from her
(how unlike Patrick and Charlotte!). Polly's greatest loss in childhood
had been to give up Graham for her father; in adulthood to give up her
father for Graham. But in the unfolding of the story, she really relinquishes neither: the Graham she leaves is later to become her husband,
and father and husband are finally joined in their encircling love of
herself. One of our last sights of Polly shows her plaiting together locks
of her father's gray and Graham's golden hair, and binding them up with
"a tress of her own" (p. 631).

As a child, a chord of Polly's passionate nature had been struck by the
biblical account of Jacob's grief over his favorite son Joseph: "if you were
to die," she tells Graham, paraphrasing Genesis, "I should 'refuse to be
comforted, and go down into the grave to you mourning' " (p. 37).
Charlotte's final words concerning Polly are a returning allusion to the
story of Jacob and Joseph—but now to its miraculously happy ending:

> In short, I do but speak the truth when I say that these two lives of
> Graham and Paulina were blessed, like that of Jacob's favoured son,
> with "blessings of Heaven above, blessings of the deep that lies under."
> It was so, for God saw that it was good. (p. 633)

The "germ of the *real*" (see above, p. 229) was planted in Polly's childhood, when Polly learned the whole range of human emotion—"joy
and grief, affection and bereavement" (p. 396); the "purely imaginary"
lies in the circumstance that Polly is then spared all the darker half of life,
achieving without compromise her heart's every desire.

Paulina Mary Home de Bassompierre and John Graham Bretton are
what Charlotte calls "natures elect" (p. 632); each has an adoring and
nurturing parent of the opposite sex; each is beautiful, gracious, and
lucky. But they are no less creatures of this wilderness world. Paulina is
spiritually more elevated than Graham—in fact she functions as a kind
of secular redeemer for him, a lesser Paul: "to develop fully the best of

his nature, a companion like you was needed" (p. 545), Lucy explains to her pretty friend, which accounts at least in part for the mirroring names: Paulina/Paul.

But as worldling Polly cannot utterly escape Lucy's (or Charlotte's) patronizing irony, which we first encounter in the fate assigned Polly's mother ("As silly and frivolous a little flirt as ever sensible man was weak enough to marry") and peaks when Lucy insists that M. Paul's "delicate, silky, loving, and lovable little doggie" reminds her of Paulina: "forgive the association, reader, it would occur" (p. 602). Though patently unfair, and very much the expression of Lucy's own high spirits at the time, the hostility of the comparison suggests that although Lucy has buried her love of Dr. John and the world he represents, she still mourns at the grave. In other scenes it is harder to establish Lucy's tone, as for example when she appears to damn with clichéd praise raptures she cannot share: " 'My lamb! my treasure!' murmured the loving though rugged sire" (p. 626). In such cases it is hard to tell what is merely bad writing—an example of the problems of presentation to which Charlotte confessed—and what is intended to give the impression of human experience cropped down to novelistic platitude. By effect, whether or not by intention, such writing underscores Lucy's judgment that Paulina is ultimately a trivial creature despite her grace, wealth, and good fortune —even because of them. In high Romantic tradition, backed by long religious tradition, the storm and pain that Lucy must endure mark at the same time her privilege. In her martyrdom she is cut out from the crowd as the special object of God's intervening hand.

The World as Wilderness

Graham is a man of this world, then: a curled darling of nature whose "prize" is Charlotte-as-she-never-was, but (insofar as she still did long for earthly happiness) fervently wished she might have been. But the world Graham represents, and in which he shines, is far larger than himself; and parts of it are far darker than his limited awareness can know or even guess. It extends from nature's elect, like Paulina, to the very depths of evil; and it embraces not only individual characters, but society as a whole, and even the realm of religion itself, when religion is misused. Such were the wandering Israelites, bowing to false gods.

Critics have agreed in finding *Villette* anti-Catholic and contemptuous

of Belgium; yet of course the case against Catholicism is blunted somewhat by the fact that Paul Emanuel is himself Catholic and that Père
Silas, despite his "crafty Jesuit-slanders," is "not a bad man, though the
advocate of a bad cause." Charlotte seems to wish to distinguish between
religion as spiritual experience—"it seemed to me that *this* Romanist
held the purer elements of his creed with an innocency of heart which
God must love"—and the Church as a bastion of power, a mighty tool
in the grip of "mitred aspirants for this world's kingdoms." The one is
true religion, whatever the creed, and helps raise the spiritual body. The
other—Catholicism as institution—is merely a "Moloch 'church' " (pp.
605–9), worshiping the very materialism that binds it to mortality:

> the CHURCH strove to bring up her children robust in body, feeble
> in soul, fat, ruddy, hale, joyous, ignorant, unthinking, unquestioning.
> . . . Lucifer offers just the same terms: "All this power will I give thee,
> and the glory of it. . . . If thou, therefore, wilt worship me, all shall be
> thine!" (p. 177)

As for Belgium, certainly it does come off poorly: *Labassecour* is a
term for a stable. A *Villette* is a little town, surely a deprecating judgment
of Brussels. And Rue d'Isabelle, the actual street in Brussels on which
was located the school the Brontës attended, becomes in the novel "Rue
Fossette," or "little ditch." And so on.[50] But the negative qualities
associated with "worldliness" are not confined to Belgium. John Bretton
and his mother, whose surname emphasizes their Britishness, have corollary limitations. Ginevra Fanshawe, though English, is a grasping and
shallow flirt; even Polly, as we have seen, can be dismissed as a silky
dog. Moreover London, itself described as "a Babylon and a wilderness"
(p. 61), was the actual scene of several key events that are fictionalized in
Villette—for example, the performance of "Vashti" (historically the French
actress Mme. Rachel) and Paul's lecture (modeled at least in part on one
of Thackeray's lectures). Both of these Charlotte experienced during her
visit to London in the summer of 1851. And the fire that brings Dr. John
and Paulina together reflects an actual event in London, as well.[51]

British Protestantism, to be sure, Charlotte preferred on principle to
Continental Catholicism; but we meet no remarkable Protestants aside
from Lucy herself, and her true kindred spirit is the Catholic Paul.
Perhaps, then, we may guess that Charlotte's expressions of scorn reflect
less her judgment on a particular place or population than a generalized
perspective on the theater of her life's experience as one vast "Villette"
or "Dura" in the province of Babylon, in which the English dwell along

with the Belgians and most of the rest of humanity. In this world Paul is
the one great exception: comic as a "bottled storm" in his mundane
proportions, but spiritually divine.

Thus although Charlotte is certainly critical of both Belgium and the
Catholic church, her censure extends far beyond either, to the very
source of their fleshly limitation—which is, ultimately, the eternal enemy "Apollyon . . . trailing his Hell behind him" (p. 644). This Apollyon (the "destroyer" from the bottomless pit in Revelation 9:11, and
Christian's great enemy in *Pilgrim's Progress*) is for Lucy centered in that
"basilisk with three heads," the Romish Trinity whose "alpha is Mammon, and its omega, Interest." These three are the suggestively named
Magloire Walravens, Modeste Maria Beck, and Père Silas.[52] As a "junta"
the three represent not only Catholic religion at its most corrupt and
superstitious, but more largely the values of the whole fallen world, in
which, as the novel's last words tell us,

> Madame Beck prospered all the days of her life; so did Père Silas;
> Madame Walravens fulfilled her ninetieth year before she died. Fare-
> well.

Not until the end of time will the meek inherit this earth. The fallen
world is not all bad, of course. Moreover Lucy and Paul themselves,
however much they challenge and surmount the values of this world, are
full of human faults. And Lucy, unlike Paul, lives on in the world,
fulfilling her apostolic role by teaching her school and writing her life.

Still, the marks of worldliness lie all about us: in the schoolgirls with
their large limbs and "thick, glossy hair" (p. 116); in the women Lucy
sees in public, "cold, rounded, blond, and beauteous" (p. 300); in the
fleshly and indolent "Cleopatra" (along with the fops who admire her);
and of course in "that snake, Zélie St. Pierre" (p. 203).

One of Charlotte's fullest studies of worldly values is Ginevra Fanshawe, whose shallowness is, however, so patent and undisguised as to
be really quite disarming. Like Polly's dead mother, she is "the child of
pleasure" for whom life can be "full" only in a ballroom; "sweet wine
was her element and sweet cake her daily bread" (p. 198). (Wine and
sweets are food specifically disliked by Lucy, for whom Ginevra regularly stands as comic foil.) But despite her prettiness, her air of the social
butterfly, Ginevra is an excellent businesswoman, for whom integrity is
a simple matter of wealth and status. She is shocked to see that an
unfortunate "nobody" like Lucy can be friends with a countess. Not
surprisingly she manages at last to become a countess herself, by marrying Alfred de Hamal, "the doll—the puppet—the manikin—the inferior

creature" (Lucy's terms). Ginevra even manages to get needed financial support from her uncle: "I'm *so* happy! I really think I've hardly anything left to wish for—unless it be a carriage and a hotel. . . ." Selfish, heartless, and acquisitive, her values are no different in essence—however much they may differ in their intensity—from those of the "basilisk with three heads." And, as with her counterparts, the world does well by her:

> . . . and so she got on—fighting the battle of life by proxy, and, on the whole, suffering as little as any human being I have ever known. (pp. 689–91)

But if Ginevra's worldliness is disarming and comic, that of the basilisk three is not. Père Silas is personally not an unattractive figure (Dr. John comments that he sees him often by the sickbeds of the poor; see p. 262), but as agent of the Catholic church—"the ruddy old lady of the Seven Hills" (p. 599)—he is leagued with the Whore of Babylon. Mme. Beck is personally more unsavory, although she quite lacks the visionary dimension: "faithless; secret, crafty, passionless," she "ought to have swayed a nation." Everything about her is down to earth:

> Interest was the master-key of madame's nature. . . . Not the agony in Gethsemane, not the death on Calvary, could have wrung from her eyes one tear. (pp. 101–2)

Her very civility is threatening:

> Madame, in all things worldly, was in nothing weak; there was measure and sense in her hottest pursuit of self-interest, calm and considerateness in her closest clutch of gain. (p. 418)

The third of this trio, however, is by far the darkest character in the book. Occupying the dead center of the spiritual wilderness, figuring the Whore of Babylon herself, is the hideous Magloire Walravens.

The chapter "Malevola" in which Lucy is sent by Mme. Beck to visit Mme. Walravens is charged with the imagery of Revelation. A lowering storm inflames the sky as Lucy approaches the presence of "Malevola, the evil fairy"—whose name means "evil-wisher" but who here expands by allusion to suggest all evil, consolidated at apocalypse. The whore in Revelation is "clothed in fine linen, and purple, and scarlet and decked with gold, and precious stones, and pearls" (18:16). This woman, despite her hideous form, is consonantly garbed:

> This being wore a gown of brocade, dyed bright blue. . . . But her chief points were her jewels: she had long, clear ear-rings, . . . she had

rings on her skeleton hands, with thick gold hoops, and stones—purple, green, and blood-red. Hunchbacked, dwarfish, and doting, she was adorned like a barbarian queen.

The interview over, Malevola turns—"a peal of thunder broke, and a flash of lightening blazed"—and then vanishes, "muttering venomously," as the storm bursts at its zenith:

> This storm had gathered immediately above Villette; . . . it rushed down prone; the forked, slant bolts pierced athwart vertical torrents; red zig-zags interlaced a descent blanched as white metal: and all broke from a sky heavily black in its swollen abundance. (pp. 562–64)

Mme. Walravens is the central figure of the "basilisk with three heads." *Walravens* means *slaughter ravens*. Here she is a kind of black bird of death, whose secular agent is Mme. Beck ("beak"), who "ought to have swayed a nation," and whose ecclesiastical agent is Père Silas, representing the Romish church. We see all three together, in person, only once in the book, and that is at the climax of Lucy's drugged night journey; but as infernal trinity they embody all that stands in opposition to Lucy's achievement of her spiritual destiny:

> There, then, were Madame Walravens, Madame Beck, Père Silas—the whole conjuration, the secret junta. The sight of them thus assembled did me good. . . . They outnumbered me, and I was worsted and under their feet; but, as yet, I was not dead. (p. 666)

Lucy's hallucinatory night journey into the festive city is spiritually a descent into the swirl of Babylon, to the whore whose throne sits atop a parodic inversion of calvary—"Three fine tall trees . . . above a green knoll" (p. 663). It is Lucy's personal version of Revelation, in which, traveling alone and incognito, she consolidates both her own error and her knowledge of the fallen world.[53] Her journey occurs on the second night after Paul's supposed departure, and in that respect suggests a kind of variant of the harrowing of hell. In this case, Lucy's journey enacts the soul's search for Christ.

Leaving her familiar neighborhood, Lucy walks abroad under a sky that "bears the aspect of a world's death" (p. 381), seeking the city park in which there lies "a huge stone-basin . . . brimming with cool water." It is the well of life she seeks, the same Charlotte had written to Ellen about, back in 1836: "I know the treasures of the Bible . . . I can *see* the Well of Life in all its clearness and brightness; but when I stoop down to drink of the pure waters they fly from my lips. . . ." (see ch. 3, p. 128).

In the Bible, Jesus had distinguished earthly waters from heavenly ones: "Whosoever drinkest of this water shall thirst again: But whosoever drinkest of the water that I shall give him shall never thirst; but the water that I shall give him shall be in him a well of water springing up into everlasting life" (John 4:13–14). Now in 1852 Charlotte has learned to distinguish between these two sources of water, figurative corollaries, for her, of human as opposed to divine love.

Dr. John had been for Lucy a source of earthly water like that which had flowed through the earthly paradise of Bretton in her childhood: he was a "goodly river on whose banks I had sojourned, of whose waves a few reviving drops had trickled to my lips." But as he turns now to join his life with Paulina's, Lucy must watch her "goodly river" depart, "bending to another course":

> It was leaving my little hut and field forlorn and soul-dry, pouring its wealth of waters far away. The change was right, just, natural; . . . but I loved my Rhine, my Nile; I had almost worshipped my Ganges, and I grieved that the grand tide should roll estranged, should vanish like a false mirage. (pp. 420–21).

These earthly waters are of course a false mirage for Lucy only if she permits herself to nourish false hopes for them. She had long known that the Bretton waters were not the water of life, and had so counseled herself on first rediscovering the comforting Bretton household in Villette.

> "Do not let me think of them too often, too much, too fondly," I implored; "let me be content with a temperate draught of this living stream: let me not run athirst, and apply passionately to its welcome waters: let me not imagine in them a sweeter taste than earth's fountains know." (p. 254)

And later she had reiterated the warning to herself:

> Great were that folly which should build on such a promise—insane were that credulity which should mistake the transitory rain-pool, holding in its hollow one draught, for the perennial spring yielding the supply of seasons. (pp. 326–27)

Thus in making her night journey into the midst of Villette, in search of the "huge stone-basin . . . brimming with cool water,"[54] Lucy is in effect reenacting her book-long (and in Charlotte's present view, her own lifelong) temptation; she is looking for the waters of life in the secular world, long to find in human love the peace and comfort that only God's love can provide.

This night journey among glittering falsities where "moonlight and heaven are banished" (p. 654) is thus a dream synopsis of Lucy's and her author's long journey through "the wilderness of SIN." Lucy's account accordingly moves into the visionary present tense. The midnight festival celebrates events in the recent history of Labassecour, when "Rumors of war" had been heard in the nation. (The quoted phrase derives from Matthew 24, in which Jesus predicts the end of the world, and his second coming.) Passing through the iron gateway of the park, Lucy enters the old landscape of spiritual bondage:

> pyramid, obelisk, and sphinx: incredible to say, the wonders and the symbols of Egypt teemed throughout the park of Villette. (p. 655).

Unseen, "safe as if masked" (this has always been Lucy's way), she moves through the scene of "chaos" and "night" to a "Byzantine building" near the park's center, where the one person who can recognize her kindly provides her with a chair. This is a M. Miret, whose name suggests "mirror"; he is in fact a kind of earthly counterpart of M. Paul. As Lucy tells us, "part of his nature bore affinity to a part of M. Emanuel's." (To glance ahead, he is "the short-tempered and kind-hearted bookseller" who leases the building in the Faubourg Clotilde in which M. Paul will establish Lucy's school.)

This seat places her within sight of the Bretton party, whom she overhears speaking of her kindly, but ignorantly (Lucy is "so little moved, yet so content," they complacently agree). But she is in her way just as ignorant of them. Watching Dr. John, Lucy fondly imagines that in some part of his heart he still keeps a place for her. More to the point, she still keeps one for him—and potentially very large it is: "I know not but its innate capacity for expanse might have magnified it into a tabernacle for a host" (p. 662). In short, at some level she still worships this false god.

Lucy has now lost all thought of her stone basin, but senses restlessly that "the night's drama was but begun," that within this "shadow of mystery" there awaited "actors and incidents unlooked-for . . . : foreboding told me as much." Straying apparently at random, she is brought at last to the object of her foreboding: Mme. Walravens surrounded by her party. Père Silas is there among the others: we are told, with considerable irony, that the church did not consider this festival "a show of Vanity Fair." Here assembled, then, is the whole "secret junta," the "basilisk" whose "alpha" is Mammon (see Matthew 6:24, "Ye cannot serve God and mammon").

Now we learn the facts behind Paul's journey. Mme. Walravens has property in the West Indies that could, under proper stewardship, be made lucrative. All three are concerned that it should be: Mme. Beck in the hope of inheriting some portion; Père Silas on behalf of the church; Mme. Walravens of course for herself. "Paul, if he liked, could make the best and faithfullest steward: so the three self-seekers banded and beset the one unselfish" (p. 668).

In a moment of further "revelation" Lucy next sees what she thinks is "mystery breaking up: hitherto I had seen this spectre only through a glass darkly; now I was to behold it face to face." What is revealed at last is "Justine Marie," namesake of the woman Paul had loved twenty years before. That earlier Justine Marie's grandmother, Mme. Walravens, had forbidden the marriage on account of her wealth and Paul's poverty; the girl had died a nun. Earlier Père Silas had informed Lucy how, after Justine Marie's death, the Walravens' family fortune had failed and Paul in "purest charity" had rescued them, how Paul had added that family to the many other charities that it was his custom to sustain. The priest had significantly warned Lucy: "he has given himself to God and to his angel-bride as much as if he were a priest, like me" (p. 569). It had been this knowledge of Paul's charities that initiated Lucy's more serious thoughts of him, in accord with the ever more significant hints that he is a figure not so much comic as divine. Paul "had laid down vengeance, and taken up a cross. . . . He had become my Christian Hero" (pp. 576–77).

Now, at this moment of Egyptian midnight, Lucy sees the younger Justine Marie, and accompanying her—yet another "revelation"!—Paul Emanuel himself. He had not yet sailed after all, but is to depart two days later on the *Paul et Virginie*. Vowing that she likes to "penetrate to the real truth," to dare truth's "dread glance," Lucy decides that she at last understands the situation, that "the revelation was indeed come." It must be that Paul loves this "girl of Villette," and is to marry her. Shaken by the erring conviction that she herself is not loved, consumed with unwarranted jealousy of this "bourgeoise belle," Lucy returns home. Even the returning moon brings no enlightenment to her spiritually darkened state.

In a sense Lucy's spiritual myopia has been Charlotte's own, as through her life and through all those earlier fictions she had searched in vain for the earthly father's love, unable to tell the false god from the true one, Bretton from Emanuel. Lucy has seen M. Paul, but she has yet to understand him. The awakening of that understanding in Lucy, and Charlotte's triumphant vision of Paul's meaning for both her novel and herself, will be the subject of the remainder of my discussion of *Villette*.

SIX

Villette, The Muse Triumphant

"O come, thou Day-spring, come and cheer
Our spirits by thine advent here;
Disperse the gloomy shades of night
Break thro' the clouds and bring us light."
  Rejoice! Rejoice! Emmanuel
  Shall come to thee, O Israel!

—thirteenth-century hymn
(2d stanza and refrain)

The Second Man Is the Lord from Heaven

I have already said that in Dr. John and M. Paul we may see a novelistic rendering of the two "bodies" described by St. Paul in 1 Corinthians 15:47, "The first man is of the earth, earthy: the second man is the Lord from Heaven." And I have made the case for such a reading of Dr. John. Now it remains to complete the evidence for thinking that M. Paul figures "the Lord from heaven." As such he is the fictional embodiment of Charlotte's ultimate muse, the redeemer of her fallen imagination.

We have seen that *Jane Eyre* was a novel dedicated to the proposition that Jane was "no apostle" and had "no vocation."[1] Her destiny was earthly marriage and sexual and domestic fulfillment, the fulfillments that in *Villette* are accorded to Paulina. And the experience that sanctified Jane's destiny was the mysterious call that came "like an inspiration." Jane explained: "The wondrous shock of feeling had come like the earthquake which shook the foundations of Paul and Silas' prison: it had opened the doors of the soul's cell, and loosed its bands—it had wakened it out of its sleep . . ." (p. 539). But in *Villette* Paul and Silas enter directly into the novel, and it is Paul's function to shake the foundations of Lucy's prison—her frozen and half-drowned state of fetal enclosure—and loose the bands of her huddled soul by means of his ardent and fiery spirit. He is Emanuel. He has come to bring Lucy rebirth and call her to the apostolic vocation that Jane Eyre did not have.

On a first of March, early in the novel, Lucy, sleeping under the dome of St. Paul's church in London, had waked to a strange sensation: "my inner self moved; my soul shook its always-fettered wings half loose; I had a sudden feeling as if I, who had never yet truly lived, were at last about to taste life: in that morning my soul grew as fast as Jonah's gourd."[2] But this is not yet the real thing. In its biblical original, Jonah's gourd, which "came up in a night," unfortunately also "perished in a night" (Jonah 4:10). And so it is now with Lucy's loosened wings: the effect is temporary, like the effect of earthly waters—one drinks them only to "thirst again." Biographically the allusion to Jonah's gourd probably points to Charlotte's memory of her own high hopes when she first went to Brussels, and her later despair after leaving it; certainly the same rise and fall describe the pattern of Lucy's experiences of exhilaration followed by loss in her journey abroad—first her excited sense of freedom, and then the loneliness and soul-hunger that overwhelmed her there. But it also points to Charlotte's more recent loneliness during the time she was writing *Villette:* to that April of 1852 when she couldn't even remember her own birthday; when "India" was "silent as the grave," and Cornhill "silent too"; when she was driven to recognize, as she wrote to Ellen, that "we must not rely upon our fellow-creatures, only upon ourselves, and on Him who is above both us and them." To her desolation at that time she alludes quite directly in the novel, in terms her publishers themselves doubtless recognized:

> Those who live in retirement . . . are liable to be suddenly and for a long while dropped out of the memory of their friends, the denizens of a freer world. . . . The letter, the message once frequent, are cut off; . . . the book, paper, or other token that indicated remembrance, comes no more. (p. 381)

The books and papers are literal—the once regular gifts of her attentive friends at Cornhill, later discontinued after Taylor's departure and Smith's absorption in other business. Charlotte well understood her situation: "Always there are excellent reasons for these lapses, if the hermit but knew them. Though he is stagnant in his cell, his connections without are whirling in the very vortex of life." But it is one thing to understand the sources of bereavement, another to cope with the bereavement itself. How is the hermit to survive such loneliness? Lucy reports that she tried various expedients "to sustain and fill existence"—reading books, studying German—but that "the result was as if I had gnawed a file to satisfy hunger, or drunk brine to quench thirst" (p. 383). Charlotte had written Ellen in March 1852 how when mail time came around "expectation would be on the alert—but disappointment knocked her down." Now Lucy is similarly tortured: "My hour of torment was the post-hour. Unfortunately I knew it too well, . . . dreading the rack of expectation, and the sick collapse of disappointment which daily preceded and followed upon that well-recognized ring" (p. 383).

Charlotte had long since learned to cope with external realities inimical to her inner self by withdrawing behind "a mask of frozen seeming, / Hiding secret fires from view." Lucy's whole character is an example of that process writ large; but now as starved "hermit" she must enforce the method even more stringently. And in her metaphoric description of what it means to do so, Charlotte recalls the fetal figure that we have seen so many times before. But this time there is a savage twist. We have seen that woman, un-reborn, may be sustained by "mother" until the male "god" comes to deliver her by means of his love. But supposing no deliverer comes? This last is the possibility Lucy now feels forced to consider.

> The hermit—if he be a sensible hermit—will . . . lock up his own emotions during these weeks of inward winter. He will know that Destiny designed him to imitate . . . the dormouse . . . : make a tidy ball of himself, creep into a hole of life's wall, and submit decently to the drift which blows in and soon blocks him up, preserving him in ice for the season.

This is the "Snowe" that names and surrounds the dormouse Lucy: "And, perhaps," she continues optimistically, "one day his snow-sepulchre will open" and the dormouse will be delivered—the spring thaw "will call him to kindly resurrection." But then again "perhaps not: the frost may get into his heart and never thaw more; when spring comes, a crow or a pie may pick out of the wall only his dormouse-bones" (p. 382). Without a doubt this was the prospect Charlotte feared for herself in the bleak loneliness of Haworth as she labored on her book. Her father, Patrick, had always disappointed her; Heger had disappointed her also, and far more pointedly. Smith would never love her, and the man who did, James Taylor, was gone forever from her life. From the world of actual men, then, from men "of the earth, earthy," she could expect no salvation for her frozen, starved, and sinking soul. But Genius she still had: it stirred in the "small, forgotten atom of life," as she had phrased it in the Eva *devoir,* in her "spark of soul, emitted inadvert from the great creative source, and now burning unmarked to waste in the heart of a black hollow." Might she not transform the Taylor who actually did love her into a figure of the divine Imagination Himself, and in doing so invoke to her own cause the Son of God who resurrects by His love, and in invoking Him, resurrect her own creative powers, and redeem them from the worship of false gods to worship of the true? In the Eva story, Genius as "Son of God" had "refined the polluted cup, exalted the debased emotion, rectified the perverted impulse." Now Charlotte's own Genius would do as much for Lucy: both as character within the novel, and as inspiration enabling its author to write it. Love was what Charlotte needed, and God is love. Both her own liberation and Lucy's would thus come through Paul Emanuel: "Behold, a virgin shall be with child, and they shall call his name Emmanuel, which being interpreted is, God with us" (Matthew 1:23, recalling Isaiah 6:14).

St. Paul's church in London provides, as we saw, the first hints of the "taste of life" that will come to Lucy's spirit. The first anniversary of that briefly liberating occasion—the first of March a year later—finds Lucy in Villette, celebrating not her own birth, but the fête day of him who will bring her rebirth. "M. Paul's fête fell on the first of March, and a Thursday" (p. 485). (Charlotte's relationship with Taylor began, we recall, on March 1, 1849—a year in which March 1 actually did fall on a Thursday.) For his fête-day present, Lucy has made Paul a watch guard, a significant gift for so watchful and guarding a man. Unlike Mme. Beck, Paul did not want or value costly gifts. He was, Lucy tells us— twice echoing Scripture—"a man, not wise in his generation, yet could he claim a filial sympathy with 'the dayspring on high'" (p. 485). The first allusion is to St. Luke 16:8, "for the children of this world are in their generation wiser than the children of light"; and the second allusion (echoing Eva's recognition of Genius as "True Dayspring from on high!") is again from St. Luke: "the dayspring from on high hath visited us, / To give light to them that sit in darkness and in the shadow of death, to guide our feet in the way of peace" (1:78–79). Lucy has from the beginning sat in darkness, a "shadow in life's sunshine," as Dr. John cruelly observed; it is Paul's function to bring light, both by reigniting Lucy's own inner flame, and by warming her with his bright, hot presence and final "deep spell of peace." Rochester had told Jane, "You are cold, because you are alone: no contact strikes the fire from you that is in you." But Lucy is never alone. God is with her: "Who is your friend, if not Emanuel?" (p. 708). In his readings from literature Paul would "flash through our conventual darkness a reflex of a brighter world" (p. 474). Like Christ, "M. Emanuel could pity and forgive," but like Christ, too, he "pierced in its hiding-place the last lurking thought of the heart," and would judge the unrepenting, dragging them "to the summit of the mount of exposure" (pp. 486–87). At his fête Lucy in a sudden fit of perversity refuses to give him her present, allowing him to think that she alone has brought him no token of regard. Three times he asks, "Est-ce là tout?" and like St. Peter (she is in fact spurred to this stubbornness by "that snake" Mlle. St. Pierre) Lucy three times denies him. Lucy and Paul break at last into an open shouting match—an index, at least, of Paul's success in rousing her long-buried fires.

Paul disapproves of Lucy's attraction to Dr. John, as part of what he rather comically insists on regarding as her shameless vanity and lust after worldly pleasures. As human lover he may be thought to be exhibiting the jealousy that Taylor apparently felt toward Smith; and Charlotte's treatment of this theme is exuberantly funny. But as the novel progresses comedy gives way to tenderness, and we recognize in Paul's busy attentions the desire to foster Lucy's happiness and protect her from the treacherous seductions of the flesh.

Charlotte handles the fine and gradually shifting balance between the human motive and the divine one with a masterful command of tone. Yet a reader familiar with the Bible should recognize quite early that Paul's function will be different from that of ordinary men. There are direct hints even at Lucy's first encounter with Paul, when she speaks of him half-ironically as "oracular," a "diviner," and "arbiter of my destiny." "The little man . . . meant to see through me," she observes: "a veil would be no veil for him" (p. 90). Charlotte is of course recalling how Taylor used to look at her in his "keen way," but in retrospect we can see that she is also alluding to 2 Corinthians 3, where St. Paul is again distinguishing the old dispensation from the new: in this case contrasting Moses, who speaks through a veil, with Christ, in whom the veil is done away, allowing us to see our own glory as a reflection of the glory of God: "But we all, with open face beholding as in a glass the glory of the Lord, are changed into the same image from glory to glory, even as by the Spirit of the Lord." (3:18).

And readers who know *Jane Eyre* should recognize in *Villette* a resurgence of key imagery that in the earlier work surrounded St. John Rivers. Early in volume 2, M. Paul finds Lucy alone and in mourning over her departure from the friendly Bretton household, and he accosts her with what she considers inadmissible obtrusiveness and intimacy. It is his metaphors that should arrest our attention. Referring to her attachment to the Brettons, he accuses her of preferring "sweet poison" to "wholesome bitters." Lucy retorts that such poison has at least the virtue of its sweetness: "Better, perhaps, to die a pleasant death, than drag on long a charmless life." But Paul assures her that if he had his way she would take her bitters. Charlotte is alluding to the "bitter physic" of *Pilgrim's*

Progress, part 2. There Christiana's son Matthew asks, "Why, for the most part, physic should be bitter to our palates?" And Prudence answers him: "To show how unwelcome the Word of God and the effects thereof are to a carnal heart." Paul continues firmly, in the spirit of the "Greatheart" that Lucy is later to call him, "and, as to the well-beloved poison, I would, perhaps, break the very cup which held it" (p. 332). (Recall that St. John's "sternness" also was that "of the warrior Greatheart, who guards his pilgrim convoy from the onslaught of Apollyon.")

In this echo-filled encounter Paul is fastening directly on Lucy's carnal longings, the old Mary-Mina death wish, and struggling to purge them away. This death wish Charlotte had already in *Jane Eyre* associated with the attractions of "poison." When Jane was watching Rochester entertain his expensive houseguests, she felt certain that she might never have his love, but could not help desiring it; her eyes insisted on following him, despite her conviction that doing so could only have lethal results for herself:

> I looked, and had an acute pleasure in looking, . . . a pleasure like what the thirst-perishing man might feel who knows the well to which he has crept is poisoned, yet stoops and drinks divine draughts nevertheless.

Such draughts are "divine" only in a grimly ironic sense, as Charlotte makes clear later in *Jane Eyre,* when she again employs the imagery of poisoned draughts. This time Jane is contemplating St. John and assessing the extent of his attraction to Rosamond Oliver—"well named the Rose of the World," as St. John avers. St. John's face has clearly expressed his inner resolution to sacrifice his heart "on a sacred altar" rather than on the altar of human love, and seeing this, Rosamond turns away "in transient petulance." Jane summarizes: "St. John, no doubt, would have given the world to follow . . . : but he would not give one chance of Heaven." Nonetheless Jane urges on him the delicious opportunity he is missing; "You ought to marry her," Jane insists. And for a moment St. John permits himself the fantasy:

> Fancy me yielding and melting . . . : human love rising like a freshly opened fountain in my mind, and overflowing with sweet inundation all the field I have so carefully, and with such labour, prepared. . . . And now it is deluged with a nectarous flood—the young germs swamped—delicious poison cankering them: . . . . She is mine—I am hers—this present life and passing world suffice to me . . .—my senses are entranced—(p. 218)

But he knows the tempting promises of human love are false for him. Though he loves Rosamond "with all the intensity, indeed, of a first passion," he knows that marriage to her would bring him a lifetime of regret. As to his life's high aspirations—"dearer than the blood in my veins"—Rosamond "could sympathize in nothing." His life's effort has been and will continue to be to prune and train the "original materials" of his natural manhood until at last—quoting 1 Corinthians 15:53–54, which Charlotte had quoted before and would quote again in *Villette*—"this mortal shall put on immortality." What, then, has St. John to do with the Rose of the World?[3]

In *Villette,* the function of Rosamond (attractive human love) is given to Dr. John, and the function of St. John Rivers (follower of Christ) belongs to Lucy herself.

The death wish that Paul is struggling to root out of Lucy is thus her mortal yearning toward "human love," toward the very carnal fulfillment that Charlotte insisted on for Jane Eyre, although she allowed St. John's triumph over such desire to have the last word in that book. By the time of *Villette,* however, she had rewritten her own story, had decided that the rivers of this world—"my Rhine, my Nile; . . . my Ganges"—were not after all for her protagonist-self. She had always feared that for herself the plunge into sexuality would result in drowning. Now she was coming again to the same judgment, with renewed force. Men like "John Bull" Bretton (p. 266), "cool young Briton!" (p. 372)—do these names perhaps echo Patrick's "Albion"?—could never understand a nature like hers, any more than a Rosamond could sympathize with the aspirations of a St. John.

Such worldlings are always trying to make the woman artist into something she is not. Lucy knows that there are in her nature elements "wild and intense, dangerous, sudden, and flaming" (p. 372), as M. Paul had all along perceived. But to Dr. John she is "inoffensive as a shadow." Because his is from first to last an "entire misapprehension of my character and nature," he "always want[s] to give me a role not mine" (pp. 454–55). To accede to the views of such misperceivers is to commit a form of spiritual suicide, to lose, as Mina had lost, one's "identity," to have one's "very way of life . . . swallowed up in that of another." St. John had feared that the seeds of his good intentions would be swamped by the poisonous overflow of sexual temptation, by the swelling waters of "human love." In drawing on the same imagery for the encounter between Lucy and Paul, Charlotte reveals her intentions for each of them. In Charlotte's early work "death" had implied physical death, although it was also a form of self-submergence; now the "death" that is to be feared is more nearly death of the creative spirit, of the God-given spark burning within. Lucy is not yet ready to be saved; she still thinks she might prefer to drink the sweet poison and submit to its consequences. Accordingly Paul's "presence utterly displeased me" (p. 332), as St. John had displeased both Jane Eyre and her author. But Charlotte has changed since she wrote *Jane Eyre,* and Lucy's change is coming.

This change is what Paul is fighting for, and his struggle underlies the progress of volume 2 of *Villette.* When Lucy receives a friendly letter from Dr. John, she is overjoyed; but M. Paul "curled his lip, gave me a vicious glance of the eye," and strode away in angry disapproval. Lucy's judgment is weighted with authorial irony: "M. Paul was not at all a good little man, though he had good points." Earlier Lucy had praised the sustenance that "Imagination" provides, likening it to the manna that God provided the Israelites in the wilderness. But now that a letter has come from Dr. John, she repudiates the "mess of that manna I drearily eulogized awhile ago." Such "spirit-dew and essence" might be healthy provender for "Heaven's Spirits," but Dr. John's letter, she exults, is "natural and earth-grown food," and as such she regards it as infinitely preferable. The author's differing estimate is implicit in subsequent events. M. Paul has a positive tantrum when Lucy gleefully receives her letter. "Raging like a pestilence" Paul storms over the school, scowling and muttering and making his large-limbed Labassecourian pupils cry—"all melting like snow-statues before the intemperate heat of M. Emanuel" (pp. 342–44). As for Lucy, we may judge the nourishing power of Dr. John's human food by its effect on her. Taking her letter to the attic in order to read it in privacy, Lucy sits, a "poor English teacher in the frosty garret, reading by a dim candle guttering in the wintry air, a letter simply good-natured—nothing more: though that good-nature then seemed to me god-like" (p. 350). In these reduced circumstances Lucy suddenly sees what she takes to be the ghostly "nun," and collapses in terror, losing her letter and, along with it, all remaining self-possession: " 'Oh! They have taken my letter!' cried the grovelling, groping monomaniac" (p. 353). It is here that Dr. John, insisting that Lucy's is a case of "spectral illusion," recommends with unwitting mockery that she "cultivate happiness" (p. 358). This Lucy undertakes to do. But events are against her. The nourishment of Dr. John's letters is suddenly withdrawn—he has met Paulina—and Lucy is left to perish like a frozen dormouse. So much for the merits of "natural and earth-grown food."

The tone now begins the shift to comedy. Suspecting that the "severe and suspicious" (p. 422) M. Paul may invade the privacy of her hoarded letters, Lucy seals and buries them. They are now in any case mere relics of a former time. But M. Paul knows Lucy's earthward (i.e., Bretton-ward) inclinations, and not being one to underestimate their danger, still snuffs about in growling disapproval: "he accused me of being reckless, worldly, and epicurean; ambitious of greatness, and feverishly athirst for the pomps and vanities of life." (He has sensed her thirst after earthly waters, "the passionate thirst of unconscious fever" that she herself reports feeling in her drugged night journey.) Lucy continues, "It seems I had no 'piety,' no 'religious meditation'[4] in my character; no spirit of grace, faith, sacrifice, or self-abasement. . . . Never was a better little man in some points," she concludes—an improvement over her previous judgment; but "never, in others, a more waspish little despot" (p. 434). His hostility mounts. When he sees Lucy at the Hotel Crécy in the company of Dr. John, "he puckered up his eye-brows, protruded his lip, and looked so ugly that I averted my eyes from the displeasing spectacle" (p. 451). And later when M. Paul thinks that the watch guard Lucy is making may be intended for Dr. John, he explodes into a very tantrum of jealous attacks on Lucy's supposed coquettishness and worldly vanities that makes for a touching and marvelously funny scene (pp. 479–82). It is at this point that his fête arrives, that Lucy recognizes in him "a filial sympathy with 'the dayspring on high,' " and knows his heart's core to be "tender beyond a man's tenderness; a place that humbled him to little children" (pp. 485, 489). Yet still she three times denies him.

We are now in volume 3, and the signs of Paul's divine dimension rapidly accumulate. He often leaves little gifts in Lucy's desk or workbasket, although "watch as I would, I could not detect the hours and moments of his coming"—an oblique echo of Matthew 25:13, "Ye know neither the day nor the hour when the Son of Man cometh." But one day Lucy catches him at her desk "doing me what good he could" (p. 479); and in the conversation that ensues Charlotte invokes 1 Corinthians 15, on which she had drawn in the climax of her poem "Retrospection" ("O death, where is thy sting?"); in her French essay on the caterpillar, years before, for M. Heger;[5] and again in *Jane Eyre,* as we have just seen. And 1 Corinthians is probably, too, the source of Genius' words in *Shirley:* "All change, and forever. I take from your vision, darkness . . . ," etc. From this fifteenth chapter comes the verse I have used to summarize the plot of *Villette* as it relates to Lucy's "being in love with 2 men at the same time"—to wit 15:47, "The first man is of the earth. . . ." It is, in short, a biblical chapter of central importance to Charlotte's imagination.

In the present scene Paul reveals one element of his affinity with Lucy: he too has buried a love. This is literally the case in that his fiancée Justine

Marie, turned nun, had been buried years before. But he has also, like Lucy, buried a way of loving. He does not, he says, wish Lucy to have a "passion" for him. Imagining that she has started at his use of a shocking word—"passion"—he defends it: "There is such a word, and there is such a thing—. . . but I only uttered the word—the thing, I assure you, is alien to my whole life and views. It died in the past—in the present it lies buried," like Lucy's letters and love of Dr. John, and like the legendary nun who lies beneath the old pear tree of the Pensionnat garden, buried long ago "for some sin against her vow" (p. 148). Passion in the carnal sense is past; for Paul and Lucy both, it is "of the earth, earthy"— and so Lucy can now condescendingly dismiss Paul's buried fiancée when she later sees her picture: the face was (Lucy tells us) "not even intellectual." Hers must have been a character without inner fire: her "very amiability was the amiability of a weak frame, inactive passions, acquiescent habits" (p. 566). In this respect Justine Marie recalls Mary Cave of *Shirley:* both are portraits drawn from Charlotte's less approving views of her own dead mother.)[6]

Having asserted that for him carnal passion lies buried, M. Paul then quotes, as applicable to himself, the words of St. Paul addressing the Corinthians:

> In the future there will be a resurrection . . . all will then be changed —form and feeling: the mortal will have put on immortality—it will rise, not for earth, but heaven.

These words in effect summarize the rest of the novel: they spell out Lucy's future—her shift from love of the first man to love of the second —as well as the intentions that Charlotte was by this time shaping for herself. Paul had begun the conversation by urging Lucy to adjust her judgments of men: "You are indifferent where you ought to be grateful," i.e., to himself, "and perhaps devoted and infatuated, where you ought to be cool as your name," i.e., to Dr. John. He concludes modestly enough: "All I say to *you*, Miss Lucy Snowe, is—that you ought to treat Professor Paul Emanuel decently" (pp. 498–99). It is now that Lucy gives him the watch guard she has made for him, and an intimate peace is established between them.

That peace is often broken, in part because there is still the question of rivalry and submission to be settled between Paul and Lucy: but to that question I will return later, as it does not bear directly on the unfolding of Paul's divinity. The next event that does bear on it occurs as Lucy again contemplates her buried love of Dr. John, mourning not only that loss, but also her general condition as one who has "no true home," which for her means that she lacks not only a place, but also a purpose. Is there "nothing to be dearer to me than myself, and by its paramount preciousness, to draw from me better things than I care to culture for myself only? Nothing, at whose feet I can lay down the whole burden of human egotism, and gloriously take up the nobler charge of laboring and living for others?" (pp. 522–23). Lucy's wording is ambiguous. It could describe either woman's domestic calling, or a missionary call not unlike St. John Rivers'. For Lucy the distinction is not yet clear; but it is clear for Charlotte. In fact Lucy's words directly echo those of Charlotte's already published poem entitled "The Missionary" (#187),[7] in which the speaker vows to renounce "Mere human love, mere human yearning" in the interests of spreading "the light of Faith."

We now learn that it was Paul who had once, early in Lucy's stay in Villette, given her a bunch of violets that she had dried and kept among her private things (pp. 528, 166)—allusions to Wordsworth's violet, emblem for young Charlotte of her creative gift. (Paul will give Lucy violets once again, at the book's end: p. 701). And we learn that Paul's "eye" has been watching Lucy's every move: a mark of his Jesuit zeal, but also a private allusion to Charlotte's own long-standing sense of being watched by a "restless eye / Which haunts my solitude"—the eye of her artistic conscience, I have already suggested; of her sense that she is steward of a buried talent that is lying in danger of atrophy. Ultimately, of course, it is the eye of God. (And so the poem makes clear.) If that eye's beam "fell on [her] from a human brow," she had written back in 1837, it would awaken her from "that wild dream / Which spellbinds every talent now," from the feelings that "enervate / And bind the heart"—that is, from her debilitating "self-locked chain" of sexual longings and fantasies and the regression and depression that accompany them. The manuscript version of the poem from which I have been quoting had concluded optimistically, in terms that suggest the ending of *Villette:* "Passion has surged itself to rest," and the "calms" that descend from hope are coming "to soothe the deep's receding swell."[8] In the novel this outline is fulfilled by Lucy's giving up "passion" for Dr. John, and by Paul's descent, like Christ's, to still the threatening waters. The "eye" that Charlotte assigns to Paul is thus to be associated in some way—though perhaps not a fully definable way—with Charlotte's own inner insistence that she not bury her talent, but rather bury the carnal desires that enchain both it and her. The call of her genius and the missionary call to God's service are thus conflated into one vocation, the fulfillment of which requires that she renounce "human love."

I have said that Paul functions simultaneously as a character among other characters in the novel; as the projection of Lucy's own fiery inner spirit, the "talent" that is buried under her snows in the early part of the novel; and as the fictional embodiment of deity—"God with us," Emanuel. The passage concerning the "eye" continues as Paul details the "affinity" that exists between him and Lucy in terms that can be read almost as an allegory of Lucy's (and Charlotte's) double being: cool surface masking inner fire. Here "Lucy" is the outer, social self, "Paul" the chafing inner talent.

> You are patient, and I am choleric; you are quiet and pale, and I am tanned and fiery; you are a strict Protestant, and I am a sort of lay Jesuit: but we are alike—there is affinity. Do you see it, mademoiselle, when you look in the glass? . . . Yes, you were born under my star!
> (p. 531)

Here the manuscript adds, although Charlotte later omitted the addition, "there is little in me which is not yours." But manuscript and published version agree about the warning to be deduced from this affinity: the bonds it forms are ill to break. For two such interconnected persons, "the threads of their destinies are difficult to disentangle; . . . sudden breaks leave damage in the web" (p. 532).

But the thread of Lucy's destiny binds itself ever more firmly into Paul's, just as it becomes ever clearer how exalted his destiny is. On May 1 he keeps his fête-day promise to take the boarders and teachers of the school for a breakfast in the country; the trip is a medley of allusions to the acts of Christ, who "suffered little children," told memorable parables gathered and stored by the apostles, fed the multitudes, and so on. Seated on a green mount, Paul "suffers" the group to gather around him; the "little ones" move closest, as they "liked him more than they feared." He tells them all a story:

> Well could he narrate: in such diction as children love, and learned men emulate; a diction simple in its strength, and strong in its simplicity. . . . I used to think what a delight it would be for one who loved him better than he loved himself, to gather and store up those handfuls of gold-dust. . . . (p. 551)

He then tells Lucy "and five others, whom I shall select" to "spread with butter half a hundred rolls." He is both a "lamb" and "our shepherd" collecting "his sheep" (pp. 552–55).

Two moments, however, tarnish the bright day for Lucy. First, during the picnic Paul asks her "how long could you remember me if we were separated?" To which Lucy answers, "That, monsieur, I can never tell, because I do not know how long it will be before I shall cease to remember everything earthly." The question recalls Christ's prophecy to his disciples of his coming death; and though it is not his death that Paul here names, but rather a trip "beyond seas for two—three—five years" (p. 555), in the event the trip will indeed bring final separation, on earth.

Lucy's second dark moment occurs after the group has returned to the school. Hearing Paul suddenly seek her presence, "striding erect and quick," the coward shrinks within her and she unaccountably flies from his presence, evading him "as I would evade the levelled shaft of mortality" (pp. 556–57). Biographically, this moment may allude to Charlotte's seemingly unaccountable recoil from James Taylor's proffered love; but in context it seems to speak a double message. First, it dramatizes Lucy's sexual fears, recalling for example the Frances whose engagement to William Crimsworth makes her "as stirless . . . as a mouse in its terror." And second, it bespeaks Lucy's intuitive recognition that Paul's embrace requires that she repudiate all claim to happiness on earth, that she embrace, or at least accept, "the shaft of mortality." It is this second aspect of meaning that Charlotte goes on to develop. Charlotte knew from the epistles of St. Paul that "the wages of sin is death; but the gift of God is eternal life by Jesus Christ our Lord" (Romans 6:23). This biblical verse is the measure against which we must now hear Lucy's concluding words: "I took my wages to my pillow, and passed the night counting them" (p. 557). The wages of Lucy's sin in rejecting Paul's love, in flying from his fiery advance, would indeed be the death of her eternal spirit; by extension of echoing analogy, the gift of Paul will be "eternal life by Jesus Christ our Lord."

Lucy has by now learned fully to distinguish Paul's husk from his kernel. The husk she describes is James Taylor's to the last fiber: "Stern, dogmatic, hasty, imperious. I only hear of you in town as active and wilful, quick to originate, hasty to lead, but slow to persuade, and hard to bend" (p. 584). But beneath that husk lies a redemptive capacity that neither Taylor nor any mere man could ever provide. In Paul's offered friendship Lucy finds "support like that of some rock" (p. 589)—"And that rock was Christ," according to I Corinthians 10:4, a passage to which St. John Rivers had directly alluded in *Jane Eyre* (p. 514), saying, "It is the Rock of Ages I ask you to lean on: do not doubt but it will bear the weight of your human weakness."

The Catholic junta now tries either to separate Lucy and Paul, or else to convert Lucy. In this context Charlotte proffers some of her own religious thinking, chiefly her ecumenical view that the differences dividing Protestant sects were unimportant compared to their unity concerning vital doctrines: "I saw nothing to hinder them from being one day fused into one grand Holy Alliance." Lucy and Paul concur at last in the publican's prayer, cited as a model for prayer by Jesus himself: "God be merciful to me, a sinner!" (p. 611; St. Luke, 18:13). We might note in passing that this prayer had marked the moment of Albion's conversion in Patrick's *Albion and Flora* years before. (In its general terms, Albion's redemption had altogether prefigured Lucy's: in Patrick's words, the Savior "in all his mediatorial glory" revealed himself to Albion, so that "light" broke in on his mind with the consolations of "the Holy Ghost, the Comforter!")

This shared prayer is prelude to still greater tenderness between Paul and Lucy, in which Paul's manner sheds the husk entirely and reveals in its place "a mute, indulgent help, a fond guidance, and a tender forbearance"—qualities precisely lacking in Taylor, as Charlotte perceived him: "What I doubted was his kindness . . . one would be thankful for a little feeling, a little indulgence," she had written Mr. Williams. But just as Lucy has begun to think Paul loves her, the announcement is made that he will soon be departing the school, bound to the West Indies.

We have now reached—by chapter 38, entitled "Cloud"—the point in the novel that stands as fictional analogue to the spring of 1851, when the news of Taylor's projected trip to India came secondhand at the very time Charlotte had been admitting to Ellen that marriage to "the little man" did not seem out of the question, that his "quiet constancy" dignified him in her eyes. From this point on, the sharp divergence of novel from life is stunning: in life, the relationship to Taylor plunged rapidly to extinction, as did the relationship to Smith, leaving Charlotte "a lonely woman," as she wrote Ellen, struggling for resignation as she brought her novel to a close.

Taylor's final visit had made Charlotte's veins run ice, had left her with the taste of bitterness and ashes, had led her finally to defend her recoil by the claim that he was "second-rate" and "no gentleman." But the novel takes a very different course. Dr. John has already found sunshine and blessedness with Paulina by the end of chapter 37: that is, Charlotte has disposed of the specter of her attachment to Smith by pairing him off with a secularly perfected version of herself and dismissing the couple to happiness ever after. With the decks thus cleared, she is free to imagine a destiny for her spiritual self, whom she knew to be a pained, flawed, defensive being; but whom she also insisted, in the strength of her fiery genius, was the chosen of God. Her agony of spirit she appears to have regarded as part of the cost.

This agony permeates chapter 38, which opens with a fervid rush of biblical language and allusion. The happiness of a Paulina is not available to a Lucy Snowe: "What then?" the narrator asks—and answers with sorrow and bitterness, "His will be done, as done it surely will be, whether we humble ourselves to resignation or not. The impulse of creation forwards it; the strength of powers, seen and unseen, has its fulfillment in charge. Proof of a life to come must be given" (p. 634).

The question of justice, human and divine, is central to Charlotte's thinking: only an eternal reward of tremendous merit could justify the carnal suffering she has endured. As she wrote Taylor, to accept the tenets of atheism would make life truly unendurable: divine justice there must be, to rectify a world so patently unfair. Accordingly M. Paul's speech at the Hotel Crécy had touched with purifying flame on the subject of "injustice," and when Lucy is commanded to write on the theme "Human Justice," the irony of the topic spurs her to action. This has been, in fact, the topic of one of Charlotte's *devoirs* for Heger in Brussels years before; and although Charlotte did not then treat the subject allegorically, the way Lucy does in the novel, both versions agree that human "justice" is not truly "just."[9]

Charlotte's passionate language in this passage begins with an echo of Revelation 19, where the "Word of God" approaches, His eyes "as a flame of fire" and his clothing "dipped in blood," and then moves on to a whole harvest of allusions: "In fire and blood, if needful, must that proof be written. In fire and in blood do we trace the record throughout nature. In fire and in blood does it cross our own experience. . . . Dark through the wilderness of this world stretches the way for most of us. . . . For staff we have His promise, . . . for present hope His providence, . . . for final home His bosom. . . . 'Art thou not from everlasting mine Holy One? WE SHALL NOT DIE!' " (pp. 634–35).

For the rest of the novel Paul Emanuel, personal beloved of Lucy Snowe, stands revealed as the type of Christ, the Redeemer who seeks his bride not in this world, but in Eternity. Paul's two roles conflate in Lucy's and Paul's last moments together. He asks her, "Be my dearest, first on earth," gathering her "home" in his embrace (p. 709); and in that he is a personal lover, offering the accepting tenderness Polly Home had always had. But as they walk back together the moon shines as it had shone in Eden when God walked in the garden at evening, lighting "a step divine—a Presence nameless." His goodness "broke on me like a light from heaven" (p. 703). "He was my king" (p. 704). Like Christ, Paul had warned her, "Be ready for me." And she had been ready— "Oh! *I* would be ready!" (p. 644). First, when he came to her before his departure: "The hour was come: we expected the master . . . with his swiftness and his fire" (p. 635); but then again, after three years, in the closing paragraphs of the book: "he is coming . . . he is coming." The seven days of apocalyptic storm that end the book place this awaited arrival not here, not now, but in the new heaven and new earth, the millennium beyond time. "Even so come, Lord Jesus," as the respective St. Johns had said at the end of Revelation and of *Jane Eyre*.

Nuns

Given his meaning, of course Paul cannot marry Lucy. Yet as "God with us" he does remain with her, both before his death and after, with a fidelity that in Charlotte's experience no mortal man had ever displayed.

For Charlotte's character Lucy, the years of Paul's absence "were the three happiest years of my life" because during those years she did not yet have to face the full price of giving up carnal love for divine: although Paul was gone she might still receive his letters (visible signs of love in this novel, as in its author's life)[10] and look forward to his return. But this is to expect the benefits of carnal love from divinity, to confuse the hope of sexual happiness with that of redemption. Indeed, in terms of Charlotte's sexual fears, such a limited consummation was in some respects ideal: to be loved at a distance, as was the departing foster child of "Master and Pupil," is a practical way both to achieve the needed nourishment and yet to avoid having one's identity swallowed up. Some such compromise she had surely hoped to work out with M. Heger after she left Brussels; his failure to cooperate led her to see him as a "Granite God," to aver that she had "prayed to stone."

But Charlotte no longer hoped for such a compromise for herself by the time she was writing *Villette*. Indeed the novel's function was to dramatize how one like her must give over all hope of human love and turn to "God alone, and self-reliance," as she had phrased it in her poem "Frances": or as she phrased it now, in a letter to Ellen as she was writing the novel (July 1, 1852), "We must not rely upon our fellow-creatures, only upon ourselves, and on Him who is above both us and them."

In *Shirley* Charlotte had written bluntly about woman's lot in life. Women must not ask for love; society permits them only to wait for it. And often love does not come. Her bitter advice to her women readers had been to "break your teeth" on the stone Fate gave you when you wished for bread; to "close your fingers firmly" on the scorpion you received in place of the egg you desired. The pain will make you "stronger, wiser, less sensitive."[11] That is, it will deepen woman's banked-up snow. But that had been the lesson of carnal love, a warning of the bitterness and pain women must endure if what they long for is the support of a Patrick, a Heger, a George Smith. Paul's love is another matter. Like the good fathers of Scripture, Paul "would give neither a stone, nor an excuse—neither a scorpion, nor a disappointment; his letters were real food that nourished, living water that refreshed" (p. 713).

Some critics have found the spectral nun intrusive in this work. The novel's psychological realism, its proximity to autobiography, its analytic narrative manner, all make the nun seem out of place—even when she is ultimately given rational explanation. And the explanation finally given seems in the event disappointingly silly. But in fact, although the nun is obtrusive to the plot, she has a profound thematic function—as I hope I have already been able to suggest. She is the wraith of Lucy's desire for sexual love, her desire to sin against the "vow" that Charlotte was making for herself in writing *Villette*.

The nun first appears to Lucy when she takes her precious letter from Dr. John into the attic to read it alone (p. 351); then again when she runs up to choose a dress to wear with him to the theater the evening they see Vashti (p. 367); then a third time as she buries the letters he sent her (p. 426). In this series the nun bears witness to three key events in the rise and fall of Lucy's sexual hopes with respect to Dr. John. For him, of course, the nun never really existed except as a function of Lucy's illness, against which he exercised his (in this case quite useless) "professional skill" (p. 364). And in a punning sense he is quite right about that nun: there never was any substance to Lucy's hopes of Dr. John.

The nun's two final appearances concern Lucy's relationship not to Dr. John but to M. Paul, and are more complex in their implications. The first of these climaxes a scene in which Lucy has been walking in the garden with Paul, hearing him assert a special "rapport" between himself and herself, an affinity that suggests that they were "born under the same star"; he claims that their connection is confirmed by their shared susceptibility to supernatural "impressions." Like Lucy, Paul has, he says, "indisputably seen a something, more than once; and to me its conventual weeds were a strange sight, saying more than they can do to any other living being" (p. 532). What they "say" we are never precisely told. But their topic is not in doubt: it concerns Paul's dead fiancée and the question of whether his commitment to her is a barrier to his love for Lucy.

The nun's final appearance is in effect a disappearance: it occurs when Lucy comes home from her apocalyptic night journey, and finds the nun's empty vestments left behind on her bed by Ginevra and de Hamal in a kind of gross, inverted parody of the graveclothes left behind by the risen Christ. The nun of sexual hope has gone off with those worldlings: only the real nun of the regenerated spirit now remains—Lucy herself, not her clothing in the generated body. That other nun, we might say, was of the earth, earthy; but this Lucy-nun is bride of the Lord from heaven.

Paul had not sailed to the Indies on the *Antigua,* as originally planned, but rather later, on the "Paul et Virginie."[12] The implication for Lucy is that she will be the "virgin" to his Paul—as Brontë herself foresaw her own fate to be that of a single and "devoted" woman. As bride of Christ, Lucy takes by implication the role and habit of a nun: Lucy as narrator speaks of her white hair beneath her "white cap, like snow beneath snow" (p. 61), and we know from *The Professor* that "a close white cap" is Charlotte's term for "a nun's head-gear."[13] But Lucy is no ghostly nun, like her who supposedly lay buried in the garden for some (sexual) sin against her vow; nor a fake nun like her who is exploded in all her debased silliness as the irreverent disguise of the book's crudest earthlings, Ginevra and de Hamal; nor, either, the lackluster nun of M. Paul's youthful engagement.

The nun Lucy will become exists on quite a different level: she is the peculiarly deserving, especially beloved helpmeet of Christ. She is "born under the same star" (and on her night journey hears the music of Bethlehem); like Him she is a person of fire and storm, set apart from the multitude. Père Silas had hailed Lucy with the "mystic phrase": "Daughter, you *shall* be what you *shall* be!" (p. 334). The phrase echoes St. Paul's self-description in 1 Corinthians 15:10, when he observes that although unworthy to be an apostle, he *is* an apostle nonetheless: "by the grace of God I am what I am: and his grace which was bestowed upon me was not in vain." Lucy, and Charlotte beyond her, is likewise the bearer of God's news. More even than a missionary, she is a female apostle of Christ, who will use her once buried talent to write her own testament—that is, the story of her salvation, the salvation of her creative power.

Lucy had not sought this apostolic role; rather it had been forced on her by divine purpose, and she acceded much against her will. Preferring shadow, she had been driven out into the sunlight. Preferring to mask her fires, she had felt them blown by stormy winds into flames of irrepressible and passionate feeling. Preferring to remain a quiet onlooker at life, she was roused at last to action.

Yet in affirming near the end, "Oh! *I* would be ready," Lucy still doubts whether the powers opposing her will not be too great. With Apollyon straddling the passage and "trailing his Hell behind him," Lucy questions, "Could my Greatheart overcome?" (p. 644). Bunyan's text as it is used here at the end of *Villette* measures by implication the distance Lucy has traveled in this story from the childhood time when she desired nothing more than the peaceful earthly paradise of Bretton: "The charm of variety there was not, nor the excitement of incident; but I liked peace so well, and sought stimulus so little, that when the latter came I almost felt it a disturbance, and wished rather it had still held aloof" (p. 7). The Bretton haven had seemed a heaven to young Lucy, but it was an inert heaven, static, untried; at best a kind that allows of fugitive and cloistered virtue. By implication it lies not far from what Bunyan called the City of Destruction. But Lucy must be stirred into journey; the stimulus for change comes from above, shaking her out of her deadly lethargy; storms shatter her calm; despite herself, she is forced into spiritual rebirth. By the time we reach the end of the book, she has traveled a long pilgrimage through "the wilderness of this world" (p. 634) to within sight of the Promised Land.

When Lucy had sought the Catholic confession, spurred by storms and by a dream that seemed a "visitation from eternity," forcing to her lips a cup "filled up seething from a bottomless and boundless sea" (p. 223), Père Silas had judged that "a mind so tossed can find repose but in the bosom of retreat, and the punctual practice of piety. The world, it is well known, has no satisfaction for that class of natures" (p. 227), which for him meant that she must enter a Catholic nunnery. And indeed she does collapse on the steps of a Béguinage—faint echo of Nunnwood—and is then protected briefly by the motherly Mrs. Bretton in her "cave in the sea." This is to be rescued from drowning, to be nestled in a womblike enclosure that is at least not quite death itself; and we have seen that on the whole this is the best help "mothers" can provide. But it is really only a kind of retreat, and retreat is not for Lucy. Her movement is toward activity: her course from the first man to the second is also a course from ice to fire, from repression to expression, from inertia to energy—indeed, from being nearly dead herself to having God die for her.

Lucy's final "confession" is to Paul rather than to Père Silas, and how different it is from her first—in motive, in spirit, in result:

> Near me, as he now sat, strongly and closely as he had long twined his life in mine . . . the very suggestion of interference . . . [roused] a fermenting excitement, an impetuous throe, a disdainful resolve, an ire, a resistance of which no human eye or cheek could hide the flame, nor any truth-accustomed human tongue curb the cry. "I want to tell

you something," I said; "I want to tell you all." . . . Warm, jealous, and haughty, I knew not till now that my nature had such a mood; he gathered me near his heart. I was full of faults; he took them and me all home. For the moment of utmost mutiny, he reserved the one deep spell of peace. (pp. 708–9)

In the "peace" that Paul provides for Lucy in departing from her, Charlotte echoes St. John 14, where Jesus, foreseeing his death, takes leave of his disciples with the assurance that "I will not leave you comfortless: I will come to you." Now he addresses them in the flesh, but later it will be in the spirit: then "the Comforter" will come, "which is the Holy Ghost, whom the Father will send in my name." And in so saying Jesus left his disciples the legacy of "peace" that Charlotte now has Paul leave Lucy: "Peace I leave with you, my peace I give unto you: not as the world giveth, give I unto you." Lucy's will not be the merely negative peace that comes of what Charlotte regarded as mindless ritual, "the punctual practice of piety," in Père Silas' phrase. The essentially worldly nature of that "peace" Charlotte had already suggested in her portrayal of Eliza Reed in *Jane Eyre*. Rather Lucy is to know the positive, deeply satisfying peace that comes to the hungry heart when it is finally and generously fed "real food that nourished, living waters that refreshed" (p. 713).

"Lucus a Non Lucendo"

We have seen how Charlotte's writing is suffused with images expressing her sense of being buried away, of needing to be "born again"—both cleansed in spirit and drawn out into the sunshine of love and recognition. "Lucy" is hidden light: like Wordsworth's violet, her potential worth is hidden from the eye; like *Shirley*'s Eva, her "spark of soul" has been left "burning . . . forgotten." Charlotte's own "snow" is the result of such "sharp lessons" as she told the Smiths she had learned long ago as a young girl, lessons that had taught her to be "very sedulously cool and nonchalant" in her pleasures. Correspondingly, when we meet Lucy she is already in a fair way to being numbed into insensibility: "A *cold* name she must have," Charlotte wrote her publishers, "partly, perhaps, on the '*lucus a non lucendo*' principle—partly on that of the 'fitness of things,' for she has about her an external coldness."[14]

In Latin a *lucus* is a wood, grove, or forest—a dark place, in short—whose name was traditionally thought to derive from the word *luceo*, in reference to "the shining or open spaces in a wood through which the light is seen," or paradoxically (as Latin commentators have regularly noted by the phrase *lucus a non lucendo*), because light is precisely what a wood excludes.[15] Similarly "Lucy" is named light (also from *luceo* or *lux*), both because she really has an inner light and—paradoxically— because her "Snowe" shrouds that light, causing imperceptive people like Dr. John to see her only as "an inoffensive shadow," a "shadow in life's sunshine."

We should recognize in the concept of the *lucus a non lucendo* Charlotte's old "forest dell"—Lowood, Nunnwood—the fetal retreat to which she has so many times alluded over the years, first in the poem "Lowood" in 1838, or perhaps even earlier, if we think of it as being implied in the image of the violet "half-hidden" that she borrowed from Wordsworth in 1830.

In *Villette* we find it again, and not only among such indirections as the "hollow" where the spectral nun and Lucy's letters lie buried, or even the Béguinage or Mrs. Bretton's "cave in the sea." The "forest dell" itself is directly present, and given the amplest treatment it ever received in Charlotte's work. By way of characterizing, in a paradigm, the course of her life experience, Lucy tells us to imagine "a dell deep-hollowed in forest secrecy; it lies in dimness and mist: its turf is dank, its herbage pale and humid." Into this familiar unborn-woman state man enters: first bringing violent pain, but then redemptive light.

> A storm or an axe makes a wide gap amongst the oak-trees; the breeze sweeps in; the sun looks down; the sad, cold dell becomes a deep cup of lustre; high summer pours her blue glory and her golden light out of that beauteous sky, which till now the starved hollow never saw. (p. 362).

Like the story of Eva, this brief account synopsizes woman's movement from unborn state ("in catalepsy and a dead trance, I studiously held the quick of my nature") to reborn state ("no human eye or cheek could hide the flame" whose outburst Paul caressingly rewards with "one deep spell of peace").

Let us take each of the two steps—the axe that opens the way into the dell, the light that floods in and nourishes it—separately. Lucy had described the hidden forest enclosure as having been opened by "a storm or an axe"—ungentle tools, and violent is their action in this book. The axe falls on Lucy in the chapter called "Reaction," when she leaves the safely calm "cave in the sea" of the Bretton household to return to Mme. Beck's school. She tells us that she "longed to leave" the Brettons "as the criminal on the scaffold longs for the axe to descend: that is, I wished the pang over." And soon enough it comes: Dr. John takes her back to the school, shakes her hand, bids her goodbye, and departs. "He was gone. The heavy door crashed to: the axe had fallen—the pang was experienced" (p. 326). In depicting this pang and the pain of "reaction" Charlotte drew on her own experience, as we have seen. Recall that in September 1851 Smith had invited Charlotte to visit again in London. Charlotte well knew by then that she must entertain no romantic hope of this delightful young man, and firmly and revealingly she responded to his offer: "No; if there were no other objection (and there are many) there is the pain of that last bidding good-bye, that hopeless shaking hands, yet undulled and unforgotten. I don't like it. I could not bear its frequent repetition. Do not recur to this plan. Going to London is a mere palliation and stimulant: reaction follows."[16]

Charlotte's own "reaction" comprised several months of extreme mental and physical anguish: her old "hypochondria" had returned when she left the Bretton-like comfort of Mrs. Smith's home and George Smith's cheerful companionship and went back to the chill loneliness of Haworth (whose fictional analogue is in this regard Mme. Beck's Pensionnat). Charlotte's letters from the fall of 1851 to the spring of 1852 speak constantly of illnesses that she identified as having their origin in "extreme and continuous depression of spirits," as she wrote Ellen on December 17, 1851. On December 31 she wrote Smith to assure him that there was no "organic unsoundness" (i.e., no consumption) in her illness: the problem was in "the nervous system," she said; and she insisted again, "Going from home is no cure."

Through January and February the suffering continued (this was also the time of Taylor's final silence), and in April Charlotte summarized to another friend, in a letter already quoted, her terrible struggle through that "winter and early spring": "Some long, solitary days and nights there were when I felt such a craving for support and companionship as I cannot express." For those four months (from November 1851 to March 1852) Charlotte, unable to put pen to paper, experienced the "craving for support" that had driven Eva to her cry: "Guidance—help —comfort—come!" And some similar miracle of descending support seems to have come now, at this time of need, to Charlotte. By late spring she had passed through her crisis sufficiently to record it that summer in the writing of *Villette;* the "storm" or "axe" that fell on her (biographically, the "burying" of her hopes with regard to Smith, the firm refusal to seek "living waters" from such "earth's fountains" as those provided by the Smith household) had painfully but effectively opened her closed-up spirit to the "high summer" of rebirth. For Charlotte, this meant than her creative power had returned; she was now, once again, able to write. By October 30 the first two volumes of her new novel were finished; by November 20 she had sent off the third and last.

In the novel, this turning point occurs in the chapter entitled "Vashti," which actually begins with the above-quoted passage concerning the axe-opened forest dell.

The light that floods in and nourishes Lucy is of course Paul himself. But Charlotte's imagery has always suggested a female involvement in this male rescue, or delivery: some mothering Hope has always at least sustained the sufferer; and here it is a female "high summer" who pours "her" golden light into the "starved hollow." Not surprisingly, female power is a crucial presence in *Villette*.

Lucy's liberation, which begins to occur in the "Vashti" chapter, takes the form of a turn from passivity and suffering to action and strength. And we may ask what Vashti herself had to do with this fulcrum of change. Lucy had been from the beginning a poor creature devoid of beauty or grace, whose one pale hope was that she might "compromise with Fate," might find a way "to escape occasional great agonies by submitting to a whole life of privation and small pains" (p. 50). But Fate had never allowed compromise to Lucy. Again and again she had been shaken out of her lethargy by storms that were cruel, but that were constructive as the axe is constructive: they opened her up. Of her childhood she had written in suggestive metaphor:

> I will permit the reader to picture me . . . as a bark slumbering . . . in a harbour still as glass—the steersman stretched on the little deck, his face up to heaven, his eyes closed: buried, if you will, in a long prayer. A great many women and girls are supposed to pass their lives something in that fashion; why not I with the rest?

This state of being "buried . . . in a long prayer" was in important ways the familiar fetal one. But for Lucy it could not last.

> Picture me then idle, basking, plump, and happy, . . . However . . . I must somehow have fallen overboard, or . . . there must have been wreck at last. I too well remember a time—a long time, of cold, of danger, of contention. To this hour, when I have the nightmare, it repeats the rush and saltness of briny waves in my throat, and their icy pressure on my lungs. (pp. 46–47)

This was the watery plunge described in "Diving," and described again, with a darker violence, in the "avenging dream" that seemed "a visitation from eternity" and led to Lucy's confession and collapse at the end of volume 1. After that, Lucy knew that whatever her preference, she was in fact a "half-drowned life-boat man" who only puts to sea in the roughest weather, "when danger and death divide between them the rule of the great deep" (p. 258).

Still Lucy herself did not perish in the "wreck." Instead she took work with the elderly and infirm Miss Marchmont (whose lover had been another false god, at least to the extent that she still thought of him "more than of God"). In this setting Lucy again lapsed into torpor, was again shaken out of it by storm: "It seemed I must be stimulated into action" (p. 50). Each time this gourdlike cycle of waxing and waning occurred, Lucy survived; each time still feeling (however wanly) "life at life's sources" (p. 48)—words that echo Charlotte's estimate of her own stricken condition in the poem "Reason," written as she was coping with the trauma of Heger: "Even now the fire / Though smothered, slacked, repelled, is burning / At my life's source." At that point in *Villette* "a bold thought" was "sent" to Lucy, telling her, "Leave this wilderness" (p. 58). In response she sailed for Labassecour and Villette.

But this was still no promised land. Here again "the negation of severe suffering was the nearest approach to happiness I expected to know," and her only pleasures were in daydreams—"the strange necromantic joys of fancy" (p. 105). Accordingly the rousing storms continued: "One night a thunder-storm broke. . . . I was roughly roused and obliged to live," and with that obligation came an aching longing "for something to fetch me out of my present existence, and lead me upwards and onwards" (p. 152). The echo is again from "Reason," where Charlotte had told how "stronger, higher, / Waxes the spirit's trampled yearning." As if in answer to this inner cry came M. Paul, who internalized the force of storm: in Lucy's comic analogy, he "fumed like a bottled storm" (p. 215).

But Paul does not act at once: something must change within Lucy herself. This is why her experience of Vashti the actress stands at the thematic center of the novel. That dramatic evening shows Lucy a new side of woman, and thus of her own potential: "The strong magnetism of genius drew my heart out of its wonted orbit . . . to a fierce light, not solar—a rushing, red, cometary light—hot on vision and to sensation" (p. 371). It both reveals to her how little affinity there is between people like herself who "belonged to storm . . . wild and intense, dangerous,

sudden, and flaming" and the "cool young Briton" who is her companion; and it provides him with a new companion in Paulina, who now
reenters the story for that purpose. In both these senses—within Lucy
and outside her—the way is prepared for Paul.

Vashti

Acting is like writing fiction in that it permits one to expand one's
experience, to play a number of different emotional roles. But it differs-
from writing in being a more flamboyant medium, requiring more direct
self-display. Significantly Lucy's first full encounter with Paul was also
her one effort at acting. Paul was directing the amateur theatricals that
the students were to present at Mme. Beck's fête; his appearance, qualities, and values Charlotte there sketched out all at a stroke: "A dark little
man he certainly was; pungent and austere. . . . Irritable he was; one
heard that, as he apostrophised with vehemence the awkward squad
under his orders" (pp. 179–80). He apostrophizes in French, but as his
words touch on the whole system of metaphors surrounding Lucy, I will
translate them as I go: "Is your flesh of snow, your blood of ice?" (p.
180) he demands. (One recalls Charlotte's words concerning Taylor:
"My veins ran ice.") "Me, I want all that to catch fire, to have a life, a
soul!" The Labassecourian girls—consistently portrayed as the living
counterparts of the "slug" Cleopatra—are of course incapable of any
such thing. But when one of them falls ill and Lucy is approached by the
little man with his "vexed, fiery, and searching eye" (p. 187) and asked
to take the actress' place, she cannot refuse. The result is stunning. This
first effect of M. Paul's intervention in her life is a paradigm of what will
follow. "What I felt that night, and what I did, I no more expected to
feel and do, than to be lifted in a trance to the seventh heaven. Cold,
reluctant, apprehensive, I had accepted a part to please another: ere long,
warming, becoming interested, taking courage, I acted to please myself."
Yet again waxing, the gourd perished in a night, however: by the next
day Lucy's old habits had reasserted themselves. Despite her now acknowledged "keen relish for dramatic expression," she resolved characteristically that "it would not do for a mere on-looker at life: the strength
and longing must be put by" (p. 197). Not so quickly would Lucy's long
habits of repression change.

But what Lucy revealed to Paul in this incident was her latent capacity
for fire—a capacity that Charlotte had always recognized in herself, but
kept icily hidden for fear of the paternal frown: Patrick's, Heger's, indeed

God's. As she had confessed to Ellen Nussey in 1836, "If you knew . . . the fiery imagination that at times eats me up . . . you would pity and I dare say despise me." It was because of her fiery imagination, Charlotte had thought, that the waters of "the Well of Life" flew from her lips.

Vashti is in a sense the personification of those devouring fires, the slender embodiment of all Charlotte's passionate hunger, roused to violent, defiant rage against the injustice of her stinted and lonely fate. Charlotte had voiced that rage before—for example in her Roe Head Journal—but never in Vashti's public way. Yet she had long known that pain can nourish the potential for violence. In an important passage in *Shirley* (p. 118), she had remarked on the "dissimulation," or masking, that must occur in those who (like herself) feel pain too keenly. Such masks are charged with a bitterness that is both necessary and justified. Suffering women "should be bitter: bitterness is strength—it is a tonic. Sweet mild force following acute suffering, you find nowhere: to talk of it is delusion. There may be apathetic exhaustion after the rack," to be sure. But "if energy remains, it will be rather a dangerous energy— deadly when confronted with injustice." Vashti is woman dangerous, warring against her griefs, and the manner of her fury recalls the demoniac wildess of Bertha: "Hate and Murder and Madness incarnate, she stood" (p. 369). But unlike Bertha she still retains the grandeur of her Brontë original, Zenobia, even down to young Charlotte's favorite adverbs: like Zenobia, Vashti moves "royally, imperially, incedingly" (p. 370).[17]

Although the fiery Vashti is modeled on the actual actress Mme. Rachel, her role had been preparing for years in Charlotte's imagination. As just observed, she links Zenobia (her strength and her unmarriageability) to Lucy (her light and fire—especially as revealed in her acting). But a nearer link occurs in *The Professor,* in the off-stage character "Lucia," whose miniature portrait the admiring Hunsden wears and shows to Crimsworth and Frances by the light of the woman-empowering moon. Looking at the portrait Frances hazards the guess that "Lucia once wore chains and broke them. . . . social chains of some sort." She sees in the face the marks of one who has made "a successful and triumphant effort, to wrest some vigorous and valued faculty from insupportable constraint." The valued "faculty" was of course artistic genius; and constraint was certainly Charlotte's estimate of the condition of her own genius, though she had not as yet experienced Lucia's success in wresting it free. But Frances' figure for such success is Charlotte's familiar one: "when Lucia's faculty got free, I am certain it spread wide pinions and carried her higher than—" and here Frances pauses. She is struggling to account for why the unconstrained Lucia must be unmar-riageable—why, although Hunsden certainly admired her, he "could not" marry her. Frances' "ingenious" suggestion is that Lucia's pinions carried her higher than *"les covenances"* (propriety) permitted Hunsden to follow. "Lucia has trodden the stage," she firmly concludes: "You never seriously thought of marrying her—you admired her originality, her fearlessness—her energy of body and mind, you delighted in her tal-ent. . .—but I am sure she filled a sphere from whence you would never have thought of taking a wife." Hunsden neither confirms nor denies Frances' speculation, but satisifies himself merely with observing how much more brilliant was Lucia's "lamp" than Frances' ever could be, to which Crimsworth responds that he wouldn't want Frances any brighter than she is. His sight, he says, is "too weak to endure a blaze" (pp. 261–62). We have already observed how by the end of *Jane Eyre* the crippled Rochester must have his lamp lit for him by Jane; and in *Shirley* how Louis[18] imagined the decidedly intimidating "fable of Semele reversed." Men of the earth, earthy, have good reason to fear brilliant women, in Charlotte's fiction: they are powerful, and they have a towering debt of female pain to repay.

Patrick had insisted in *Albion and Flora* that the reason "intellectual ladies" on the whole remained single was "not because men feared them, but because they could not love them." But Charlotte seems to suggest that the failure to love is at least related to fear, for it is a kind of impotence. Such men can't even tell a flame when they see it, just as they can't recognize a pearl of great price unless a rich setting alerts them to its value. Cool young John Bretton is untouched by Lucy for the same reason that he is unimpressed by Vashti: for "natures of that order" his sympathies were "callous." Accordingly he judged Vashti "as a woman, not an artist: it was a branding judgment" (p. 373). Like Lucia, Vashti is one of those who spurn *"les covenances";* whereas it is on *"les covenances"* that men like Dr. John build their whole lives.

But Paul judged Lucy as an artist—and a fiercely ambitious one—from the moment he saw her act in the school theatrical; and he had the good sense to be threatened. "I watched you," he told her afterward, "and saw a passionate ardour for triumph in your physiognomy. What fire shot into the glance! Not mere light, but flame" (p. 216). Lucy quite enjoys this new experience, "to see one testily lifting his hand to screen his eyes" from Lucy's "obtrusive ray" (p. 483)! Graham might always be giving her a role not hers; but Paul saw through the role behind which she had always hidden, and demanded that she "play" her real, fiery self. In a remarkable literalizing of the implicit figure, the theater of Vashti's performance actually does burst into flame—and it is in the succeeding "blind, selfish, cruel chaos" that Dr. John meets Paulina and walks out of Lucy's life. It is only the Lord from heaven, the descending spirit of Genius itself, that can afford to love a woman like Lucy.

Charlotte's mind, then, had been well prepared for what she saw when in June 1851 she attended two performances by Mme. Rachel. She described the experience to several of her correspondents; one of the most vivid of these occurs in her last letter to Taylor—the one he never answered. "Rachel's acting," she told him, "transfixed me with wonder, enchained me with interest, and thrilled me with horror. The tremendous force with which she expresses the very worst passions in their strongest essence forms an exhibition as exciting as the bullfights of Spain and the gladiatorial combats of old Rome, and (it seemed to me) not one whit more moral than these poisoned stimulants to popular ferocity. It is scarcely human nature that she shows you; it is something wilder and worse; the feelings and fury of a fiend. The great gift of genius she undoubtedly has; but, I fear, she rather abuses it than turns it to good account."[19]

Like Rachel, Vashti was not "good"—"though a spirit, she was a spirit out of Tophet" (p. 371). But she was certainly fascinating, compelling. The key to Vashti's meaning for Charlotte is precisely her unfeminine anger, her violent and unyielding battle against her fate: "I have said that she does not *resent* her grief. No; the weakness of that word would make it a lie. . . . Before calamity she is a tigress; . . . on sickness, on death itself, she looks with the eye of a rebel. Wicked, perhaps, she is, but also she is strong; and her strength has conquered Beauty, has overcome Grace, and bound both at her side, captives peerlessly fair, and docile as fair" (p. 370). So much for such pallid feminine virtues as Charlotte might, in weak moments, have unworthily coveted for herself. The artist in her must both judge and be judged differently from the woman: Zenobia is no docile "Mary"! In the old rivalry between Zenobia and the Marys, this Zenobia is certain victor. Consider how many of the key women in *Villette* are Marys: Maria Marchmont, Justine Marie, Modeste Maria Beck, Paulina Mary Home. Vashti can be victor over these and all who are like them because she has one unanswerable weapon: she is prepared to give up the love of her "king"; to relinquish what Patrick in *Albion and Flora* had praised as woman's proper "weapons," namely "softness, tenderness, and grace"; to repudiate the ladylike habits of submission that are essential to the Mary role. A Mary must be willing to merge both herself and her God into the person of her worshiped lover. This had been the child Paulina's tendency, who seemed to have "no mind or life of her own," but to prefer to "live, move, and have her being in another."

But Vashti's name denotes her lineage of female independence, for Vashti was the queen in the biblical Book of Esther who relinquished the king's (her husband's) bed and favor by rebelling against his authority.

The biblical account is worth recalling here. King Ahasuerus, who "reigned from India even unto Ethiopia," was holding a lengthy feast; and one day "when the heart of the king was merry with wine," he commanded his chamberlains "to bring Vashti the queen before the king with the crown royal, to shew the people and the princes her beauty; for she was fair to look on. But the queen Vashti refused to come at the king's commandment by his chamberlains: therefore was the king very wroth, and his anger burned in him."

Accordingly Ahasuerus asked his wise men, "What shall we do unto the queen Vashti according to law, because she hath not performed the commandment of the king Ahasuerus by the chamberlains?" Recognizing the extent of the threat posed by such insubordinate behavior, the wise men assured their king that Vashti had wronged not only the king himself, but also "all the princes" and "all the people that are in all the provinces of the king Ahasuerus. For this deed of the queen shall come abroad unto all women, so that they shall despise their husbands in their eyes, when it shall be reported, The king Ahasuerus commanded Vashti the queen to come in before him, but she came not." The evil would spread through all of Persia and Media, they feared, arousing "contempt and wrath."

Therefore they advised the king to "let there go a royal commandment from him, and let it be written among the laws of the Persians and the Medes, that it be not altered, That Vashti come no more before the king Ahasuerus; and let the king give her royal estate unto another that is better than she." This the king did, in order that "all the wives shall give to their husbands honour, both to great and small," and that "every man should bear rule in his own house" (Book of Esther 1:1–22). This is the last we hear of Vashti in the Bible; it is Esther, of course, who comes forward to take her place.

Charlotte well knew that Patrick Brontë concurred in the view that women who relinquish their properly submissive "softness, tenderness, and grace" forfeit the love of men. Doubtless she had personal experience to guide her; but she had also his little educational story, *Albion and Flora*. Recall that it had been that work that had originally prompted Charlotte to divide her heroines into two opposing kinds—the Marys men love and the Zenobias they do not. The lovable Marys she had always associated with Esther. John Martin's famous painting of Queen Esther was copied by Branwell and assimilated by both children to the imagery of Angria. When Mary knelt to Zamorna on behalf of her father—"My King, my Husband, my very Deity, smile at me once more"—Charlotte likened her to Esther "supplicating . . . for the devoted Hebrews."[20] When Zamorna offered to reward Mina's self-obliterating fidelity, he asked: "Come, Esther, what is thy petition?"[21] Even Jane Eyre, teasing the overweening Rochester before the false marriage, addresses him playfully, but significantly, as "King Ahasuerus."

It is sexual love, the king's bed, that women must relinquish if they are to survive and flourish; but to do so requires a kind of rebellion against *"les covenances,"* and rebellious women are sure of condemnation. Zenobia had been wicked—"a beautiful intellectual woman, but an infidel"; the brilliant Lucia had soared irredeemably beyond *"les covenances";* Zenobia's descendent Bertha, starved for love, was degraded to a beast, crawling and roaring like some female Nebuchadnezzar. All of these unlovable women were expressions of Charlotte's sense that her "fiery imagination" cut her off from love, that her creative energies rendered her unworthy and unwomanly, that they were—like the sexual fantasies they so often expressed—rooted in evil and insubordination. Clearly Charlotte sensed that her "darling" imagination could not be redeemed unless her experience of sexual desire were redeemed with it. Indeed her imagination, she was beginning to see, might well be not only cleansed but actually freed if she could somehow dissociate it from the fleshly masculine imperative.[22]

We can trace in her novels the course of her efforts in this matter. In *The Professor* she had pictured a marriage of Master and Pupil so "unromantic" as to be virtually asexual. In *Jane Eyre* she had imagined a marriage between two people, both of whom had experienced symbolic castration: Rochester of course far more directly, but Jane also, metaphorically. With *Shirley* Charlotte seemed for the first time to defend sexual love directly. But even here there are ambiguities. "Love is a divine virtue," Caroline claims, asserting that those who think it shameful betray their own degradation. It is essentially a high and holy feeling that has apparently little to do with sex. Shirley condemns the dirty-minded: "in their dense ignorance they blaspheme living fire, seraph-brought from a divine altar." Such blasphemers, the girls agree, confound the holy flame that is love with something that is not love at all, but rather "sparks mounting from Tophet!" (pp. 356–57).

Shirley's words echo Byron's poem "The Giaour":

"Yes, Love indeed is light from heaven;
    A spark of that immortal fire
With angels shared, by Allah given,
    To lift from earth our low desire."
                              (ll. 1131–34)

But the implied sublimation is central to Charlotte's imagination as it never was to Byron's. Both seraph and altar return in the Eva *devoir,* where they are literalized programmatically. And Genius' mission as described in that essay ("he refined . . . exalted . . . rectified . . . purified, justified, watched, and withstood") is inherited in *Villette* by Paul, who at once purifies Lucy's love (in turning away from "passion" and the earthy Bretton) and sanctifies her inner fires. Of course he never takes her to bed.

The pivotal moment in the Vashti evening occurs when Lucy sees that Vashti has chosen the unwomanly weapons of a Zenobia and yet not been "soon vanquished," as Patrick had predicted. Rather she has "conquered Beauty" and "overcome Grace." She is a rebel against male expectation—not a lady but a fighter. She is by no means exempt from pain, but she does not accept it passively: rather she assaults her fate with mutinous rage. Watching Vashti in her agonized struggle—"she rends her woes, shivers them in convulsed abhorrence"—Lucy asks a question on whose implications the whole book turns: "Well, if so much of unholy force can arise from below, may not an equal efflux of sacred essence descend one day from above?" (pp. 370–71).

Love may be resurrected from earth to heaven, if its sources be not the sexuality of Tophet but the spirituality of a divine altar. Might not the sources of Imagination be similarly redeemed? Charlotte's word "efflux," with its pun on "lux" (Lucy, summer light), carries the force of her point: Lucy need not be a *lucus a non lucendo.* Her "sad, cold dell" may become a "deep cup of lustre" after all. As Lucy later says, Paul's love "broke on me like a light from heaven" (p. 703).

Preparation for this moment had all along been the function of storms: they were God's way of opening His reluctant vessel, of bringing her at last under the "axe," sign of her painful privilege. They had been God's way of ravishing her stubborn soul: "too terribly glorious, the spectacle of clouds, split and pierced by white and blinding bolts" (p. 152). The whole process had been predicted, right down to its vocabulary, in Charlotte's poem "The Missionary" (#187): the "sacred steel / . . . struck my carnal will," her speaker in that poem had said. The calm of reticence, the hope of earthly happiness that "I loved well, and clung to

fast" must "axe-struck, perish"—leaving "no joy on earth to cherish."
The joy now to be cherished must be the prospect of divine approval:

> Then for my ultimate reward—
> Then for the world-rejoicing word—
> The voice from Father—Spirit—Son:
> "Servant of God, well hast thou done!"

Alone in Haworth, after the departure of Taylor and the disenchantment
with Smith, Charlotte must have seen this prospect open before her;
certainly some experience of resignation ("Do not rely on fellow creatures") accompanied the returning power of her pen that summer of
1852. "For to be carnally minded is death; but to be spiritually minded is
life and peace" (Romans 8:6).

Through her character Jane Eyre, Charlotte had desired the carnal
"master" in preference to St. John's spiritual one, seeking to suggest
through the device of the supernatural "call" that this choice had God's
sanction. But I have already argued (in chapter 4 above) that Charlotte
was, in this choice, at odds with her "muse"—that is, with her own
sense of what was in the best interests of her inner, creative life. Not
only did she literally give the missionary St. John the last word in that
novel, even actually conflating his climactic words with those of scrip-
tural Revelation, but she provided another index of her own estimate as
well. Responding to the supernatural call, Jane found Rochester, and was
reunited with him, at Ferndean—a place significantly "deep buried in a
wood."[23] The very name means "forest dell," and its unhealthiness for
living things Rochester had already established in the most striking terms
earlier in the book. To send mad Bertha to this "retired and hidden"
spot, he had said, would be "indirect assassination." Richard Chase is
surely right that *Jane Eyre* ends in a curbing of the *élan vital*—an "indirect
assassination" of it, one might say. But he is wrong in assuming that this
élan is male sexual energy. If anything it is female creative and intellectual
energy that is sacrificed: it is Jane's own soaring spirit that in this conclusion bends down to enter the Ferndean door of death.

So long has Charlotte's "restless" spirit lived underground that at the
outset of *Villette* it actually prefers shadow to sunshine, as we have seen.
Nothing less than the spirit of God is required to deliver it from the
womb/tomb in which it lies buried like the legendary nun who sinned
against her vow. Only by putting the axe to "carnal will" can Charlotte's
hitherto hidden "spark of spirit" be opened to the descending "golden
light" of God's love. In corollary imagery, only then can Lucy's "buried
talent" be retrieved and put to use: "I will be your faithful steward,"

Lucy tells Paul as he departs on his long journey; "I trust at your coming the account will be ready" (p. 704). That "account," in a pun that builds with wonderful suggestiveness on the pun on "talent," is the account of her life: *Villette*. A wise virgin, she has kept her lamp "chastely lucent," as the finished novel itself attests.

Paul's Names

Paul's full name is "Paul Carl (or Carlos) David Emanuel" (p. 494), and of these four names the last three are quickly explained. The two variants "Carl (or Carlos)" are stems of one root: in English this is Charles, of which the feminine form is Charlotte or Caroline. The name in all its forms is a tie connecting Charlotte to her characters: to Charles Wellesley and Caroline Helstone, for example. In this novel Charlotte has Lucy rather coyly acknowledge, "I was like my uncle Charles" (p. 65). The presence of "Carl (or Carlos)" in Paul's name suggests what Paul himself suggests to Lucy: "We are alike—there is affinity" (p. 531). As "Genius" he is a function of his author, and figures Charlotte's Muse. "David," of course, means "beloved"—as by Lucy he surely is. Moreover Jesus, though the son of God, was "made of the seed of David according to the flesh" (Romans 1:3). In fact Jesus' last words in Revelation, excepting the final apocalyptic "Surely I come quickly," refer to this family connection: "I am the root and offspring of David" (22:16).

The name Emanuel, "God with us," should by now need no further explanation.[24] But why did Charlotte choose the Christian name *Paul* for her hero? What is curious is not the choice itself—the allusion is obviously to St. Paul the missionary apostle—but rather the astonishing range of good reasons Charlotte had for choosing it.

For one thing, Lucy's experience of expanded spirit under the dome of St. Paul's cathedral in London was apparently Charlotte's own: she alludes to it also in *The Professor*. Then it is important that St. Paul was a teacher, like Heger, indeed like Charlotte herself, and that he was a special bearer to mankind of the Holy Ghost, sent by Jesus to open the eyes of the Gentiles, "to turn them from darkness to light" (Acts 26:18) and to encourage them to "abound in hope, through the power of the Holy Ghost" (Romans 15:13).

Moreover Charlotte seems to have heard, in St. Paul's account of the storm and shipwreck he suffered on his way to Rome, an echo from her mother's life and also her own. Telling of her experience of childhood "wreck," Lucy strikingly avoided interpretation: we were given nothing of the literal circumstances. Instead, she quotes almost verbatim from Scripture:

> I even know there was a storm, and that not of one hour nor one day. For many days and nights neither sun nor stars appeared; we cast with our own hands the tackling out of the ship; a heavy tempest lay on us; all hope that we should be saved was taken away. In fine, the ship was lost, the crew vanished. (p. 47)

Charlotte's words come from Acts 27:19–20, except that she has revised the ending: in Scripture, although hope was taken away, Paul restored it. Having been reassured by "the angel of God, whose I am," he could tell the crewmen, "I exhort you to be of good cheer: for there shall be no loss of any man's life among you." And so it was: the ship was lost, but no one perished. The point in *Villette* would seem to be that this early Lucy had as yet no Paul aboard her own ship of life. Apparently Charlotte judged the same of her younger self, too. It was precisely St. Paul who had voiced in Scripture the accusation against what Charlotte saw so often and painfully as her own case, condemning those who "worshipped and served the creature more than the Creator" (Romans 1:25). And of course it was St. Paul who propounded so repeatedly the distinction Charlotte seized on for her own case between the "first man" and "the second," between the letter and the spirit, the wisdom of this world and that of the next, the children of flesh and the children of promise, the "carnally minded" which is death and the "spiritually minded" which is life and peace. Like St. Paul and Silas in Acts 16, Charlotte would now truly burst her prison and shed her bonds: like their jailer (and Bunyan's Christian), she wanted to know "what must I do to be saved?" The novel's conclusion suggests that what she must do is learn to embrace the proffered love of Emanuel—who in dying for her will (alas) leave her alone on earth, but with the prospect of eternal union in Heaven.

Earlier I said that Paul's and Lucy's early peace was often broken because the question of rivalry and submission remained still unsettled between them; and I postponed discussion of this question because it did not bear directly on the unfolding of Paul's divinity. But it does bear on M. Paul's relation to St. Paul—and specifically on what would now be termed their sexist views. Those views, and the process of Paul's retraining, account for much of Charlotte's comedy in *Villette*—which is surely her funniest as well as her most somber novel.

Charlotte had already called attention to St. Paul's sexism in *Shirley*, in the crucial central chapter that also criticizes Milton's vision of Eve ("It was his cook he saw") and substitutes for it Shirley's—and Charlotte's—vision of the grand woman-Titan "Nature." That vision is followed by a much earthier event: the women's encounter with the chauvinist Joe Scott, Robert Moore's foreman, who refuses to engage Shirley, even though she is his boss' boss, in any conversation about politics. Women, he smugly claims, are incapable of understanding such masculine topics, and he quotes "the second chapter of St. Paul's first epistle to Timothy" as his authority: "Let the woman learn in silence, with all subjection. I suffer not a woman to teach, nor to usurp authority over the man; but to be in silence. For Adam was first formed, then Eve."

It is Caroline (in this respect she is a Lucy-to-be) who points out the implications of such a stand for Protestants: for if one allows the right of private judgment in the first place, why should not women exercise it as well as men? Shirley summarizes Caroline's argument: "You might as well say, men are to take the opinions of their priests without examination" (pp. 370–71). So ends the debate in Shirley; but *Villette* takes it up again, and gives it much fuller and more complex treatment. There Paul and Lucy must settle both of the parallel issues between them. First there is the issue of personal supremacy: Paul must be brought to respect Lucy as his human equal, to adjust his original view that she must be "kept down." (Mme. Panache is given the off-stage role of the woman toward whom he cannot change his views, one whose "long, free step—almost stride" invariably made Paul "snatch up his papers and decamp on the instant" (p. 504). Hers is the role of a Zenobia ever unlovable). And second, there is the parallel matter of religious independence: Paul must learn to respect Lucy's Protestant convictions. Both issues are settled together through the progress of volume 3, as Lucy grows in confidence and stature, and Paul emerges from being comic provocateur to become the Christian Hero who justifies the names David and Emanuel.

But as type and justification of Christian authorship, St. Paul was not only a sexist, but specifically the grand progenitor of Patrick Brontë as published author. In fact it was specifically as St. Paul's apostolic descendant that Patrick saw himself. In his preface to *Cottage Poems* (1811) he defended his poetic effort by reference to St. Paul's self-description in 1 Corinthians 9:22:

> The Great Apostle says, "I am made all things to all men, that I might by all means save some:" and may not the Author, acting from the same good motive, endeavour to walk in the same steps?[25]

In his preface to *The Rural Minstrel* (1813) he adduced the same model, saying "the author" had endeavored "as nearly as he could, to copy after the great Apostle. . . ."[26] And in his preface to *Albion and Flora* (1818) he yet a third time identified his writing with St. Paul's: "In this, though following at an immense distance, he has endeavoured to walk in the footsteps of him of Tarsus. . . ."[27] Patrick followed his mentor's example not only in religious authorship, but in his attitude toward women, as we have seen. In this respect, too, then, there lurks behind the M. Paul whom Lucy successfully educates the Patrick whom Charlotte must have long despaired of changing.

Yet she clearly loved the chance to try, even by proxy. Her text, in drawing the battle lines between Lucy and Paul, was significantly not St. Paul's epistles themselves, but Patrick's *Albion and Flora* yet again. And here she has a romping good time. Had Patrick written condescendingly that "lovely, delicate, and sprightly woman, is not formed by nature, to pore over the musty pages of Grecian and Roman literature, or to plod through the windings of Mathematical Problems"? Charlotte had long ago created in Zenobia a woman who did just those things, and did them as well as any Mme. de Staël—whose illustrious example may well have provided a bone of contention in the parsonage household, to judge by the tenacity with which Charlotte all her life worried it. Now in *Villette* Lucy discloses to us a Paul more intolerant even than Napoleon had been (who exiled the difficult lady): Paul "would have exiled fifty Madame de Staëls, if they had . . . outrivalled, or opposed him" (p. 504). When Paul undertakes to teach Lucy arithmetic (those "windings of Mathematical Problems"!), he is indulgent to a flaw so long as she is stupid and slow to learn.[28] But then—"strange grief!" cries Lucy—"when my faculties began to struggle themselves free, and my time of energy and fulfillment came . . . there flowed out the bitterest innuendoes against 'pride of intellect.' I was vaguely threatened with, I know not what doom, if I ever trespassed the limits proper to my sex, and conceived a contraband appetite for unfeminine knowledge" (p. 508).

Nor does Charlotte leave Patrick's "musty pages of Grecian and Roman literature" unturned. "In M. Emanuel's soul," Lucy tells us, "rankled a chronic suspicion that I knew both Greek and Latin. As monkeys are said to have the power of speech if they would but use it, and are reported to conceal this faculty in fear of its being turned to their detriment, so to me was ascribed a fund of knowledge which I was supposed criminally and craftily to conceal." Repeatedly Paul tries, by pouncing on her unawares, to catch her in her forbidden knowledge. And "there were times," Lucy acknowledges, "when I would have given my right hand to possess the treasures he ascribed to me. . . . I could have gloried in bringing home to him his worst apprehensions astoundingly realized" (pp. 511–12). But alas, it is out of her power—as it would have been out of Charlotte's. It was Branwell, precious Branwell, now dead of his own puerile excesses, whom Patrick had taught the coveted Latin and Greek. With the injustice that Charlotte felt characterized so much else in his treatment of herself, Patrick in his treatment of "intellectual ladies" had held true to his own misguided precepts.

Accordingly "women of intellect" are Paul's final target, his last retreat once he has learned that he cannot surprise his prey in the secret possession of her Greek and Latin. "Here he was at home. A 'woman of intellect,' it appeared, was a sort of . . . luckless accident, a thing for which there was neither place nor use in creation, wanted neither as wife nor worker. . . . He believed in his soul that lovely, placid, and passive feminine mediocrity"—Patrick had actually written "softness, tenderness, and grace"—"was the only pillow on which manly thought and sense could find rest for its aching temples; and as to work, male mind alone could work to any good practical result" (p. 513). "Truly his bark was worse than his bite," Lucy concludes of Paul, refusing either to placate or directly to nettle. But Charlotte had already barked at her game and also bitten him, using the highly capable tooth of comedy—a woman of intellect's revenge.

But in one thing Patrick was right about intellectual women: "In general they have remained single." Patrick had maintained that this was because men "could not love them"; Charlotte had grown to suspect that, despite disclaimers, it might well be because men feared them. But St. Paul had named a deeper reason, and a far more compelling one, in arguing the innate superiority of the virgin state. "The Children of this world marry . . . but the worthy neither marry nor are given in marriage: they are the children of God, being the children of resurrection" (Luke 20:34–36). Accordingly (as Charlotte had long known) the married woman "careth for the things of this world, how she may please her husband." But "the unmarried woman careth for the things of the Lord" (1 Corinthians 7:34). And "things of the Lord" are the proper business of the woman of intellect, the woman artist whose fiery imagination has been redeemed from the Tophet of sexuality.

What Paul can do for Lucy in this world is to prove that she is indeed lovable, and then leave her with meaningful work to do: "you shall mind your health and happiness for my sake, and when I come back—" To Paul's hint concerning his return—we might call it his second coming—Lucy had answered in the language of Jesus' parables, "I will be your faithful steward" (p. 704).[29]

Appropriately, considering her apostolic calling, the work Paul has left for Lucy is teaching; and the address of the school he has prepared for her is 7 Faubourg Clotilde. This address has led one critic to speculate that Brontë meant to allude to a Clotilde who was a "famous warrior maiden," and that in Clotilde's name Lucy will "begin an Amazonian independence." The number seven, the same critic further observes, was "considered by numerologists to signify wisdom."[30] These are happy possibilities. But in the context of this novel the number seven seems more likely to have been meant to recall the times of creation and apocalypse, or more largely the realm of Time altogether, as distinct from Eternity. And the name Clotilde almost certainly had a very different set of associations for Charlotte, associations drawn from French history. (Charlotte's figure for Amazonian independence is in fact Penthisilea, who is associated in this novel with the strident Mme. Panache.)

To understand the meaning of Clotilde for Charlotte, we must go back for a moment to the scene of Lucy's nervous collapse in the face of the two interrogating professors for whom she eventually wrote her essay "Human Justice." The rattled Lucy could at first remember nothing: "They went on to French history. I hardly knew Mérovée from Pharamond" (p. 579). But Charlotte herself knew that Mérovée, after whom the Merovingian dynasty is named, and Pharamond were fifth-century kings. And St. Clotilde (475–545) was the wife of a third early French monarch, the Merovingian King Clovis. That Charlotte associated King Clovis with M. Paul is evidenced by the fact that in her manuscript of *Villette* Paul's home was located in "Rue Clovis," a name she later changed to "Rue des Mages" ("Street of the Magi"), presumably in deference to the important scene she was constructing around the ghastly Malevola who lived next door. Clovis' widow Clotilde fulfilled after her husband's death a life of austerity and good works that resulted in her canonization. Thus for Charlotte the name Clotilde suggested not Amazonian independence, but rather Christian widowhood-cum-sainthood. If bereavement must be the condition of Charlotte's life as woman, still as an artist her work had the most elevated spiritual heritage and potential.

At one level, then, Paul's death leaves Lucy a "widow" destined to a life like St. Clotilde's of austerity and good works. At a still deeper level of religious suggestion Paul dies the death of Jesus, and Lucy as his nunlike "bride" lives on in her conventual white cap. At this level the "real food that nourished, living water that refreshed" that she receives from him have sacramental implications associating them with the saving body and blood of Christ.

But finally we may observe that in drowning at sea, Paul fulfills the destiny of all those Brontë heroines who have drowned in the stormy carnal waters of time and space and sexual passion. The seven-day (7 Rue Clotilde!) "destroying angel of tempest" that drowns Paul prefigures the apocalyptic second coming ("when I come back—" Paul had hinted); it looks forward to the "new heaven and a new earth" that will replace those that shall have passed away, to the millennium when there will be "no more sea" (Revelation 21:1). Then will the Spirit and the Bride together say "Come," and go forward, united forever, into Eternity.

At this level Lucy's story has been a synopsis of Charlotte's, who saw in the biography of her own creative imagination (from birth to rebirth) in turn a kind of reenactment of biblical history, such that her fire of creative energy was in its redemptive potential an inner Moses (with Vashti as his "magian power" or "rod"—see *Villette,* p. 371) leading her out of the bondage of earthly love, through the bitter salt sea of time and space, across the "wilderness of SIN," toward the promised land of Salvation and rebirth in Christ.[31]

As Paul takes Lucy to preview her future life and bids her goodbye, the text reverberates with biblical suggestiveness. Hearing Paul approach, Lucy thinks that the sound of his shoe must be that of "the master-carpenter." Then Paul himself arrives in "bridegroom-mood" (p. 694). His whispered "Trust me!" breaks in her "the seal of another fountain" (p. 695), and she weeps as he tells her, "I come to justify myself" (p. 697). Days before, Paul had told her, "Be ready for me," and she had affirmed, "Oh! *I* would be ready." Now without reserve of any kind Lucy confirms, "I was ready" (p. 697); and Paul takes her to see the place he has prepared for her. The experience is like being born again: "I can no more remember the thoughts or the words of the ten minutes succeeding this disclosure, than I can retrace the experience of my earliest year of life" (p. 702). As they return together to the Pensionnat Lucy feels like Eve in unfallen Eden, walking in the company of "a step divine—a Presence nameless." Paul had deemed her born under his star, Lucy recalls; now "he seemed to have spread over me its beam like a banner" (p. 710). The striking analogy recalls the Song of Solomon: "and his banner over me was love" (2:4).[32]

That her art was her religion was of course one of Charlotte's earliest aesthetic doctrines, implicit already in the figure of Aaron's rod in the poem "Retrospection" (1835). But for years she had feared that she might be working in the service of false gods after all—though surely the creative spirit was godlike, whatever the source of its power. This conviction animates, for example, even Charlotte's description of Lucy writing her mundane French exercises: "I got books, read up the facts, laboriously constructed a skeleton out of the dry bones of the real, and then clothed them, and tried to breathe into them life, and in this last aim I had pleasure" (pp. 580–81). But in the character of Paul she has at last found a way to justify her old perception that " 'Tis my religion thus to love"—a way, that is, to love a man who has the attractions of the father yet is not a false god; even a way to see her love reciprocated as divine power operating through her talent, no longer "buried" but wisely invested at last.

Mother, for One Last Time

We have seen that for Charlotte the mother gives birth, but only the father can bring rebirth. Yet as Lucy struggles toward regeneration, toward the liberation of her creative fires from the powers of Tophet, she too—like so many Brontë heroines before her—has special aid from a mothering female force who descends to her from above.

Under the titles of "Imagination" and "the Ideal," versions of the "mighty Mother" are periodically astir in *Villette,* keeping Lucy's head above water as she awaits the coming of the Lord. They are in effect female variants of the "efflux . . . from above" at which Vashti's powers had hinted, encouraging figures that labor on her behalf against the harsh and numbing effect of "the rude Real," "Reason," the "World." One night when Lucy has been struggling to repress her passionate longings, "something like an angel—the Ideal—knelt near . . . shedding a reflex from her moonlight wings and robe over the transfixed sleeper." That her power is "Hope" Charlotte shortly makes explicit: "By which words I mean that . . . the night filled me with a mood of hope" (p. 153). Later, when "Reason" has been forbidding Lucy to write Dr. John letters that would reveal the fullness of her heart, Lucy admits that "Reason might be right"—but who can blame us, she asks, if we are "glad at times to defy her . . . and give a truant hour to Imagination . . . our divine Hope." Reason is a cruel "step-mother" whose ill-usage, "her stint, her chill, her barren board, her icy bed" would long ago have killed Lucy were it not for a "kinder Power" whom Lucy envisions in terms familiar to readers of Charlotte's earlier works: "Then, looking up, have I seen in the sky a head amidst circling stars, of which the midmost and the brightest lent a ray sympathetic and attent. A spirit, softer and better than Human Reason, has descended with quiet flight" (p. 328).

Of course Reason had been right, as far as wordly reality is concerned. For Lucy to have given expression to her feeling for Dr. John in her letters to him could in the long run only bring her more pain, even threaten submergence. (Reason and its ally pride had always been defenders against that fate.) Still in this passage "Imagination" does have about her something of the "divine," something that is not at all necromantic daydream, as Charlotte's imagery makes clear. The visionary female presence that had revealed herself in Charlotte's poems and novels in past years, through the various forms of rainbow, moon, or landscape, had always figured Nature. But here she is less natural than celestial: she is a "daughter of Heaven," a "good angel," a "divine, compassionate, succourable influence!" to whom Lucy vows, "When I bend the knee to other than God, it shall be at thy white and winged feet, beautiful on mountain or on plain" (p. 329). One editor observes that in this phrase we may hear a reminiscence of Isaiah 52:7, "How beautiful upon the mountains are the feet of him that bringeth good tidings."[33] And surely that editor is right. But there is still more to the echo, for those words of Isaiah were quoted and their meaning expanded by St. Paul; in Romans 10:15 he uses the image to celebrate the role of apostles and missionaries carrying the word of God out into the world. How shall the people hear God's word unless someone is sent to preach to them, he asks: "And how shall they preach, except they be sent? as it is written, How beautiful are the feet of them that preach the gospel of peace, and bring glad tidings of good things!" Indeed this moonlight-winged "Ideal" and the "daughter of Heaven" who is "Imagination" are angelic analogues of the apostolic woman writer herself, whose creative fires have been lit from the altar of God.

This angelic power is not "Genius." For Charlotte Genius, like God, is always male. But Charlotte had come to believe that faith is related in an important way to Genius. If we look back to Charlotte's French essay, "The Death of Moses," we may see that the power she here names "Imagination" she there named "Faith." In that essay the opposition had been not between Reason and Imagination or the Ideal, but between Reason and Faith; "Reason," she wrote in Brussels, cannot comprehend the mysteries of Revelation. But "Happily Faith comes to man's aid, an angel . . . , a seraph, who soars to the seventh heaven, to the very throne of the Eternal."[34] This seraph is the female counterpart of Genius, mother figure to his father figure: the "true" mother of the female artist, in contrast to the cruel stepmother, Reason. Like her sister Emily, Charlotte now saw "Reason" as a dark and unwelcome agent of material reality, a false mother in contrast to whom Faith (faith in God, in self-reliance) was true mother. But unlike Emily, Charlotte did not see that mother figure as divine. In "faith" lay woman's access to divinity; but divinity itself was a father to Charlotte, who never did doubt that the deep source of her creativity lay beyond herself, in a "god" for good or ill.

In *Villette,* biblical echo and religious imagery dominate every other kind. Accordingly both Eve and the Virgin Mary are merged in Lucy herself so that the "Resurgam!" of all womankind is imaginatively effected through Lucy's resurrection from the half-drowned, near-dead state of fetal inertia. As Eva had met the descent of Genius with the Virgin Mary's words at her Annunciation, so Lucy's embrace in the arms of Emanuel occurs significantly on the Feast of the Assumption (p. 693) —the day that celebrates the taking up of the Virgin Mary into heaven. "I shall arise"—*Resurgam!*

Once the sacrificial axe had severed the connections between Charlotte's art and her carnal will, once the destiny of the Missionary was allotted not to a male "Greatheart" like St. John or the male hero of her poem "The Missionary," but rather to her heroine, the novelistic embodiment of herself, Charlotte could envision herself, as artist, as a nun dedicate to her eternal Bridegroom. Through Lucy she could be at last both beloved by the Father and also be like Patrick a writer-teacher who walks in the footsteps of the great Apostle. And M. Paul, in turn, can shed at last his misogynist wolf's clothing to stand revealed as the Lamb of God.

But having found at last the perfect Father, has Charlotte lost interest in her actual mother, dismissed her as an essentially unworthy rival for fatherly affection, merely a Justine-Marie of too-acquiescent habits? There may be truth to such a view of Charlotte's attitude, but it would be partial truth only. The nun who was buried alive for a sin against her vow stands for all women—Maria Brontë foremost among them—who have lost themselves to the power of male sexuality. Lured into sexual danger, whether literally like Elizabeth Hastings at the grave of Rosamund Wellesley, or figuratively like Lucy-Charlotte, led "along the track of revery, down into some deep dell of dream-land" (p. 184), they stand at the edge of annihilation, ready to plunge into the waters of unconsciousness, equally the repository of infantile memory and the source of sexual longing. When Lucy finds refuge at the Brettons, she describes her "cave in the sea" as a nether world (like Angria) from which she could hear the storms of outside life "withdrawn far, far off, like a tide retiring from a shore of the upper world—a world so high above, that the rush of its largest waves, the dash of its fiercest breakers could sound down in this submarine home, only like murmurs and a lullaby" (pp. 258–59). It is in this context, I think, that we must hear the imagery of Charlotte's poem "Diving" (#117):

> Look into thought & say what dost thou see
>   Dive, be not fearful how dark the waves flow[.]

In those depths come no winds of inspiration, no breeze of life:

> What had I given to hear the soft sweep
> Of a breeze bearing life through that vast realm of death
> Thoughts were untroubled & dreams were asleep
> The spirit lay dreadless & hopeless beneath[.]

This is the context as well of another poem (#140), untitled, written that same spring of 1837 in which "Diving" was written. It begins "Is this my tomb?" and concludes:

> Past, Past, forgotten I am here
>   They dug my chamber deep
> I know no hope I feel no fear
>   I sleep—how calm I sleep!

Womb and tomb, the places of memory and the preconscious sources of those desires that lure women back toward death, all converge in Charlotte's imagination and coalesce in her imagery. Compare Charlotte's concept of the "deep dell of dreamland" to her words concerning memory in *The Professor*. There she commented concerning certain precious sensations, "treasure them, Memory! seal them in urns and keep them in safe niches" (pp. 57–58). This imagery is then echoed in *Shirley*, in the "black hollow" where the un-reborn Eva lives, and now in *Villette* in the "deep hollow . . . hidden partly by ivy and creepers" (p. 424) in which Lucy buries her letters and in which the nun was said to have been buried. All these dells, both watery and mossy, are places of un-reborn female enclosure, variants of Lowood, Nunnwood, the fragile retreat of Mrs. Bretton's "cave in the sea." Variants, too, of "that forest dell where Lowood lay" and where Helen Burns' mortal remains lie buried in *Jane Eyre*. And of the assassinating Ferndean as well. These are the dark loci of sexual fantasy and desire, the deep-hollowed *lucus a non lucendo* where "talent" lies spell-bound, the deep-buried fires that are hidden beneath the weight of pain-induced snow. On such female graves (really it is the "normal" condition of woman's life that they figure) Charlotte had for years been writing "Resurgam!" But not until the Eva *devoir* did she begin to see a way to make her redemption of her mother through the power of art (by her mother I mean of course both Maria Brontë and the struggling "mother" internalized in Charlotte herself) coincide with the redemption of herself as intellectual woman, as artist.

Shortly after Charlotte finished *Shirley,* Patrick for the first time gave her her mother's papers to read. She found the "mind whence my own sprang" to be "of a truly fine, pure, and elevated order. . . . There is a rectitude, a refinement, a constancy, a modesty, a sense, a gentleness about them indescribable. I wished that she had lived, and that I had known her."[35] We have seen that Charlotte discovered in that good woman no divine dimension. Yet Maria Brontë had left her daughter the message that she now found, in writing her final novel, the most crucial of her life. The message was not left among Maria's letters or papers, but was carved on her memorial tablet in the Haworth church. "Here lie the remains of Maria Brontë," the tablet reads, "Departed to the saviour . . . in the 39th year of her age." And then it adds the motherly message of Faith:

> Be ye also ready: for in such an hour as ye
> think not the Son of Man cometh: Matthew XXIV.44.

The "golden light" that in *Villette* floods into the deep-hollowed dell was for Charlotte the light of Faith wedded to Genius. After her stormy pain and loneliness, this light figures the triumphant return of her ability to write: a female apostle, she writes her experience of God. So virginal Lucy writes her life in a nun's white cap, her white hair lying "like snow beneath snow." The opened dell is of course not only the opened hiding place of Lucy's power, but also a type of the grave that Christ opens at Resurrection, when the dead arise and the mortal shall put on immortality, when the man of the earth, earthy, is succeeded by the lustrous Lord from heaven. Now Lucy-Charlotte writes words; but—a wise virgin— she is "ready" for the hour when the Son of Man cometh; then her words will give way to the Word.

On November 20, 1852, Charlotte sent off to Cornhill the last volume of *Villette.* On December 13 Arthur Bell Nicolls, her father's curate who had loved her, unobserved, these several years, declared his love for her and proposed marriage. Under no illusion that she loved him, yet valuing his devotion as she had earlier found herself unable to value Taylor's, after long indecision she married him at last on June 29, 1854.

To what extent, if any, Charlotte felt that she too had now sinned against her vow we will never know. I am inclined to guess that her marriage to Nicholls, by putting an end to the fusion her imagination had finally effected between lover and muse, would have had to put an end to her art. Perhaps it hastened also the end of her life. Despite her husband's loving solicitude and tender care, Charlotte died nine months after her marriage, possibly from complications of pregnancy. It may be that precisely because Nicholls was good to her as a husband, making her feel cherished by a man of body and blood, he reinstated within her the old opposition between outer male (source of love) and inner "male" (source of art), between the Patrick she wanted to be loved by and the Patrick she wanted to be like. The evidence of her last letters (February 1855) suggests that her husband fed her plenteously the food of love for which she had hungered all her life. But alas, she could not take it when it came. She died rejecting his food—literally, she died vomiting.[36]

In *Villette* Charlotte had distinguished between the food of earth and the food of heaven, between the "savoury mess of the hunter" and the manna "gathered amongst gleaning angels"—the latter being, as she there observed, "an aliment divine, but for mortals deadly." In March 1855 Charlotte Brontë exchanged Nicholls' food for "aliment divine." Like her mother before her, she "departed to the saviour . . . in the 39th year of her age."

SEVEN

Conclusion

Holy Ghosts

The "Holy Ghost" of my title was for Charlotte Brontë the traditional member of the Christian trinity, somewhat transmuted to meet Charlotte's own needs (as in her emphasis on its association with "Genius") but still recognizable as the power that impregnated Mary mother of God, and as the Comforter whom Jesus promised to send to the apostles after his death. But for Emily the "Holy Ghost" was more nearly the spectral relic of a lost life—a "Ghost" because in its separateness it is the emblem of all death, and "Holy" because the life it departed was divinity itself: "Being and Breath," what Coleridge called the infinite "I AM," the originating center of all that either "is" or "does." In divinity, being and doing unite: Being is the Breath that gives life and inspires art. For Emily this total Being is female in just the sense that humankind's earliest deities may have been female: aspects of the eternal Mother, the "principle of life / Intense," in Emily's phrase.

But as we have seen, the elements may break apart, male element from female. Emily found that in such case male doing, divorced from female being, must either perish in utter annihilation or else wander in uncentered destructiveness. As Blake agreed, "male forms without female counterparts" are "Cruel and ravening with Enmity & Hatred & War" (Four Zoas). In Emily's theology the male loosed from his source in being is death itself, and so is the created world that he stands for, in Emily's revision of the traditional gender associations of nature. That is, nature is death not only in that it is the realm of mortality, but also in the Neoplatonic sense that to be born into nature is to die out of some fuller life.

Thus although for both sisters the creative force through whom one writes novels and poems was the Holy Ghost—as active doer, as Genius or visitant—only for Emily was that Ghost a figure of death.

In Emily's poem "No coward soul is mine," the mother-world of "Undying Life" that "pervades and broods" with "wide-embracing love" stands in contrast to the "storm-troubled sphere" of violent doing and impoverished being. Certainly Charlotte agreed with her sister that the father-world is a storm-troubled sphere. We have seen how consistently she associated the stormy with the masculine, from the earliest Glasstown fictions where as false god he nearly drowned her or swallowed up her being, through to *Villette,* in which storms—now the painful but stirring instrument of the true God—rouse the sinking Lucy and fan her faltering flame of life. With her fires aroused, she can *act.* The pun on "act" (act on stage/act as doing) is latent, but crucial to Charlotte's thinking; it allows us to recognize the full importance of the example that Vashti provides.

In Vashti woman's male element reigns absolute; she is an *act*ress "wild and intense." Charlotte has Lucy confide that she had "seen acting before, but never anything like this." Describing Vashti's effect on her audience, Charlotte draws on an imagery she normally reserved for masculine act. Vashti "disclosed power like a deep, swollen river, thundering in cataract, and bearing the soul, like a leaf, on the steep and steely sweep of its descent." Her male element empowered to the limit, Vashti is a kind of female storm, a woman's doing pursued almost to the extinction of her being, "an inordinate will, convulsing a perishing mortal frame." As such she is almost not a woman at all, but pure act, pure "artist" housed in a female body. Dr. John could hardly miss the point more completely when he judges her "as a woman, not an artist." As woman's action incarnate, an "unholy force," "torn by seven devils," Vashti is Charlotte's female version of Emily's Heathcliff. Stirred by Vashti's example (the fierce little actress is a "rod of Moses" that can part and remingle the Red Sea: free the Israelites, punish the Egyptians), Lucy is enabled to cope with and respond to the "bottled storm" that is Paul Emanuel. She learns to use her talent and render her account to the true God who she now feels is "with her" at long last—God with us, Emanuel. That "account" is the novel *Villette,* the figuratively rendered testament of Charlotte's own "Resurgam."

Lucy's refusal to give up her woman's clothing when acting a male role in the play performed at Mme. Beck's fête works like a miniature prophecy and defines the difference between Lucy and Vashti. Lucy consistently refuses to give up her female being; for Charlotte this meant that she refused to give up the hope of being loved. (It was a similar refusal that led Charlotte to depict St. John Rivers as an unacceptable alternative for Jane Eyre: there St. John represents Jane's temptation to take the road of male doing at the cost of female being, to fulfill an apostolic mission at the price of being lovable and loved.) Lucy's reward for her tenacious hold on her female "being," even as she gives full play to her desire to act, comes in her last encounter with M. Paul. As she grows more aggressive he grows more accepting. In this scene she gives, for the first time in her life, wholly unimpeded expression to "a fermenting excitement, an impetuous throe, a disdainful resolve, an ire, a resistance of which no human eye or cheek, could hide the flame, nor . . . curb the cry." At this, the novelist is released within her: "All leaped from my lips. I lacked not words now; fast I narrated; fluent I told my tale; it streamed on my tongue. . . . truthful, literal, ardent, bitter." Here St. Paul's injunction against female speech—quoted at the very center of *Shirley*—is resoundingly repudiated at last.

Now Charlotte's fictional Paul in effect redeems the errors of the historic saint. Instead of striving to repress Lucy's passionate verbal action, M. Paul welcomes it with the rapt happiness of a proud mother: "I merited severity," thinks Lucy, but "he looked indulgence. . . . I was full of faults; he took them and me all home. For the moment of utmost mutiny, he reserved the one deep spell of peace." As Lucy is energized into her fullest "doing," Paul wells up into his fullest "being," uniting in his presence both mother-love and father-power. Such union recalls the God who walked among his creatures in Eden before the Fall: "a step divine—a Presence nameless."

The novel that results from God's being "with" Charlotte brings to fruition all Charlotte's long history of fascination with gender inversions: the Zenobia who seemed to have a "masculine soul" in her female "casket"; the choice of those ambiguous pseudonyms when publishing the sisters' poems; the union of male and female selves in *The Professor;* the power reversal that comes in *Jane Eyre* when Jane assumes the role of Albion and departs the grieving Rochester; the "fable of Semele reversed" in *Shirley*. The Eva allegory had marked the first occasion on which no gender inversion was necessary. The reason was that with this allegory Charlotte transformed her longed-for beloved much the way Emily had transformed the dazzling sun: she internalized him, rendered him figurative. Now for the first time Charlotte fully embraced what I have been calling her male muse. For Charlotte this could occur only after she had learned to regard her experience of Genius, her fervent ambition to do "man's work," not as something that drove paternal love away but rather as a source of that necessary love. Her experience as artist could be a version of all creation's experience of God; the descent of her male muse could now be understood as a type of the descent of the Holy Ghost into the receptive human spirit.

By contrast, Emily's final act as artist was a stirring denunciation of masculine "act." In September 1846, after she had finished *Wuthering Heights,* Emily wrote in her Gondal notebook one long, last, rambling and nearly illegible poem (#192),[1] spoken by a man who, somewhat like Heathcliff after his loss of Cathy, has left "home" and is fighting in a brutal foreign war that means nothing to him. The fiction is set in Gondal, but the condition of the speaker is that of Emily's own male energy cut off (perhaps by the writing of her novel) from his source in her being and now abandoned to mere purposeless violence. His "hate of rest," the speaker says in significant metaphor, has "weaned me from my country's breast" and brought him to this condition of ruthless anarchy. Enacting her art, the figure implies, Emily has lost touch with her own center of being.

Twenty months later, seven months before her death, Emily returned to this poem and reduced it to its sharp, bitter core of statement. This revision (#193) appears to have been the last thing she wrote—the last cry of her ghostly male element in its separateness. Both the original and the reduced versions borrow the meter and some of the imagery of Shelley's "Lines Written Among the Euganean Hills." Shelley, generalizing from the political unrest he sensed in Italy in order to comment on the whole human condition, foresaw the revolution that must follow from oppression. The aristocratic lords, enemies of the people, he saw as "sheaves" lying ripe for "destruction's harvest home":

> Men must reap the things they sow
> Force from force must ever flow.
> (ll. 231–32)

Emily's poem employs a similar technique of generalization—the "date or clime" of her story is unimportant; it is a story of "our own humanity." And it draws on the same imagery of harvest:

> It was the autumn of the year
> When grain grows yellow in the ear;
> Day after day, from noon to noon
> The August sun blazed bright as June.

But her expression of horror goes far beyond Shelley's. In words that recall the ferocity of the blood-red sun draining blood and drinking tears in "Stars," she associates life in this father-world of alienated action with the evil harvested at apocalypse. The female breast that the speaker has lost touch with ("weaned . . . from my country's breast" in the earlier version) is now distantly recalled through the figure of the "panting earth" whose "milky" corn has already been brutally threshed in a harvest of destruction:

> . . . we with unregarding eyes
> Saw panting earth and glowing skies;
> No hand the reaper's sickle held,
> Nor bound the ripe sheaves in the field.
>
> Our corn was garnered months before,
> Threshed out and kneaded-up with gore;
> Ground when the ears were milky sweet
> With furious toil of hoofs and feet[.]

As if in acknowledgment of his alienation from his female element, from the ground of his "being," Emily's speaker concludes:

> I, doubly cursed on foreign sod,
> Fought neither for my home nor God.(#193)

This "foreign sod" is the correlate of Heathcliff's "abyss . . . where I cannot find you," which was also the "abyss" Catherine faced in having gone too far over into the father-world by marrying Edgar, only to find herself "an exile, and outcast," wrenched from her "all in all." For Emily this is only an extreme form of the more general truth: that to be born is to leave the mother home and live in the "foreign sod" that is the world.

For Emily the female element is Holy in its wholeness. It is palpable in the "fulness of being" that several critics have observed in Catherine on Heathcliff's first arrival and in their childhood freedom of play together, before the falling apart that reached its crisis when Catherine— for whom Heathcliff is in effect a ghost already—could "neither lay nor control" him. Fully realized Being thus lies in "that glorious world" that Catherine longed for; it is the perfection of the "soul's bliss" that buoyed the dying Heathcliff as he felt himself nearing Catherine's presence.

God for Emily is Being in the full ascendant, from which pervading vantage it "Changes, sustains, dissolves, creates and rears" (in the words of "No coward soul") much as for Coleridge the secondary Imagination, echoing the infinite "I AM," "dissolves, diffuses, dissipates, in order to recreate."[2] For Emily as for Coleridge as for Winnicott: "After being— doing and being done to. But first, being." However, for Emily, unlike Coleridge or Winnicott, the doing that properly comes "after being" is not what one does as artist working in the world of time and space. The world of human endeavor, of life and art, Emily judged alien to her being and to Being itself. In the realm of the world, doing is in the full ascendant; this was the very father-world in which she had been orphaned when Maria Brontë died. To participate in it was to contribute to her own further fragmentation and decay. It was to deny the "God within my breast." To practice her art was thus for Emily to loose fatally the anchor that secured her to "Undying Life"—to the "steadfast rock of Immortality."

The Romantic Search for Being

Much of Emily's and Charlotte's feeling about their female "being" was personal to themselves, reflecting their differing responses to their mother's early death and the dominant character of the father who survived her, as well (no doubt) as their differing attitudes toward the brother who offered so much hope and brought such disappointment. Equally personal was their experience of their own inner power, of the active or "male" element in themselves that makes poems and novels—each one's male muse.

Yet much that we might imagine as unique to the Brontës—uniquely female, or of the special Brontë family experience—may be found in other writers of their time, male writers as well as female, writers with healthy, living parents as well as those whose parents died young. Certain Emily Brontë, missing her mother and drawn to join her in death, yearned retrospectively for the happiness she had felt as an infant at her mother's breast; and accordingly resisted growing up, and fiercely resented the masculine world of getting and spending that seemed so disloyal to her mother's memory and so alien to the comforts her mother had once provided. But the Romantic poets all shared Emily's yearning and resentment in greater or lesser degree: Wordsworth and Shelley as we have seen, and Byron in some of his moods. These English poets the Brontës had read since childhood, and they influenced the ways in which both sisters framed their thought.

Charlotte too certainly traveled her own path, first trying to please a father who seemed to disapprove of her fiery intellectual ambitions, then finally taking joy in the conviction that God the Father was both pleased and approving, and also the source of those very ambitions and the talent that enacted them. It was her own great victory to find that her muse was no less than the Word Himself. Yet her journey from father to Father, like Emily's journey from mother to Mother, had widespread literary analogues. Lucy's progress in *Villette* from the stinting and painful worship of a false god to the releasing and rewarding love of the true

God was certainly autobiographical, and in its structure and imagery very much the product of Charlotte's own deeply private struggles in life and art. Yet its structure is prefigured not only in Bunyan's *Pilgrim's Progress,* which she certainly knew well and drew on consciously, but also in Richardson's *Clarissa,* which she seems not to have considered in any way a model. Many of the strategies that we have seen employed by both Emily and Charlotte are present in that novel, although it was published a full century before the Brontës' novels, and written by a man.

Others shared the Brontës' gender perspectives as well. Bernardin de St. Pierre, the popular and influential French romantic novelist whose writing the Brontës probably first met in Belgium (M. Heger presented St. Pierre's complete works to Charlotte in Brussels) also saw the intruding father-world as the source and corollary of human corruption. This is a central theme of his novel *Paul et Virginie,* after which Charlotte named the ship that carries M. Paul away to his duties and to death in *Villette.* In St. Pierre's novel young Paul and Virginia are raised by their mothers in an idyllic island setting of love and peace, until storms herald the approach of their sexual maturity (with all that it implies about the demands of reality—marriage, financial burdens, ties to European society). They fall victim at last to coercive pressures from the island's priest and governor, paternal powers both, the human agents of time and fate. Only in death can the young people and their mothers recover the paradise they have lost, for life on earth moves unrelentingly toward sorrow.

Similarly, a childlike yearning toward the eternal mother and a fierce resentment of the intrusive, world-oriented father possesses Goethe's famous character Werther. His story evidently touched a raw cultural nerve, for the romantic suicide that concludes *The Sorrows of Young Werther* generated an international epidemic of imitative attempts. Chateaubriand's autobiographical character René is likewise tortured by the emptiness of workaday life and longs for healing union with the sister who has been a mother to him. In short, the Brontë sisters shared with other writers of their time not only their sense of deep tension between the realms of the mundane and the eternal, but even their association of these realms with parental genders—with father and mother respectively.

Why should a whole century of our history—the "pre-Romantic" and Romantic period, which was marked by vigorous optimism concerning spiritual liberty, equality of opportunity, the brotherhood (even the sisterhood) of humankind—have been pervaded also by alienation and emptiness, by a sense of the world's worthlessness, by the attractions of death? It is of course beyond the scope of this book to answer such questions. And they surely have many different kinds of answers beyond those that literary history could provide.

Yet one answer is sure to be associated with the "disappearance" of God the Father—the regulator of desire, the principle of authority and reason. Certainly the revolution that was Romanticism left Western man in the position of the Oedipal son who had succeeded in killing his father and was now left alone to face what he had long mythologized as the great mother. By "mother" he meant all that unbounded physical world that was not himself—Mother Earth, Mother Nature, from whose womb he was born and to whose bosom he must return, in an inexorable cycle in which the mother endures but the generations of her children come and go, dust to enveloping dust. Certainly it was a contradictory and discomfiting spot to be in: to be the perceiving center of one's universe and yet, in oneself, a mere vanishing speck in that universe. I have already suggested (in my chapters on Emily Brontë) that this circumstance contributed to the renewed importance of the muse among the male Romantics. As mediator between the individual man and the vast world of his perceptions, the muse was the projection of the poet's own spiritual or transcendent "being," yet also emblem of the "being" of that vast universe surrounding him, the earth that seemed both inviting in her beauty and fecundity, and frightening in her associations with death. As man luxuriated in the seeming limitlessness of his powers of discovery and of his instrumental achievements in that vast outer world—in his male element of doing as it appeared able to quell or control the world outside him—he seemed to grow increasingly insecure concerning the female element of his inner being, increasingly cut away from his own deep source.

Emily's experience of this insecurity led her to denigrate all male doing that was not directed to recovery of being, all activity that pointed outward toward the world, as Lockwood's did: "I am of the busy world," Lockwood concludes at last, "and to its arms I must return." Man's true condition, in Emily's eyes, was Heathcliff's, with Catherine dead. For him "the entire world" was then no more than a "dreadful collection of memoranda that she did exist, and that I have lost her!" (p. 394)

We have seen how this elegiac spirit pervades Romantic poetry ("Where is it now, the glory and the dream?"). As its subject is creativity itself, the recovery through "doing" of that "being" that precedes it and is its source, Romantic art is to some extent at odds with its own impulses. It is act dedicated to the inauthenticity of action. This is another way of understanding the Romantic fascination with the ineffable and the unfinished: the poem as fragment, the unheard melody as sweetest, the "noisy years" of life as "moments in the being / Of the eternal Silence." The less the commitment to doing, the elegiac posture seems to suggest, the greater the possibility of access to being.

The insecurity that Charlotte experienced was not Romantic in that special sense that Emily's was, but has been familiar to women across many historical periods. Charlotte feared that if she exercised her own male element of doing, the men in her life would punish her by finding her unlovable; or else they would expunge her female element entirely, swallow up her "very being" into their own stormy selves, as she supposed had been her mother's fate. We have seen Charlotte's creative life as a progress in her determination not only to avoid that fate, but to revive her mother as an inner source of love ("*I* care for myself," says Jane Eyre at the critical moment) that will permit her to depart the false god who threatens to swallow her, and to seek the true God who will feed her with His love. Paul Emanuel "wrote as he gave and as he loved, in full-handed, full-hearted plenitude. . . . ; his letters were real food that nourished, living water that refreshed." As this "God with us" balances male and female elements within Himself, so He permits the same to Charlotte, who becomes as novelist His apostle—the bearer of His word, a missionary among the unenlightened.

Romantic Speech

We have seen that for the Romantic poets, the connection between childhood entitlement and the artist's vision lies in the fact that they have a common source. In Romantic theory the unconscious or deep self that is the source of inspiration is also the earliest historical self, the child who fathered the man. The incestuous love for sister or mother substitute (the female muse) is a way of expressing the longing for a return to the unconscious "deep" self that is beyond language because antecedent to it: prelinguistic.

From the root *fari* (to speak) we derive both *infant,* the unspeaking, and *ineffable,* that which is beyond speech, an etymological connection that it was left to the Romantics to elevate to a vividly felt theoretical one. The infant trails clouds of glory in part because he comes from the realm beyond words. Therefore is he, in Wordsworth's daring figure, an "eye . . . deaf and silent" (that is, neither hearing speech nor offering it), which "reads" the "eternal deep" not as one reads words, but as having direct experience of "the eternal mind."

Since Wordsworth's point is that our experience of this capacity evades language, we may not get very far in any effort to translate or state Wordsworth's ultimate meaning. But a curious and difficult passage of some twenty-five lines in book 3 of *The Prelude* may be of help. Addressing Coleridge there—"O Friend!"—Wordsworth summarizes his poem so far. He has "retraced . . . The glory of my youth" and told of "genius, power, / Creation and divinity itself / . . . for my theme has been / What passed within me." And here he pauses to generalize:

> O Heavens! how awful is the might of souls,
> And what they do within themselves while yet
> The yoke of earth is new to them . . .
> This is, in truth, heroic argument,
>   . . . but in the main
> It lies far hidden from the reach of words.

Wordsworth then attempts to touch on the source of his conviction concerning that original "might" of the soul—his conviction that what might be called the "unconscious" self (although that is not his term) is rooted in infantile experience. Here is Wordsworth's own difficult phrasing, which, despite its difficulty, he kept unaltered from 1805 right through to 1850:

> Points have we all of us within our souls
> Where all stand single; this I feel, and make
> Breathings for incommunicable powers.

We "stand single" in the double sense that each person is "himself" and not something else—not "the principle of life," for example—and that each is at the same time central and unique, not merely mingled as one indifferent object among a universe of objects. There is a universe and each "singleness" is at its generative center: the universe is "ours" in the way that we say in theological terms that creation is God's. The word *breathings* subsumes the idea of God's "breath of life" to that of the artist's "inspiration": to "make breathings for incommunicable powers" is thus to claim for the infant (as father of the artist and source of his powers) God's power to breathe life; it is to locate "inspiration" at the source of one's own outward-breathing breath. And all of this Wordsworth expresses in a verb ("make breathings") that points to the preverbal in another sense—to the energized air, exhaled as breath, out of which audible speech is made. This "breath" is all language in potential, before its fragmentation into the particulars of this or that articulate word-forming sound. To move from breath to sound is to move from the limitlessness of potential to the finite of actuality. In Blake's terms it is to move from eternal ever-opening center to finite circumference. If the billowing energy then retreats or is withdrawn, there remains only an empty shell—the hardened "veil" of nature, in Blake's mythology.

Wordsworth's passage closes with six lines that differ slightly in the 1805 and 1850 versions, but whose gist in both is that although the poet must now quit this theme or subject, he is not hopeless of being understood, despite the incommunicability of his topic. For each person may draw on his own experience, his own memory of having once had godlike power, and so recognize those powers, within each of us, which we bring with us on entering the world of nature and taking our own natural form. I quote the 1805 version:

> Yet each man is a memory to himself,
> And therefore, now that I must quit this theme,
> I am not heartless; for there's not a man
> That lives who has not had his god-like hours,
> And knows not what majestic sway we have
> As natural beings in the strength of Nature.[3]

It should be clear that in this case the problem in communication does not originate from the fact that we are cut off from one another (that "all stand single," and that "each man is a memory to himself"), but rather from the ineffableness of the subject matter. Indeed it is because each has his own memory of the experience of "awful . . . might" in this state of singleness ("the might of souls / And what they do within themselves while yet / The yoke of earth is new to them") that Wordsworth may hope to be understood. Although the experience is beyond speech, we each have had it, and although no one else's words will "communicate" to us what it is, we may each have recourse to our own recollections of what it was to be "god-like," to have had "majestic sway."[4] Thus does the "ineffable" have its origins in the experience of infancy and remain inaccessible to ordinary consciousness as it is inaccessible to language. What we are conscious of we may put into words. But what we "know" in the "recesses" of our nature, in the "hiding-places of man's power" (*Prelude*, book 12, l. 297), we may not put into words; it is "unconscious" in the sense of being unspeakable. It may eventually be utterly lost to us if we allow the world to be too much with us, if we lay waste our powers, ignore them, or deny their call. To do so is to enslave the mind, to oppress it "by the laws of vulgar sense," and hand it over to "a universe of death."[5] This is the prison house that in the Intimations Ode rises up around the growing boy: the loss of one's touch with being.

The function of Romantic poetry was to give access to this silent preverbal realm, to those godlike hours when our Being was whole, as yet unshadowed by the prison house. The subject of Romantic poetry was thus the artist's encounter with this source within him or her self. Emily's victory was to find a way to draw this poetic function and subject into the novel, to give narrative form to the experience that "in the main/ . . . lies far hidden from the reach of words." We have seen that in order to do this she placed the words—the narrative itself—in the mouths of persons who do not in fact see or understand. From Lockwood's own largely discredited mouth comes every single word in Emily's novel. Much of the time he is supposedly quoting Nelly, who understands perhaps a little more than he, but is still certainly a member of the world from which Catherine and Heathcliff must depart to find the Being that is Emily's own creative source. From Catherine herself we hear very little, and that little does not tell of the reunion that is the novel's point and center.

We have seen that Charlotte hated Heathcliff. And she was troubled by the heterodox views in Emily's poetry. Yet in Charlotte's late addition to *Shirley,* written as she was editing her dead sister's work, she shows that she was beginning to learn from Emily the most important lesson of her mature authorial life—namely, how to recover and redeem the full energies of her muse, that she might speak without fear of male reprisal. The secret lay in uniting in her imagination the two masculine forces that had seemed always before to be at war over the body of her self and writing, and giving full fictional life to the resulting figure. This she achieved at last in Paul Emanuel. He is the paternal lover Charlotte needed to please and appease, and he is also the masculine element within Charlotte herself, the ambitious muse who had stirred his restless wings so often and for so long within her breast, the "Genius" whose union with Eva will redeem all humanity. Having achieved this vision of lover and muse in one, she could write her own testament with rushing self-confident freedom: "All leaped from my lips."

In Charlotte's final novel the ghosts of M. Heger and of Patrick Brontë, who stands haunting behind Heger, are assimilated to the Holy Ghost, through which Charlotte fulfills the apostolic mission: "Go ye therefore and teach. . . . and lo, I am with you" (Matthew 27:19–20). Although treading on the very borders of sacrilege, she never quite crosses them. Instead, in Paul Emanuel she renders one of the "roundest" male characters in Victorian fiction. Domesticated by the sharp eye of comedy, Paul is a thoroughly believable presence in the real world; he participates fully in the "actual" realm of time and story. Yet equally he retains, and through the course of the novel he gradually reveals, a divine dimension that gives *Villette* its "preternatural" power (George Eliot's admiring term). This crucial aspect of M. Paul's meaning can be stated only indirectly: a character in a novel cannot "become" God. Nor is it quite correct to say that Paul does so. And yet . . . like a poet Charlotte "says" what cannot be said.

Woman's Place

From the realm of the "hiding places of man's power" the male writer projects the muse. Such "hiding places" are female space, in a sense: certainly the image is familiar in women's writing, as for example in Doris Lessing's description of the "dark empty space" in which Martha Quest's "whole self cleared, lightened, . . . became alive and light and aware."[6] But these must not be thought of as places to which females are "confined," either in the social sense (women should be, not do) or in the more theoretical or metaphoric sense of woman as the "absent Other" that language "kills" by replacing. One way of understanding the traditional perception that transcendence is ineffable—beyond speech, uncapturable by language, to be pointed toward through the agency of symbol and in the spirit of faith—is to understand that when "being" is objectified as the "absent Other" it is of course lost to him who objectifies. Insofar as language only records absence, and it is female "being" that is absent, then any user of language is a mere Heathcliff as Emily understood him to be after Catherine's death—a disembodied phallus, doing cut off from being, fretful energy in search of its own lost essence. Sundered from its source in being, doing is truly at a loss. As Wordsworth saw, the prison house shades close with tragic speed and force around little actors who, in conning their parts, are at strife with their own blessedness.

I have argued above that the yearning that characterizes Romanticism (and is echoed in the writers' urgent evocation of their muses) is a yearning for wholeness of being, and may express the Romantic artist's awareness that in the increasingly secular modern world with its emphasis on the instrumental—industry, physical power, technical achievement, the exploitation of vital resources—being has been diminished at the expense of doing, so that the balance must be rectified. Clearly there can be no creative doing, no "creation," much less "recreation," without being. Emily Brontë spoke for the male Romantic writers as well as for herself in insisting that to be physically alive is not necessarily fully to "be." Partly because of her mother's early death she found in the outer, temporal world less of the divine presence than they did, and thus found the argument for alienation and withdrawal, and eventually for silence and even death itself, more compelling than it was for most of them.

Yet Emily demonstrated that even in narrative the pen that records absence may at the same stroke invoke what is absent. Although *Wuthering Heights* is storylike in its hold on our interest, its structure is not linear but vortical. It works like a prophetic poem whose "rough basement" (in Blake's phrase) is ordinary English, but whose receding center of meaning points as visionary poetry does toward the state of unalloyed Being that Blake called "Eternity." Recall J. Hillis Miller's observation that the unitive "origin" of the pervasive doublings and repetitions that organize Emily's novel is absent because it is "prior even to language." "Storytelling is always . . . constructed over a loss," he concluded, a loss that by its very nature may not be represented within the story. Yet in Virginia Woolf's work Miller recognized "the possibility that repetition in narrative is the representation of a transcendent spiritual realm of reconciliation and preservation, a realm of perpetual resurrection of the dead."[7] The "dead" that needed resurrecting was for Emily personally her lost mother, and for the Romantics generally, the lost mother-world of being. Indeed among English novelists it was not Woolf but Emily Brontë who first discovered and employed this resurrecting device. Brontë's method was to take the linearity and dualism that are often associated with male structures of thought and to make of them a pathway to the realm of the lost—to what Wordsworth said we "know" in "the recesses of our nature." This truth, or lost "origin," is unitive and nonlinear because Eternal: related to what Goethe called the "Ewig-Weibliche," or eternal feminine. For Emily it is the unspoken center toward which her doublings point and in which they are reconciled and fulfilled.

The biographical corollary of this fictional method was in Emily's case a driving need for privacy—a privacy that provides (to paraphrase Wordsworth) the "hiding places of woman's power." This too we may call female space, or woman's place. Women's need for it can best be understood in relation to the rest of their psychological and moral development. As Freud saw, the male child creates his identity through separation from the mother, forming a self whose relation with others is rooted in disengagement and results in the possessiveness, rivalry, and aggression that it is the job of civilization and the superego to regulate.

But the female child, in Freud's view, was hampered in her development because unable to establish such clear separation. Recent feminists like Nancy Chodorow and Carol Gilligan have revived Freud's insights concerning female development, but revised our understanding of their implications. Chodorow and Gilligan have taught us to recognize that because the female child's development leads her "not through aggression to separation but through differentiation to interdependence,"[8] the female self relates to others by what Gilligan calls an "ethic of caring." This ethic grows not from some universal female philosophy, but from women's primal experiences of relationship with their mothers, their consequent sense of being joined to others in a web of connectedness. This web society has made it women's duty, and their own early development has made it to a great extent also their habit and pleasure, to help maintain. But it has its costs.

Man's achieved separateness ill serves his ultimate needs, if we may judge from the work of the male Romantic poets, who reinvented the muse to reconnect them to female origins, earth, and eternity even as they variously enacted the modern mythos of the artist as wounded isolate. Similarly, women's connectedness ill serves the creative needs of women artists, who typically require more than they are likely to get of that male isolation. In Woolf's famous image, they need "a room of one's own." If the male artist's need is to recover his touch with being, the female artist's is to clear a space for doing. She must be able, on occasion, to withdraw from the web of relationships, the ethic of caring, in order to do her creative work undisturbed. The mythos concerning women is that they (more than men) are in touch with the unconscious wellsprings of instinct, dream, and memory—as also with the world of nature, whose metaphoric gender they share. In domestic terms they (more than men) are bound into the networks of family and community. As women knit into this web of caring, the Brontës certainly were in touch with nature, dream and memory; but through their male muses they vigorously expressed those elements of selfishness, assertiveness, isolation, and arrogance that were necessary to the survival of their creativity.

Robert Southey wrote to Charlotte Brontë, in what have survived as perhaps the most famous lines penned by that poet laureate, "Literature cannot be the business of a woman's life, and it ought not to be. The more she is engaged in her proper duties, the less leisure she will have for it." Charlotte spoke for many a creative woman, beleaguered from within and without, when she responded in muffled apologetic rebellion that she had striven to feel deeply interested in "all the duties a woman ought to fulfill," but could not always do so: "for sometimes when I'm teaching or sewing I would rather be reading or writing."[9] Given her deep commitment to duty, and her lifelong yearning after fatherly approval, one cannot wonder that Charlotte's muse finally had to incorporate the prerogatives and male authority of Godhead itself. But Emily scornfully pictured in Lockwood the kind of drawling dandy who thinks of having "leisure" for literature. As Charlotte recognized, Emily's muse could be a swart and savage giant, one whom men like Southey had better let alone.

Emily and Charlotte Brontë spoke for women, and women's needs, in their choice of muses and in their understanding of how the muse functioned for them in their work. As savage giant or secret visitant, Emily's muse embodied the creative woman's need for privacy, for distance from the human network. Her companionship with him, in excluding all other community, allowed her to envision and evoke the realm of the ineffable. But Charlotte's muse was a decidedly public figure, designed to right long-standing public wrongs. In summoning to her book and then reeducating the erring misogynist St. Paul, then transmuting him into a figure for her own "Genius," who proves to be no less than the saving Word Himself, Charlotte undertook to stake for all futurity woman's claim not to the silence of eternity but to confident human speech. "I lacked not words now; . . . fluent I told my tale." That fluency she had resurrected from her mother's and sisters' deaths and from the deepest wells of her own pained experience and redeemed through the "Holy Ghost" that was her own "Genius." With St. Paul she could say at last, quoting from her favorite fifteenth chapter of 1 Corinthians:

> By the grace of God I am what I am: and his grace which was bestowed upon me was not in vain; but I laboured more abundantly than they all: yet not I, but the grace of God which was with me.

❦ NOTES

Introduction

1. In this study I do not treat the work of the youngest Brontë sister, Anne. Although Anne shared the labor and love of the more gifted Emily and Charlotte, she did not, as they did, raise through her writing the large aesthetic questions of her time or change the course of literary history.

2. Concerning Mrs. Brontë's illness, see Rhodes, "A Medical Appraisal of the Brontës," p. 102.

3. Gérin, *Emily Brontë*, p. 18.

4. "Extract from the Prefatory Note to 'Selections from Poems by Ellis Bell,' " printed in Appendix 1 to Brontë, *Wuthering Heights*, p. 446 (see my bibliography). Further page references to *Wuthering Heights* will be given in the text. Throughout this book, all quotations from the Brontë novels are taken from the Clarendon edition (Oxford University Press), under the general editorship of Ian Jack, published over the years from 1969 (*Jane Eyre*) to the present (the last of the series, Anne Brontë's *The Tenant of Wildfell Hall*, is forthcoming).

5. Gaskell, *Life of Charlotte Brontë*, p. 197. The biography was first published in 1857, two years after Charlotte's death.

6. D. W. Winnicott, "Creativity and Its Origins," in Winnicott, *Playing and Reality*, pp. 65–85.

7. A similar priority obtains in the human embryo. Morphologically all embryos are female until the fifth or sixth week of fetal life, when fetal androgen first begins to take effect, differentiating the male from its female origins.

8. Bloom, "The Internalization of the Quest-Romance," p. 3.

9. Shelley, "A Defence of Poetry," in Perkins, *English Romantic Writers*, p. 1084.

10. I refer to M. Heger and George Smith.

11. Gérin, *Emily Brontë*, p. 123.

12. This point is made by Dr. Lucile Dooley, who was one of the first psychoanalysts to write about the Brontës. See "Psychoanalysis of Charlotte Brontë," pp. 221–72; and her "Psychoanalysis of the Character and Genius of Emily Brontë," pp. 208–39. Other important psychological studies include those by Charles Burkhart, *Charlotte Brontë: A Psychosexual Study of*

her Novels; Moglen, *Charlotte Brontë: The Self Conceived;* and Maynard, *Charlotte Brontë and Sexuality.*

13. Concerning Wordsworth's stoicism, and its roots in a somewhat similar need, see Perkins, *The Quest for Permanence,* especially ch. 3, "The Wordsworthian Withdrawal."

14. As Girard observes in *Deceit, Desire, and the Novel,* p. 287: "The will to make oneself God is a will to self-destruction which is gradually realized."

15. Letter to Williams, November 2, 1848, Wise and Symington, *The Brontës: Their Lives, Friendships & Correspondence* (hereafter LL), 2: 269.

16. Kingsley, *Charles Kingsley,* 1:78. Interestingly, Charlotte uses nearly the same figure in writing of the fictional Shirley (who was modeled, she told Mrs. Gaskell, on her sister Emily). At one point Shirley's expressive face is "a poem—a fervid lyric in an unknown tongue" (p. 418), and elsewhere an inspiring setting makes "life a poem, for Shirley" (p. 437).

17. Swinburne was perhaps the first critic to suggest that *Wuthering Heights* should be considered a dramatic "poem." See his essay, "Emily Brontë."

18. Clayton's *Romantic Vision and the Novel* offers an excellent discussion of the problems of representing transcendence in the novel. Partly because he is not concerned with the issue of the muse, his reading of Emily Brontë's work differs somewhat from mine, and he does not address Charlotte's work at all. But his book is important for all students interested in the Romantic novel from *Clarissa* to *Women in Love.*

1. Emily Brontë's Poetry

1. The numbering of Emily's poems follows Hatfield, *The Complete Poems of Emily Brontë;* all quotations are from this edition.

2. See the entire passage on Dorothy as William's muse in Wordsworth, *The Prelude,* Book 14, ll. 232–66.

3. Sir Herbert Read is one of several who have argued that Shelley harbored a suppressed incestuous love for his sister. See Thorslev, "Incest as Romantic Symbol," p. 57, n. 5.

4. McGann, *Fiery Dust,* p. 189.

5. Margaret Homans summarizes these issues as they concern women writers in the first chapter of *Bearing the Word.* For readers interested in the problems that women writers face in imagining a muse for themselves, DeShazer offers a brief and useful summary of the muse's history and of some reasons why modern women writers often prefer to think of their muses as female; see *Inspiring Women,* ch. 1.

6. Shelley's "On Love," first published in 1829; quoted from Perkins, *English Romantic Writers,* pp. 1070–1071.

7. This essay was first published in 1832; quoted from *Ibid.*, pp. 1068–1070.

8. Graves, *The White Goddess*, p. 12.

9. *Ibid.*, pp. 500–501.

10. Homans' *Women Writers and Poetic Identity* is one of the few recent studies giving sensitive and detailed attention to Emily Brontë's poetry, especially in its relation to issues of gender. I think Homans was the first to make it explicit that "Brontë's masculine visitants are comparable to a masculine poet's muse" (p. 104). But I cannot share Homans' view that Emily struggled with her muse to gain control over language. Chiefly we differ in our view of (1) the extent to which even male Romantics felt that they controlled language, and (2) the extent to which Emily allowed the "dualism of language" (p. 38) to give priority to the male.

Edward Chitham and Nina Auerbach are also among the important new critics giving attention to Emily's ties to Romanticism. See Chitham's chapter on "The Development of 'Vision' in Emily Brontë's Poems" in Chitham and Winnifrith, *Brontë Facts and Brontë Problems* and his new biographical study, *A Life of Emily Brontë;* and Auerbach's chapter 13 on Emily in her *Romantic Imprisonment.*

11. *Wuthering Heights* was so described in a review in *The Leader,* December 28, 1850, p. 953.

12. To William Smith Williams, August 14, 1848, LL 2, 245.

13. Deutsch, *The Psychology of Women,* 1:228, 86.

14. The practical facts of Emily's poetic career are quickly summarized. According to Hatfield, the earliest extant poems date from 1836, when she was turning eighteen. From then to twenty-two was a period of vigorous experimentation. In Brussels (during 1842) when she was twenty-three and twenty-four, poetry came almost to a halt. But on her return she made steady growth, and in February 1844 (at twenty-five) she went back over all her earlier poems and transcribed a selection of them into two notebooks. From that point on, the only new poems to survive appear in one or the other of those notebooks. The one Hatfield labels "ms A" is headed simply "E.J.B. Transcribed February, 1844," and contains thirty-one poems, many of them obviously highly personal and none containing Gondal references. The other notebook—"ms B"—is headed "Emily Jane Brontë. Transcribed February 1844 / GONDAL POEMS," and contains forty-five poems. Although she did not transcribe her poems in the order in which they had been written, she did retain, in copying them, the original dates on which they had been composed or completed, so that we may reconstruct with some confidence the process of her poetic development.

The retrospection of 1844 either caused or reflected a critical point in her work, for it ushered in the poetry of Emily's twenty-sixth year, unquestionably the summit of her poetic achievement. From this year derive most of the poems for which she is best known. Then in the autumn of 1845, shortly after Emily turned twenty-seven, Charlotte discovered Emily's notebooks and read them. After this Emily wrote only two or three more poems and her novel, which together ended her creative life.

The question of the relevance of Emily's poems to her biography has been much discussed. I find Denis Donoghue's view the most convincing. Some poems undoubtedly record personal experience; but even her openly fictional speakers, Donoghue argues, are really "extreme functions of Emily Brontë's own personality. She does not release them: she endows them not with free will but with her own will in diverse forms. When they speak, therefore, what we hear is a kind of ventriloquism." See Donoghue, "The Other Emily," p. 171.

15. Emily's late biographer Winifred Gérin attributes the final silence to loss of inspiration: "her visions had deserted her" (*Emily Brontë*, p. 252). But Gérin offers no evidence for this view beyond the fact that Emily stopped writing. And it is clear now that she did stop. It was thought for a time that she might have begun and then destroyed another novel; but this theory is persuasively dismissed by Inga-Stina Ewbank in her introduction to the Oxford edition of *Wuthering Heights,* pp. xxii–xxiv. However, Ewbank's observation that "only a year of life remained" to Emily after completing *Wuthering Heights* (p. xxiii, n.) is mistaken. In fact, nearly two and a half years remained, for the novel was finished and ready to be sent to readers by July 4, 1846, as Ewbank herself notes on p. xiv, whereas Emily did not die until December 19, 1848.

16. This quotation and the next are from Wordsworth's own notes to his Intimations Ode.

17. Lewin, *The Psychoanalysis of Elation,* p. 144.

18. Rizzuto, *The Birth of the Living God,* pp. 184–85. Two seminal explorations of the importance of mother-infant mirroring are chapter 9 of Winnicott's *Playing and Reality* and Kohut's *The Analysis of the Self.*

19. Ratchford, *Gondal's Queen,* p. 87.

20. A seminal discussion of this figure appears in Abrams' "The Correspondent Breeze," pp. 25–43.

21. Denis Donoghue brilliantly demonstrates how this poem does "the traditional work of metaphor, but in slow motion, and by degrees. The process of metaphor is the process of transformation, metamorphosis. Metaphor acts suddenly, in a flash; the poem achieves a metaphorical object, but slowly, earning the right to do so as it moves along, stanza by stanza" ("The Other Emily," p. 170).

22. Blake, "All Religions Are One." Blake's original line was "The true Man is the source, he being the Poetic Genius," Perkins, *English Romantic Writers,* p. 49.

23. Homans, in *Woman Writers and Poetic Identity*, pp. 113–15.

24. Hewish, *Emily Brontë*, p. 80.

25. In this connection compare also Blake's use of the striking word "stain'd" in the "Introduction" to *Songs of Innocence,* where in order to "write" his songs, that is to enter them into the records of time, the piper must "stain" the clear water. Such diction reminds us of the Romantic doubt whether poetry itself did not obtrude upon the silence that Carlyle called "deep as Eternity."

Emily and Charlotte Brontë both knew "Adonais" very well. Emily borrowed the "frozen cheek" of Adonais to use in *Wuthering Heights*. And I will show in chapter 3 how Charlotte adapted the final stanza for a poem of her own.

26. Emily's ideas continue to echo Wordsworth's. Emily's "deep fountain" is Wordsworth's "fountain-light of all our day," just as his "shadowy recollections" are what her "Faithful . . . spirit" "remembers."

27. Emily knew the text. She alludes to Lear's curses against his daughters in *Wuthering Heights*, p. 21.

28. The theme of a "perished faith" that can yet "spring" to new life (#169) appears in several poems. A related idea appears in #177, where dying is compared to a "seed" falling from its "parent tree" and springing to "glorious birth."

29. Contrast Homans' view in "Repression and Sublimation of Nature in *Wuthering Heights,*" pp. 9–19. Homans overlooks the sense in which nature is masculine for Emily (the dazzling sun, the wooing winds). Sublimating the natural by rendering it figurative is Emily's way not of "killing" the mother, as Homans argues, but of translating the temporal world (the father's realm and consort) into the eternal (the realm of the undying Mother).

30. The line "Fate is strong, but Love is stronger" comes from one of a pair of poems (#186 and #187) that Charlotte later published together under the title "The Two Children." But these two children are less separate characters than aspects of one child's experience: in this they look forward to the Catherine who will insist, "I *am* Heathcliff." One might almost think of the children as Blakean "Visionary forms dramatic," eternal principles perceived in human shape. The boy is a "sunless human rose," in effect the composite child's natural or physical being, subject to time and fate. The girl is a "Spirit of Bliss," in effect the child's visionary capacity. As aspects or doubles of one another, these children are variations on the idea of the Romantic muse as I have been developing it. It is especially interesting that Emily's speaker tentatively offers the term "Guardian angel," for as Otto Rank has observed, "belief in a guardian spirit . . . is closely related to the double motif," of which the Romantic muse is also a version. Muse, double,

guardian spirit—all are as Rank explains them expressions of the human need to defend against the prospect of death (Rank, *The Double*, p. 50).

31. "Biographical Notice of Ellis and Acton Bell," reprinted in Appendix I of the Oxford edition of *Wuthering Heights*, pp. 435–36.

32. In an excellent recent book on Emily Brontë, Stevie Davies observes astutely that Emily's rage against her sister's intrusion was doubtless fueled in part by "a sinister sense of excitement at having been discovered and praised, and feeling her worth recognized" (Davies, *Emily Brontë*, p. 50).

33. Letter to Williams, September 1848, LL 2: 256.

34. The novels were undertaken not because the book of poems failed, but for much more positive reasons. Well before the poems were published (May 1846) each of the sisters was at work on a "prose tale"; in fact by April 6, 1846 Charlotte was already seeking a publisher for "three distinct and unconnected tales" that she described as "preparing for the Press." These were Charlotte's *The Professor*, never published in her lifetime; Anne's *Agnes Gray*; and of course Emily's *Wuthering Heights*. All three sisters must have worked on their novels at tumultuous speed; certainly each was drawing on a personal experience that pressed heavily on her mind at the time.

For discussion of dating, see the Oxford edition of *Wuthering Heights*, pp. xiii–xvi, to which I add only the observation that Charlotte's discovery is not likely to have predated her final letter to Heger, considering that letter's relentlessly despairing tone.

2. *Wuthering Heights*

1. Brontë, *Wuthering Heights*, p. 351. Further page references will be given in the text.

2. In "The Date of Heathcliff's Death," pp. 15–19, Daley demonstrates that Heathcliff was dead by April 15 at the latest.

3. Miller, *Fiction and Repetition*, p. 61.

4. *Ibid.*, p. 202.

5. In *Madwoman in the Attic*, p. 265, Gilbert and Gubar discuss Heathcliff as replacement. For a view of him as alien "Other" see Bersani, *A Future for Astyanax*.

6. Harpham has observed that in a sense Heathcliff "represents origin itself" (*On the Grotesque*, p. 210, n.).

7. In *Bearing the Word*, Homans brilliantly distinguishes between the first Catherine and the second on the grounds of their relation to patriarchy. The first never fully accepts the father-world, but the second does accommodate to it—over the dead body of her mother. (In this respect, I would argue, the second Catherine parallels Emily Brontë as novelist writing for the public.) But I think that Homans mistakes the meaning of both Heathcliff and the

ghost-child. To argue that "the first Cathy dies into the literal nature she loves . . . merging in her death with the moors" (p. 82), is to miss the sense in which Cathy joins in death not mother earth but maternal "Undying Life"; in other words, it is to lose sight of the visionary dimension of the novel.

8. Freud, *Complete Psychological Works*, 17:253.

9. The "frozen cheek" echoes Shelley's "Adonais" (stanza 11), also a poem of reunion beyond death. More on this later.

10. In *Bearing the Word* Homans suggests that the ghost-child is born at Catherine's death: "Dying as she gives birth, she is released to become the ghostly child who appears to Lockwood" (p. 82). But that ghost-child was "born" much earlier: it is already haunting her here, and has been wandering for "twenty years" by the time Lockwood encounters it in 1801. (The implications of this dating I will consider a little later.)

11. This moment and language, like those of Lockwood's dream, had already been experienced and recorded years before, when Emily was nineteen. See especially poems #15 and #29 (numbering follows Hatfield, *The Complete Poems of Emily Brontë*).

12. As children, finding consolation in one another in their shared room the night of Mr. Earnshaw's death, Nelly overheard them "comforting each other with better thoughts than I could have hit on; no parson in the world ever pictured Heaven so beautifully as they did, in their innocent talk" (p. 54). In retrospect we may guess that they were already constructing their "heaven," and that it was not at all Nelly's, even then.

13. Again I must differ with Homans' interpretation in *Bearing the Word*. Homans sees this "witch" as "a female outlaw like [Catherine] herself, . . . a Fury with the power to refute the patriarchal laws of ownership" (p. 80). But I see little support in the text for a reading that allies Nelly with Catherine in such a way. Catherine's hostility to Nelly as "witch" is consistent with her quite accurate perception that Nelly has always been the enemy of Catherine's own deepest values.

14. Cecil has pointed up many of these important areas of contrast in *Early Victorian Novelists*, and they have been frequently observed since.

15. Sanger, "The Structure of *Wuthering Heights*."

16. In *Psychoanalysis and Feminism* Mitchell summarizes the way culture depends on exogamous marriages like that of Hareton and the second Cathy: "the systematic exchange of women is definitional of human society. . . . marriage laws and the intimately related taboos on incest are set up precisely to prevent any circular fixation" of relationship within the family (p. 372). The love of Heathcliff and the first Catherine is an extreme case of incest: not just brother-sister, but self-self.

17. This ability to render dimensions of human experience figuratively accounts, I think, for the novel's continuing ability to evoke, and success-

fully to sustain, an extraordinarily wide variety of interpretations, from the Marxist reading offered by David Wilson in 1947 ("Emily Brontë: First of the Moderns") to such feminist or deconstructionist readings as those of Gilbert and Gubar, Bersani, and Homans. Kermode even chose this novel as the text on which to test his theory concerning the pluralities of meaning available in a classic *(The Classic)*. But Miller, whose analysis in *The Disappearance of God* has been seminal for students of Emily Brontë, has more recently concluded that "the text is over-rich" (*Fiction and Repetition*, p. 52). Perhaps the problem lies in our expectations about genre: would anyone call Coleridge's "Rime of the Ancient Mariner" or Blake's "The Tyger" "over-rich"?

18. In Blake's terms, to participate in Eternity one must annihilate "selfhood" (for Blake the "selfhood" is roughly the self in its separated condition, as fallen fragment) in an act of apocalyptic reunion like that of Milton and his sixfold emanation Ololon at the climax of Blake's visionary prophecy *Milton*. From the perspective of ordinary society and of the merely mortal self, this self-sacrifice or "annihilation" looks like death, although Blake's point was that it is absolutely the opposite. Perhaps we may see a related idea in Wordsworth's "Tintern Abbey," where he claims that his "little, nameless, unremembered, acts / Of kindness and of love" are the basis from which he rises to "become a living soul" who can "see into the life of things."

19. Quoted in Gérin, *Emily Brontë*, p. 127.

20. *Brontë Society Transactions*, vol. 12, no. 5, p. 385; my translation.

21. Spacks points to the striking sterility of their love, and its destructiveness (*The Female Imagination*, p. 137). Spacks' discussion of the novel demonstrates the complex ways in which it dramatizes adolescent resistance to the process of growing up, the choice of narcissism over social maturity.

22. Freud, *Complete Psychological Works*, 14:222.

23. Shelley, "Alastor," ll. 211–13, in Perkins, *English Romantic Writers*, p. 962.

24. Ewbank, *Their Proper Sphere*, p. 110, seems to see in it a true peace.

25. Miller, writing of the absent "origin" in *Wuthering Heights*, observes: "If 'something' is incompatible with any sign, if it cannot be seen, signified, or theorized about, it is, in our tradition, no 'thing.' It is nothing" (*Fiction and Repetition*, p. 67). But Emily Brontë's work suggests that it is also "everything," in a way that Juliet Mitchell helps clarify: "In discovering through absence his subjectivity, the baby . . . must for ever desire the non-relationship and non-identity of Zero. So must romantic poets and mystics: to be in a state of unity, 'at one with the world,' is to be the asubjective zero from whence we came" (*Psychoanalysis and Feminism*, p. 386).

26. I will discuss this poem in my conclusion.

3. Charlotte's Early Work

1. Charlotte's poems are published and numbered in Newfeldt, *The Poems of Charlotte Brontë*. Hereafter, poems that appear in this edition will be quoted from it and cited by poem number directly in the text.

2. Published in Wise and Symington, *The Miscellaneous and Unpublished Writings of Charlotte and Patrick Branwell Brontë*, 1:24–35. Hereafter abbreviated as SHB [Shakespeare Head Brontë].

3. Obviously Arthur and Charles function as versions of Patrick and Charlotte, although as privileged brother and paternal stand-in Arthur also absorbed some of Charlotte's feelings about Branwell.

4. Patrick Brontë, "The Maid of Killarney; or, Albion and Flora: A Modern Tale; In Which Are Interwoven Some Cursory Remarks," originally published in 1818, reprinted in Turner, *Brontëana*, pp. 131–99. The passages quoted below occur on pp. 177–78.

5. Brontë, *Shirley*, pp. 61–62. Further page references will be given in the text. In LL 1: 99, Ellen Nussey is quoted as saying that Charlotte's models for Helstone were Hammond Roberson and Patrick Brontë. Both men were thought to bear a striking resemblance to the duke of Wellington, whom Charlotte has Shirley herself compare to Helstone: "They positively *are* rather alike; . . . a pair of human falcons" (p. 630). In Charlotte's fiction the "falcon eye" is a regular attribute of the father-lover figures.

6. Letter dated November 18, 1812, LL 1: 20.

7. Quoted in Alexander, *The Early Writings of Charlotte Brontë*, p. 21. Alexander suggests that the magazines belonged to Charlotte's "mother or her aunt." But there is no reason to think that Aunt Branwell's things suffered shipwreck, and the "Mary Cave" of *Shirley* is a fictional variant of Maria Brontë, not of her spinster sister, Aunt Branwell.

8. SHB 1: 361.

9. Brontë, "The Foundling," SHB 1: 241, dated June 27, 1833.

10. Charlotte included this poem in her 1833 story "The Secret"; the story is printed in Holtz, *Two Tales by Charlotte Brontë*, pp. 50–51.

11. Brontë, "Mina Laury," *Five Novelettes*, p. 165.

12. Brontë, "Characters of Celebrated Men," SHB 1: 39. Patrick Brontë really did write such poetry. See for example his "Cottage Poems" (1811), in Turner, *Brontëana*, pp. 24, 41.

13. SHB 1: 202–13, dated August 1832.

14. SHB 2: pp. 11, 12.

15. Charlotte, in a letter to Ellen Nussey, July 2, 1835, LL 1: 129.

16. All quotations in the last three paragraphs (except that concerning Zenobia's "masculine soul") are from "A Peep Into a Picturebook," SHB 1: 357, dated May 1834. The noted exception is from SHB 2: 37.

17. "The Spell," pp. 83–84. The term "Egyptian bondage" had been on Charlotte's mind for at least a year, as she had Zenobia use it ironically to describe her marriage to Percy in a story written in June 1833 (SHB 1: 258).

18. The quoted words are from "Albion and Marina."

19. Brontë, "My Angria and the Angrians," SHB 2: 3–4.

20. Over time Charles Wellesley evolves into Charles Townshend, yielding the initials *C. T.*, which in turn come to stand for *Charles Thunder,* a name Charlotte chose because *Brontë* is associated by sound with the Greek word for thunder—one more connection between Patrick and storm.

21. John Martin's famous picture of Esther was copied by the Brontë children.

22. "My Angria," p. 29.

23. Most of the loose sheets that comprise Charlotte's Roe Head Journal are to be found in The Bonnell Collection, now housed at the Brontë Parsonage Museum in Haworth, England.

24. "Roe Head Journal."

25. Chapter 30: "that Impulse was the most intractable, the most capricious, the most maddening of masters . . . ," etc.

26. "Roe Head Journal."

27. LL 1: 139, May 10, 1836.

28. LL 1: 143.

29. LL 1: 147.

30. LL 1: 153, February 20, 1837.

31. "Passing Events," dated April 1936 (*Five Novelettes,* p. 68).

32. "The Return of Zamorna," SHB 2: 281–314. The manuscript is undated; the editors of the SHB derive the date December 1836/January 1837 from the evidence of related stories. (SHB 2: 281), and Christine Alexander agrees, proposing "c. 24 December 1836" (*Early Writings,* p. 156).

33. "Passing Events," *Five Novelettes,* p. 46.

34. "Mina Laury," *Five Novelettes,* passim.

35. She speaks of her "hypochondria" in letters to Miss Wooler, quoted in Gérin, *Charlotte Brontë,* p. 114, and to Ellen, LL 1: 166.

36. Bonnell Collection, 98b. Charlotte later used the lines in her conclusion to "The Teacher's Monologue," #191.

37. The prose passage is reproduced in Neufeldt, pp. 422–23, as context for the poem that concludes it.

38. Mary Taylor observed of the Brontë family that "Cowper's poem 'The Castaway' was known to them all, and they all at times appreciated, or almost appropriated it" (LL 1, 137). Charlotte comments in detail on Cowper and "The Castaway" in *Shirley.*

39. Bonnell ms. 125/1.

40. Lodge's essay "Fire and Eyre" and Heilman's "Charlotte Brontë, Reason and the Moon" are both immensely useful and suggestive. They are among the few studies that demonstrate the importance of reading Charlotte's imagery. But concerning the meaning of the moon, both authors are mistaken because they do not know enough about Charlotte's whole system. To understand the moon's appearance, one must recognize that she always functions as some form of "woman-power."

41. The nominal speaker in this poem is as usual Arthur Wellesley, later called Zamorna; but it is obviously Charlotte herself who pleads and is answered by the mother. Arthur, of course, would never be told that his mind was not exalted enough for laurel. Indeed just the preceding month, in "Albion and Marina," his literary successes had "wreathed laurels of fame round his brow."

42. My translation from the original in Bonnell ms. 115.

43. Brontë, *The Professor*, pp. 178–79.

44. Bonnell ms. 113/7.

45. Du Fresnay, *Geography for Youth*, p. 45.

46. Charlotte also knew of an actual family named *Eyre*. See Fraser, *The Brontës*, p. 229.

47. Du Fresnay, *Geography for Youth*, p. 174.

48. "Captain Henry Hastings" appears in *Five Novelettes*, pp. 171–270.

49. Elizabeth, the name of the second Brontë sister, who died in 1825, was one of the names Charlotte often used for characters in whom she represented aspects of herself. On the ms. of *Shirley* she made a revealing error in writing "Elizabe—" for Caroline. One may see on the ms. where she lined it out and corrected herself (BM add. ms. 43477, 1:179).

50. "Captain Henry Hastings," p. 242. Gérin so judges; see her introduction in *Five Novelettes*, p. 173. And Christine Alexander also feels that this story expresses Charlotte's "faith in her brother despite social misfortune" (*Early Writings*, p. 189).

51. The moon directly aids her escape: "She lingered for a moment—she could not go—a cloud just then crossed the moon—[in the momentary darkness] she was gone. . . . There he remained where she had left him for hours . . . Lady Rosamund's tomb alone proclaiming in the moonlight 'I shall arise.' " *Five Novelettes*, p. 257.

52. The quoted words are from "Mina Laury," *Five Novelettes*, pp. 147, 165.

53. "Captain Henry Hastings," p. 225. Further page references for this story will be given in the text.

54. The theme of sibling rivalry is carried into other elements of this story, and regularly appears in Charlotte's early narratives. Where a story is told concerning two brothers, it is invariably the younger brother with

whom she identifies, the one with less status or privilege: Charles Wellesley rather than Arthur, William Percy rather than Edward, for example.

55. Recall again that Patrick was thought to be, like Wellington, a "human falcon." (See *Shirley,* p. 630.)

56. LL 1: 173; to Henry Nussey, March 5, 1839.

57. "Caroline Vernon" is included in Brontë's *Five Novelettes.* Further page references to this story will be given in the text. Caroline Vernon was, however, the name of a real woman, although Charlotte may or may not have known this. She was the wife of Robert Percy Smith, whose brother the Reverend Sydney Smith (1771–1845) was a brilliant wit and onetime Brontë neighbor: he was from 1806 to 1826 resident clergyman at Foston-le-Clay in Yorkshire, and in 1828 was presented with a prebend in Bristol Cathedral.

58. LL 1: 206–7, May 15, 1840.

59. "The Duke of Zamorna," SHB 2: 349–50.

60. To Ellen Nussey, August 4, 1839, LL 1: 164.

61. To Ellen Nussey, August 7, 1841, LL 1: 218.

62. To Branwell, May 1, 1843, LL 1: 297.

63. To Emily, May 29, 1843, LL 1: 299.

64. May 22, 1843, LL 1: 298.

65. See, e.g., the one on Napoleon, "Le Morte de Napoleon," dated May 31, 1843, in which she writes of his exiled state: "perhaps he suffered too that thirst of heart, that hunger of soul, which torture the exile, far from his family and from his fatherland."

66. As Gérin suggests she did (*Charlotte Brontë,* p. 252).

67. January 23, 1844; LL 1: 276–77.

68. Separately published as "Master and Pupil" (#205).

69. Gilbert and Gubar suggested that the wound represents Charlotte's sense that ambition is "an impulse of disease" for a woman, in that it "can only lead to grief, to an inevitable separation from her master—that is, from the literary tradition which has fostered her" (*Madwoman in the Attic,* p. 330). But for Charlotte the "master" she must give up is the man she loves, and not at all "literary tradition." In her imagery the "inward wound" is the pang one receives in forgoing carnal love precisely in order *to pursue* spiritual or intellectual goals.

70. Heger's manner of paternal intimacy may have been seductive, especially for vulnerable young women like Charlotte; but I do not think that anyone has ever suggested that he literally seduced Charlotte. The poem should be read as "prophecy" (in Blake's sense) rather than "history."

71. Bonnell Collection, ms. 118.

4. *The Professor, Jane Eyre, Shirley*

1. Ewbank, observing this split, describes it well: the hero and heroine "have natures and careers so similar as to make them one character distributed over two sexes" (*Their Proper Sphere,* p. 157). Keefe makes a similar point in *Charlotte Brontë's World of Death,* p. 85.

2. Brontë, *The Professor,* p. 23. Further page references will be given in the text.

3. This tale is printed in Holtz, *Two Tales by Charlotte Brontë.*

4. The numbering of Charlotte's poems follows Neufeldt, *The Poems of Charlotte Brontë.* All quotations from her poetry are from this edition.

5. Brontë, *Shirley,* p. 276. Further page references will be given in the text. The social and psychological implications of the mermaid as metaphor for woman (as she is feared and disparaged by men) are suggestively explored by Dinnerstein in *The Mermaid and the Minotaur,* and her summary of the implications of this fish-woman is remarkably apt for Charlotte's use of the figure. The treacherous mermaid who lures voyagers to their death, writes Dinnerstein, is the "seductive and impenetrable female representation of the dark and magic underwater world from which our life comes and in which we cannot live" (p. 5).

6. Brontë, "Caroline Vernon," *Five Novelettes,* pp. 352, 354.

7. For one further, oddly obtrusive example, note that Crimsworth voices Charlotte's judgment on Branwell, whose affair with Mrs. Robinson resulted in his being sent home in disgrace from Thorpe Green in July 1845. Crimsworth speaks: "Limited as had yet been my experience of life, I had once had the opportunity of contemplating, near at hand an example of the results produced by a course of interesting and romantic domestic treachery. . . . it was very loathsome. I saw a mind degraded by the practice of mean subterfuge, by the habit of perfidious deception, and a body depraved by the infectious influence of the vice-polluted soul. I had suffered much from the forced and prolonged view of this spectacle . . ." (p. 187). The account is entirely gratuitous, except as it evidently relieved Charlotte's personal feelings.

8. Even the name Charlotte chose for Frances' and William's child—Victor—serves this fantasy in echoing the name of the Hegers' fifth child, Victorine (a girl), born shortly before Charlotte's final departure from Brussels.

9. Rich, *On Lies, Secrets, and Silence,* pp. 89–106. The lines quoted below appear on p. 106.

10. Chase, "The Brontë's, or, Myth Domesticated," pp. 102–19.

11. Brontë, *Jane Eyre,* p. 576. Further page references will be given in the text.

12. Critics have generally not noticed that this passage echoes the climax of "Albion and Marina," or, observing the echo, they have missed its

implications. See, e.g., Robert Keefe, who in *Charlotte Brontë's World of Death* notes the analogy but finds it flawed in that Bertha Mason died, but Jane's beloved Rochester did not.

13. Brontë, "Caroline Vernon," p. 302. Interestingly, Louisa then proposes that if this fails, she might act the Othello to his Desdemona and smother him with his pillow—a role reversal that had also crossed Frances' mind in *The Professor*.

14. Gérin, *Charlotte Brontë*, p. 329.

15. When Jane must face the terrible truth of Rochester's deception, she describes her response—a version of the old depressive "hypochondria"—in one dense paradigm: "Self-abandoned, relaxed and effortless, I seemed to have laid me down in the dried-up bed of a great river; I heard a flood loosened in remote mountains, and felt the torrent come." An "unuttered prayer" (her old friend "virtue") saves her from total annihilation, but not from a heavy dose of those waters. To describe their overwhelming effect Charlotte turns from her own words to paraphrase Psalms 69:1: "it came: in full, heavy swing the torrent poured over me. The whole consciousness of my life lorn, my love lost, my hope quenched, my faith death-struck, swayed full and mighty above me in one sullen mass. That bitter hour cannot be described: in truth, 'the waters came into my soul; I sank in deep mire: I felt no standing; I came into deep waters; the floods overflowed me' " (pp. 374–75). This Rochester is not yet the "master wave" that will bear Jane to a "calmer current." For that transformation the intervention of Bertha is required.

16. For a discussion of Charlotte's self-division that addresses the problems inherent in female quest romance, see Melodie Monahan, "Heading Out Is Not Going Home: *Jane Eyre,*" *Studies in English Literature* (Autumn 1988), 28(4):589–608. But let me reemphasize the important fact that for Charlotte "quest" as religious mission *paralleled* (and was a way of talking about) "quest" as artist. Both are matters of "vocation."

17. Ratchford, *The Brontës' Web of Childhood*, pp. 62, 204–7.

18. Both quoted phrases are from *Villette*, p. 392.

19. At the early Rochester's approach Jane had quailed to see "his face all kindled" and his "eye flashing" (p. 343). But the later Rochester's countenance reminds her of "a lamp quenched, waiting to be relit—and alas! it was not himself that could now kindle the lustre of animated expression: he was dependent on another for that office" (p. 562). If we recall Zamorna's appearance in the juvenilia—"Fire! Light! . . . Zamorna's self, blazing . . . like the sun"—we know how to read the meaning of Rochester's quenched lamp.

20. Rosamond Oliver inherits the name and some of the meaning of the Rosamund Wellesley whose name is inscribed on the gravestone in "Captain

Henry Hastings." Both are versions of woman as sexual being, whether seducing or seduced. Both figure the sensuality that weighs against the lift of wings—though Rosamund Wellesley to some extent resisted this role in resisting Zamorna.

21. For a different reading of the meaning of fire and ice in *Jane Eyre* and *Villette,* see Nina Auerbach's stimulating discussion in chapter 12 of *Romantic Imprisonment.*

22. Brontë, *Shirley,* p. 336. Further page references will be given in the text.

23. Charlotte's allusions to Robert's desire for a home are pointed, and they bracket the story of Caroline and Robert: pp. 96, 681. They are presumably meant to indicate that Robert does have the underlying capacity to give and receive love.

24. Or a "Virgin Mary" for his worship—"Rose céleste," as he says, half-playfully offering to "kneel and adore" (pp. 690–91). Here Charlotte is implicitly contrasting Caroline with such worldly roses as Rosamund Wellesley and Rosamond Oliver.

25. Holgate, "The Structure of *Shirley,*" makes the case that Caroline is first modeled on Ellen Nussey, later on Anne Brontë. It is not, however, this level of modeling—e.g., eye color—with which I am concerned.

26. Volume 1 contains the first eleven chapters (numbered 1–11); volume 2 contains the twelfth through twenty-third chapters (numbered 1–12); and volume 3 contains the twenty-fourth through thirty-seventh chapters (numbered 1–14). I might observe that the halfway number, eighteen, is also Caroline's age.

27. Agnes and Mary Grey are the names of Anne's heroine and her sister. Curiously, two sisters named Agnes and Mary Gray (note the different spelling) were the nursemaids who cared for Lord Byron as a child. It is interesting to speculate whether Anne was aware of this fact. Thomas Moore mentions Mary Gray by name in his biography of Byron, a book that the Brontës certainly did know. But Moore does not mention Agnes by name, nor does he reveal that Byron accused Mary Gray of having abused him sexually as a child.

28. Charlotte told her publisher that "if this character had an original it was in the person of a clergyman who died some years since at the advanced age of eighty. I never saw him except once" (letter to Williams, September 21, 1849, LL 3: 23). But Ellen Nussey (LL 1: 99) claimed that Charlotte's models were both Hammond Roberson and Patrick Brontë.

29. This is the only poem of those that Charlotte attributed to Emily for which there survives no manuscript in Emily's own hand. After observing this fact, Hatfield adds that to him the poem seems "to express Charlotte's thoughts about her sister, rather than Emily's own thoughts," and that "it

would have been in keeping with the editorial liberties she took in other connections to offer such an interpretation of her sister in the guise of Emily's own words" (Hatfield, *The Complete Poems of Emily Brontë*, p. 255). My own guess is that some original did exist, but that Charlotte did not approve it, or felt that it could only contribute to a greater misunderstanding (i.e., disapproval) of her sister; that accordingly she rescued what she could, altered the rest as necessary, and destroyed the evidence of what she had done. I suggest this elaborate theory because certain of the lines sound so very much indeed like Emily, and others so very unlike her. The opening, for example, is a typical Emily opening in its headlong vigor of image, diction, and rhythm, as well as in the idea that it states:

> Often rebuked yet always back returning
> To those first feelings that were born in me . . .

And elsewhere in the poem one can hear odd echoes from other of Emily's work—e.g., the lines from the fourth stanza, "I'll walk where my own nature would be leading: / It vexes me to choose another guide" echoes "Was I not vexed, in these gloomy ways / To walk unlit so long?" from "My Comforter" (#168). On the other hand some parts of the poem, and especially its concluding stanza, sound a note of lumbering piety that one never hears in Emily's verse:

> What have those lonely mountains worth revealing?
> More glory and more grief than I can tell:
> The earth that wakes *one* human heart to feeling
> Can centre both the worlds of Heaven and Hell.

30. Study of the rather complex patterns of repagination of the manuscript in the British Museum has led me to conclude that the Eva essay was the last of several late additions, following even the "superior men" passage that was late added to volume 2. The renumbering that begins there runs down to the Eva essay, stops for its duration, then resumes. The place occupied by the Eva essay seems originally to have been held by a "letter," to judge by Charlotte's use of that word, which she later lined out. Correspondence with her publishers indicates that the letter was originally offered in French, and that the essay was substituted for it in mid-September. The new material was considerably longer than what it replaced: what had been a letter-length two and a half pages of material (according to the ms. numbering, from the bottom of p. 657 to the middle of p. 660) grew, in revision, to fill an essay-length eight pages. It was presumably then, also, that Charlotte altered her title for this chapter from "Le Cheval Dompté" (a work by the seventeenth-century cleric Bossuet, still mentioned in the chapter) to its present one, "The First Bluestocking." Readers interested in questions con-

cerning alterations in the manuscript will find the manuscript carefully described in Rosengarten and Smith's introduction to the Clarendon edition of *Shirley,* although the editors do not posit the thematic connections that I do among these late additions, nor do they connect them to the patterns of renumbering.

31. If she knew Byron's "Heaven and Earth," which derives from the same text, she did not here draw on it so far as I can see.

32. Charlotte's French essay "The Death of Moses" shows how interconnected were the story of Moses and her developing ideas about her own role as artist; I will return to the topic of the artist as God's prophet or missionary at the end of chapter 6.

33. Letter to Williams, November 6, 1852, LL 4: 18.

34. Charlotte described the event in a letter to Emily, September 2, 1843, LL 1: 303.

35. The phrase is from the poem "Reason" (#111), and will return in *Villette.*

36. "Captain Henry Hastings," *Five Novelettes,* p. 269. Rochester also calls Jane a "nonnette," or little nun (p. 160).

5. *Villette*

1. Letter dated November 3, 1852, to Smith.

2. *Daily News,* February 3, 1853. *The Christian Remembrancer* of April 1853 likewise complained of a "want of continuity."

3. To Lucy Baxter, March 11, 1853; quoted in Allott, *Critical Heritage,* p. 197.

4. To Smith, December 6, 1852.

5. As Colby early recognized in his important essay *"Villette* and the Life of the Mind," "through her most complex heroine, Charlotte Brontë obviously means to depict something of the creative act itself" (p. 417). Peter Allan Dale, who is one of the few critics to discuss *Villette* as a novel of religious crisis, is also sensitively aware of Charlotte's concern in this novel with the processes of her own art. But Dale sees what I have called Charlotte's "woman's testament" as doomed (heretical) by its own ambition: "This writing, which strives to become a better Word than God himself has vouchsafed, is the image, the idol, whose worship Brontë most fears" ("Heretical Narration," p. 20). In *Charlotte Brontë and Sexuality,* John Maynard argues sensibly and eloquently that Charlotte's understanding of human sexual needs and feelings was profound and healthy. But in recognizing the sweet sensuality of Lucy's last meeting with Paul, Maynard neglects the

extent to which this depiction of mature and tender human love stands (like the marriage in Revelation) as a figure for the love of God and (wo)man.

6. Letters of May 12 and 20, 1851, LL 3: 232–4. Unless otherwise noted, letters may be located by date in the volumes of LL.

7. Brontë, *Villette*, p. 485. Further page references will be given in the text.

8. Letter of April 2, 1849, LL 2: 320.

9. Letter of May 8, 1849, LL 2: 329.

10. Letter of July 26, 1849, LL 3: 9.

11. Letter of December 4, 1849, LL 3: 53.

12. Gérin, *Charlotte Brontë*, p. 402.

13. *Ibid.*, p. 439.

14. Quoted in *ibid.*, p. 434.

15. Mrs. Brookfield, quoted in *ibid.*, p. 432.

16. Quoted in *ibid.*, p. 436, n.

17. Letter to Ellen Nussey, June 21, 1850, LL 3: 121.

18. *Ibid.* The passage from Smith's letter to Mrs. Ward is quoted from Gérin, *Charlotte Brontë*, p. 436, n.

19. Quoted in Gérin, *Charlotte Brontë*, pp. 364–65.

20. Letter of October 23, 1850, LL 3: 173.

21. Letter of November 6, 1850, LL 3: 177.

22. Letter of January 30, 1851, LL 3: 205.

23. Letter of February 5, 1851, LL 3: 207. Of course what she alludes to (now with painful humor) is a version of Bertha Mason's fate: going mad from solitary confinement.

24. Letter of March 11, 1851, LL 3: 211.

25. Letter of March 22, 1851, LL 3: 214.

26. Letter of March 24, 1851, LL 3: 214.

27. Letter of March 28, 1851, LL 3: 215.

28. Letter of March 31, 1851, LL 3: 216.

29. Letter of April 5, 1851, LL 3: 220.

30. Letter of March 22, 1851, LL 3: 214.

31. Letter of April 5, 1851, LL 3: 220.

32. Letter of April 5, 1851, LL 3: 221.

33. Letter of April 9, 1851, LL 3: 222.

34. Letter of April 12, 1851, LL 3: 223.

35. Letter of April 23, 1851, LL 3: 229.

36. Letter of November 15, 1851, LL 3: 290.

37. Letter of March 4, 1852, LL 3: 320.

38. Letter of March 7, 1852, LL 3: 321.

39. Letter of April 12, 1852, LL 3: 330.

40. Letter of July 1, 1852, LL 3: 341.

41. The phrase is from *The Professor,* p. 30.

42. Fannie Ratchford long ago observed his connections to Zamorna, in *The Brontës' Web of Childhood,* pp. 230–34.

43. The words again recall Charlotte's characterization of Heger as a false god in her poem "Reason."

44. Letter to Smith, November 3, 1852, LL 4: 16.

45. Letter to Smith, December 6, 1852, LL 4: 23.

46. Sinclair, *The Three Brontës,* p. 177: "There is no sign in the beginning that this detestable Lucy is to be the heroine. But in Chapter Four Polly disappears and Lucy takes her place."

47. There exist two fragments of material relating to little Polly, published among other fragments as Appendix 1 to the Oxford edition of *Villette.* The salient features in both fragments relating to Polly are the child's passionate attachment to what she loves—in the first, her father; in the second, her doll.

48. For a different view, see Martin, *Accents of Persuasion:* "From her initial misjudgment of Polly" Lucy "constantly misjudges" (p. 147). I think that Charlotte expects the reader to see as mask what Martin takes as Lucy's real feeling.

49. Gaskell, *The Life of Charlotte Brontë,* p. 379. Janice Carlisle describes the relationship well in saying that Paulina is "a projection of Lucy's most gratifying self-image" ("The Face in the Mirror," p. 280).

50. Dunbar notes Charlotte's French sarcasms in her useful essay, "Proper Names in *Villette.*"

51. George Smith wrote Charlotte an account of a theater fire at which he had been present. Charlotte responded by observing that such occasions "while startling people out of their customary smooth bearing, elicit genuine touches of character." Both Smith and "the panic-struck young lady" whom he had helped on that occasion "revealed themselves according to their different natures," Charlotte concluded. "It is easy to realize the scene" (letter of August 9, 1851, LL 3: 270). Obviously she did so in *Villette.*

52. The full names of the first two may be found on pp. 667 and 98–99, respectively. Charlotte may have intended her readers to recall in this "secret junta" the three great enemies of the Lamb, who are to be defeated at the Last Judgment: the Beast, his false prophet, and the workshipers of his image (Revelation 19:20). The basilisk is a fabulous animal with a three-pointed crest and (in medieval descriptions) three-pointed tail, traditionally thought to symbolize the devil, or an infernal inversion of the qualities of the Trinity.

53. It is useful to recall Charlotte's description of her infernal "dream" in her Roe Head journal (see my chapter 3, above): it "acted upon me like opium & was coiling about me a disturbing but fascinating spell. . . ." With its associations of Egyptian bondage, false gods, etc. this trip of

Lucy's seems a fictional equivalent of those early journeys to "the world below."

54. Possibly this stone basin is one of the sources of the name de Bassompierre?

6. The Muse Triumphant

1. Brontë, *Jane Eyre,* p. 514. Further page references will be given in the text.

2. Brontë, *Villette,* p. 64. Further page references will be given in the text.

3. This exchange occurs on pp. 475–79 in *Jane Eyre.*

4. I translate the French terms.

5. Her language in this essay looks ahead in many suggestive ways to the later work, especially to *Villette.* She writes, for example, of the chrysalis, that for a month it "remains deprived of light, of movement, of life. And then? The warmth of summer begins; . . . the principle of life is revived, the insect moves within its tomb, at last it breaks its coffin and escapes." Transformed into a butterfly, it "has quitted its materialistic existence and launched itself upon a life entirely spiritual." Charlotte then draws the moral for mankind: "his ordinary life is the life of the caterpillar." But "Faith" teaches him of what is to come: and in quoting the "voice" of Faith, Charlotte paraphrases Scripture. "The body is sown in corruption, it is raised in incorruption; . . . it is sown a natural body, it is raised a spiritual body. In a moment . . . we shall all be changed, for the trumpet shall sound and the dead shall be raised incorruptible." "La Chenille," translated by Dr. Phyllis Bentley.

6. One should note also that Justine is the name of a dying mother in an untranscribed poem that sounds very much as if it were based on Charlotte's memories, or on stories she later heard, of her own mother's death (Bonnell ms. 91 [1]). The daughter in that poem is named Mina, and the son (demoted to foster son) like Henry Hastings is a man of "withering crimes."

7. The numbering of Charlotte's poems follows Neufeldt, *The Poems of Charlotte Brontë.*

8. So worded in Bonnell ms. 97. Neufeldt's published version (#135) differs slightly, and offers additional lines anticipating the turn from Dr. John to Paul Emanuel in *Villette:* "Kneel . . . / And ask thine unseen Father's care / To fill the void of earthly love." An earlier ms. variant also published by Neufeldt (p. 427) has a pessimistic conclusion: "No strength will to the rescue come."

9. See *Brontë Society Transactions,* vol. 12, no. 2, pp. 89–90; translated by

Dorothy Cornish. The original French essay was written on October 6, 1842.

10. Through Paul's letters Charlotte also inevitably alludes to gospel, perhaps especially to her own favorite Epistles of St. Paul.

11. Brontë, *Shirley,* pp. 117–18. Further page references will be given in the text.

12. The ship is named for a novel by Bernardin de St. Pierre, of which more in my conclusion, below.

13. Brontë, *The Professor,* p. 79. Further page references will be give in the text.

14. November 6, 1852; LL 4: 18.

15. William F. H. King, *Classical and Foreign Quotation* (New York 1887), p. 311.

16. September 22, 1851, LL 3: 279.

17. See the several descriptions of Zenobia in Charlotte's "Passing Events" *(Five Novelettes),* passim.

18. Louis is another fire figure, if he is named for the "Roi Soleil" who took the sun for his royal emblem. (The sun was Zamorna's emblem too.)

19. Letter of November 15, 1851, LL 3: 290.

20. "My Angria," SHB 2: 29.

21. "Mina Laury," *Five Novelettes,* p. 163.

22. I think that Mary Jacobus was brilliantly right in her observation that the subject of *Villette* is "repression itself" ("The Buried Letter," p. 59). And she may be right that Romanticism and feminism are repressed, depending on how one defines these terms. But the root repression is certainly sexual: like St. John in *Jane Eyre,* the would-be apostle must forego human love.

23. *Jane Eyre,* p. 550. The phrase "indirect assassination," below, is from p. 383.

24. It should be noticed that on the back of the last sheet of the manuscript of some material later omitted from *Villette* is written: "The rumor that M. Alpha was outside had run through the Salle and there was a crush in the direction of the door" (Bonnell ms. 125/2, quoted in the Oxford edition of *Villette,* p. 764). This suggests the possibility that Charlotte had at one time considered naming her hero "M. Alpha," as in "I am Alpha and Omega" (Revelation 1:8).

25. Turner, *Brontëana,* p. 20.

26. *Ibid.,* p. 71.

27. *Ibid.,* p. 133.

28. Compare Rev. Helstone, in *Shirley,* who "couldn't abide sense in women."

29. Charlotte seems to have conflated for her purposes several of Jesus' related parables concerning separations and returns, masters and servants,

bridegroom and virgins—notably those of Matthew 24 and 25 and Luke 12 and 15.

30. The quotations are from Dunbar, "Proper Names in *Villette*"; subsequent critics appear to have followed Dunbar's lead in this matter.

31. A related synopsis of Judeo-Christian history from Moses to the advent of Christ is told in Charlotte's French essay "The Death of Moses," translated by Dr. Phyllis Bentley in *Brontë Society Transactions*, vol. 12, part 65, pp. 366–75.

32. Possibly Charlotte imagined Paul's comforting answer to Lucy's "Do I displease your eyes much?" as those of the repeated refrain in the Song of Solomon—"Behold, thou art fair, my love; behold, thou art fair" (4:1). Even the watch guard Lucy made Paul may echo the "one chain of thy neck" with which "thou hast ravished my heart, my sister, my spouse" (4:9). (Lucy does call herself Paul's sister" [p. 592], and her gift of the chain is a defining moment in the growth of their love.) In a work so shot through with biblical allusion, it is hard to know where the echoes cease.

33. *Villette*, ed. G. Tillotson and D. Hawes (Boston, Mass.: Houghton Mifflin, 1971), p. 197, n.

34. Brontë, "Death of Moses" (see note 31, above), p. 370.

35. Quoted in Fraser, *The Brontës*, p. 359.

36. What little is known concerning the physical cause(s) of Charlotte's death is carefully summarized by John Maynard in *Charlotte Brontë and Sexuality*, pp. 218–24.

7. Conclusion

1. The numbering of Emily's poems follows Hatfield, *The Complete Poems of Emily Brontë*. All quotations from her poetry are from this edition.

2. Samuel Taylor Coleridge, *Biographia Literaria*, ch. 13.

3. Entire passage: ll. 170–95 (1805); ll. 170–96 (1850).

4. Cf. Wordsworth's view concerning the evolution in each person of powers of spiritual love which each of us must evolve alone; none can help in this inevitably private work: 1805 *Prelude*, book 13, ll. 188–97.

5. These last words are quoted from the 1805 *Prelude*, book 13, ll. 139–41. In the 1850 version (book 14, ll. 154–60) "laws" become "weight"—just as "custom" was a "weight" in the Intimations Ode.

6. Lessing, *The Four-Gated City*, pp. 38, 36.

7. Miller, *Fiction and Repetition*, p. 202.

8. Gilligan, *In a Different Voice*, p. 47.

9. Southey's letter and Charlotte's answer are quoted in Gérin, *Charlotte Brontë*, pp. 110–111.

ᐳ WORKS CITED

Abrams, M. H. "The Correspondent Breeze: A Romantic Metaphor." In M. H. Abrams, ed., *The Correspondent Breeze: Essays on English Romanticism*. New York: Norton, 1984.

Alexander, Christine. *The Early Writings of Charlotte Brontë*. London: Blackwell, 1983.

Allott, Miriam. *The Brontës: The Critical Heritage*. London and Boston, Mass.: Routledge and Kegan Paul, 1974.

Auerbach, Nina. *Romantic Imprisonment: Women and Other Glorified Outcasts*. New York: Columbia University Press, 1986.

Bersani, Leo. *A Future for Astyanax: Character and Desire in Literature*. Boston, Mass.: Little, Brown, 1976.

Bloom, Harold. "The Internalization of the Quest-Romance." In Harold Bloom, ed., *Romanticism and Consciousness*. New York: Norton, 1970.

Bonnell manuscript collection in the Brontë Parsonage Museum, Haworth, England.

British Library manuscript collections.

Brontë, Charlotte. "La Chenille." Trans. Phyllis Bentley. *Brontë Society Transactions*, vol. 12, no. 5.

Brontë, Charlotte. *Five Novelettes: Passing Events, Julia, Mina Laury, Captain Henry Hastings, Caroline Vernon*. Ed. Winnifred Gérin. London: Folio Press, 1971.

Brontë, Charlotte. *Jane Eyre*. Ed. Jane Jack and Margaret Smith. Oxford: Clarendon Press, 1975.

Brontë, Charlotte. "La Justice Humaine." Trans. Dorothy Cornish. *Brontë Society Transactions* (1952), vol. 12, no. 2.

Brontë, Charlotte. "La Morte de Moïse." Trans. Phyllis Bentley. *Brontë Society Transactions*, vol. 12, no. 5.

"La Morte de Napoleon." Trans. Margaret Lane. *Brontë Society Transactions*, vol. 12, no. 4.

Brontë, Charlotte. *The Professor*. Ed. Margaret Smith and Herbert Rosengarten. Oxford: Clarendon Press, 1987.

Brontë, Charlotte *Shirley*. Ed. Herbert Rosengarten and Margaret Smith. Oxford: Clarendon Press, 1979.

Brontë, Charlotte. *The Spell: An Extravaganza*. Ed. G. E. MacLean. Oxford: Oxford University Press, 1931.

Brontë, Charlotte. *Villette*. Ed. Herbert Rosengarten and Margaret Smith. Oxford: Clarendon Press, 1984.

Brontë, Emily. *"Lettre." Brontë Society Transactions* (1955), vol. 12, no. 5.

Brontë, Emily. *Wuthering Heights*. Ed. Hilda Marsden and Ian Jack. Oxford: Clarendon Press, 1976.

Burkhart, Charles. *Charlotte Brontë: A Psychosexual Study of Her Novels*. London: Gollancz, 1973.

Carlisle, Janice. "The Face in the Mirror: *Villette* and the Conventions of Autobiography." *English Literary History* (1979), vol. 46.

Cecil, Lord David. *Early Victorian Novelists: Essays in Revaluation*. Indianapolis, Ind. and New York: Bobbs-Merrill, 1935.

Chase, Richard. "The Brontës, or, Myth Domesticated." In William Van O'Connor, ed., *Forms of Modern Fiction*. Minneapolis: University of Minnesota Press, 1948.

Chitham, Edward. *A Life of Emily Brontë*. London: Basil Blackwell, 1987.

Chitham, Edward and Tom Winnifrith. *Brontë Facts and Brontë Problems*. London: Macmillan, 1983.

Clayton, Jay. *Romantic Vision and the Novel*. Cambridge, England: Columbia University Press, 1987.

Colby, Robert A. *"Villette* and the Life of the Mind." *PMLA* (September 1960), vol. 75, no. 4.

Dale, Peter Allan. "Heretical Narration: Charlotte Brontë's Search for Endlessness." *Religion and Literature* (Autumn 1984), vol. 16, no. 4.

Daley, A. Stuart. "The Date of Heathcliff's Death." *Brontë Society Transactions* (1976), vol. 17, no. 1.

Davies, Stevie. *Emily Brontë: The Artist as a Free Woman*. Manchester, England: Carcanet Press, 1983.

DeShazer, Mary K. *Inspiring Women: Reimagining the Muse*. New York: Pergamon Press, 1986.

Deutsch, Helene. *The Psychology of Women*. 2 vols. New York: Grune and Stratton, 1944.

Dinnerstein, Dorothy. *The Mermaid and the Minotaur*. New York: Harper and Row, 1976.

Donoghue, Denis. "The Other Emily." *The Brontës: A Collection of Critical Essays*. Ed. Ian Gregor. Englewood Cliffs, N.J.: Prentice-Hall, 1970.

Dooley, Dr. Lucile. "Psychoanalysis of the Character and Genius of Emily Brontë." *Psychoanalytic Review* (April 1930), no. 17.

Dooley, Dr. Lucile. "Psychoanalysis of Charlotte Brontë, as a Type of the Woman of Genius." *The American Journal of Psychology* (July 1920), vol. 31, no. 3.

Du Fresnay. *Geography for Youth*. Dublin, 1795.

Dunbar, Georgia S. "Proper Names in *Villette.*" *Nineteenth-Century Fiction* (1959–1960), 14:77–80.

Ewbank, Inga-Stina. "Introduction." In Hilda Marsden and Ian Jack, eds., *Wuthering Heights,* pp. xiii–xxiv. Oxford: Clarendon Press, 1976.

Ewbank, Inga-Stina. *Their Proper Sphere: A Study of the Brontë Sisters as Early-Victorian Female Novelists*. Cambridge, Mass.: Harvard University Press, 1968.

Fraser, Rebecca. *The Brontës: Charlotte Brontë and Her Family*. New York: Crown, 1988.

Freud, Sigmund. *The Complete Psychological Works*. 24 vols. London: Hogarth Press, 1955.

Gaskell, Elizabeth. *The Life of Charlotte Brontë*. Ed. Alan Shelstone. Middlesex, England: Penguin English Library, 1975.

Gérin, Winifred. *Charlotte Brontë: The Evolution of Genius*. London: Oxford University Press, 1967.

Gérin, Winifred. *Emily Brontë: A Biography*. Oxford, England: Clarendon Press, 1971.

Gilbert, Sandra and Susan Gubar. *The Madwoman in the Attic: The Woman Writer and the Nineteenth-Century Literary Imagination*. New Haven, Conn.: Yale University Press, 1979.

Gilligan, Carol. *In a Different Voice: Psychological Theory and Women's Development*. Cambridge, Mass.: Harvard University Press, 1982.

Girard, René. *Deceit, Desire, and the Novel*. Baltimore, Md.: Johns Hopkins University Press, 1965.

Graves, Robert. *The White Goddess*. New York: Vintage, Random House, 1948.

Harpham, Geoffrey Galt. *On the Grotesque*. Princeton, N.J.: Princeton University Press, 1982.

Hatfield, C. W. *The Complete Poems of Emily Brontë*. New York: Columbia University Press, 1941.

Heilman, Robert B. "Charlotte Brontë, Reason and the Moon." *Nineteenth Century Fiction* (1960), 14:283–302.

Hewish, John. *Emily Brontë: A Critical and Biographical Study*. London: Macmillan, 1969.

Holgate, Ivy. "The Structure of *Shirley.*" *Brontë Society Transactions* (1962), vol. 14, no. 2.

Holtz, William, ed. *Two Tales by Charlotte Brontë: "The Secret" and "Lily Hart."* Columbia: University of Missouri Press, 1978.

Homans, Margaret. *Bearing the Word*. Chicago, Ill.: University of Chicago Press, 1986.

Homans, Margaret. "Repression and Sublimation of Nature in *Wuthering Heights.*" *PMLA* (January 1978), vol. 93, no. 1.

Homans, Margaret. *Women Writers and Poetic Identity*. Princeton, N.J.: Princeton University Press, 1980.

Jacobus, Mary. "The Buried Letter: Feminism and Romanticism in *Villette.*" *Women Writing and Writing About Women* Ed. Mary Jacobus. London: Croom Helm, 1979.

Keefe, Robert. *Charlotte Brontë's World of Death*. Austin: University of Texas Press, 1979.

Kermode, Frank. *The Classic: Literary Images of Permanence and Change*. Cambridge, Mass.: Harvard University Press, 1983.

King, William F. H. *Classical and Foreign Quotations*. New York, 1887.

Kingsley, Charles. *Charles Kingsley: His Letters and Memories of His Life*. Ed. by his wife. 2 Vols. London, 1879.

Kohut, Heinz. *The Analysis of the Self*. New York: International Universities Press, 1971.

The Leader. December 28, 1850.

Lessing, Doris. *The Four-Gated City*. New York: Bantam Books, 1970.

Lewin, Bertram. *The Psychoanalysis of Elation*. New York: Norton, 1950.

Lodge, David. "Fire and Eyre: Charlotte Brontë's War of Earthly Elements." In Ian Gregor, ed., *The Brontës: A Collection of Critical Essays*. Englewood Cliffs, N.J.: Prentice-Hall, 1970.

Martin, Robert B. *Accents of Persuasion*. London: Faber and Faber, 1966.

Maynard, John. *Charlotte Brontë and Sexuality*. Cambridge: Cambridge University Press, 1984.

McGann, Jerome. *Fiery Dust: Byron's Poetic Development*. Chicago, Ill.: University of Chicago Press, 1968.

Miller, J. Hillis. *The Disappearance of God,* Cambridge, Mass.: Harvard University Press, 1963.

Miller, J. Hillis. *Fiction and Repetition: Seven English Novels*. Cambridge, Mass.: Harvard University Press, 1982.

Mitchell, Juliet. *Psychoanalysis and Feminism*. New York: Pantheon, 1974.

Moglen, Helene. *Charlotte Brontë: The Self Conceived*. New York: Norton, 1976.

Neufeldt, Victor A., ed. *The Poems of Charlotte Brontë*. New York: Garland Press, 1985.

Perkins, David. Ed. *English Romantic Writers*. New York: Harcourt Brace Jovanovich, 1967.

Perkins, David. *The Quest for Permanence*. Cambridge, Mass.: Harvard University Press, 1959.

Rank, Otto. *The Double*. Ed. and trans. Harry Tucker, Jr. Chapel Hill: University of North Carolina Press, 1971.

Ratchford, Fannie E. *The Brontës' Web of Childhood*. New York: Columbia University Press, 1941.

Ratchford, Fannie E. *Gondal's Queen*. Austin: University of Texas Press, 1955.

Rhodes, Dr. Philip. "A Medical Appraisal of the Brontës." *Brontë Society Transactions* (1972), vol. 16, no. 2.

Rich, Adrienne. *On Lies, Secrets, and Silence: Selected Prose 1966–1978*. New York: Norton, 1979.

Rizzuto, Ana-Maria. *The Birth of the Living God*. Chicago, Ill.: University of Chicago Press, 1979.

Sanger, Charles Percy. "The Structure of *Wuthering Heights*." In William M. Sale, ed., *Wuthering Heights*, 2d ed. New York: Norton, 1972.

Showalter, Elaine. *A Literature of Their Own: British Women Novelists from Brontë to Lessing*. Princeton, N.J.: Princeton University Press, 1977.

Sinclair, May. *The Three Brontës*. Boston, Mass. and New York: Houghton Mifflin, 1912.

Spacks, Patricia Meyer. *The Female Imagination*. New York: Knopf, 1975.

Swinburne, Algernon Charles. "Emily Brontë." *The Athenaeum*, June 16, 1883.

Thorslev, Peter L., Jr. "Incest as Romantic Symbol." *Comparative Literature Studies* (1965), vol. 2.

Turner, J. Horsfall, ed. *Brontëana: Rev. Patrick Brontë's Collected Works*. Vol. 1. Bingley, England: T. Harrison & Sons, 1898.

Wilson, David. "Emily Brontë: First of the Moderns." *Modern Quarterly Miscellany* (1947), 1:94–115.

Winnicott, D. W. *Playing and Reality*. New York: Basic Books, 1971

Wise, Thomas James and John Alexander Symington. *The Brontës: Their Lives, Friendships and Correspondence*. 4 vols. Oxford, England: The Shakespeare Head Press/Blackwell, 1932.

Wise, Thomas James and John Alexander Symington. *The Miscellaneous and Unpublished Writings of Charlotte and Patrick Branwell Brontë*. 2 vols. Oxford, England: The Shakespeare Head Press/Blackwell, 1936 and 1938.

INDEX